DOCTRINE OF THE SPIRIT-FILLED CHURCH

DOCTRINE OF THE SPIRIT-FILLED CHURCH

Francis Vlok

ELM HILL

A Division of
HarperCollins Christian Publishing

www.elmhillbooks.com

Doctrine of the Spirit-Filled Church

Published in Nashville, Tennessee, by Elm Hill, an imprint of Thomas Nelson. Elm Hill and Thomas Nelson are registered trademarks of HarperCollins Christian Publishing, Inc.

All Scripture quotations, unless otherwise indicated, are taken from the King James Version. Public domain.

Scripture quotations marked NASB are from New American Standard Bible˚. Copyright © 1960, 1962, 1963, 1968, 1971, 1972, 1973, 1975, 1977, 1995 by The Lockman Foundation. Used by permission. (www.Lockman.org)

Scripture quotations marked NIV are from the Holy Bible, New International Version˚, NIV˚. Copyright © 1973, 1978, 1984, 2011 by Biblica, Inc.˚ Used by permission of Zondervan. All rights reserved worldwide. www.Zondervan.com. The "NIV" and "New International Version" are trademarks registered in the United States Patent and Trademark Office by Biblica, Inc.˚

Scripture quotations marked NKJV are from the New King James Version˚. © 1982 by Thomas Nelson. Used by permission. All rights reserved.

One Lord, One Faith by W.A.C. Rowe
Puritan Press LTD, Bradford, Yorkshire, England
Used by permission.

Library of Congress Cataloging-in-Publication Data

Library of Congress Control Number: 2018962330

ISBN 978-1-595559494 (Paperback)
ISBN 978-1-595559906 (Hardbound)
ISBN 978-1-595559685 (eBook)

CONTENTS

PART 6

PART 7

PART 8

PART 9

PART 10

PREFACE

Throughout the church age, many righteous and devout men have penned the doctrine of the church. More concisely, they have reduced to the written form, the doctrine, as their denomination has perceived it should be. There are numerous volumes written to explain the interpretations of a specific denomination's principles and beliefs. These men are to be applauded for their contribution in assisting their denomination in abiding by the truths they believe.

In all the research and studying done over more than forty years and being a member of the Spirit-filled church during that time, it has been difficult to come upon a true record of the doctrine of the Spirit-filled church as declared in the Holy Writ. There are numerous study aids, a few books that give an outline of the doctrine of a Spirit-filled church, and some unfortunate works that are not in line with the Word. However, a complete work that details the *apostles' doctrine* was not found. Hence, the reason for this book.

In an attempt to compile the Spirit-filled church's doctrinal tenets as found in the Bible, a few basic standards had to be applied. First, the Bible is the only true record and reference for every tenet and its explanation. Second, no tenet should be adopted if it does not have a biblical basis for its existence. Third, there should be no interference or changes made to the words that the Bible uses for distinctive offices. An example of this is found when certain denominations will not use the title of "apostle" but change it to "bishop." Likewise, hierarchy is added to the layers of the Bible's appointees, such as cardinals, archdeacons, etc.

There is only one divine basis for any doctrinal tenet, and that is the holy Bible. Every teaching in the Holy Writ should form the basis of each tenet. This is so because the Bible is God's message to man, while everything man has penned is man's message to men.

Mention must be made of the denominational works already completed by many scholars and theologians throughout the history of the church. Within these works, there are sections that have been excellently explained, many of which align, in part, with the Spirit-filled doctrine. These have been used to assist in explaining certain universal doctrinal statements.

This book is meant for ministers, Bible students, and laymen who are seeking answers to the biblical doctrinal tenets, termed *the apostles' doctrine.* (Acts 2:42)

It is written for all members of the church, but more precisely, for members of the Spirit-filled churches, namely the members of the original apostolic churches throughout the world that were started as a result of the Welsh Revival of 1901–1904. From these original apostolic churches the Pentecostal denominations were formed, then the Charismatics, and now the independent Spirit-filled churches. It is for them that this work is intended.

The study of God's Word is vital for a believer to become sanctified and mature in Christ. Every ordained minister whom Christ has placed in the ministry should be a diligent student of His Word, so that they are never in danger of leading the flock of God down a crooked path. History records the many who have neglected the study of the Word, and the results have proven their misguided adaptation of the Word's principles and truths. This is particularly evident in the many "independent" Spirit-filled churches that are mushrooming throughout the world. Each one has a particular variance or inclination that separates them from the other, and it is never completely rooted and grounded in the *apostles' doctrine.*

The doctrines of Christ, or the teachings of Christ, are all included in the *apostles' doctrine*. While every born-again believer should immerse themselves in the study of God's Word, it should be the particular effort of the minister to saturate himself in the fullness of God's message found in the Holy Writ. There is nothing more noble and fulfilling for any human being than to spend time, under the anointing of the Holy Spirit, studying the Word. John Dick has said in one of his *Lectures on Theology*, "To know this mighty Being, as far as He may be known, is the noblest aim of the human understanding; to love Him the most worthy exercise of our affection, and to serve Him the most honorable and delightful purpose to which we can devote our time and talent."

This volume bases its foundation on the *apostles' doctrine* born out of the Welsh Revival that began in 1901. After centuries of Roman Catholic domination of the world, in the sixteenth-century Martin Luther boldly broke the stronghold of the Roman Catholic faith and began the establishment of the reformed movement. During that century, this escalated with men such as John Calvin, and the church embarked on the journey of the Protestant movement. All the while that they moved away from the Roman Catholic and Anglican denominations, they never fully abided by the *apostles' doctrine*, and the evidence of the Holy Spirit's indwelling power was never experienced through the manifestation of the gifts of the Holy Spirit.

From 1901, the Holy Spirit began moving in a miraculous way throughout the world. The start of the Holy Spirit's outpouring occurred in a small Welsh town, Penygroes, where believers seeking a deeper walk with God were baptized with the Holy Spirit. Almost simultaneously the Holy Spirit began moving in the United States, and the outpouring of the Holy Spirit's *fire* (Luke 3:16) ignited believers across the oceans and denominational barriers. Believers from every denomination began experiencing the mighty baptism of fire with a new stream of purpose and spiritual influence in the churches. All the while this divine experience took place, opposition from the established mainstream denominations forced these Spirit-filled believers to leave their membership. The first Spirit-filled churches to be formed were called Apostolic Churches. Their abiding doctrine was immersed in the *apostles' doctrine*.

It took a mere ten years for the Holy Spirit's work to spread throughout most of Europe and many parts of the United States. The rapid outpouring of the Holy Spirit had gained such momentum that by 1914 Spirit-filled believers had established what is known today as the Pentecostal denomination. This denomination was, in its inception, highly condemned by the mainline denominations. It was in the late 1940s that the World Council of Churches adopted a resolution that the Pentecostal denomination be recognized as an acceptable denomination of the Christian Church, and that it is not a sect operating outside the origins of the original church that was based on the Apostles' Creed and early teachings of the church. By the middle of the 1950s, the Apostolic and Pentecostal churches were virtually spread worldwide.

In the early 1970s the Holy Spirit again moved in a mighty way, and many mainline church members experienced the same outpouring as those in 1901 and onwards did. The manifestation of the gifts of the Holy Spirit, the abundant joy, and the exuberant praise and worship that these "charismatic" members of the mainline churches began to manifest was not eagerly accepted. This caused many unpleasant rifts between the conventional church attendees and the new Spirit-filled members. The expulsion of these members was again evident as divisions in the mainline churches were experienced. This led many to leave the mainline churches and the Pentecostal movement, and they started the formation of what is today known as "independent" Spirit-filled churches.

With the continued growth of the Spirit-filled churches, and in particular the independent churches, the focus has shifted dramatically from the *apostles' doctrine* to many variances of it. This being so, it is vital that the Spirit-filled church returns to its origin. Hence, the purpose of this book, *Doctrine of the Spirit-Filled Church*.

The timing of this book is never more perfect than now. With the soon return of the Lord Jesus Christ who will receive His bride, the church, it is only appropriate that the *unity of the faith* be restored and that Spirit-filled believers return to the biblically established church. How devastating it will be if Spirit-filled believers are called by Jesus at the Judgment Seat of Christ and are asked by Him, "Why didn't you build the church according to My instructions?"

This book is written in chapter and verse, as guided by the Holy Spirit. It was never intended to be written this way, until the Holy Spirit instructed it to be so. It is therefore presented in this way, in obedience to the Holy Spirit's instruction and guidance.

The Tenets of the Apostolic Church

The following tenets were set into the foundation of the Apostolic Church that was formed in 1916. It was first originally written in Welsh and translated into English in 1920.

1. The unity of the Godhead and the Trinity of the persons therein.
2. The utter depravity of human nature, the necessity for repentance and regeneration, and the eternal doom of the finally impenitent.
3. The virgin birth, sinless life, atoning death, triumphant resurrection, ascension and abiding intercession of our Lord Jesus Christ; His second coming and millennial reign upon earth.
4. Justification and sanctification of the believer through the finished work of Christ.
5. The baptism with the Holy Ghost for believers, with signs following.
6. The nine gifts of the Holy Ghost for the edification, exhortation, and comfort of the Church, which is the Body of Christ.
7. The Sacraments of Baptism by immersion and the Lord's Supper.
8. The divine inspiration and authority of the Holy Scriptures.
9. Church government by apostles, prophets, evangelists, pastors, teachers, elders, and deacons.
10. The possibility of falling from grace.
11. The obligatory nature of tithes and offerings.

WORD CLARIFICATION

Apostolic – Referenced to the original structure of the church as found in the New Testament. There should have been the continuance of this divine organism throughout the church ages and should be in operation today.

Apostolic Church – This is a fellowship of Spirit-filled believers who conform to the *apostles' doctrine.* It is biblically structured and has all its doctrinal tenets anchored in God's holy Word. It has no affiliation to a denomination who are called "New Apostolic" and "Old Apostolic" churches.

Believer – born-again believer – A person who accepts if: you *confess with your mouth the Lord Jesus and believe in your heart that God has raised Him from the dead, you will be saved. For with the heart one believes unto righteousness, and with the mouth confession is made unto salvation....* (Romans 10:9–10 NKJV)

Charismatic believers – Born-again Spirit-filled believers who, after they were baptized with the Holy Spirit during the 1970s, left their mainline denominations and have since established independent and nondenominational churches.

Inerrant – inerrancy – Pertaining to the holy Word; it is complete in its entirety and without fault.

Infallible – With reference to the Holy Bible and the fact that there are no omissions, errors, or untruths contained in it.

Omnipotent – As relating to God; He is all-powerful and there is no power greater than His, neither is there any event that is out of His control.

Omnipresent – As relating to God; everywhere all the time. There is never a place created that He is not present.

Omniscient – As relating to God; He is all-knowing all the time. There is never anything at any given moment about which God is unaware, even before it takes place. He has foreknowledge, insight, and future knowledge of everything that was, is, and will be.

Pentecostal – The denomination of born-again Spirit-filled believers established in countries throughout the world, their origins founded upon the original Apostolic Church that started in 1901.

Saints – Those *dead in Christ* and those alive who will be raptured at the return of Jesus Christ, their bodies changed from mortality and corruption into immortality and incorruption, to rule with Christ forever.

Sovereign – God alone has all power and authority, and no one will ever usurp His rule. He alone is the decider and implementer of His decisions.

Spirit-filled believer – A person who is born-again and is baptized with the Holy Spirit, has the Holy Spirit in their body (1 Corinthians 6:19), and manifests the gifts of the Holy Spirit.

Spirit-filled church – An assembly of Spirit-filled believers who worship God, exalt Jesus Christ as Lord, and have the gifts of the Holy Spirit in operation during meetings and in their daily lives.

About the Author

Francis Vlok was born in South Africa in 1947 and educated at Cambridge School, East London. After graduating from high school, he continued his studies attending night classes and graduated from the East London College with an associate banking degree.

It was during 1972 that he was called into the ministry. After being a youth pastor for two years, he continued with his ministerial studies and graduated from the Methodist Church of South Africa in 1977.

While studying for the ministry, he was baptized with the Holy Spirit on January 5, 1975 in his brother's home in Kathu, South Africa. After completing his studies, he and his wife went to Israel in 1977. While visiting the excavations at Qumran, the Lord spoke clearly to him that he was to discontinue everything and complete all unfinished business. The Holy Spirit told him that the Spirit would strip from him all Protestant veneer and spiritually reveal to him the perfect will of God for the church.

He requested a release from his obligations to the Methodist church, and for the next six months he and his wife, Sandra, sat under the ministry of the Holy Spirit as the Spirit revealed to them the perfect will of God. They set about visiting denominations asking what their doctrinal tenets were and, after months of searching, they walked into the Christian Fellowship in Retief Street, Pietermaritzburg, South Africa. It was here that he discovered how the fellowship functioned under God's perfect will. They became members in 1978. This denomination, The Christian

Fellowship, was established by apostles from the Apostolic Church of Great Britain who were sent by God to South Africa in 1962 to lay the foundation of the perfect will of God in that country.

He was called into the ministry in 1979 through the office of two apostles, Reginald Evans and Cyril Wilson, and ordained in 1980. Two years later God sent him to another city, Port Elizabeth, where the Holy Spirit led him to start an assembly. This was the fulfillment of his ministry as an apostle. The fellowship in Port Elizabeth grew to maturity and after seven years, they had several ordained elders and ministers.

During the period from 1979 to 1995, he lectured at the Christian Fellowship's School of Ministry. His continuous studying and teaching of the Word paved the way for him to be the assistant to the president of the fellowship, Apostle Cyril Wilson, in the rewriting of the fellowship's constitution and the establishment of the biblical tenets, beliefs, and principles.

He also wrote the book, *The Perfect Will of God,* which laid down the doctrinal tenets pertaining to the structure and operation of the church as found in the New Testament. This book is still available today.

In 1987, he was appointed vice president of the Christian Fellowship, South Africa.

The Holy Spirit continued to use him to mature the local assembly in Port Elizabeth until 1993 when he was called by the Holy Spirit to relocate to the United States.

The call to go was clear, but without the long-term vision being revealed as to exactly what he would be doing when he arrived in the United States. He moved to Mississippi, US, and was asked to preach in various Pentecostal churches. After almost four years of ministering, in 1999, God called him out from the itinerant ministry. The moment he stopped preaching in various churches, a group of believers from two cities, fifty miles apart, simultaneously contacted him in March 1999 asking him to start a Spirit-filled fellowship that stood for the perfect will of God.

The beginnings of the fellowship were almost identical to the church in the book of Acts. They went from house to house for six months. Thereafter, they searched for a venue between the two cities and settled in a rented building in the village of Pachuta, Mississippi. The word "Pachuta" is derived from the native Indian language which means, "where the pigeons come home to roost." The small fellowship grew slowly, but the presence of the Holy Spirit constantly encouraged them to continue steadfastly in the perfect will of God. At the conclusion of a midweek Bible study, a member of the fellowship approached him and said that God has told her to give four acres of land to the fellowship.

Three years later the fellowship was still a handful of Spirit-filled believers. However, the members inquired from him as to when they would construct their own church building. Francis was reluctant to build because he had not received anything from the Lord about the work other than that it was to start. While visiting one of the members, Mildred Rhoden, she informed him that there were five ladies in Pachuta who had gathered every week for thirty years asking God to bring a Spirit-filled church that stood for the perfect will of God to Pachuta.

While in prayer for God to reveal His purpose to him, Francis received the revelation from the Holy Spirit that God had brought him and his wife, Sandra, seven thousand miles to Pachuta so that God could fulfill His promise to the five women who prayed for thirty years and establish a Spirit-filled church in their village. Francis and Sandra then realized why God had uprooted them from South Africa and brought them to the United States.

Today the Christian Fellowship has a small assembly in Pachuta that is fulfilling the perfect will of God in accordance with God's promise to five ladies' answered prayers. They have their own land and building, and the ministry has developed today to where an evangelist, David Chandler, has been sent to Guyana, South America, several times, and the local Pachuta fellowship supports the Guyana ministry. It also supports the ministry in South Africa.

For more than forty years Francis has been ministering and, during this time, God instructed him to look after himself and his family without receiving any remuneration from the church. By the grace of God, he has been able to support them and work in the church. He maintains that as Apostle Paul stated, his hands supplied his sustenance while he ministers, and he is no man's debtor.

He has authored a book, *The Perfect Will of God*, and has now fulfilled his longtime mission of writing the *Doctrine of the Spirit-Filled Church*.

PART 1

1. DOCTRINE – Introduction
   The introduction references the importance of the **place** doctrine has, the **purpose** in the church, and the **protection** it has of the church.
2. DOCTRINE – The essence and nucleus of doctrine explains the meaning of sound doctrine based on God who is love.
3. DOCTRINE – Intrinsic doctrinal beliefs—where it began.
4. DOCTRINE – God's and man's instruments focus on the work of the Holy Spirit in believers' lives and the methodology man implements to receive the contents of sound doctrine.
5. DOCTRINE – Of the Spirit-filled church refers to the original apostolic Spirit-filled church from the Day of Pentecost and its development through the centuries. It explains the move away from the Holy Spirit's revelation to a legalistic and humanistic church governed by man's ordinances. The conclusion of this chapter directs believers to the return of the church to the revealed truth from the Holy Spirit as it once again is beginning to understand the Godhead's work amongst believers and, in particular, the work of the Holy Spirit from 1900 until today.

CHAPTER 1

INTRODUCTION

*Doctrine – Its **Place** in the Church*

1. Doctrine is vital to the church. It focuses as a light, guide, and premise from which the church should function.
2. Doctrine is the extrapolation of the Word of God and detailed in such a way that members of the church are made aware of the spiritual intentions of each word within the Holy Writ.
3. Doctrine's place in the church must be the reenforcement of the foundation—the Word of God—upon which members build their faith. (Jude 1:20) *Faith is ... evidence of things not seen...* (Hebrews 11:1), and doctrine helps the believer focus on the light that guides him on the path, illuminating the way for him. It helps expose the path that is entrenched in the firm foundation of biblical principles that undergird the believer's faith.
4. Doctrine never divides; it distinguishes truth from error. Truth from error is exposed when *sound doctrine* is applied. (2 Timothy 4:3–4) The Word of God is the *plumb line* and the only reference believers need to guide their faith along the path of truth.
5. Doctrine never divides; it separates assumption from fact. Too many assume that God will never banish a sinner to eternal

damnation. Yet the Word clearly states, and it is therefore a doctrinal fact, that *the wages of sin is death.* The Word declares, *He who believes in the Son has everlasting life; and he who does not believe the Son shall not see life, but the wrath of God abides on him.* (John 3:36 NKJV)

6. Doctrine never divides; it guides. Life's all-consuming passions easily sway a loose and unbridled belief. It is *sound doctrine* that guides the believer along *the straight and narrow.*

7. Doctrine that is rooted in the depth of the Word contains intrinsic elements that prevent it from being corrupt and apt to divide.

8. The error that causes confusion and division is highlighted when believers become skeptical and doubt the truth. These two hindrances—skepticism and doubt—temper the solidity of *sound doctrine*, and the error of "basic doctrine" becomes the measurement of a skeptical believer's beliefs.

9. Lewis Sperry Chafer emphasizes that "since doctrine is the bone structure of the body of revealed truth, the neglect of it must result in a message characterized by uncertainties, inaccuracies, and immaturity...."

10. Basic doctrine is the extraction of parts or the altering of stated Word-based truths to pacify the skeptic and is the reason why so many believe that doctrine divides. It is not doctrine that divides; it is the unwilling mind of the skeptic and doubting believer who refuses to accept the inherent truth in the Word spoken by Almighty God. The impending result: believers who desire to accept basic doctrine have a *form of godliness, but denying the power thereof....* (2 Timothy 3:5)

11. If basic doctrine causes such cataclysmic division, how much more does the "lack of doctrine" make *shipwreck* of a believer's faith? Too many avoid the premise of *sound doctrine,* and because of the application of misguided faith from basic doctrine, many believers reject any form of doctrine, resulting in their walk of faith being exposed and *tossed to and fro, and carried about*

with every wind of doctrine.... (Ephesians 4:14) There is no reinforcement to the foundation of their faith.

12. There is, however, a need to sound a warning: doctrine must not be the method or the overriding and dominant reason why a person becomes a believer. Sound doctrine's place is the explanation that enhances their understanding of what they believe.

13. It is by faith and through God's grace that believers are born again (Ephesians 2:8, Romans 10:9–10), cleansed in the shed, precious blood of Jesus (1 John 1:7), and baptized with the Holy Spirit to worship and glorify Him (Luke 3:16). They serve Him because they love Him. Believers testify about Jesus because, in their heart, they yearn to do this.

14. Believers don't serve God, worship Him, and testify about Jesus because doctrine tells them to do this. Their motivation and inspiration is from the Holy Spirit who will *guide you into all truth....* (John 16:13)

15. Believers are constrained by the love *of* God, *for* God, and *through* God to serve Him. It is done because they are cognizant of the mercy that flows from the Godhead and have experienced the grace of the Lord Jesus Christ that has redeemed them from the *curse of the law.* (Galatians 3:13)

16. Doctrine can be compared to the rail tracks on which the train runs: they guide and keep the train on track. The believer is the train, empowered by the power source (the engine) the Holy Spirit, filled with the love of God, and zealous to serve God as it races along the tracks.

17. Let doctrine always be the guide that keeps a believer *on the straight and narrow....* Let the power source, the Holy Spirit, lead him in the path of righteousness, and let the love for God compel him to *follow in His steps....*

18. Doctrine's place is therefore signified by its ability to give direction and discipline to believers in how they operate in accordance with God's Word. Regrettably, many believers allow emotional

tendencies and experiences of the flesh to enter the realm of their walk with God. The operation of the Holy Spirit's gifts, the time for holy worship and praise, is often infected by the mind/soul, and believers do not *worship the Father in spirit and in truth....* (John 4:23–24)

19. Conversely, if believers are bound by legalism and "doctrinal" parameters preventing them from the liberating freedom of the knowledge that *whom the Son sets free is free indeed*, they stifle the move of the Holy Spirit and limit His ability to achieve His mission.

20. Doctrine, in the eyes of those who believe this way, is then defined as chains that shackle the believer, and these constraints are not doctrine but rather rules and laws that inhibit spiritual growth in Christ. God's Word states, *Christ is the end of the law for righteousness* ... and as such, believers are filled with the Holy Spirit, not legalistic laws and rituals, and can now *mount up on wings as eagles....*

21. It behooves believers, therefore, to understand that doctrine is important to every believer. It must not be the binding force that *quenches* the Holy Spirit. It should be the illuminating beam that shines forth on the path of righteousness for every born-again believer to safely walk in the presence of the Lord.

22. Doctrine's place is settled by the instruction in the Bible: *follow after sound doctrine....* There can be no variance or accusation against doctrine. It must be present in the church because it is present in the Holy Writ.

23. The place it occupies is one of importance because it is the Word of God being placed in its correct order, and the very Word is the measurement by which all tenets are extrapolated.

24. A worthy example of this is found in the very first verse of the Bible. The condemnation that God did not create the heavens and the earth is a direct accusation against the Word, making it out to be a lie. *In the beginning God created the heavens and the earth....*

(Genesis 1:1 NKJV) There is no biblical evidence of evolution. Neither is there any evidence of cataclysmic explosions that thrust a ball of matter into the cosmos that became planet Earth. In the *doctrine of creation,* it is emphatically declared that Jesus, the Word, created the entire world, heaven, earth, that which is under the earth, and all things on earth. (Colossians 1:16)

25. Therefore, believers take the aspects and tenets of sound doctrine and place them in accordance with Divine will and not mankind's wishes.

26. Church foundations become shaky when they build their faith on shifting sands, such as shallow and basic doctrine. Within believers' hearts, controversy is birthed as they question the basis of certain tenets that have no biblical reference.

27. The threat that causes such controversy is the intuition of man's intellect that wants to dissect the essence of the doctrine and apply it to human standards. *God is Spirit* and as such, the tenets are rooted and grounded in Him, not human intellect.

28. The premise that believers must never seek to include God in their plans, but rather seek to place themselves in His purposes, is never more apt.

*Doctrine – Its **Purpose** in the Church*

29. The basis of every doctrinal statement is none other than the biblical evidence of its existence. It is the only reference needed to substantiate its purpose.

30. Any deviation from God's Word or man-made inclusion into church doctrine causes the members to be... *tossed to and fro and carried about with every wind of doctrine, by the sleight of men....* (Ephesians 4:14)

31. Doctrine's purpose in the church is simple and easy to entreat: it is the believer's confession in Jesus Christ as the only begotten Son of God, and His finished work of redemption on the Cross.

32. Every doctrinal tenet *must* reference *Jesus Christ and Him crucified.*

33. The absolute truth in this statement and the full understanding of its message is what forms every other tenet. Its purpose is, therefore, to anchor every believer's born-again spirit in the infallible love of God, who is love, keeping him secure until the *Day of Jesus Christ.*

34. The doctrinal path that stems from Calvary's crimson flow gathers its momentum in the River of Life as it meanders through the Word and intertwines every teaching God breathed into saintly scribes who diligently penned His eternal purposes for mankind.

35. God's purposes for man are found in His message which are rooted and grounded in His never changing eternal love, mercy, and grace. Hence the relevant purpose that doctrine declares: *In him we live and move and have our being....* (Acts 17:28) There is no other righteous pathway; it is the only way. Doctrine therefore purposes that man walk circumspectly ... *in His steps....*

36. In every activity which man involves himself, a code of conduct and a script that directs his path is made available with the express purpose of preventing unnecessary stumbling or perversion. Likewise, the purpose of doctrine is to illuminate the path of a righteous man and keep his feet on solid ground.

37. Again, the analogy of the rail tracks: the purpose of doctrine is to keep the believer within the constraints of the Holy Spirit's leading. Doctrine purposefully channels a believer along the path that is embedded in the Holy Writ. It keeps him from going astray and falling into unscriptural practices.

38. The ultimate purpose of sound doctrine is to direct believers along the path of righteousness that constantly points them to Calvary's Hill and Christ's finished work on the Cross. The resounding

voice of triumph echoing from the empty tomb heralds the proclamation that believers are treading the path of truth and life. Sound doctrine paves the way, and sound doctrine engraves each footstep with a nail imprint so purposefully that there is no fear, doubt, or unbelief in the unquestionable fact of the risen Savior's victory over death and the grave.

Doctrine – Its **Protection** of the Church

39. What would man believe? What path must he follow to keep him from falling into unrighteousness? It can only be the divine teaching found in the holy pages of the Bible. Herein is found the protection from a sinful way. Added to this, the believer is led by the Holy Spirit to the teachings in the Word that detail their beliefs. This sovereign protection is from God Himself, via His Holy Word. Walking in His ways and believing in Him is the scaffolding every believer needs to protect him from the wiles of the devil.

40. Sadly, in the church many are led away by false teachers. They develop *itching ears* to hear only what entices them into self-gratification. Many are led away to *believe a lie*. However, when surrounded by the intrinsic truths of the indelible Word, an everlasting protection from His everlasting arms secures the believer and anchors him in the undisputed fact that *Christ Jesus came into the world to save sinners....* (1 Timothy 1:15)

41. The true corporate church owes the world no apology; neither does it owe the world any explanation. Its doors are open to *anyone*, and the invitation to all is without intimidation or pecuniary interest. It is focused on the eternal purposes of God, and those who accept its message walk by faith in the belief and promises from the mouth of God: *Neither shall any man pluck them out of my hand....* (John 10:28) Doctrine assures the believer of the Holy

Spirit's mantel that protects him from *dashing his foot against a stone....* Doctrine declares to the world what saints believe. The world must either accept it or reject it. Doctrine is direct and without hypocrisy, it needs no intellectual interpretation; it is sound and easy to be entreated. Regrettably, the *wise of this world* find it difficult to accept it, and willingly cast it aside for their own gain.

42. The members of the church should be equally cognizant of the teachings and explanations the educated hierarchy deliver as well as to those who are well versed and experienced, although uneducated. There should be a holy reverence for those entrusted with the Word by God. The church should always measure the message against the spiritual depth of the preacher and the anointing he carries, instead of his diplomas and degrees. It is useless for members to adhere to the educated preacher if he is unholy and spiritually lukewarm. It is within the grasp of every believer to listen to "fishermen" (Apostle Peter, Apostle John), a "tax gatherer" (Apostle Matthew), as it is important to take heed what the "physician" (Luke) says, and humbly turn to the Holy Writ rather than the *wise according to the flesh* (1 Corinthians 1:26–31 NKJV).

43. *They continued steadfastly in the apostles' doctrine....* (Acts 2:42) This was the plumb line of their walk in Christ. It never wavered or sowed confusion. This doctrine rooted and grounded believers. It protected them daily from wolves in sheep's clothing (Matthew 7:15). Believers' reference wasn't man's worldly wisdom. It wasn't from a collection of wise sayings worldly men had declared to the ignorant to help them walk a better life. A believer's reference is their Holy God's Holy Word that stands the test of time and is eternal in its application. There they hide in the *cleft of the Rock ...* and dwell ... *in the secret place of the Most High....* (Psalm 91:1)

44. Sound doctrine, according to the Word, is the fortress that protects the church from meandering along a path of false and crooked teaching. "What does God's Word say?" is the question

that echoes every time someone needs direction. How blessed the church is today to have centuries of guidance and teaching in *sound doctrine* that protects it on every one of life's flanks.

45. So daunting and profound is the Word of God that every nation is guided by it in some way or another. The basis of what is good or evil is determined by God's standards of what is good or evil. In their ignorance and their unsaved state, the world follows many doctrinal teachings that they willingly apply to protect them from untoward wrongdoing.

46. On the contrary, in the divine organism of the body of Christ, the church abides in the full extent of obedience as it follows true doctrine.

47. Doctrine surrounds every belief and principle that guides the believer. Compromise is not an option. *Following after righteousness* is not a choice for a believer. It is a doctrinal standard taught in the Word, and believers are to *cut off the weights and sin that so easily besets* ... and *continue steadfastly in the **apostles' doctrine, fellowship, breaking of bread**, and **prayers**....*

48. It is an absolute decree of God's merciful and loving expression of His love towards mankind that He never leaves them destitute. His divine oracle and ever-abiding presence covers them with the mantel of His protection. Doctrine is the extrapolation of the Word and sets the "rail tracks" within which man lives.

49. Within the holy pages of the Majestic Word, man finds the deep revelation about God, from God. Lewis Sperry Chafer says, "The Bible is that message and, while man cannot originate any similar truth, he, though finite, is privileged by the gracious illumination of the Spirit to receive, with some degree of understanding, the revelation concerning things which are infinite."

50. Believers never should apologize for what they do in Christ. There is no need for them to answer any question regarding their righteousness and conduct because the Word declares, *Their righteousness is of me, saith the Lord....* (Isaiah 54:17)

51. The protection doctrine affords a believer is peace of mind. Its covering is likened to the veil covering the Holy of Holies: impregnable. If a person enters the place of God's divine presence without the protection of His anointing, then he who does this will suffer the same wrath an unrighteous High Priest suffered.

52. Doctrine roots and grounds the believer. Their foundation cornerstone is Jesus Christ, and believers build upon the foundation of apostles and prophets.

53. Faith is the premise from which doctrine operates. Faith in God and His Word, belief in the promises of Calvary's sacrifice, and the guarantee of eternal life in Christ Jesus propel the believer to walk daily under the covering of the church's doctrinal tenets.

Doctrine is the explanation of the intrinsic truths in the Bible.

CHAPTER 2

Doctrine – Its Essence and Nucleus

1. While the Holy Word of God consists of many separate books, the ultimate reference that each one presents are the same: glorify God Almighty and conform to His righteousness.
2. These two aspects referenced in the Word are made possible for every created human being through the essence of God's nature. Love is Who He is. God is not a God of love: He is *agape* (love).
3. God immerses His love (Himself) into every person who accepts Him by faith.
4. The nucleus of God's message is intertwined in and around one core premise: *For God so loved the world that He gave His only begotten Son....* (John 3:16 NKJV)
5. Every tenet that doctrine has emanates from this premise. There is a fundamentally entrenched basis for this message: *God manifest in the flesh: The Lamb of God who takes away the sin of the world: For God so loved the world that He gave His only begotten Son....*
6. The transformation of a man's spirit from death to life is based upon the following statement and belief by faith: *If you confess*

with your mouth the Lord Jesus and believe in your heart that God has raised Him from the dead, you will be saved. (Romans 10:9 NKJV) This is nothing short of *Jesus Christ and Him crucified.*

7. This faith-applied declaration is the beginning of the doctrinal message. Every tenet is rooted and grounded in this rich texture that nourishes every aspect of the church's beliefs.

8. Calvary's Cross and Golgotha's Hill is for the church the most holy expression of God's divine love for man. It is an "emblem of suffering and shame," and a place of victory over sin and death. In addition, they are the door to the heart of Almighty God to everyone who believes.

9. There is no other way to be reunited with God. Neither is there any other way for man to be saved. Worse still, rejection of Calvary and the Cross opens the alternate door to eternal judgment.

10. It must be the starting point of every believer's walk. Likewise, it is the focal point of every believer's daily walk in Christ.

11. The confession that a person makes stating their belief in Jesus Christ and Him crucified culminates in the statement that they believe in a glorious demonstration of God's power, namely, the resurrection of Jesus Christ from the dead.

12. The statement that a person confesses *Him crucified* always directs him to the result of the crucifixion, namely, Jesus' resurrection. The death and resurrection go together as hydrogen and oxygen do to form water. Christ's death and resurrection are summed up in the word *crucified.*

13. It is therefore only appropriate that the Holy Writ contains a verse that brings everything together for a believer. The illustration of Love, and the effects of this Love, are found embedded in these sacred words, *For He made Him who knew no sin to be sin for us, that we might become the righteousness of God in Him.* (2 Corinthians 5:21 NKJV)

14. *The gospel of Christ ... is the power of God unto salvation to everyone that believeth....* (Romans 1:16) This is a conclusive statement that gives assurance to everyone who believes. It is the confirmation clause that in the crucified Christ, man has a redeeming power that flows like a crimson river from Calvary's Hill into the life of a faith-filled heart, bringing salvation through the blotting out of sin. This is unbridled power that can come from nowhere else, except from *Jesus Christ and Him crucified.*

15. Having this "cornerstone" of a believer's faith steadfast and unmovable, each tenet reaches forth to the teachings of Jesus and the apostles and expounds the Word regarding a particular doctrine. While the teachings unfold the deep truths of the tenet, they must always look to the Cross as the nucleus from which the tenets emanate.

16. God's mercy transcends human comprehension. God's love is immeasurable. God's forgiveness is impartial. These vital truths must be clearly understood.

17. They are experienced in the heart (spirit-man) and are freely given when a converted sinner is standing before the Heavenly Father at a spiritual "Calvary's Hill" and confessing *Jesus Christ as Lord.*

18. It is not found in manuscripts or books. It is not apportioned to a person who studies and takes a test, getting the answers correct. It is encountered when repentant sinners stand before the Father and confess Jesus Christ as Lord and believe in their hearts that God raised Jesus from the dead.

19. Thus, the confession that the sinner believes Jesus was crucified, and that God raised Him from the dead, becomes the birthplace and nucleus of his faith. He dares not wander from it.

The Essence of Sound Doctrine

20. Doctrine can never replace the infallible Word of God. It must reference the Word in every description and explanation it makes about the Word.

21. Salvation is not wrought through doctrine. Salvation comes from Jesus Christ and His finished work on Calvary. His finished work on Calvary is not a doctrinal statement, it is the Word of God; *Christ died for the ungodly. He offered Himself once, for all….*

22. Doctrine takes the Word of Almighty God and unveils deeper truths and meaning that lies in the depth of God's unsearchable ways; *Oh, the depth of the riches both of the wisdom and knowledge of God! How unsearchable are His judgments and His ways past finding out!* (Romans 11:33 NKJV)

23. Furthermore, doctrine draws from the Holy Canon various scriptures that are of like-mindedness, in harmony of meaning, and that contribute to the greater explanation of a subject. It cannot be tainted by human interpretation. Doctrine conforms to God's desire for man, and His will that is detailed in His Word. Therefore, all doctrine does is unveil God's purpose and will for man.

24. Doctrine cannot be man's attempt to suggest to God his will for man. It must always be God revealing His will to man. Put another way, it is not man taking from God what man wants, but it rather explains God giving to man His will.

Summary

25. In conclusion, it is imperative that every born-again believer fully understands that every aspect of his acceptance and continued walk in the Lord is based on the fundamental root of walking in

the steps of the Master by *faith*. The Word declares, *Without faith it is impossible to please him....* (Hebrews 11:6)

26. By faith man accepts God's salvation offer through Jesus Christ. By faith man walks according to His precepts. By faith man follows the Holy Spirit's guidance and teaching.

27. The yearning within the spirit of the born-again believer to *grow in the grace of the Lord Jesus Christ* compels him to *study to shew thyself approved unto God....* (2 Timothy 2:15)

28. This yearning can sometimes be infected by false teaching which causes shipwreck. Hence the need for sound doctrine to be the parameters within which believers walk.

29. Doctrine is the basis for the explanation of what the newly born-again believer has experienced, as well as the "rail tracks" that keep him in the right direction.

30. Doctrine does not replace faith; it enhances the believer's knowledge of his faith.

31. Doctrine does not save the lost soul and spirit; it enables the saved soul and spirit to walk circumspectly in the Word.

32. Doctrine always points to the hill called Mt. Calvary. It is always rooted and grounded in Jesus' finished work.

33. Doctrine must separate truth from error. It must distinguish between faith and unbelief.

34. Doctrine explains God's will for man, detailed and explained in more depth. It should never be man's desire to fit God into his plans, but rather man fitting himself into God's purpose for his life.

The Church's Effective Operation

35. The early church that was established on the Day of Pentecost lived and operated under the leading of the Holy Spirit. The Holy Spirit led men to record the principles and beliefs by which every member of every local assembly should function. Furthermore,

the Holy Spirit led the men to lay the ultimate and only doctrinal foundation for the church. (2 Peter 1:21)

36. For the first one hundred years, there was only one "denomination," one doctrine, one faith, which was entirely focused on one Lord.

37. Every believer followed the same apostles' doctrine and contended for *the faith*. It did not matter whether a believer worshipped in Rome, Jerusalem, Corinth: the same principles and doctrine were adhered to.

38. Likewise, the same teachings found in the New Testament, from Matthew to Revelation, were applied by every believer.

39. Having said this, it must be understood that in every local assembly throughout the church, the same tenets and principles were operational.

40. In every assembly, the gifts of the Holy Spirit were operational. In every assembly, the ministry of the gospel of Jesus Christ was preached. In every assembly, the elders laid hands on the sick, the deacons served the widows, and the fivefold ministries were operational. (Ephesians 4:11)

41. Absolute acceptance and implementation of every ministry and office in the church was evidenced. There was no casting aside of certain ministries; all were operational all the time.

42. The sacred words contained in the pages of the Holy Writ were not given to man so that he can pick and choose which of them he thought would best suit his congregation. These are entirely God's words to the church.

43. Therefore, today, every church, local assembly, and fellowship of the saints should be functioning according to the New Testament's instructions.

44. There is no reason, neither is there evidence that gives permission for local denominations to carve out sections of the Holy Writ because it doesn't suit their people or "fit their culture."

45. There is only one age for the church, and that is the Apostolic Age. Departure from this basic foundation is the reason for the

ineffectiveness of the church's operation and the lack of impact it has on the unsaved.

46. If every word in the New Testament is for the church, then why is it not in operation in every local assembly today? Who gives man the right to discard some of the teachings and guidance found in the holy pages?

47. After all, what will be the basis of the ruling of the final dispensation of this age? Will it not be Jesus Christ ruling in righteousness over all mankind during the Millennial Reign? And upon which principles will He base His rulership? They will be from the Word of God.

48. Anyone who has removed the principles and teachings of the church's functions and pushed them aside declaring they don't need them today will answer to Jesus for their omission of His teachings. In addition, anyone who adds to these teachings found in the Word of God is as answerable to Jesus.

49. Every *one jot or one tittle* (Matthew 5:18) contained in the New Testament should be evidenced in every local assembly across the world that sets forth to proclaim the truth of the gospel of Jesus Christ.

The Absolute and Sure Foundation

50. The Psalmist asks the question, *If the foundations be destroyed, what can the righteous do?* (Psalm 11:3) The ultimate purpose of the church's enemy is to destroy the solid foundation upon which believers stand. When this is done, the enemy sows fear, doubt, and unbelief in the believer's soul.

51. However, even though society, filled with sinful intent, has tried to destroy righteous truths, shrouded the foundation pillars with humanism, compromise, and blatant denial of the truth, they will

not be able to utterly destroy the foundation of righteousness, justice, and peace.

52. The Holy Spirit-filled believer reaches deep into the Word and strips the evil veneer, sinful dirt, and corrupt attempts that try to tarnish the holiness and righteousness of the foundational pillars and uncovers God's truth. These words have been declaring the incorruptible message throughout the ages: *Nevertheless the solid foundation of God stands, having this seal: The Lord knows those who are His....* (2 Timothy 2:19 NKJV)

CHAPTER 3

INTRINSIC DOCTRINAL BELIEFS –
WHERE IT BEGAN

1. The underlying premise uttered by God, *I change not ... (Malachi 3:6)*, sets the record of impartiality and parity for all mankind. There is *no variation or shadow of turning* with God.
2. Thus said, the charge to born-again believers is to conform to God's holy teachings and follow after His righteousness. Doctrine unveils these teachings and assists every generation to walk in His unchangeable steps.
3. However, millenniums, centuries, and decades in man's traditions, culture, and philosophies can erode the essence and dogma of truth. It was, and is, in the best interest of every generation of born-again believers that from the earliest days, men have been drawn to pen the intrinsic truths of Jesus' teachings.
4. The preservation of these truths was sealed in the earliest writings available to the church. They have stood the test of time and still hold the timeworn sails of the Christian church steady on its course.
5. The basis for the declaration of the gospel of Jesus Christ, *We were reconciled to God by the death of his Son ...* (Romans 5:10), rests on the pillars that undergird the essence of Christian doctrine.

These intrinsic values/beliefs/tenets are entrenched, immovable, and unchangeable.

6. These pillars of truth must be openly declared, confessed, and truly believed.

Jesus' virgin birth
Jesus' death on the cross
Jesus' resurrection from the dead
Jesus is the Son of God

7. From the earliest writings, men who were led by the Holy Spirit declared unequivocally these truths. The first account that contains these four pillars is recorded in the church's first message ever preached by Apostle Peter on the Day of Pentecost.

Acts 2:27 *The Holy one*
Acts 2:23 *The crucified One*
Acts 2:24 *The resurrected One*
Acts 2:33 *The Father's promise to His Son fulfilled.*

8. From this premise, writers declared their belief and commitment to these doctrinal truths.

9. With these witnessed, testified, and believed holy truths so convincingly evident in the early church's faith, the first writers, Mark, Matthew, Luke, and much later John, were drawn by the Holy Spirit to record the gospels. Their aim was to give an accurate eyewitness account of the teachings and ministry of the Savior, Jesus Christ. Apostle John emphatically declares this: 1 John 1:1–3 (NKJV)

That which was from the beginning,
which we have heard, which we have
seen with our eyes, which we have

looked upon, and our hands have handled,
concerning the Word of life-
The life was manifested, and we have seen,
and bear witness, and declare to you that
eternal life which was with the Father and
was manifested to us-
That which we have seen and heard we
declare to you, that you also may have
fellowship with us; and truly our fellowship
is with the Father and with His Son Jesus Christ.

10. To preserve these truths, the writers of the New Testament were led by the Holy Spirit to give detailed instructions and teachings on the Christian life which is, in the church age, by *faith in Jesus Christ and His finished work on Calvary,* and no longer earned on the basis of obedience to the Law and Commandments, for *Christ is the end of the law for righteousness....* (Romans 10:4) Hence flowed the writings of the New Testament to the early church.

11. These holy anointed writings are the Word of God to everyone who believes. They rivet the believer's faith in Jesus Christ. Therefore, the statement by Apostle Paul: *There are some who trouble you and want to pervert the gospel of Christ. But even if we, or an angel from heaven, preach any other gospel to you than what we have preached to you, let him be accursed ...* (Galatians 1:7–8 NKJV) is not one made in arrogance and jealously. It is declared with such forcefulness so that it can turn the wayward believer back onto the path of the truth.

12. The New Testament writings became the anchor for the early church, which stayed the course. However, as the church grew and spread across the known world culture, religion, and heritage caused many to misinterpret the holy Word of God. To settle any misunderstanding and confusion, church leaders gathered to

make "Statements of Belief." Thus, flowed declarations on what the church based its beliefs.

13. Contained in the first statements of belief/faith, such as the Apostles' Creed and the Nicene Creed which date back to the first three hundred years of the church, are the four core tenets/pillars expressed in fundamental terms.

14. What now followed was the worst error that has ever invaded the church's holy estate: man began to dissect and give his worldly interpretation of the Word of God and the creeds.

15. Subsequently, faith was exchanged for intellect, belief was exchanged for evidence, and trust in God was exchanged for trust in human folly.

16. Even though the four pillars of the Christian faith have been battered by so many interpretations, cultural and traditional influences, there has been throughout the ages those whom God has chosen to preserve the intrinsic message contained in the four pillars.

17. Therefore, with these intentions imbedded in the believer's heart, namely to find the essence of biblical truth expressed in doctrinal terms, man must return to the eternal Word of God, cast aside man's interpretations, and delve into the riches of the Holy Writ to no longer conform to this world: *And be not be conformed to this world, but be ye transformed by the renewing of your mind, that ye may prove what is that good, and acceptable, and perfect will of God ....* (Romans 12:2)

18. The only measurement that can be trusted is the Word of God. The only plumb line of truth is the Word of God. The only reference man can make is to the Creator of all things, Jesus Christ and His finished work.

19. Having the absolute truth declared from the holy God, it is important to seek the depths of His Word knowing that ... *deep calleth unto deep* ... (Psalm 42:7) and ... *the secret things belong*

to the LORD our God, but those things which are revealed belong to us and to our children.... (Deuteronomy 29:29 NKJV)

20. The word *doctrine* is derived from the Greek word *didasko*. The Greek meaning translated into English is "teacher" or "teachings." (Acts 5:34) It is used both as a subject "lesson" being taught, and for the person "giving the lesson." Hence the word *doctor*, or one who has been educated to make a specialized declaration with authority on a particular subject ("teacher").

21. Derived from this origin *didasko*, the word *didache* is used to imply the "content" of the subject, namely its "teachings" or "doctrine" (Acts 2:42)

Conclusion

22. There is no choice in the matter but to return to the origin of the teachings (doctrine) for the church.

23. It does not matter what man has done or invented for their denomination. What matters is the truth and the application thereof.

24. Every believer has the right and the privilege to know these truths. Thus said, once they are known, the challenge is for every believer to *live, move, and have their being* in them.

25. *Cutting off, laying aside, returning to the stronghold*, and *standing fast in the liberty* should draw the believer to *hunger and thirst*, to crave, yearn, and search the holy, pure, and undefiled Word of God until they find the essence of God's *didasko*.

26. The inerrant, holy, undefiled, everlasting, and Holy Spirit-anointed Word of God is: *the declaration of who God is, and how He deals with man's sin and sins*. Upon this immovable foundation, and in these truths, the New Testament doctrine is "soundly" constructed.

CHAPTER 4

God's and Man's Instruments

1. *All Scripture is given by inspiration of God ...* (2 Timothy 3:16), and ... *holy men of God spake as they were moved by the Holy Ghost.* (2 Peter 1:21) Herein lies the declaration that roots and grounds the content of the Bible.
2. It is from the Messenger—the Holy Spirit who imparts the message, the Word of God, into the heart of man—who is equipped to receive this eternal declaration: *Forever, O Lord, thy word is settled in heaven.* (Psalm 119:89)
3. The question that needs to be answered is this: How does the infallible eternal God, who is almighty, reach the heart of fallible man, and what does fallible man need to be used of God and receive the message?
4. Henceforth, it is needful to remain within the Holy Writ and consider how this process takes place and what instruments are used to expound the doctrinal truths within, so that all born-again believers can continue *steadfastly in the apostles' doctrine....* (Acts 2:42)

God's Instruments

Revelation

5. The primary instrument used by Almighty God is *revelation.* Divine revelation from God to man is: "God's disclosure of Himself and of His will to His creatures." (*Webster's Encyclopedic Dictionary*) Revelation is God opening, showing, and declaring that of Himself and His creation to man which was previously unknown. The information, insight, and knowledge so declared by God is beyond human knowledge, common sense, and education.

6. God needed a receptacle for His divine revelation concerning Who He is and how He deals with man's inherent sin and subsequent sins. He chose man as this receptacle conduit to declare His righteous purposes, as well as His intended forthcoming dealings with righteous saints. The only way He can declare His sovereignty, His holy estate, His deity, and His power is via direct revelation from His heart into the heart of man.

7. To clarify what spiritual revelation from God is, Lewis Chafer says, "A divine revelation is accomplished whenever any manifestation of God is discerned or any evidence of His presence, purpose, or power is communicated."

8. Revelation is divided into two parts: that which has already been revealed, and that which is now being revealed to the church. These two forms of revelation need to be separated to ensure that there is no confusion regarding the unchangeable Word of God.

9. First, the Holy Writ, the Canon, the Bible, or better still the *inspired Word of God,* is complete. It needs no further additions, subtractions, or modifications. What God has revealed to *holy men of God* is *forever settled in heaven.* (Psalm 119:89) This is declared revelation and needs no additions or subtractions in its contents.

10. Revelation is never conceived in man's mind. It is declared from the heart of God to man. The Bible is, therefore, holy *words*

declared by God to mankind. It is that which is revealed by God to man for man's instruction and benefit.

11. Lewis Chafer continues, "There is a limitless yet hidden spiritual content within the Bible which contributes much to its supernatural character.... The natural capacities of the human mind do not function in the realm of spiritual things. The divine message is presented ... *not in words which man's wisdom teaches but which the Holy Spirit teaches, comparing spiritual things with spiritual....* " (1 Corinthians 2:13 NKJV)

12. Second, ongoing or progressive revelation is never conceived by man's intellect. It is that which is unknown to him in his puny mind, and subsequently *enlightened* (illuminated) by the *wisdom from above* (by God) into the spirit of mortal man. (John 16:12–15)

13. This revelation concerns the eternal relationship between God and man, and how God imparts greater clarity to him and gives *spiritual discernment* regarding the deep truths embedded in His Word.

14. Without doubt, there is no way the human mind can comprehend the intimate and depths of God's eternal Word unless they are revealed to him by the Holy Spirit. *Now we have received, not the spirit of this world, but the Spirit who is from God, that we might know the things that have been freely given to us by God.* (1 Corinthians 2:12 NKJV)

15. Consequently ... the *natural man does not receive the things of the Spirit of God, for they are foolishness to him; nor can he know them, because they are spiritually discerned.* (1 Corinthians 2:14 NKJV)

16. God does not use a particular class of person, a special standard of education, or an esteemed socialite to impart revelation. God uses the righteous standing, the upright intentions, and the holy estate of a believer's heart to impart revelation. It is the condition of the heart that determines the ability to receive from God.

17. When man *hungers and thirsts after righteousness and seeks the Lord while He may be found,* his intentions are rewarded. God *is a rewarder of them that diligently seek Him.* (Hebrews 11:6)

18. The progressive revelation concerning the operation and effectiveness of the perfecting of the church has been and is *... revealed unto his holy apostles and prophets by the Spirit.* (Ephesians 3:5)

19. Revelation is still operational today because God's Word has *depth of the riches both of the wisdom and knowledge of God ...* (Romans 11:33) embedded in the divine message, which is *enlightened* (revealed) into the heart of righteous persons who *... hunger and thirst after righteousness.* (Matthew 5:6) *For I am not ashamed of the gospel of Christ, for it is the power of God unto salvation.... For therein is the righteousness of God revealed from faith to faith....* (Romans 1:16–17)

20. The prayer for the righteous one to receive revelation is expressed by Apostle Paul: *that the God of our Lord Jesus Christ, the Father of glory, may give to you the spirit of wisdom and revelation in the knowledge of Him, the eyes of your understanding being enlightened that you may know what is the hope of His calling....* (Ephesians 1:17–18 NKJV)

21. Revelation is used by God to direct and enhance the believer's understanding of God's will for them. (Philippians 3:15–16) Again, the Word says, *But God has revealed them to us through His Spirit. For the Spirit searches all things, yes, the deep things of God* (1 Corinthians 2:10 NKJV).

22. To conclude, the finality of the Holy Bible is without question. It is complete in its sixty-six books and needs no additions or deletions. The revelation that flows thereafter to man is the impartation of the spiritual intentions, so that man's *understanding* may be *enlightened* through the Holy Spirit, in order that he can fully comprehend the unchangeable truths within the Bible. Because God's infinite wisdom and knowledge are far beyond the finite capacity of the human soul and spirit, God uses revelation to declare and clarify that which man cannot fathom out on his own.

Inspiration

23. The word used only once in the Bible which has deep meaning concerning the mode of God's impartation of His Word is *inspiration.* Apostle Paul declares, *All Scripture is given by inspiration of God....* (2 Timothy 3:16)

24. The literal translation of the word *inspiration* so used in the Bible is: *the breath of God, breathed by God,* or more accurately translated, *God-breathed.*

25. The exposition of the literal translation can be likened to the day God formed Adam from the dust of the ground and *breathed into his nostrils the breath of life; and man became a living soul.* (Genesis 2:7)

26. The life-giving breath from Almighty God burst forth into the frame God created, and *life* ignited every cell and blood vessel with *power to live.* Likewise, God *breathed forth* His Word through the Holy Spirit into men's hearts, and God's life-giving spiritual utterances were revealed to holy men of God who diligently penned God's Words. (2 Peter 1:21)

27. Consequently, the Word of God is eternally a life-giving word that will never *pass away.* Every word recorded in the pages of the Holy Writ is *life,* and they *live and breathe life.*

28. The words contained in the pages of the Bible are not man's interpretation of what God wanted to say, neither are they man's thoughts of what God intended. They are life in its holiest and purist form, and they are eternally spoken from the heart of God and as such, recorded. They are outside the frame of mortal man, and diligently recorded by obedient *holy men of God.*

29. The God-breathed Word is from a holy source, namely God's heart. The life contained in the Bible is eternal and never changes, neither does it cease in its power and effect. Thus said, because it is *given by inspiration of God* (God-breathed), it has the effect of spiritual enlightenment.

30. Every syllable contains the everlasting presence of Almighty God, which illuminates God's will, His way, and His works with man. *Thy word is a lamp unto my feet, and a light unto my path* (Psalm 119:105). It enlightens the way for man, exposing truth from error. It illuminates man's spirit to fully comprehend God's will and thereby gives a clear message of His works.

Anointing

31. The seal of God's approval and the separation of a man for the purpose of receiving revelation, inspiration, and instruction from God is embodied in God's anointing of that person.

32. *He has anointed Me to preach the gospel....* (Luke 4:18); *Now He who establishes us with you in Christ and has anointed us is God, who also has sealed us and given us the Spirit in our hearts as a guarantee....* (2 Corinthians 1:21–22 NKJV); *Touch not mine anointed....* (Psalm 105:15)

33. The effectiveness and sufficiency of this infallible promise is sealed in these words: *But the anointing which you have received from Him abides in you, and you do not need that anyone teach you; but as the same anointing teaches you concerning all things, and is true, and is not a lie, and just as it is taught you, you will abide in Him.* (1 John 2:27 NKJV)

34. Consider the process emanating from God's heart. He desires that man knows and understands more of His Word. He chooses a vessel—*You did not choose Me, but I chose you ...* (John 15:16 NKJV)—to whom He will impart His revelation and message. Now God *seals* the person with His anointing. Next, He equips the person with His holy anointing so that the person understands the spiritual intentions of His purposes ... *But you have an anointing from the Holy One, and you know all things....* (1 John 2:20 NKJV)

35. The physical anointing God instructed the Jews to perform and the manufactured anointing oil/paste was critical to God. God's instructions in Exodus chapter 30:22–38 had to be followed to the letter. If it was not done exactly as God had prescribed, the recipients were ... *cut off from his people*.... (Exodus 30:33)

36. Likewise, the Holy Spirit's anointing of a person is the *Holy One's* (1 John 2:20) holiest act of *consecration* (Exodus 30:30) and unification of the person's spirit/heart with the Holy Spirit, so that the individual can be a sealed, sanctified, and the holy vessel readily equipped to perform God's intention for the specific revelation or task.

37. The church's acceptance by faith of this spiritual application is critical for ... *the effectual working of his power*.... (Ephesians 3:7)

38. Apostle Paul was saturated in the Holy Spirit's anointing which is evidenced by his labors and the miracles God wrought through him. His message to the church is ... *Christ crucified* (1 Corinthians 1:23). Therein he declared the faith. This message was under the anointing of the Holy Spirit and it was readily received ... *as it is in truth, the word of God, which also effectively works in you who believe* .... (1 Thessalonians 2:13 NKJV)

39. Every born-again believer must willingly approach the presence of the *Holy One* with this attitude: *present your bodies a living sacrifice, holy, acceptable unto God, which is your reasonable service* .... (Romans 12:1) When believers do this, the *oil of the anointing* flows from the fountain of grace and drenches their words and deeds in the Holy Spirit's revealed intentions.

40. These three instruments—revelation, inspiration, and anointing— are not conclusive and wrap up the totality of God's divine ability to impart His purpose for man. The declaration that God's divine utterances are "inerrant" and "infallible" must be accepted as ... *the way, the truth, and the life* .... (John 14:6)

41. These three instruments used by God do, however, shed light onto the path that paves the way for man to stand *steadfast* and

unmovable.... Knowing that emanating from God's heart, the impartation of His will is encased in these three characteristics, unequivocally settles the premise that God's message is truth. It is His truth, and the truth is declared through the *mouth* of man. (Acts 1:16)

42. It is needful to consider the application of the following three instruments God applies towards mankind.

Love, Mercy, and Grace

43. God is love. All His infinite attributes that are presented to man are encapsulated in who He is, namely love. He shows mercy towards man's sin-stained generations, and ultimately in the finished work of Calvary, shows grace towards mankind.

44. The moment the divine Savior exited the tomb, grace was shed abroad towards man because of what Jesus accomplished on the Cross and in His resurrection. *All have sinned and come short of the glory of God.* There has never been or will ever be anyone born who is not covered under the fallen nature of sin. Neither is there anything possible that mankind can do to eradicate that sin nature and be accepted by God who is pure, holy, and undefiled.

45. The grace of the Lord Jesus Christ and the impartation, therefore, is entirely a God-created act. Man has absolutely no part in its origin and can claim no ownership to any part of its application and result. It is wrought entirely through the finished work that Christ accomplished on Calvary. It is wholly the God-ordained gift towards fallen mankind. This is grace personified.

46. Grace, while being the object of God's divine love for man that induces mercy, should never be seen as an abstract tangent that God imposes upon fallen man to afford him the opportunity of escaping everlasting damnation. It is the ultimate act of perfect divine love that is expressed through the heart of a loving God

who is ... *not willing that any should perish, but that all should come to repentance....* (2 Peter 3:9)

47. To receive this magnificent expression of love and mercy, man reaches forth and accepts by faith the finished work Jesus Christ accomplished on the Cross. In this horrific death and glorious resurrection, God took care of the sin-stained heritage infested in man's nature and offered His Son as the propitiation for their sin, which paved the way for His grace to be freely offered to whosoever will receive it.

48. *That in the ages to come He might show the exceeding riches of His grace in His kindness toward us in Christ Jesus. For by grace you have been saved through faith....* (Ephesians 2:7–8 NKJV)

49. Grace is not the cold, hard, and loveless instrument God has made available for the salvation of mankind. It is, in fact, the most sublime, beautiful, and ultimate gift that God could make available to mankind. It embodies the fullest expression of love and mercy which ... *in Him we have redemption through His blood, the forgiveness of sins, according to the riches of His grace which He made to abound toward us in all wisdom and prudence....* (Ephesians 1:7–8 NKJV)

Man's Instruments

Faith

50. *But without faith it is impossible to please Him, for he who comes to God must believe that He is, and that He is a rewarder of those who diligently seek Him.* (Hebrews 11:6 NKJV)

51. No ritual, deed, or intention can ever please the righteous God. It is in the immeasurable power of faith the size of a *grain of mustard seed* that man uses which is pleasing to God.

52. Faith is man's demonstration that he believes in God's promises,

is prepared to live by the consequences of his actions resulting from his faith which are *foolishness to the world*, (1 Corinthians 1:27–28 NKJV), and he trusts God to bring about the things man *hoped for*. (Hebrews 11:1)

53. Even though the Word is filled with evidences that God's promises are *yea and amen*, too few are prepared to ... *walk by faith, not by sight*. (2 Corinthians 5:7) Jesus' question is being put to believers every day: *Do you believe that I am able to do this?* (Matthew 9:28 NKJV) This question demands that believers trust God to bring about His will in their lives. Faith is from God who gives it to believers to believe and trust Him (Romans 12:3).

54. Such trust, an integral ingredient of faith, is the demonstration by the believer that they differ from the world as they declare: *Some trust in chariots, and some in horses; but we will remember the name of the Lord our God*. (Psalm 20:7 NKJV)

55. Believers root and ground their faith in the finished work of Calvary. They accept by faith the cleansing flow of the crimson tide flowing from Calvary's crucifixion. They believe that once repentance is done, sin is washed away. It is faith in Jesus' finished work that brings about the new birth. This doctrinal tenet is the nucleus from which every other tenet springs forth.

56. The only basis by which believers can walk in *His steps* is by faith in *things unseen*. The age-old phrase that has echoed through the church age is as relevant today as it was when first uttered: "Bring nothing, no deed or offering into His presence. Yet, bring everything—faith."

57. Doctrine is sealed in the premise of the believer's faith that God has said it and that settles it. When a doctrinal tenet is drenched in the Holy Writ, then faith is all that is required to unlock the door and enter the presence of almighty God.

Holiness

58. *Be ye holy, for I am holy.* (1 Peter 1:16) This is a commandment from the Holy God to His children. There is no "right of choice" and conversation about the merits of either being holy or not. *Being holy* ... is the spiritual state in which the believer must walk.

59. Doctrine is understood, and revelation is received, when this holy state is embedded in man's spirit. The channel which the Holy Spirit uses to reach the heart of man is the holy condition of his spirit ... *but holy men of God spake as they were moved by the Holy Ghost....* (2 Peter 1:21)

60. Holiness is described as the condition that is "morally and spiritually excellent." It is the result of the divine cleansing of a man's spirit by the love, mercy, grace, and forgiveness that streams from the Holy Godhead.

61. From the moment the sinner repents and accepts Jesus Christ as Lord, their spirit is born again and is washed in the precious blood of Jesus which produces a *holy* and undefiled spirit within. Now follows the command, *Be holy,* namely walk in this pureness and righteous condition and ... *present your bodies a living sacrifice, holy, acceptable to God, which is your reasonable service. And do not be conformed to this world, but be transformed by the renewing of your mind....* (Romans 12:1–2 NKJV)

62. The condition of man's spirit—holy—is what God seeks in the one through whom He desires to reach the lost and impart His will. God cannot impart His sacred, pure, and holy message through an unholy vessel of dishonor. The ritualistic cleansing of the vessels in the temple by the children of God while under the Law was a prerequisite God demanded before the people could enter His holy presence. Now, God's *better covenant* requires that man constantly remain holy.

63. Further attributes such as obedience, humbleness, steadfastness, and willingness to learn are as important and must be in man's

tool chest for him to receive the deep things from God. These additional attributes are explained in broader detail in the doctrinal tenets.

Prayer

64. The ultimate favor passed on to man when they are born-again is the restored intimate communion he has with God through prayer. This divinely imparted gift to a redeemed soul is the reconciliation he has craved for from the time of the fall in the Garden of Eden.

65. The darkness of the separation that hindered the lost soul is now destroyed as the believer *looks to Jesus* (Hebrews 12:1–2) and through His wonderful name, man can once again speak to God in prayer and supplication with thanksgiving, praise, and worship.

66. Believers are exhorted to *pray without ceasing*.... (1 Thessalonians 5:17) They are called to ... *seek the Lord while He may be found, call upon Him while He is near* and to stand firm on the promise that *the effectual, fervent prayer of a righteous man availeth much*.... (James 5:16)

67. The prerequisite and instruction given to man when he prays is pure and undefiled in its application: *Ask the Father in my name*.... (John 16:23) Not only is this how man must pray, it gives the assurance ... *Whatever you ask the Father in My name He will give you*....

68. How privileged believers are to know that they can come to the Father in Jesus' name and confess their sins, and then have the assurance: *He is faithful and just to forgive us our sins, and to cleanse us from all unrighteousness*.... (1 John 1:9) This is done when the individual enters the presence of the Father and seek His forgiveness.

69. This is an instrument freely given to man who has been reconciled to God through the shed blood of Jesus. It is the privilege every Spirit-filled believer does not take for granted because they are fully cognizant of the price the Father paid to once again have this divine communion with man.

70. Many books have been written about prayer. However, it should never be forgotten that God restored the relationship with man when He sent His Son to the Cross. It took a sacrifice and a resurrection for man to once again be reconciled to God. God did this because He loves so much and desired to commune with him again. Prayer is a God-initiated act and a God-thing that draws man from the shadows of life into His glorious light.

Fasting

71. To many this is a lost and forgotten instrument that is available to man to strengthen and cleanse the spirit and soul. It is biblical and right that Spirit-filled believers obediently follow the teachings of Jesus, as well as apply what He personally did.

72. In every respect of the command that believers fast, it should never be from a platform of boasting and adoption of an attitude that exalts the person fasting. (Matthew 6:16–18) This is a private matter between God and the believer. It is never displayed or paraded as a sign of spiritual superiority.

73. This is a discipline and a sacrifice the believer makes to bring his body into subjection to his spirit. Believers are instructed to *lay aside every weight and sin.* This is done when the flesh is denied its habits and the believer spends time on his knees before God, seeking the cleansing flow of the Holy Spirit that can flush out the dross and *loads* that weigh them down. (Acts 13:2–3, 14:23)

Conclusion

74. The Holy Spirit's work of imparting a holy message to mortal man is precious to the Godhead. It is done with precision and purity. God's sovereignty is perfectly expressed when the vessel He chooses receives it by faith and in all holiness. Every generation that is charged with the responsibility of declaring God's message should join alongside the saints of old and affirm; *Therefore we also, since we are surrounded by so great a cloud of witnesses, let us lay aside every weight, and the sin which so easily ensnares us, and let us run with endurance the race that is set before us, looking unto Jesus, the author and finisher of our faith, who for the joy that was set before Him endured the cross, despising the shame, and has sat down at the right hand of the throne of God.* (Hebrews 12:1–2 NKJV)

CHAPTER 5

DOCTRINE OF THE
SPIRIT-FILLED CHURCH

1. Man's interference throughout the centuries has eroded the Apostles' Doctrine declared in Acts 2:42. This being said, it is important to set the doctrinal foundation on the correct platform as it was originally laid out by the apostles from the Day of Pentecost.

2. There can never be enough credit given to the many bastions of old who dedicated themselves to preserving the intrinsic truths embedded in the Holy Word. Men who were led of the Holy Spirit diligently penned the Apostles' Doctrine in an attempt to keep the truths in the forefront of believers' minds.

3. Regrettably, because of myriad unsavory influences, the primary one being self-gain and benefit, the numerous denominations, schisms, and compromises were tabled in "church meetings" to set a book of rules fashioned only in part from the Bible. History is strewn with these diabolical calamities that poisoned the hearts of thousands of believers who were ... *never able to come to the knowledge of the truth....* (2 Timothy 3:7, 4:3–4)

4. Now the questions every believer who is thirsting after the truth asks, "What did the Apostles' Doctrine declared in Acts 2:42

contain?" "If it is in the Bible, is it not supposed to be applied in the church today?"

5. These questions demand answers. This is so because every man who has been called by God to hold an office in the church of Jesus Christ will give an account of their motives and actions as an ordained *minister of Jesus Christ*.... (Romans 15:16)

6. The Apostles' Doctrine is what is contained in the ensuing pages. The question regarding the application of every instruction in the Bible needs to be addressed here. The reason for the discussion on this subject is to explain how worldly influences, and not Word influences, have been incorporated in the church, and corrupted the truth to the extent that many *believe a lie*....

7. During the first and second century, every local assembly in every country witnessed the Spirit-filled move of God in their midst. The fruit of the Spirit was evidenced daily in the believers' walk with the Lord. The manifestations of the Gifts of the Holy Spirit were not absent in any assembly. Likewise, the fivefold ministries of apostle, prophet, evangelist, pastor, and teacher were vibrantly active all over the church.

8. These mentioned above embody the Spirit-filled church. These are the experiences of the early believers: they witnessed chains falling off, the prophetical utterances that no one will perish in a ship destined to be wrecked, that the lame walk, and their prayers shook the roof under which they stood or kneeled while praying.

9. The Spirit-filled church experienced *great power and great grace.* (Acts 4:33) The world could not understand a believer's peace of mind; neither could they grasp the miraculous demonstration of the Holy Spirit as it worked through God's chosen servants. (Acts 4:13–22)

10. Because the world could not understand the Spirit nor receive the *things of the Spirit of God* (1 Corinthians 2:14), they liked what they saw, yet they did not fully comprehend the Holy Spirit's actions through holy believers who dedicated themselves to the

gospel. Consequently, the world adopted many Christian church practices without accepting the power of the Holy Spirit whom Jesus Christ promised His believers, and they created a *form of godliness* ... and denied the power of the Spirit-filled walk with God. (2 Timothy 3:5)

11. Into this man-made structure many labeled "the church," worldly lust and pecuniary interest spearheaded growth.

12. The creation of Roman Catholicism; the breach from it through a king's lust who formed the Anglican/Episcopal denomination; the Reformation that tried to straighten the crooked path the church was walking; and the Protestant establishment that sealed the break from Catholicism all fell short of the original Apostles' Doctrine.

13. The primary exclusion from all these denominations was the submission to the Holy Spirit's leading and manifestation amongst the believers. Added to this exclusion, they all banished the fivefold ministries, adopting titles and rank that were nowhere to be found in the Scriptures. These denominations literally banned and abolished the use of spiritual gifts, as well as watered down the holy Word of God by declaring it to be man's expression of what God intends.

14. *In due season,* when God had tolerated their false doctrine long enough, the Holy Spirit once again was manifested amongst and in believers' lives. This was the outpouring of the Holy Spirit throughout the world which began at the turn of the twentieth century. God laid the groundwork for the reestablishment of the Spirit-filled church as it was in the Apostolic Period that followed from the Day of Pentecost until around AD 100.

15. These vibrant Spirit-filled churches were first called *Apostolic* churches. And they were Apostolic in their functioning and leadership from apostles, prophets, evangelists, pastors, and teachers who obediently followed the Holy Spirit's leading. These Apostolic believers were baptized with the Holy Spirit, and

the church structure was laid upon the *foundation of apostles and prophets* who were "set" in the body of Christ and spoke with *one mind, one mouth* ... from *one Lord*.

16. Sadly, after a few decades, too many Spirit-filled believers sought the favor of man rather than be a servant of the Most High God. (Galatians 1:10) Henceforth many departed from *the faith* (Jude 3), and the decaying process of worldly influences caused the Spirit-filled church to discard some of the fivefold ministries such as apostles and prophets. They adopted new titles, structured their "groups" under the governance of "spiritual boards" and "deacons." The office of elder as an overseer of the flock was thrown aside. Pentecostalism became the new name.

17. Worse than this, many Spirit-filled denominations presented a "better-than-thou" arrogance. This was evident when many "main line" churches began to experience the outpouring of the Holy Spirit in the latter part of the twentieth century. The Pentecostals looked across the aisle to these precious souls, and the lack of love and humility drove these new groups from the Pentecostals.

18. The result was plain to see: these believers who had received the baptism with the Holy Spirit had nowhere to go. Their main line church denomination wanted nothing to do with them, and the Pentecostals showed them minimum love. They forged their own group: the charismatics.

19. As with all things with God, He always has a remnant that clings to the truth. There are those who still choose the Apostolic path. These are the ones who take God at His word and *follow in His steps*.

The Original Apostolic Spirit-Filled Church

20. The reasons for the many variances amongst the Spirit-filled churches revert to the foundational principles from which many

have strayed. The remnant, however, has not strayed from the foundation that was so diligently laid by the Holy Spirit at the beginning of the twentieth century.

21. Jesus Christ is the *chief cornerstone,* and from this cornerstone the structure is laid upon the foundation of apostles and prophets. (Ephesians 2:20) Even to this day, the remnant church has apostles and prophets. The rest of the Spirit-filled church has bishops—no elders, no teachers; only deacons, pastors, and evangelists.

22. The underpinning of the *chief cornerstone* of the remnant church is the holy, divine, sovereignty that the Father vested in His Son. Jesus is the Christ. He is the Word become flesh, and He is the Lamb slain from the foundation of the world. Henceforth, every utterance that flows from preachers must exalt *Jesus Christ is Lord, to the glory of God the Father....* (Philippians 2:11)

23. This is the nucleus from which everything else stems. The evidence of this belief is found in God's Word: *For He made Him who knew no sin, to be sin for us, that we might become the righteousness of God in Him.* (2 Corinthians 5:21 NKJV)

24. It is not only about the miracles, the healings, the prospering of the believer, and the utterances the Holy Spirit has for the body of Christ. These are the result of the believer focusing on something much more precious. It is about the relationship the believer has with the holy Jesus Christ. It is the compelling thirst and hunger *... that I may know him and the power of his resurrection....* (Philippians 3:10) Furthermore, it is the dogmatic declaration that *... I have been crucified with Christ; it is no longer I who live, but Christ lives in me....* (Galatians 2:20 NKJV)

25. Apostle Paul's repeated statement to the church—*Jesus Christ and Him crucified*—needs to be studied so that the believer will *know whom* (he has) *believed and am persuaded....* (2 Timothy 1:12) Apostle Paul writes under the anointing of the Holy Spirit to the churches and, in particular, the church in Corinth, stating the message he was charged with by Jesus on the road to

Damascus... *to turn them from darkness to light, and from the power of Satan to God, that they may receive forgiveness of sins and an inheritance among those who are sanctified by faith in Me....* (Acts 26:18 NKJV)

26. This message is exactly what he proclaimed everywhere. He never strayed from the fact that Jesus suffered and died for the sin of the world. *But we preach Christ crucified....* (1 Corinthians 1:23) What then is this message that consumed and convinced him to proclaim it every time he opened his mouth?

27. The sacred words in 1 Corinthians 2:2 need careful examination, for they are the pivotal declaration from which everything else flows.

28. JESUS. The Holy name, the Holy One is emphasized and it proclaims Him to be the Chosen One. His name is given from the Father in heaven ... *and shall call his name JESUS....* (Luke 1:31) Notice the capitalization of the spelling of JESUS: it proclaims the *fullness of the Godhead....* (Colossians 2:9) In His Name everything is embodied, and power resides in His Name and is available to every believer.

29. His name, JESUS, is Who He is. The angel expresses to Mary that the One she will carry in her womb will be conceived by the Holy Spirit. Jesus was God-conceived, God-endowed, and God-sent... *that holy thing* (Luke 1:35) ... states the angel ... *shall be called the Son of God* (Luke 1:35). He is holy, divine, righteous, pure, and the complete expression of the Godhead in the flesh. He is the deity in the physical presence of man ... *For in him dwelleth all the fullness of the Godhead bodily....* (Colossians 2:9) And all this is in His Name: JESUS.

30. Apostle Paul declares the full title of the Savior as he writes his letter to the Corinthians: *Jesus Christ.* He is emphatic on Whom he constantly focuses as he walks in the crooked and perverse Corinthian society.

31. He fully comprehended the depth, length, and breadth of his

Savior's name and the work He accomplished at Calvary. He understood that the name "Jesus," even though used by many in that day, was more than a name/word attached to the holy One. This was the Father's chosen name for His chosen Son.

32. In that name the Godhead functions in its fullness, even to this day.

33. The title attached to the name of Jesus—*Christ*—is the highest honor with which any name can be adorned. It is so, because the honor is bestowed by the Most High God on Jesus, not from any human soul or flesh. It is God-ordained and God-given. He is the Christ, the Bible proclaims it, and it is revealed to His disciples: *You are the Christ, the Son of the living God....* (Matthew 16:16–17 NKJV)

34. "Christ" – the anointed One. His anointing is without height, depth, or breadth. It is eternal and extends beyond time, because it is from the Eternal God ... *He has anointed Me....* It is the "holy anointing" from the *Spirit of the LORD* that endowed Jesus to *heal the brokenhearted* and *set at liberty those who are oppressed....* (Luke 4:18 NKJV)

35. Again, the word "LORD" (Luke 4:18 NKJV) is entirely capitalized, indicating the entire Godhead is responsible for the proclamation that Jesus—the Christ (anointed One)—has the full authority and support of the entire Godhead. This anointing is not a suggestion from man. It is not a "good idea" conjured in the soul of a wise human; it is directly from the throne of Almighty God.

36. "And Him." Nothing emphasizes the holy deity of Jesus Christ more than His holy name given from the Godhead. Yet nothing more emphasizes the human life of Jesus than these two words (*and Him*). "Him" is masculine, denoting the human gender of the Christ. It focuses the believer's attention of the fact that Jesus was very God, and very man.

37. Apostle Paul is emphatic in this statement: Jesus, the anointed Son of God, is also the Son of Man. And in His entirety, He was slain for man's sin. His death was the death of the Son of God and

the Son of Man ... *Jesus Christ and Him* ... is the proclamation of the delivery of the promise of the Father: *Behold the Lamb of God which taketh away the sin of the world....* (John 1:29)

38. "Crucified." What a Savior! The slain Lamb is nailed to the cross and dies a ruthless death at the hands of human hatred. Yet the message does not end at the cross. "Crucified" embodies all the work at Calvary and the Garden Tomb. Stating that Jesus Christ was crucified can only point to the result of the crucifixion: the resurrection of the *Lamb slain from the foundation of the world....* (Revelation 13:8)

39. The huge battle that raged at the cross between Jesus and Satan culminates in Jesus' exodus from the tomb. The victory wasn't won by Satan at the cross; it was won by Jesus at the tomb. Much more needs to be explained about the doctrine of eternal life and the resurrection from the dead, and therefore is covered further on. Suffice to say, it starts with the "crucified" at Calvary's Hill, and culminates with ... *I am He who lives, and was dead, and behold, I am alive forevermore. Amen. And I have the keys of Hades and of Death....* (Revelation 1:18 NKJV)

40. Thereafter, with the foundation firmly entrenched, the Apostolic church follows the original biblical structure for the church. It is governed by and designed on scriptural principles under the leadership, authority, and guidance of the fivefold ministries found in Ephesians 4:11: *And He Himself gave some to be apostles, some prophets, some evangelists, and some pastors and teachers....*

41. The man-made offices of pope, cardinal, reverend, and bishop are not evident in the remnant Apostolic church. The fivefold ministries and the support of elders and deacons, helps, and governments are the only offices and positions operating in it. Furthermore, the ministries are not held in tandem, and neither are they interchangeable. A man is called by God, is "set" in the

body of Christ, and given one ministry. Again, much more on the subject is included under the doctrine of the church.

42. The remnant Apostolic church conforms to the perfect will of God (Romans 12:1–2). Every aspect of the operation of the Holy Spirit is evidenced in the lives of these believers. The manifestation of the gifts of the Spirit and the evidence of the fruit of the Holy Spirit is apparent in their daily walk.

43. This glorious presence of the Holy Spirit is manifest in their lives because they have been baptized with the Holy Spirit as prophesied by John the Baptist ... *He* (Jesus) *shall baptize you with the Holy Ghost and with fire....* (Luke 3:16)

44. The Spirit-filled church conforms fully to biblical teachings regarding the necessity to be born again. *Do not marvel that I said to you, 'You must be born again.'* (John 3:7 NKJV) This is the first step man takes towards God to be saved.

45. Too many believe that when they confess Jesus Christ as Lord, the Holy Spirit enters their heart simultaneously as the Spirit of Christ enters their heart. (Galatians 4:6) Yes, the Holy Spirit is in their heart, as He accompanies the Spirit of Christ, yet there is more to follow: *Ye shall receive power after that the Holy Ghost is come upon you....* (Acts 1:8) This is the baptism with the Holy Spirit that the Spirit-filled church experiences which is the infilling of the Holy Spirit in their bodies: *Your body is the temple of the Holy Ghost which is in you....* (1 Corinthians 6:19)

46. These biblical beliefs are the differences between the Spirit-filled believer and all others who confess Jesus Christ as Lord.

47. It is this Apostolic and Spirit-filled endowment and profession wherein the Holy Spirit *reveals* the perfect will of God (Romans 12:2) that permits the doctrine of the Spirit-filled church to henceforth follow.

PART 2

6. DOCTRINE – Of God. The introduction of this tenet focuses on the eternal existence of God and the four absolutes pertaining to God.
   a. God is eternal.
   b. God is omnipresent.
   c. God is omnipotent.
   d. God is omniscient.
7. DOCTRINE – The Godhead. The explanation of the Godhead is a revealed truth that can only be accepted by faith. Their unity of essence and their unilateral affirmation of all they do is found in the Bible. Within the Godhead dwells the divine characteristics of wisdom, mercy, truth, faithfulness, and glory.
8. DOCTRINE – The Nature of God. God's nature has five attributes:
   a. Love
   b. Divine
   c. Holy
   d. Pure
   e. Righteous

CHAPTER 6

THE DOCTRINE OF GOD

1. God is. It is a doctrinal *fact* that God is the eternal and everlasting existing Spirit that holds all things in His hands. *The eternal God is your refuge, and underneath (are) the everlasting arms....* (Deuteronomy 33:27 NKJV)

2. It is not a fact that God exists simply because the Bible says so. The Bible exists because God exists. It is God who *breathed* His word into existence for man's benefit. (2 Timothy 3:16) The incorruptible Word is therefore eternal, as the One who uttered it into existence is eternal. *Forever, O Lord, Your word is settled in heaven....* (Psalm 119:89 NKJV)

3. The very existence of God is not a fantasy; it is a fact. God is *Alpha and Omega* (Revelation 1:8) which literally means: "without beginning and without end." Likewise, it is also accepted as meaning, "before the beginning and after the ending."

4. God is Spirit. Norman Geisler, in his *Systematic Theology* (Volume Two), quotes Stephen Charnock ... "God is a pure Spirit, He has nothing of the nature and tincture of a body ...whoever conceives Him as having a bodily form ... instead of owning His dignity, detracts from the super-eminent excellency of His nature and blessedness."

5. God declared in the Word that His understanding is *infinite* (Psalm 147:5). God is One, referring to His entirety as being unified in all His essence and nature. Because He is infinite in His understanding, all His attributes are therefore infinite. They are identical because whatever God possesses is what He is. All His attributes refer to His one essence. This, therefore, declares that if God is infinite in one attribute, He must be infinite in all attributes, since He is an indivisible Being.

6. When focusing on God as a Being, there should be a clear understanding that He is an essence and a substance, and not of a mere idea or a personification of an idea. God is Spirit, and as such He transcends human comprehension known in man's puny mind as substance. In essence, God's nature is Who He is, and substance is the product of His divine handiwork ... *For by Him all things were created that are in heaven and that are on earth, visible and invisible, whether thrones or dominions or principalities or powers. All things were created through Him and for Him....* (Colossians 1:16 NKJV)

7. While the Word declares God is Spirit, He is also of substance, namely spiritual substance, which is invisible and untouchable (Colossians 1:15). God's ability to show Himself physically and visibly is apparent when He appeared to Moses on Mount Sinai demonstrating His glory to Moses (Exodus 33:18–23). Furthermore, Jesus is the bodily representation of the Godhead, for Jesus is *the image of the invisible God* (Colossians 1:15) and ... *in him dwelleth all the fullness of the Godhead bodily....* (Colossians 2:9)

8. Unlike kings and rulers today who inherit their rulership, God is ruler. He has the supreme ownership and rulership of everything He has created, because He was before what He created.

9. To begin this explanation, the Word is clear that God is "before" "previous" "prior" to all things. Before anything existed, God is ... *Even from everlasting to everlasting, You are God....* (Psalm

90:2 NKJV) Jesus prays to the Father ... *before the foundation of the world....* (John 17:24) God is ... *I AM....* (Exodus 3:4)

10. Spirit-filled believers never question God's eternal existence. Neither do they need an explanation of God's sovereignty and rulership throughout His eternal reign. Their acceptance and spiritual application of who God is is rooted in the premise that God the Holy Spirit, who dwells in them, reveals to them all truths pertaining to God. (John 16:13) It is a personal witness through God's revelation to them that God is the great *I AM.*

11. All the attributes pertaining to God are identical: His power, everlasting existence, knowledge, wisdom, and His glory are identical to His Being because whatever God has, that He is (Revelation 5:12).

12. The doctrine of God is rooted in the four "absolutes" that encompass God. He is: *eternal, omnipresent, omniscient,* and *omnipotent.* These four absolutes are all orchestrated from the nucleus, *Love,* which is who God is (1 John 4:8).

God Is Eternal

13. Too little is understood about the eternal absolute of God. The human mind cannot fully grasp an eternal state. It is so because everything that involves human life is measured in "time." God has no "time" measurement. He is outside of this limiting incarceration that is peculiar to man and His earthly creation. In fact, God has no measurement of any kind (distance, space, time) that can be applied to any one of His absolutes and attributes.

14. God existed before man, and thus existed before the matrix of time was formulated ... *And now, O Father, glorify Me together with Yourself, with the glory which I had with You before the world was....* (John 17:5 NKJV) Jesus asked His Father to manifest this glory which they had together before time was in existence.

15. God in His eternal absolute can purpose the eternal condition of the human soul ... *who has called us with a holy calling, not according to our works, but according to His own purpose and grace which was given to us in Christ Jesus before time began....* (2 Timothy 1:9 NKJV)

16. W.A.C. Rowe in his book, *One Lord One Faith, says:* "He is the forever, unchanging God. The eternal One goes on through the ceaseless ages in His greatness, goodness, and glory. Nevertheless, all these qualities of absolute deity have been brought to bear upon man in exceeding gentleness and tenderness (2 Samuel 22:36)."

17. God made infallible promises, and one of these is eternal life in Him ... *in hope of eternal life which God, that cannot lie, promised before the world began....* (Titus 1:2)

18. In the vast subject of the doctrine of creation pertaining to man, God's eternal existence produces ages, dispensations, and periods involving man on this earth. These are measurements that endeavor to explain God's creation, both physical and spiritual. Furthermore, if God is the Creator of these periods, then He is also the Creator of time. To create these things, He had to be before they were created. Therefore, He is before what He created, and is outside of His created time.

19. The warp of time must be excluded from the expression that God is eternal, for eternity does not have a measurement of any sort. It is a perpetual duration.

20. As eternal God has no commencement, and is always in the "now" when mankind relates to His existence ... *I AM....* (Exodus 3:14) God is unchangeable and was, is, and will always be the same sovereign, almighty, and holy God. Everything about God is always constant and eternal. (Psalm 102:27)

21. *For I am the LORD, I do not change....* (Malachi 3:6 NKJV) *Jesus Christ the same yesterday, and today, and forever....* (Hebrews 13:8)

22. Everything that can be seen, touched, and experienced will

wither, tarnish, wilt, or fade from man's memory. Yet God in His eternal and immutable state will not, and cannot, change or become irrelevant because He is always in the *now*. Whatever the born-again believer is about, God is *now* in that event in their life.

23. His infinite existence has no parts, because if God had various parts, He would not be infinite. Therefore, it is fundamentally true that He who has no parts cannot change. There is nothing about God that wilts, tarnishes, or fades away. He is eternal in His ever-now—*I AM*—presence and is forever the same.

24. In His immense love for His highest creation, mankind, God willingly bestows this glorious "absolute" upon him. His Word promises ... *that whoever believes in Him should not perish but have everlasting life....* (John 3:15–16; Romans 6:23 NKJV)

25. Spirit-filled believers who operate in the Apostles' Doctrine (Acts 2:42) receive by revelation from the indwelling Holy Spirit the *deep things of God*. God's eternality is so all-encompassing that the Spirit-led believer is immersed in the spiritual endowment of the Eternal Holy Spirit. Their very ability to function under the anointing of the Holy Spirit is the recognition that an eternal Spirit dwells within their bodies. (1 Corinthians 3:16)

26. These believers do not rely on their physical experiences or emotional encounters. The basic premise from which they launch their faith is vested in the knowledge that the God they serve is eternal and therefore can do according to His good pleasure as and when He so chooses.

27. Unlike other denominations that align themselves with human intellect and instruction, apostolic believers have no question about the eternal state of God. Like the bastions of old, when the church was born on the Day of Pentecost, believers still, today, experience the eternal indwelling Spirit flooding their being and, without question, know that the eternal Spirit resides in them.

28. Apostolic believers do not only believe God is eternal; they live and breathe His eternal existence that resides in them. (Acts 17:28)

29. This leads them to have a holy reverence for God because they do not show "lip service" but in their heart, they know that He is eternal. As such, the apostolic believer should move gingerly and with caution towards every deed and command the Holy Spirit infuses in their spirit.

30. In essence they are in awe at the eternal existence of God, and have a reverence for revealed truth the Holy Spirit imparts to them.

31. For them, God's eternal existence needs no explanation. There is no discourse to prove God's eternal state; neither is there any rational discussion demanded. Spirit-led believers *receive by revelation* the eternal existence of God and unconditionally accept it (Galatians 1:12).

32. The character trait that inevitably flows from such a heart is humbleness. It is knowing that so great an eternal God chooses to dwell in them that they abase themselves in His presence, and ... *therefore humble yourselves under the mighty hand of God....* (1 Peter 5:6 NKJV)

God Is Omnipresent

33. *Am I a God near at hand, says the LORD, and not a God afar off? Can anyone hide himself in secret places, so I shall not see him? says the LORD. Do I not fill heaven and earth? says the LORD....* (Jeremiah 23:23–24 NKJV)

34. By God's own word, He is omnipresent. The ever-present and all-present God in His fullness is constantly everywhere.

35. David declares ... *Where can I go from Your Spirit? Or where can I flee from Your presence? If I ascend into heaven, You are there: If I make my bed in hell, behold, You are there. If I take the wings of the morning, and dwell in the uttermost parts of the sea, even there Your hand shall lead me, and Your right hand shall hold me. If I say, "surely the darkness shall fall on me," even the night*

shall be light about me: indeed, the darkness shall not hide from You, but the night shines as the day; the darkness and the light are both alike to You. (Psalm 139:7–12 NKJV)

36. When considering God's omnipresence, the word that aligns itself with His all-encompassing existence in and everywhere is *immensity.*

37. Norman Geisler says: "God is not in space nor is He limited by space: He is present at every point in space, but He is not part of space or limited to it, He transcends all space and time."

38. The acceptance of God's omnipresence is both encouraging and frightening. To the believer, the fact that God is always present in every thought and deed encourages him to ... *Whatsoever thy hand findeth to do, do it with thy might....* (Ecclesiastes 9:10) Conversely, if the believer does not reverence the presence of God in everything they do, and they sin, then the witness of God's presence, no matter where they are, brings them into reality that God's convicting power of the presence of sin is a frightening thing.

39. As an indivisible Being, God is not separable; namely, one part of God cannot be separated from Him and be in one place while the rest of Him is elsewhere. He is always in His fullness everywhere all the time.

40. God's immensity is the ultimate word to describe His ever presence in His fullness everywhere.

41. *God, who made the world and everything in it, since He is Lord of heaven and earth, does not dwell in temples made with hands. Nor is He worshipped with men's hands, as though He needed anything, since He gives to all life, breath, and all things....* (Acts 17:24–28 NKJV) Furthermore ...*The whole earth is full of His glory....* (Isaiah 6:3 NKJV)

42. God's omnipresence displays more than the human mind can comprehend. First, it is the manifestation of His glory. His Spirit is the witness to Spirit-filled believers that the God they serve

is glorious and holy. He is untouchable and so glorious that He cannot be taken for granted. God is to be constantly recognized by the believer as the glorious God who manifests His glory in the fullness every time. In this glory, there is divine revelation that empowers the believer to experience the "fullness" of God's presence. (Colossians 1:9–17)

43. Second, God's omnipresence is witnessed when believers look on His creation. They are in awe of His mighty power that flung the stars into the heavens, fashioned the landscapes of earth, and breathed the breath of life into a human body. No human being can do any of these things. It is from nothing that God spoke into existence all things.

44. In all things God is always all-present, whether spiritually or materially ... *Do I not fill heaven and earth says the LORD....* (Jeremiah 23:24 NKJV)

45. All the above statements are affirmed by the Spirit-filled believer. However, the Spirit-filled believer believes that the Holy Spirit, who is of the Godhead, dwells in their bodies (1 Corinthians 3:16). This is the experience they receive the moment they are baptized with the Holy Spirit by Jesus Christ (Luke 3:16).

46. The Holy Spirit, who is omnipresent throughout the entirety of God's creation, now resides within the believer. This infilling only takes place when the believer is baptized with the Holy Spirit and is contrary to other denominations that believe the Holy Spirit is received within the believer when they are born again.

47. The omnipresence of God the Holy Spirit now resides in the Spirit-filled believer's body, and as such the Gifts of the Holy Spirit are manifested in their fullness by the indwelling Holy Spirit through the believer. (1 Corinthians 12:1–13)

48. God's omnipresence throughout the world is now more personal to the Spirit-filled believer in that the glorious presence of the Holy Spirit is now not only upon them but also within them.

49. This was the basis of the birth of the church of Jesus Christ on

the Day of Pentecost. These born-again believers experienced the Holy Spirit's presence surrounding them, and then by faith they received the Spirit who took up residence within them. Henceforth, the apostolic church functioned under the anointing of the Holy Spirit as He operated through them. (Acts 2:1–4)

50. Even though many denominations have strayed from this vital truth and experience, there is still today a remnant that follows in the fullness of the apostolic doctrine that was birthed when the omnipresent Holy Spirit took up residence within the human frame. (Acts 2:42)

51. It is God Himself who now resides in man, and not merely around man.

God Is Omnipotent

52. God is all-powerful, all-consuming everywhere at the same time. He is never less powerful in one place than the other and is never less effective in other parts of His creation when He is doing something in a part of His creation.

53. Not only is God simultaneously all-powerful in every part of His creation, but God is self-sufficient and unlimited in every aspect of His Being. He has no need of anyone to instruct Him or support Him with an additional power source.

54. There is nothing God cannot do. Neither is there anything God needs to do. Impossible in man's thought is possible with God. He has power to do, choose, and not do and refuse to do.

55. *Behold, I am the LORD, the God of all flesh. Is there anything too hard for Me....* (Jeremiah 32:27 NKJV)

56. The Spirit-filled believer is ever conscious of the almighty power existent in their God. In addition to this awareness, they comprehend that this power and ubiquitous presence never leaves them, because within them dwells this power: *But if the Spirit of*

Him who raised Jesus from the dead dwells in you, He who raised Christ from the dead will also give life to your mortal bodies through His Spirit who dwells in you. (Romans 8:11 NKJV)

57. Furthermore, these Spirit-filled believers cling to God's word that God can, and will, defeat Satan and all the evil he has spewed on mankind. The indwelling power of the Holy Spirit supplies the believer's every need (Philippians 4:19) and reigns victorious in their life ... *Nevertheless I am not ashamed, for I know whom I have believed and am persuaded that He is able to keep what I have committed to Him until that Day....* (2 Timothy 1:12 NKJV)

58. The word that is aligned to God's omnipotence is that fact that He is infinite. *Great is our Lord, and of great power; his understanding is infinite.* (Psalm 147:5) Thus said, God is unlimited in His power and His understanding of all things. He possesses foreknowledge and He can direct His power in any direction His infinite knowledge desires.

59. God's infinite existence allows Him to be limitless in every aspect of every attribute in His nature. He is absolute in all His thoughts and actions. This stems from an intrinsic holy manifestation of whom He is that demonstrates His glory. God is, in essence, all good. He will defeat evil and rule in righteousness which is determined in His time. It will take place because God is omnipotent and never fails to perform His promises: *For I know whom I have believed and am persuaded that He is able to keep what I have committed to Him until that Day....* (2 Timothy 1:12 NKJV)

60. God, who raised His Son, Jesus Christ, from the dead, now speaks to believers through His risen Son, and has seated Jesus Christ on the highest seat of honor, power and authority (Hebrews 1:1–3, 13).

61. William Rowe says it best: "He meets every need and every exigency. Man is made a free-will agent; if he falls, then a full salvation is ready. God's ways are not temporary expedients; splendid after thoughts: they are ways of foreknowledge and

predestination (Isaiah 46:10). Crowning the sun of all God's qualities and abilities is His perfect and holy will (Romans 12:2). He executes His counsels and judgments and carries out His eternal purpose and *none can stay His hand. God ruleth overall,* planning, controlling and achieving. Truly, He is the *El Shaddai,* the All-Sufficient Lord. (Genesis 17:1)"

God Is Omniscient

62. God is all-knowing. This transcends human comprehension because man can only see and know *in part* (1 Corinthians 13:12) that which is of God. Only God knows Himself and all other things.

63. God has full knowledge of all things, whether they be in the past, present, or future, and He knows them perfectly in His very eternal existence (Isaiah 46:9–10). Furthermore, God does not have a thought process in the manner man thinks. He has instant and immediate full thought on everything, from the past, in the present, and regarding the future. There is no process He applies. Everything is immediately available to Him without any sequence or process.

64. William Rowe explains God's omniscience as: "God knows all the needs of all His creatures (Matthew 6:8). His mind is Infinite, comprehending all things from eternity to eternity. His knowledge and His understanding are limitless (Psalm 147:5)."

65. Referencing God the Father, God the Son, and God the Holy Spirit, the most sublime aspect of their existence is the fact that they know each other perfectly, and only they have this perfect knowledge of each other. There is one undivided divine nature in the Godhead which exists and manifests itself in three personal subsistences: *All things have been delivered to Me by My Father, and no one knows the Son except the Father. Nor does anyone*

know the Father except the Son, and the one to whom the Son wills to reveal Him.... (Matthew 11:27 NKJV)

66. God's all-knowledge is not the result of Him having reasoned things to be; neither does God have this infinite knowledge from experience.

67. It is outside man's intellect for him to comprehend that everything that has happened in the past is fully known by God. Likewise, everything that is in the present anywhere and all things that are going to be are fully known by the omniscient God.

68. It is worthy to join in the accolade expressed by the Psalmist: *O LORD, You have searched me and known me. You know my sitting down and my rising up; You understand my thought afar off. You comprehend my path and my lying down, and are acquainted with all my ways. For there is not a word on my tongue, but behold, O LORD, You know it altogether. You have hedged me behind and before and laid Your hand upon me. Such knowledge is too wonderful for me; it is high, I cannot attain it....* (Psalm 139:1–6 NKJV)

69. *Oh, the depth of the riches both of the wisdom and knowledge of God! How unsearchable are His judgments and His ways past finding out!* (Romans 11:33 NKJV)

LORD GOD ... Lord God

70. The Word is emphatic in its proclamation that God is Father, Son, and Holy Spirit. The extrapolation of the word "GOD" (all capital letters) which is used numerous times in the Old Testament is the explanation of the *Godhead*. When used this way ("GOD"), it refers to God in His most holy, almighty, sovereign, and divine nature.

71. Furthermore, GOD is the definitive explanation in Hebrew as JEHOVAH. When translated into all capitals it embraces the full

extent of God as "creator" and "revealer." The first description of this is found in Genesis 2:4, when the writer uses "LORD God" to explain God as both "revealer" and "creator." The Hebrew word for God as "creator" is "Elohim." The Hebrew word for "revealer" is "Jehovah," which is translated as LORD.

72. It is used this way (LORD God) in Genesis 2:4 to explain that the entire Godhead in His most holy, eternal, almighty, sovereign, and divine nature is the one who reveals His creation to man.

73. Henceforth, whenever the translation renders all capitals for GOD and LORD, it is declaring that the full capacity of the eternal Godhead is involved.

74. The rendering of these two words in all capitals, LORD GOD, is the translation of the word "Jehovah" that contains every provision for man. It is the sum total of the seven compound names wrapped up in Jehovah:

75. Jehovah-Jireh means "provider" (Genesis 22:13–14). Jehovah-Rapha means "healer" (Exodus 15:26). Jehovah-Nissi means "banner" (Exodus 17:15). Jehovah-Shalom means "peace" (Judges 6:23–24). Jehovah-Raah means "shepherd" (Psalm 23:1). Jehovah-Tsidkenu means "righteousness" (Jeremiah 23:6). Jehovah-Shammah means "present" (Ezekiel 48:35).

CHAPTER 7

THE GODHEAD

1. Herbert Lockyer says: "The Godhead composed of three Persons coeternal, coequal; and the same in substance but distinct in subsistence permeates the Bible. This sacred doctrine is above reason."

2. The entire explanation of the Godhead is a revealed truth that can only be accepted by faith. Their unity of essence and their unilateral affirmation of all they are and do is found in the holy pages of the Bible.

3. The Godhead is Who God is. This One God is unique in all His qualities and power. The power source that flows from the divine nature and deity within the Godhead possesses the same qualities and has the same abilities when used by the Father, the Son, or the Holy Spirit. Each member of the Godhead does not have its own unique qualities, deity, or measure of power distinct from the other; they all function and operate from within the same source.

4. However, each Member of the Godhead, the Father, the Son, and the Holy Spirit has a unique application of these qualities and power. Therefore, the source is the same, yet with a different application by each Member of the Godhead.

5. The words "Trinity" or "Triune" God are not entirely biblical in their definition of God, neither are they found in the Holy Writ. While expressing the Godhead's nature and divinity in one accord, these word-definitions could be interpreted as separating the power and operating abilities of each Member of the Godhead. It does, at times, incorrectly portray the emphasis that each Member of the Godhead has its own independent power and methodology.

6. The "oneness" of the Godhead is a fundamental teaching of the Holy Writ. Anyone who opposes this vital teaching violates God's emphatic statement in His opening of the Ten Commandments: *I am the LORD your God....* (Exodus 20:2)

7. Thus said, the Hebrew declaration—*Hear, O Israel, the LORD our God, the LORD is one* (Deuteronomy 6:4 NKJV)—is the truthful statement that God is Creator and revealer. It further supports the statement: *Let Us make man in Our image....* (Genesis 1:26 NKJV) *Then the LORD God formed man of the dust of the ground....* (Genesis 2:7 NKJV)

8. This confirms that God is the One who reveals Himself and creates all things. The One who creates is the Son of God, *the Son of His love* (Colossians 1:13 NKJV). *All things were made through Him ...* (John 1:3 NKJV), *For by Him all things were created that are in heaven and that are on earth, visible and invisible....* (Colossians 1:16 NKJV)

9. The opening salvo of the Holy Writ that bursts onto man's eyes in Genesis 1:1 ... *In the beginning God created the heavens and the earth* ... announces for the first time the word "God." The Hebrew word used in this context is "Elohim." The full translation for Elohim is "Eternal One Who Created." This rendering makes an emphatic declaration of the eternal existence of the Godhead. Father, Son, and Holy Spirit have always been in existence and will always be one.

10. Wayne Grudem, in his book, *Systematic Theology*, gives an interesting explanation regarding a more apt rendering of the

completeness of the Godhead which enables man to comprehend the equality and full measure of the Godhead. He says, "The Father is 'fully' God. The Son is 'fully' God, and the Holy Spirit is 'fully' God."

11. God is One LORD, explained in the New Testament as the Godhead; namely Father, Son, and Holy Spirit. (Romans 1:20, Colossians 2:9) The Spirit-filled church emphatically believes in one eternal God.

12. The fullest understanding of the Godhead is beyond the understanding of mankind and can only be given to him by revelation from the Holy Spirit. Herbert Lockyer says, "The sacred mystery of the trinity (Godhead) is one which the light within man could never have discovered."

13. The Word reveals God as being eternal in unity as three Persons (1 Peter 1:2). These three Persons, who are one in substance and essence, have entity in the most perfect unity of thought and purpose (1 John 5:7), and they are equal in glory, majesty, and power.

14. Their inseparable and indivisible nature of One causes the presence and action of One to implicate the presence and action of the Others.... *But when the Helper comes, whom I shall send to you from the Father, the Spirit of truth who proceeds from the Father, He will testify of Me.* (John 15:26 NKJV)

15. Stephen D. Renn, author of *The Expository Dictionary of Bible Words*, describes the definition of God when termed *YHWH* occurring one hundred and eighty times in Genesis in the Old Testament, "God has appeared to Abraham and his descendants by the name 'God Almighty,' but has not made Himself known to them as 'LORD.' The uniqueness of God's revelation to Moses lies not in the mere knowledge or articulation of the name *YHWH*, but rather in the divinely given insight that *YHWH* is the ever-present, all-powerful God, the redeemer of His people, and the One who keeps His solemn promises pledged under the oath

of the covenant. Such a revelation had not been imparted to the patriarchal predecessors of Moses—they only had the promise."

16. God's progressive revelation of Who He is continues through the New Testament, and culminates in the exaltation that Jesus Christ, the Son of God, has the fullness of the Godhead bodily in Him. (Colossians 1:19, 2:9)

17. Consequently, all the Godhead, both power and authority, now reside in Jesus Christ who has been given the highest elevation by the Father who seated Him at His own right hand and sealed Jesus' office of authority and power with the scepter of righteousness. (Hebrews 1:8–13)

18. It is vital that Spirit-filled and Holy Spirit-led believers understand that within the Godhead there is perfect equality of all things pertaining to their deity. The divine nature intrinsic in the Godhead is equal in all three Persons. The Bible is emphatic and saturates the pages of the Holy Writ with the fact that the operation of the Godhead composed of the three Persons who are coeternal and coequal, and even being the same in substance yet distinct in subsistence, always functions this way.

19. The operation of the entire Godhead is inevitably present when God's divine deity is in operation. This is no more apparent than at Jesus' baptism. (Matthew 3:16–17)

20. William Rowe says: "While each Person is verily God, each Person is not God apart from the other two Persons; they are inseparable. They are not three Gods, but One."

21. The striking manifestation of the Godhead's equal and distinct operational abilities is experienced at the birth of the church in Jerusalem on the Day of Pentecost. It was Jesus Christ, the Holy Son, who said, *Behold I send the Promise of My Father upon you; but tarry in the city of Jerusalem until you are endued with power from on high....* (Luke 24:49 NKJV)

22. The Father purposes salvation for mankind and *sends forth His Son*. The Son was always with the Father who sent Him at the

appointed time into the world, giving Him a name that is above every other name, JESUS. Jesus is the embodiment of God in the flesh … *I and My Father are one*….

23. The Son fulfilled the Father's will and created all that is apparent to mankind. Then `*In these last days* … (Hebrews 1:2 NKJV) and *… when the fullness of the time had come, God sent forth His Son*…. (Galatians 4:4 NKJV) Jesus Christ is the fulfillment of the Father's predestined will … *Blessed be the God and Father of our Lord Jesus Christ, who has blessed us with every spiritual blessing in the heavenly places in Christ, just as He chose us in Him before the foundation of the world … having predestined us to adoption as sons*…. (Ephesians 1:3–5 NKJV)

24. The Holy Spirit is commissioned by the Father and the Son to reveal the intent and purposes of God the Father to mankind. He is also the comforter and teacher of all things pertaining to God. The Holy Spirit's anointing that is in every Spirit-filled believer reveals (teaches) to him all truth (1 John 2:27).

25. It is therefore correct to state that all things are from the Father (1 Corinthians 8:6 NKJV), through the Son, and revealed to mankind by the Holy Spirit.

26. This subject is so vital to the Spirit-filled believer that they approach it with reverence and humility, because they know they are entering the very essence and nucleus of who God is.

27. These believers know that their most important discourse with God is when they *enter into thy closet, and when thou hast shut thy door* (prayer) … (Matthew 6:6), that they reverently approach the Father in the name of Jesus and worship Him in spirit and in truth as the Holy Spirit gives them utterance. Herein is the blending of man's spirit with the Holy God in the entirety of the Godhead.

28. Henceforth, the scriptural word for "the Three-in-One," "Trinity," or "Triune" God is the "Godhead" and as such, the doctrine of the Spirit-filled church applies this biblical word.

Characteristics Applicable to the Godhead

29. *Wisdom.* God's wisdom is outside of human measurement. He is the very embodiment of wisdom which encompasses every thought and action emanating from Him ... *in whom are hidden all the treasures of wisdom....* (Colossians 2:3 NKJV)

30. The length, breadth, and depth of God's wisdom is impossible to fully comprehend: *Oh, the depth of the riches both of the wisdom and knowledge of God! How unsearchable are His judgments and His ways past finding out!...* (Romans 11:33 NKJV)

31. *For the LORD gives wisdom; from His mouth come knowledge and understanding* (Proverbs 2:6 NKJV). Every act and word from God is wise. In essence, He is the source of all true wisdom, and therefore everyone else who has wisdom has received it from God.

32. God's wise and knowledgeable applications are always correct because He knows which means are the most effective to achieve a perfect end. God's omniscience enables Him to be wise.

33. Wisdom is the application of knowledge. It is also using knowledge perfectly and in the correct manner. God never makes a mistake or gives the wrong instruction: He has perfect wisdom ... *But the wisdom that is from above is first pure, then peaceable, gentle, willing to yield, full of mercy and good fruits, without partiality and without hypocrisy....* (James 3:17 NKJV)

34. *Goodness.* God is ready to deal with man kindly, gently, and in goodness. More appropriately, God always deals with man in this manner. He is unchanging in His goodness towards mankind, and He was, is, and will always be this way ... *For I am the LORD, I change not* .... (Malachi 3:6) *The goodness of God endureth continually....* (Psalm 52:1)

35. There is no place on earth where mankind dwells that is void of God's goodness ... *The earth is full of the goodness of the LORD*.... (Psalm 33:5 NKJV)

36. The evidence of the enduring goodness is demonstrated by those who are led by the Holy Spirit's indwelling fruit (Galatians 5:22).

37. *Mercy.* God's mercy is poured out on those who are guilty of sinning against Him. Mankind, in his inherent sin, is utterly guilty of transgressing God's righteousness and holiness. He is therefore at the mercy of God to be forgiven. God alone has this power to forgive sin.

38. From the throne of God in heaven, namely the highest seat of authority, God has the mercy seat upon which the sacrificed blood of His Only Son was placed as the sufficient offering that invokes God's mercy to all who approach Him by faith ... *And the blood of Jesus Christ His Son cleanses us from all sin.... He is faithful and just to forgive us....* (1 John 1:7, 9 NKJV)

39. *Faithful.* God is the only true faithful companion man can fully trust. He has promised those who walk in His steps that He ... *will never leave thee nor forsake thee.....* (Hebrews 13:5) He is completely reliable and steadfastly constant, always fulfilling His promises.

40. God is faithful because He is unchanging and will always show the same faithfulness to every generation ... *Therefore know that the LORD your God, He is God, the faithful God who keeps covenant and mercy for a thousand generations with those who love Him and keep His commandments....* (Deuteronomy 7:9 NKJV)

41. *Truth.* The Scriptures declare that He is *the only true God* (John 17:3). John says ... *that we may know Him that is true* (1 John 5:20 NKJV). This translation into the English language of "true" is the same meaning attached to "genuine" and "real." For God in Jesus Christ is truthfully "real and genuinely" *God manifested in the flesh.*

42. Jesus makes the personal declaration that He is the truth: *I am the truth ...* (John 14:6), and has testified and witnessed to the truth. God is, in essence, wholly truth personified in Jesus Christ.

43. *Glory.* The overriding characteristic that is unique to God is His glory. No one anywhere and nothing ever created can claim the majesty and the magnificence of His glory (Psalm 145:5). Everything else is counterfeit. *The brightness of His glory* (Hebrews 1:3), Jesus, the Christ (anointed One), and the holy presence of the Holy Spirit causes believers to fall prostrate before Him.

44. His glory is the evidence of His impeccable reputation and requires the utmost honor and reverence from believers.

45. God's glory fills the expanse of His creation, manifesting itself in every crevice, mountaintop, and valley. Furthermore, the *Shekinah* glory impregnates the spirit of the Spirit-filled believer who radiates the Holy Spirit's presence.

46. God's glory manifests to the believer that He is present. The glory of His presence produces spiritual light that enlightens the believer's path, enabling them to walk in His righteousness. Wayne Grudem says, "It is very appropriate that God's revelation of Himself should be accompanied by such splendor and brightness, for this glory of God is the visible manifestation of the excellence of God's character."

47. Unbelievers shun God's glory, while believers run towards the *Light of the world....*

God the Father

48. Fatherhood is the most responsible role the Godhead can deliver. God the Father denotes the custodianship of man who accepts His offering as their provider, protector, and supplier of their every need.

49. Fatherhood is rooted in the very nature of God. Spirit-filled believers confess that ... *there is one God, the Father, of whom are all things, and we for Him....* (1 Corinthians 8:6 NKJV)

50. God the Father is the eternal *Elohim* and source of all life. In Him

all things are purposed and brought about. It is the highest form of *agape* ever expressed and is the fulfillment of the Father's unique function as the "parent" over His children, namely His sons and daughters.

51. Wayne Grudem states it as, "What then are the differences between Father, Son, and Holy Spirit? There is no difference in attributes at all. The only difference between them is the way they relate to each other and to the creation. The unique quality of the Father is the way He *relates as Father* to the Son and the Holy Spirit."

52. God is Father to all mankind, and operates equally and with equal measure when dealing with man*: Have we not all one Father? Has not one God created us?* (Malachi 2:10 NKJV)

53. Consequently, God the Father relates to mankind as the Father who is personal ... *Thou art my father, my God, and the rock of my salvation....* (Psalm 89:26)

54. God's Fatherhood relationship is "one-on-one" with every human. His caring and provisions are unlimited and impartial... *For your heavenly Father knows that you need all these things ...* (Matthew 6:32 NKJV) and as such ... *my God shall supply all your need according to His riches in glory by Christ Jesus....* (Philippians 4:19 NKJV)

55. Creation, including mankind, is entirely at the discretion of the Father's will. He orchestrates every action and predestines their beginning and end through His omniscient and omnipresent foreknowledge: *Are not two sparrows sold for a copper coin? And not one of them falls to the ground apart from your Father's will. But the very hairs of your head are numbered. Do not fear therefore; you are of more value than many sparrows....* (Matthew 10:29–31, 18:14 NKJV)

56. Therefore, all things pertaining to creation and mankind are at the discretion of the Father's will. This is the overriding attribute of the Father's function, namely that He wills (His intention and purpose) and knows all things at all times.

57. In this divine will that the Father has, He is abundant in mercy (2 Corinthians 1:3). Judgment, condemnation, forgiveness, and an unlimited supply are all contained in His mercy. (Luke 6:36)

58. These characteristics are all bound together in the indivisible chord of the Father's unconditional love. (Hebrews 12:6)

God the Son

59. Pertaining to the Godhead, the Son is first expressed as *the Word ... In the beginning was the Word, and the Word was with God, and the Word was God....* (John 1:1 NKJV)

60. The Son (the Word) has always been of the Godhead, and in fulfilling the will of the Father *the Word became flesh and dwelt among us....* (John 1:14 NKJV) Thus, the eternal existence of the Son is expressed prior to His human Sonship as *the Word.*

61. From the outset *the Word* was the creator of all things ... *All things were created through Him and for Him* (Colossians 1:16 NKJV) *... One Lord Jesus Christ, through whom are all things, and through whom we live....* (1 Corinthians 8:6 NKJV)

62. To fulfill the eternal purposes of God, the Father sent forth His Son (*the Word*) into the world ... *to make all see what is the fellowship of the mystery, which from the beginning of the ages has been hidden in God who created all things through Jesus Christ; to the intent that now the manifold wisdom of God might be made known by the church to the principalities and powers in the heavenly places, according to the eternal purpose which He accomplished in Christ Jesus our Lord.* (Ephesians 3:9–11 NKJV)

63. Of Jesus Christ, the only Son begotten of the Father: *For this purpose the Son of God was manifested, that he might destroy the works of the devil....* (1 John 3:8) Jesus, the Son, did this when He offered Himself as the sacrifice for sin.

64. Spirit-filled believers confess that the Lord Jesus Christ is the Son

of God (Romans 1:4) who is both Lord and Christ (Acts 2:36), and that the Word of Eternal God emphatically teaches that Jesus Christ is the only begotten Son of God and He is unequivocally God (John 10:30).

65. Furthermore, Spirit-filled believers believe in Jesus Christ's incarnation and virgin birth (Matthew 1:20). Jesus Christ lived a sinless life on earth, was crucified, and raised from the dead.

66. Once the Son had accomplished the Father's purpose He ascended into heaven, and the Father exalted Him and gave Him the seat of honor and authority and said... *Sit at My right hand, till I make Your enemies Your footstool....* (Hebrews 1:13 NKJV)

67. Henceforth, the Son is now the Apostle and the High Priest, advocate, and intercessor for the saints.

God the Holy Spirit

68. The Holy Spirit is sent by the Father and the Son to reveal to believers the deep things of God (1 Corinthians 2:10–11). He convicts the sinner and comforts the believer (John 16:7–14).

69. The Person of the Holy Spirit is of absolute equality with the Father and the Son and is equal to them as to source of all power and blessing (John 14:16–17, 26).

70. While the omnipresence of the Holy Spirit has always been with mankind, His working is upon them. Nevertheless, from the birth of the church on the Day of Pentecost, the Holy Spirit is now resident in the believers who experience, through faith, the baptism with the Holy Spirit. The evidence of His indwelling is manifested by the initial physical sign of speaking with other tongues as the Holy Spirit gives utterance (Acts 2:4).

71. The Holy Spirit's omnipresence will continue eternally throughout all generations of man.

72. The Holy Spirit possesses all the attributes of Deity. He is the Spirit of life (Romans 8:2), He is truth (John 16:13), holiness (Ephesians 4:30), is eternal (Hebrews 9:14), and is omniscient and omnipresent (Psalm 139:7).

73. Possessing these attributes of Deity, the Holy Spirit performs those acts and revelations that pertain to God only. No human being can do what God can. Man can make, but God creates. Creation was the prerogative of the divine Deity and implemented by the Spirit at creation (Genesis 1:1).

CHAPTER 8

THE NATURE OF GOD

1. The Word declares ... *For My thoughts are not your thoughts, nor are your ways My ways, says the LORD. For as the heavens are higher than the earth, so are My ways higher than your ways, and My thoughts than your thoughts....* (Isaiah 55:8–9 NKJV)

2. The essence of God's nature, His thought process, and the actions resulting from His nature are completely opposite to man's nature. Man's nature stems from the stained "sin nature" inherited from Adam and Eve's fall into sin and death in the Garden of Eden. God's nature is unblemished.

3. The original nature that was given to Adam when God created him was perfect. However, Adam's nature had to be proved (tested) to qualify its righteous and pure condition. Until Adam's nature had gone through the test, it was "innocent." This innocence kept it in a perfect state, namely without sin.

4. The test God laid on Adam's heart and soul hinged on one attribute: be obedient to God's command: *But of the tree of the knowledge of good and evil you shall not eat....* (Genesis 2:17 NKJV)

5. Adam disobeyed God's command and ate of the tree of knowledge of good and evil. This resulted in the contamination of Adam's

nature, and the sin of disobedience permeated his natural abilities. *For in the day that you eat of it you shall surely die.*

6. Thus, Adam exchanged his "innocent" nature for one that acquired knowledge of good and evil. His nature had to be tested to prove that it was worthy of its innocent state. He failed by disobeying God's one command.

7. Since then, now residing in man is the sin-stained nature that is contrary to God's nature.

8. God purposed through His Son, Jesus Christ, a reconciliation of the relationship with mankind. Jesus took upon Himself the sin of mankind and was condemned to hell to pay the punishment of a sinner, and more so the sin-stained nature of mankind.

9. Jesus perfected the process, and man can now be restored to their original state before God. This state is the acceptance of Jesus Christ as Savior, and once this is done, God in Jesus Christ and God the Holy Spirit once again dwells within a man's spirit. Ultimately, it is the indwelling nature of God that now resides within man's spirit.

10. What now follows is the application of God's indwelling nature within man. This implementation of God's nature by man in their daily life is what ultimately draws him to have a closer relationship with Jesus Christ.

11. What then are the contents of God's nature that man must pay the closest attention to as he *draws nigh unto God?* (James 4:8) There are five fundamental attributes (or elements) in the distinctive nature of God as revealed in the Bible. These attributes require a gracious response of the people to His grace as they become molded into His likeness. God's nature consists of five intrinsic attributes:

Love

Divine

Holy

Pure

Righteous

12. To express each attribute in the fullest extent, it is important to understand them. They must be considered from God's perspective and not analyzed by man's intellect. God's ways are higher than man's ways and His thoughts are above man's thoughts. Therefore, God's nature must be examined from His Word. Therein is hidden the foundation of every attribute and the effect it must have on mankind.

13. At the outset, let it be known that God is indivisible and completely One. When considering His attributes, the intention is not to dissect God into various parts but merely establish His total uniqueness.

14. Apostle Paul exhorts the brethren to ... *look not at the things which are seen, but at the things which are not seen....* (2 Corinthians 4:18) Here he relates the trials and struggles the believers endure in the physical and visible ("seen") aspects of life to the indwelling Holy Spirit's conquering power. His focus is not fixed on the sufferings or victories of the flesh, but rather on the unseen attributes of God's nature within him. His relationship with Jesus Christ is more valuable to him than any "seen" accomplishment or struggle.

15. The application of God's nature in a believer's life is the most effective testimony they can have. Hence, the Word declares ... *For in Him we live, and move, and have our being....* (Acts 17:28)

16. When the five attributes are mentioned in the Bible, it is vital that they are measured against the four "absolutes" that constitute God's infinity.

17. Man has no vocabulary to express the "existence" of God. Man's finite mind cannot fully comprehend the infinite God.

18. God is outside of "measurement." God is beyond man's capability of categorization. Nothing is measurable against God's actuality as an infinite Being.

19. The four "absolutes" pertaining to God, in human terms, are defined as:

Eternal
Omnipotent
Omnipresent
Omniscient

20. These absolutes are the circumference that encircles God's nature. They are a binding cord that holds the eternal state of God's nature intact. They surround the five attributes like a fortress wall that shields God's infinite nature.

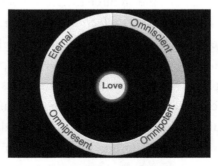

God Is Love

21. Within the circle of God's four absolutes resides the center of who He is—love. God is not a God of love; He is love (1 John 4:8). The remaining attributes contained in His nature are intrinsically wrapped in love. Hence, love is the center of all that God is. Love is therefore ... *a wheel in the middle of a wheel....* (Ezekiel 1:16 NKJV)

22. If there has ever been an attack on the Godhead, then it is the deceit and confusion Satan sows in peoples' minds regarding who God is. The divine, holy presence of God flows from the very Being of who God is. *God is Love*; He is not the God who loves, He is entirely Love.

23. The Greek declaration of the loosely translated word "love" into the English language dilutes the very essence of who God is. Flesh to flesh, the word is "Eros" in Greek, but translated as "love." This is directed at the feelings between a man and a woman. Brotherly love, "Phileo," which is also translated as "love," is the expression for the feeling between people, kinship, and is charitable in its application. Finally, the love that is God is "Agape," yet translated as "love."

24. At the outset, let it be known and believed that there is no fruit or by-product of God that is "Agape." God's eternal Spiritual existence, omniscience, omnipotent, and omnipresence is altogether Agape.

25. The awesome, unexplainable ever-present presence and involvement in every aspect of all of creation and act of God is immersed in this one revelation: God is Love. Every human being has a constant demonstration of Agape when they view God's creation. Every minute detail of the magnificent creation leaves man aghast as they absorb the manifestation of the love that divinely formed the habitat and cosmos.

26. Yet the personal experience every person has when they encounter Agape as the Holy Spirit reveals who God is immerses them in

the unending love. Love/Agape opens the door to man's spirit to expose God to him. This is the relevance Jesus referenced when He told Nicodemus, *You must be born again.* It is because *God so loved the world ...* that the Holy Spirit reveals Agape—God—and this Agape bursts forth into the heart/spirit of the person. Apostle Paul says *Christ in you, the hope of glory.* Love/agape takes up residence in the born-again believer's spirit, and they are now a *new creation.* (2 Corinthians 5:17)

27. God is Spirit (John 4:24), and the intrinsic attribute that constitutes God is entirely agape. To illustrate the explanation further, water constitutes both the elements of hydrogen and oxygen, which are two atoms that form a liquid substance of water when combined. Conversely, God is entirely agape, and it contains only one element: love/agape.

28. The nature of God must therefore be anchored in who God is. It is because God is love/agape that the spiritual attributes of righteousness, holiness, pureness, and His divine presence flow from His heart to mankind. His absolutes of eternality, omnipresence, omnipotence, and omniscience are the effects of the composition of who He is. The entire Godhead, Father, the Word (Son), and Holy Spirit are entirely love.

29. Every activity the Godhead undertakes is propelled by their unconditional love that always has a desire to replenish, build, mature, and improve a believer's life.

30. To adequately describe the qualities of this love, man must forgo his human and carnal aspiration of love. God is Spirit, and His agape can only be *spiritually discerned* (1 Corinthians 2:14).

31. When a Spirit-filled believer gets a glimpse of this immense agape, it raises him up on eagles' wings. (Isaiah 40:31) Such revelation exposes him to the deepest intentions of God's divine purposes for him.

32. God—Agape—desires a spiritual personal relationship with His creation. He desires a righteous, sanctified, and holy spirit/

heart to be intricately fused in His love. His ultimate desire is not for wealth, health, or pleasures forever more for His children. (He has the windows of heaven wide open, and they are already being poured out [Malachi 3:10]). What He desires is a spiritual relationship with a holy saint.

33. The entrance into His presence brings spiritual light (Psalm 27:1), and this light brings the Spirit-filled believer into a place where he abandons everything he desires for himself and pours out his being (everything he is) so that God can work through him to perform His will. The source of love is God, and from the pinnacle of this source a river begins to flow through the Spirit-filled believer's life, touching others *for Christ's sake* (2 Corinthians 12:10). The Spirit-filled believer has no idea, or even concern, for God's intentions in using him as a river of life. His only focus remains on the source, agape/love, which flows through him.

34. When Spirit-filled believers reach this height in their relationship with Agape, then they know the measure of their insignificance compared to God's all-in-all love. Agape breaks through the barriers of self-will, self-righteousness, and selfishness. It bursts asunder the hindrances of "I can't," "I'm not worthy," and "My past is too corroded by sin," as it gushes forth like a river of living water nourishing all who cross his path... *He who believes in Me, as the Scripture has said, out of his heart will flow rivers of living water. But this He spoke concerning the Spirit, whom those believing in Him would receive; for the Holy Spirit was not yet given, because Jesus was not yet glorified....* (John 7:38–39 NKJV)

35. Spiritual agape knows no boundaries. It is most active expressing its truest intentions when the Holy Spirit exposes this love to a person kneeling at the Cross. Furthermore, agape demonstrates its deepest intentions when a Spirit-filled believer confesses his sins, and the crimson flow of the Blood of the Cross cleanses him of all sin. (1 John 1:7) Even more so, Agape fulfills its fullest intentions

when He casts a repentant heart's sin into the sea of forgetfulness and remembers them no more.

36. Apostle John exalts God and who He is, Agape to the loftiest pedestal, and crowns biblical teaching by focusing on love. Love is the foundation of everything God intended ... *For God so loved the world....* (John 3:16, 17:23, 1 John 3:16)

37. Apostle John continues his declaration on love by embracing God's agape that is continually being demonstrated towards us and, consequently, that same agape flows through believers towards brothers and sisters in Christ ... *In this the love of God was manifested toward us, that God has sent His only begotten Son into the world, that we might live through Him. In this is love, not that we loved God, but that He loved us and sent His Son to be the propitiation for our sins. Beloved, if God so loved us, we ought also to love one another....* (1 John 4:9–11 NKJV)

38. The human mind cannot fully comprehend or express the contents of the statement *God is love.* Agape lovingly recognizes, reveals, and redeems the sinner's condition. It removes every hindrance which sin encapsulates in a repentant man's heart. It is a lightning strike on the repentant heart immediately removing the impediment of inherent sin, and a gentle rain of blessed assurance, comfort, and caring for His beloved that culminates in the promise of eternal life to everyone who believes. Consequently, to them who shun this precious gift, they are left to the peril of their unrepentant condition, and subsequently must face His wrath and judgment ... *He who believes in the Son has everlasting life; and he who does not believe the Son shall not see life, but the wrath of God abides on him....* (John 3:36 NKJV)

39. Extending from this inner circle of love, and surrounded by the four absolutes, reside the remaining attributes of God's nature.

CHAPTER 9

THE NATURE OF GOD –

CONTINUED

God's Nature Is Divine

1. Continuing the doctrine of God's nature, God's holy word declares that His nature is *divine:* Apostle Peter refers to God's nature ... *As His divine power has given to us all things that pertain to life and godliness, through the knowledge of Him who called us by glory and virtue, by which have been given to us exceedingly great and precious promises, that through these you may be partakers of the divine nature, having escaped the corruption that is in the world through lust.* (2 Peter 1:3–4 NKJV)

2. Ancient translators have used the Greek word *theios* to mean "Godhead." The more accurate translation is "divine nature" and is used only twice in the Bible. It signifies the "totality" of the deity of the Godhead. "Divinity" (*theios*) is the expression emphasized in the Greek as One who is above all things, without beginning and end, and is entirely sovereign, sacred, and unique. There is only One God, and it is the divine God, Creator of all things. When extending the word *theios* to *theotes,* this all-encompassing

declaration is also understood to mean the "Godhead" in the New Testament, namely "all of God."

3. Thus the Bible correctly records that God's nature is divine, meaning it is rightly emphasizing that God is totally sovereign and sacred, and there is none other like Him.

4. The only One to whom this adjective can be applied is God. Nothing else ever created and nothing else sculptured from man's hands out of the most precious of commodities can ever be declared divine ... *Therefore, the One whom you worship without knowing Him, I proclaim to you.... For in Him we live and move and have our being.... Therefore, since we are the offspring of God, we ought not to think that the Divine Nature* (Godhead, or the all-encompassing God) *is like gold or silver or stone, something shaped by art and man's devising....* (Acts 17:23–29 NKJV)

5. It is therefore correct to declare that God's nature is divine, encompassing every aspect of Him, and each attribute in His nature is divine. Divinity can only be ascribed to God, the eternal, the omniscient, omnipotent, and omnipresent One. He alone as Creator of all things is the Supreme Being.

6. Delving a little deeper into God's divine nature, the first description worthy of consideration is the expression used, the "*deity*" of God. When applied to God, it expresses the uniqueness of God as the Supreme Being, Creator, and Eternal One. Human comprehension of God's eternal existence cannot be fully explained, and thus "deity" is used to denote His fullness in all things.

7. "Deity is the term that defines the essence of God and the quality of the Divine. It is a character trait that makes God who He is and sets Him apart as worthy of worship." (*The International Standard Bible Encyclopedia*, Volume D–E)

8. Furthermore, God's divine nature is *sovereign*. There is nothing that is not under His control or ever happens without His knowledge. He alone is the Supreme Commander who orchestrates

His universe, His earthly creatures and their habitat. He alone has the supreme authority to control everything He has made.

9. Sovereignty is God's control or governance over all things. He is the ruler over all reality. Because God is divine, He has dominion over all things. His words and actions are final, and He needs no one and nothing to tell Him what to do. His declaration, decisions, and instructions are without questioning. No one can ever question God's judgments and His rulership and ask ... *If He takes away, who can hinder Him? Who can say to Him, what are You doing?* (Job 9:12 NKJV) *...As for the Almighty, we cannot find Him: He is excellent in power, in judgment and abundant justice....* (Job 37:23 NKJV)

10. In His sovereignty God encompasses all wisdom and is the Source of it. Embodied in this immeasurable wisdom, God orchestrates His sovereignty for the benefit of mankind.

11. In His matchless sovereignty, God is revered, honored, and worshipped by everyone. His wisdom, power, strength, and glory are the description of Who He is because His divine nature is sovereign.

12. God's sovereignty is best described in His holy word ... *Then I looked, and I heard the voice of many angels around the throne, the living creatures, and the elders; and the number of them was ten thousand times ten thousand, and thousands of thousands, saying with a loud voice: 'Worthy is the Lamb who was slain to receive power and riches and wisdom and strength and honor and glory and blessing!" And every creature which is in heaven and on the earth and under the earth and such as are in the sea, and all that are in them, I heard saying: "blessing and honor and glory and power be to Him who sits on the throne, and to the Lamb, forever and ever!"...* (Revelation 5:11–13 NKJV).

13. To expand the explanation further, God's divine nature is *sacred.* It is eternally divine and thus eternally sacred. It is inherently

blameless and without blemishes. From His throne, His divine utterances are sacred and therefore without question.

14. In contrast to the worldly decrees that are termed "sacred" and are declared from earthly kings, and stem from a sin-stained heart, the sacred decrees from God's throne are from a pure, wise, and holy King and Lord. The subjects ruled by an earthly king question the decrees from their king. On the other hand, the decrees from God are never questioned by believers.

15. God's instructions are sacred and followed by believers because every utterance from the holy throne is saturated in God's divine holiness, wisdom, glory, and power.

16. So sacred are His words He is present in them ... *In the beginning was the Word, and the Word was with God, and the Word was God.... And the Word became flesh....* (John 1:1; 14 NKJV)

God's Nature Is Holy

17. The most sublime attribute of God's nature is the fact that He is holy.

18. To fully define this holy state is impossible. However, the following explanation declares God's holiness best. Dr. Herbert Lockyer says: "As the absolute holy One God is free from evil and hates and abhors sin. (Leviticus 19:2) He is 'glorious in holiness.' (Exodus 15:11) As the sun cannot darken, so God cannot act unrighteously, 'He is the Holy One.' (Job 6:10) Holiness is His inward character—not merely a trait of His Being, but His very essence—not one of a list of virtues but the sum of all excellencies rather than an excellence."

19. When God's holiness begins to be understood in man's finite mind, holiness provokes a holy reverence (fear) within the human soul and spirit. God's holiness is His spiritual covering, His

indwelling dynamo, the instigator of His thought process, and the reason for His actions.

20. It is not merely the understanding on the part of man to declare that God is a holy God. God Himself declares that He is holy. *For I the LORD am holy....* (Leviticus 20:26) Again, God declares...*For I am God and not man, the Holy One in your midst....* (Hosea 11:9 NKJV)

21. God's most emphatic intrinsic attribute that separates Him from mankind is His holiness. It is the essence of who He is, and holiness can never be abandoned or ignored in everything God is and does.

22. Jesus Christ, the holy One (Luke 1:35), declares that His Father is holy: *Holy Father....* (John 17:11) The Son of Man is not slack concerning the reference to His Father's holy nature; He addresses God the Father by acknowledging the Father's highest attribute, namely His holiness. Furthermore, when teaching the Jews to pray, Jesus directs them to proclaim that their heavenly Father's name is incomparable and unique: *Hallowed be thy name....* (Matthew 6:9)

23. In an attempt to acknowledge God in His unique and most significant attribute, the seraphim who are charged with the custody of the holy throne of God circle the throne, and the only accolade they voice in His presence is *Holy, holy, holy is the LORD of hosts; the whole earth is full of His glory....* (Isaiah 6:3 NKJV)

24. The seraphim do not address God's unlimited power, His omnipotence, omniscience, omnipresence, or His eternal state. They are engulfed in God's holy state.

25. God's holiness is above man's finite intellect. His unlimited holiness knows no boundaries, and it is far deeper and higher than the human mind can reach. In an attempt to explain God's holiness, it is best to divide God's holiness into three categories: spiritual, sacred, and separate.

26. *God is Spirit* ... (John 4:24) and the Godhead—Father, Son, and

Holy Spirit—are holy. God is the source of holiness. He has been and will always be holy. The intrinsic measure of God's spiritual existence is His holiness.

27. God does not have to do anything to prove He is holy. He does not have to explain how He is holy because God is infinitely above human comprehension, and therefore His perfect holiness is outside man's intellect. It is man's acceptance, by faith, that God, whom man serves, is beyond the grasp of the human definition of perfect holiness.

28. God is viewed in the human spirit as the matchless and incorruptible source of spiritual edification. The command ... *Be holy, for I am holy* ... (1 Peter 1:16 NKJV) resounds in the human spirit, knowing that the source of the holiness God is exacting from His children is Himself.

29. Holiness and any reference to it is intrinsically blended into who God is. Man cannot mention God without referencing the fact that He is holy. This attribute is the spiritual presentation of the entire constitution of God. As Spirit, there is not one aspect of Almighty God that is not holy ... *No one is holy like the LORD....* (1 Samuel 2:2 NKJV)

30. God's Spirit permeates every corner of His creation. There is never a place He has created that can hide from His presence. In the vast expanse of His creation, in the heavens, the cosmos, or within the human frame, God's Spirit is presented as holy.

31. Man's response to God and His holiness is first the acceptance that wherever God is spiritually evidenced, there His holiness is. The untouchable spiritual presence is discerned in the human spirit when man realizes the corruptible sinful state he is in as opposed to the holy spiritual attribute within the Holy God's presence.

32. The acknowledgement and acceptance that God's holy presence is everywhere is the reason why mortals bow down and worship God ... *Exalt the LORD our God, and worship at His footstool— He is holy....* (Psalm 99:5 NKJV) Their acknowledgment of

God's holiness reaches into man's spirit and demands attention. This results in the second step man takes: they either reject or accept God's holiness. Believers receive the holy presence of God and surrender to the Holy Spirit, and worship God *in spirit and in truth*.... (John 4:24)

33. Man's spirit is the receptacle and place that responds to God's holiness. Because God is Spirit, it interacts with man's spirit to direct their decisions and activity. This spiritual interaction is confirmed ... *But he who is joined to the Lord is one spirit with Him*.... (1 Corinthians 6:17 NKJV) *My spirit has rejoiced in God my Savior*.... (Luke 1:47 NKJV) Apostle Paul states ... *whom I serve with my spirit*.... (Romans 1:9 NKJV)

34. Not only is the holy attribute spiritual, it is also sacred.

35. There is no comparison or measure the human frame can conjure up to match the sacred holiness of God. It is sacred because it is unique to God. His very being is entirely holy, making it sacred, which is without measurement. God's sacredness is peculiar to Him, and it has no equivalent.

36. It is so sacred that whoever attempts to mimic His sacred holiness or even consider declaring that they are as sacred are nothing but self-righteous and self-indulgent.

37. Every "sacred" edifice created by human hands, every utterance declared by the human tongue proclaiming that they are as sacred as God are a mere shell by comparison to the intrinsic sacredness attributed to God's holy nature.

38. In this declaration that God's holy nature is sacred, every created being must show respect and honor to God. It is not only fitting that believers show the highest level of respect: God's sacred holiness demands it.

39. It is therefore, without contradiction, that He who is holy speaks words that are holy. God's words are for the believers who understand that His words flow through their spirit, and that they

have been uttered from their sacred God who is incomparable and unique.

40. The ultimate definition of God's sacred holiness is best expressed when declared "incomparable" and "unique."

41. This holy attribute is not only spiritual and sacred: it is also entirely separate.

42. There is nothing and no one who can claim their holy existence as emanating from their own doing. God alone is holy, and His very Alpha and Omega existence (without beginning and without end) is holy. God's holy state is separate from everything else.

43. *Come out from among them and be separate, says the Lord ...* (2 Corinthians 6:17 NKJV) is the command God gives to His children. This separation is necessary for the believer to ... *be holy, for I am holy...* (1 Peter 1:16 NKJV) He instructs the children to separate themselves like this because He is separate from all sin and uncleanness.

44. God's separateness is unique to Him because it is impossible for Him to be contaminated. He is the Author of His distinguishable trait of holiness which separates Him from everything else. God did not have to create holiness: He is holy. Neither did God have to acquire holiness: He is inherently holy. God did not have to sacrifice any other attribute so that His holiness could be separated from all else: He is holy and therefore separated from all frailty and sin.

45. Consequently, on the great Day of the Lord and at the Great White Throne Judgment, Holy God, represented by His eternal holy Son, Jesus Christ, will take His place as the holy God and judge according to the standard of His holiness ... *Who shall not fear You, O Lord, and glorify Your name? For You alone are holy...for Your judgments have been manifested....* (Revelation 15:4 NKJV)

46. Such, then, is the holiness of God. It is immeasurable, all-encompassing, and intrinsically existing in every aspect of His holy nature.

CHAPTER 10

THE NATURE OF GOD –
CONTINUED

God's Nature Is Righteous

1. The dominant reflection cast from every word in the Bible relates to the absolute righteousness of God and the utter depravity of the human soul ... *There is none righteous, no, not one....* (Romans 3:10 NKJV) God alone is righteous (Romans 3:21–23).

2. God's righteousness is above comparison, and no creature has this inherent attribute; only God is inherently righteous ... *Righteous are You, O LORD, and upright are Your judgments....* (Psalm 119:137 NKJV) The very foundation of God's dealing with man from His heavenly spiritual throne contains this attribute ... *Righteousness and justice are the foundation of Your throne....* (Psalm 89:14 NKJV)

3. Unlike man, God's righteous nature did not need a sacrifice to afford Him righteousness; neither did God need to repent of anything to make Him righteous. He is righteous, and the basis of the relationship and the fellowship man has with God is founded upon man repenting of his inherent sin, exercising his faith in the finished work of Calvary, accepting Jesus Christ as Lord, and in

so doing ... *might become the righteousness of God in Him*....
(2 Corinthians 5:21 NKJV)

4. Righteousness is explained as one who does justly and right. It is the "rightness" exercised in every thought and action. In this definition, God is always just and right ... *The just LORD is in the midst thereof: he will not do iniquity: every morning doth he bring his judgment to light, he faileth not....* (Zephaniah 3:5)

5. Being righteous indicates that God's righteous nature permanently operates justly, and henceforth He always does what is right. While God's holy nature explains His intrinsic attribute of who He is, righteousness is the attribute that explains God's nature in His dealings with mankind.

6. Furthermore, God is righteous because of His mercy and justice. The Old Covenant was the basis of God's mercy towards His people, affording them the privilege of learning righteousness. Now in Christ Jesus our Lord, the Better Covenant extends God's mercy to all humanity when He sent Jesus as the sacrifice for "whosoever will."

7. Because of the declaration of man's faith in Christ's finished work on Calvary ... *so also by one Man's obedience* (Jesus obediently giving His life on the cross) *many will be made righteous....* (Romans 5:19 NKJV)

8. God declares that He alone is the only One who deals justly with mankind ... *and there is no other God besides Me, a just God and a Savior: There is none beside Me....* (Isaiah 45:21 NKJV)

9. This emphatic statement by God regarding His uniqueness relates to the fulfillment of His promise ... *If we confess our sins, He is faithful and just to forgive us our sins and to cleanse us from all unrighteousness....* (1 John 1:9 NKJV)

10. Conversely, if God is to deal justly with a repentant heart, He will mete out the same just judgment on the unrepentant heart ... *Oh, let the wickedness of the wicked come to an end, but establish the just: for the righteous God tests the hearts and minds. My defense*

is of God, who saves the upright in heart. God is a just judge, and God is angry with the wicked every day.... (Psalm 7:9–11 NKJV)

11. This "anger" God shows towards the wicked is manifested during the Great Tribulation when God deals justly with the wickedness of the sinner... *since it is a righteous thing with God to repay with tribulation those who trouble you....* (2 Thessalonians 1:6 NKJV) Furthermore ... *You are righteous, O Lord, the One who is and who was and who is to be, because You have judged these things. For they* (the wicked) *have shed the blood of saints and prophets, and You have given them blood to drink. For it is their just due....* (Revelation 16:5–6 NKJV)

12. God does not have to prove to anyone that He is righteous. His "right" dealing with mankind's sin, the fulfillment of every promise He has made, and the ever-present witness of the Holy Spirit proclaims His righteous nature.

13. The intrinsic righteousness God's nature possesses, and because of it, He is enabled to always be right in everything He does or says. All His judgments are right, and all His promises are *yea and amen* (2 Corinthians 1:20). It is everlasting ... *His righteousness endures forever....* (2 Corinthians 9:9 NKJV)

14. God does not only always do the right things; He always does things right.

15. His righteous nature produces mercy that is shown to all mankind. This *mercy* produces *grace* that is shed abroad in every repentant sinner's heart. Because of the grace that is shown, God's *forgiveness* gushes forth into the repentant sinner's spirit and soul as the blood of Jesus Christ cleanses him of all sin. Without hesitation, the righteous nature of God blots out the iniquity within the repentant heart, and the repentant sinner is *justified* and declared *righteous* in God's eyes. (Titus 3:4–7) Consequently, God's righteous nature that produces mercy reaches into the miry clay and plucks the sin-stained soul from the devil's clutches and places it in the palm of His hand ... *But God who is rich in mercy, because of His*

great love with which He loved us, even when we were dead in trespasses, made us alive together with Christ (by grace you have been saved), and raised us up together and made us sit together in the heavenly places in Christ Jesus.... (Ephesians 2:4–6 NKJV)

16. God shows mercy because He deals justly and rightly with every repentant sinner's heart ... *Have mercy upon me, O God, according to Your loving-kindness; According to the multitude of Your tender mercies, blot out my transgressions....* (Psalm 51:1 NKJV)

17. Mercy can only be shown to the guilty. Innocence needs no mercy. The just God deals justly, and with loving-kindness fulfills His promise ... *If we confess our sins, He is faithful and just to cleanse us....* (1 John 1:9 NKJV) God honors His word, and constantly shows mercy towards the guilty heart that repents: *For His mercy endures forever....* (Psalm 118:1 NKJV)

18. It is because God's nature is righteous that He shows mercy that produces this immeasurable pardon towards the repentant heart. The moment the individual repents, confesses their sin, and seeks God's forgiveness, the Father applies the blood of Jesus that blots out the iniquity within the heart ... *The blood of Jesus Christ his Son cleanseth us from all sin....* (1 John 1:7)

19. The righteous God demands that the believer be righteous, for without the righteousness of God residing in the believer's heart, there can be no relationship and fellowship between God and man. Created man has no righteousness of his own; it is imputed to him by God and as such, man is wholly dependent on God's grace ... *that we might become the righteousness of God in Him....* (2 Corinthians 5:21 NKJV)

God's Nature Is Pure

20. The intellectual and worldly dictionary expresses *pure* as something or someone being *flawless, perfect, genuine, and*

virtuous. Taking these interpretations of *pure* to its logical conclusion, the Holy Writ must surely reference these adjectives, and it does.

21. God's *pure* nature is flawless, without spot or blemish. The Word declares: *The words of the LORD are pure words, like silver tried in a furnace of earth, purified seven times....* (Psalm 12:6 NKJV) God's "words" are pure. They can only come from a pure heart, a pure state of being, and a pure motive.

22. Every utterance and every action emanating from God's heart is flawless in its intent and application. It is never contaminated by impure intentions or motives.

23. The eternal existence of God makes the declaration that God's purity is flawless a unique statement. God has been and always will be flawless. This is what supports the definition of Him being pure.

24. God is forever without spot or blemish. God's nature is untarnished. The very presence of Jesus on earth manifested the purity of the Godhead, because ... *He who knew no sin ...* (2 Corinthians 5:21 NKJV) was the only One who can be acclaimed as ... *for such a High Priest was fitting for us, who is holy, harmless, undefiled* (pure and flawless), *separate from sinners, and has become higher than the heavens....* (Hebrews 7:26 NKJV)

25. God is apart from sin. Sin has no ability to tarnish His existence. Sin cannot enter the realm of God's pureness, because unlike mankind, His nature is pure and without any flaws through which sin can enter. Hence, God's pure attribute is termed flawless.

26. Satan constantly seeks for the flaw in mankind's nature. He searches the actions of mankind to determine their intentions. Once he has established the kink in man's armor, he enters through the flaw and sows his evil intentions that provoke sinfulness. God has no kink in His nature. Satan can never find a foothold in God's pure nature. God is above any approach from Satan. And Satan knows this fact.

27. In as much as God's nature is flawless, so is it perfect ... *Your*

Father which is in heaven is perfect.... (Matthew 5:48) Perfection is outside of measurement. There are no degrees of perfection. Hence, God's pureness is unblemished and never contaminated by the slightest taint of imperfection.

28. Because God's nature is pure, thus perfect, all His ways are therefore perfect. *As for God, His way is perfect....* (Psalm 18:30; 2 Samuel 22:31 NKJV) There are never any imperfect, guile-infested motives aligned in God's ways. Every way intended and implemented is perfect from its inception.

29. It is a foregone conclusion that if God's ways are perfect, then His works are perfect. *He is the Rock, His work is perfect.* (Deuteronomy 32:4 NKJV) Flowing from the pure heart that has perfect intentions, perfect works emanate.

30. This state of perfection is constantly applied in all God's intentions and works. He is beyond variance in His nature and character ... *Every good gift and every perfect gift is from above, and comes down from the Father of lights, in whom there is no variation or shadow of turning.* (James 1:17 NKJV)

31. God's pure nature has yet another explanation: it is genuine. In God's pureness, the flawless, perfect pureness is instigated from God's heart. This is not a copied or adapted pureness: it is genuine (real) pureness.

32. Flowing from His nature, every commandment God produces is from a genuine heart that desires ultimate blessings for His people ... The *commandment of the LORD is pure* (genuine)*, enlightening the eyes....* (Psalm 19:8 NKJV) The Psalmist continues, *Your word is very pure ...* (Psalm 119:140 NKJV), emphasizing that it is more than refined—it is the genuine article.

33. From every vantage point God establishes a pure motive, and His observation and evaluation of each circumstance is from a genuine heart: *You are of purer* (free from defect or filth, i.e. genuine) *eyes than to behold evil, and cannot look on wickedness....* (Habakkuk

1:13 NKJV) God does not even consider or perform acts of wickedness. He is repulsed by evil and wickedness.

34. God never considers any compromise of His pureness, because His genuine purity does not contain elements that permit an imitated and inferior pureness to match or influence His genuine purity.

35. Because God's nature is pure, it is unquestionably virtuous. The moral soundness of every aspect of God reflects His pure nature. The character traits that are produced from His excellent uprightness declare His virtuous intentions ... *But the wisdom that is from above is first pure, then peaceable, gentle, willing to yield, full of mercy and good fruits, without partiality and without hypocrisy....* (James 3:17 NKJV)

36. God's infinite virtue, which never varies, has always been in existence and will continue forever. It is in this pure attribute that He can perform His miraculous perfect will in and through believers.

37. The ultimate result of God's virtue is found in His pure desire to always do good things for mankind. Evil intent does not have the slightest probability of invading God's pureness.

38. In conclusion, God's nature is pure. This attribute contains biblical evidence that illustrates God's pureness as flawless, perfect, genuine, and virtuous. What then is the impact that His pure nature has on believers who *follow his steps...?* (1 Peter 2:21)

The Impact of God's Nature on a Believer's Walk in Christ

39. Residing in every born-again believer, God's nature must flow through every word and deed performed. When His nature is evidenced, it is the manifestation of His indwelling existence within the believer's heart ... *But if the Spirit of Him who raised*

Jesus from the dead dwells in you, He who raised Christ from the dead will also give life to your mortal bodies through His Spirit who dwells in you.... (Romans 8:11 NKJV)

40. The definition of "pure" in the human spirit, soul, and body means it is "free from any contamination." It is not intermingled with any other substance contained in the original carnal nature, but purely God's nature operating within the born-again spirit.

41. The old nature, or carnal nature, that is now subjected to God's nature must no longer exhibit its immoral, blemished, corrupt, and defiled conduct. The indwelling Holy Spirit who has implanted God's nature in the believer gives life to the believer in its purest form.

42. The foundation of a believer's faith becomes immovable when the declaration is made that ... *it is God who arms me with strength and makes my way perfect....* (Psalm 18:32 NKJV) The initial step of recognizing that, in himself, the believer has no ability to bring the carnal nature to perfection opens the pathway for God's nature to begin the reformation of his ways.

43. Once the recognition that it is God who now dwells within him ... *the steps of a good man are ordered by the LORD....* (Psalm 37:23 NKJV)

44. The sanctification of man's soul begins as the purifying process of God's nature starts to refine the believer's walk. The immoral state of the carnal nature is imprisoned, and God's pureness becomes the moral compass that directs *the steps of* the *good man*. The result of walking in Christ's steps and being led by the Holy Spirit compels the believer to ... *behave wisely in a perfect way ... walk within my house with a perfect heart....* (Psalm 101:2 NKJV)

45. This moral cleansing requires that saints ... *keep (yourself) pure....* (1 Timothy 5:22) This moral purity occurs when the believer is ... *casting down arguments and every high thing that exalts itself against the knowledge of God, bringing every thought into captivity to the obedience of Christ....* (2 Corinthians 10:5 NKJV)

46. This purifying process God's nature brings about in the believer's life causes immoral thoughts and actions to cease. To the pure *all things are pure, but to those who are defiled and unbelieving nothing is pure; but even their mind and conscience are defiled....* (Titus 1:15 NKJV)

47. Because the soul is made pure, the thoughts and deeds should align with God's flawless pureness, causing it to be blameless. Now God's command becomes the pivotal compass point ... *I am Almighty God, walk before Me and be blameless....* (Genesis 17:1 NKJV)

48. The Word promises ... *Behold, God will not cast away the blameless....* (Job 8:20 NKJV)

49. Flowing through the believer's spirit, God's purifying nature eradicates guilt. God's forgiveness is without partiality to the one who repents and confesses their sin. There is no stain of guilt that lingers, neither any condemnation laid at the repentant heart's door ... *If we confess our sins, He is faithful and just to forgive us our sins and to cleanse us from all unrighteousness....* (1 John 1:9 NKJV) This promise is supported by the statement ... *There is therefore now no condemnation to those who are in Christ Jesus....* (Romans 8:1 NKJV)

50. The pure attribute of God's nature should be so interwoven in the believer's soul and spirit that no corrupt thought or deed is produced. It remains in an incorruptible state so long as the believer declares ... *I will set nothing wicked before my eyes; I hate the work of those who fall away; it shall not cling to me. A perverse heart shall depart from me; I will not know wickedness....* (Psalm 101:3–4 NKJV)

51. The result of the moral state, the blameless conduct, the guilt-free conscience, and the incorruptible soul and spirit confirms the believer is capable of walking undefiled before God. Ultimately, man is to be holy. Oswald Chambers, in his daily reading book, *My Utmost for His Highest*, states, "We must remind ourselves of the purpose of life. We are not destined to happiness, nor to

health, but to holiness. At all costs, a person must have a right relationship with God. God has only one intended destiny for mankind—holiness. His only goal is to produce saints."

52. It is Jesus Christ who, through the shedding of His blood, enabled repentant souls to become a pure undefiled believer ... *who gave Himself for us that He might redeem us from every lawless deed and purify for Himself His own special people, zealous for good works....* (Titus 2:14 NKJV)

53. When the heart is undefiled and pure in all its motives, then this scripture becomes a reality in the believer's life ... *Blessed are the pure in heart* (undefiled), *for they shall see God....* (Matthew 5:8)

PART 3

The Doctrine of Jesus Christ

11. DOCTRINE - The Divine Person, the Son.

    Jesus is God manifest in the flesh. Jesus is the only begotten Son of God. His deity is declared and found in the Bible when Apostle John declares in the opening salvo of his majestic account of Jesus, the Divine Person: *In the beginning was the Word and the Word was with God, and the Word was God.*

12. DOCTRINE - The Divine Person, the LORD Jesus Christ.

    Believers know and seek a relationship with Jesus who is their Lord and Savior. He is the anointed Lord who is the head of the church.

    The Word made Flesh

    The miraculous conception and perfect salvation plan is invested in Jesus Christ. There will never be any explanation as to how this took place, and yet it stands as the pillar of the Christian faith that Jesus was made flesh.

    The Divine Person: Jesus Christ's two natures

    a. The Divine Nature

    b. The Human Nature

13. DOCTRINE – The Lord Jesus Christ's Eternal Work

There is no greater or more outstanding proclamation than the fact that Jesus was raised from the dead by the glory of the Father. It is the most significant and ultimate expression of God's power and love that is presented to mankind who accepts by faith the conclusive fact that Jesus was raised from the dead.

This chapter expounds the place to which Jesus ascended, His exaltation to the highest seat of honor, and His current position of Apostle and High Priest. His prophetical, priestly, and kingly offices are also discussed to help understand the significance of the eternal spiritual office He occupies and His spiritual office of advocate and His intercessory role.

CHAPTER 11

THE DOCTRINE OF JESUS CHRIST

The Divine Person, the Son

1. *You are the Christ, the Son of the living God....* (Matthew 16:16 NKJV) Without hesitation and disbelief, Spirit-filled believers echo this statement about Jesus. The entire relevance of the gospel message is based on this declaration by faith that Jesus is the only begotten Son of the living God.

2. *Concerning his Son Jesus Christ our Lord* ... (Romans 1:3), there can be no salvation unless the Lord Jesus Christ is received, accepted, and believed to be the Person He is declared to be in the Holy Writ.

3. Jesus is neither a myth nor a figment of imagination; He is a fact, a real person and a figure who has influenced every nation on earth. There has never been, and never will be, anyone who has accomplished what Jesus has. Everything Jesus did is saturated with the very essence of His nature and deity, namely love. He has, and still does, change innumerable lives, turns hatred into love, drenches His presence into believers' hearts, and turns man's despair into hope.

4. History records the beginning of change as it hangs on the hinges of a stable door in Bethlehem. The greatest act of love is expressed on a cruel cross outside the walls of Jerusalem, the city of peace. It was here that the miraculous resurrection event occurred, death was conquered, and eternal life freely offered to "whosoever" accepts Him by faith.

5. John Richter says it the best, "His pierced hands lifted empires off their hinges, turned the stream of centuries out of its channel, and He still governs today.

6. "Countless figures who attempted to shape history through their dictatorial force and unnecessary slaughtering of human flesh on the battlefield have never amounted to anything as huge as Jesus Christ achieved through His love. One such ruler, Napoleon, as carnal as he was, declared, 'I founded a great empire, but upon what did I depend? Upon force. Jesus founded His empire upon love, and to this very day millions will die for Him. Jesus Christ was more than man.'"

7. Now comes this statement that surpasses every attempt by man's puny mind to express the magnitude of Jesus' existence. The Holy Writ proclaims that He is ... *declared to be the Son of God with power according to the Spirit of holiness, by the resurrection from the dead....* (Romans 1:4 NKJV)

8. It is fitting that consideration of this vast subject begins with its focus on the glorious Person of the Lord Jesus Christ. Throughout the entire Word of God, there is a golden thread that pertains to Jesus Christ. The Old Testament declares Him to be the exalted divine Person whose ... *name shall be called Wonderful, Counselor, The mighty God, The everlasting Father, The Prince of Peace....* (Isaiah 9:6)

9. Flowing through the Word, countless prophetical references are made about Him. One such exaltation is declared ... *Behold the virgin shall conceive and bear a Son, and shall call His name Immanuel* (God with us).... (Isaiah 7:14 NKJV) The

highest accolade that could be given to Him came from His own Father ... *This is my beloved Son, in whom I am well pleased....* (Matthew 3:17)

10. The affirmation of Jesus Christ's deity does not culminate there. Apostle John boldly unsheathes the *two-edged sword* (Hebrews 4:12) as he announces in the opening salvo of his Holy Spirit-inspired gospel record whom Jesus is ... *In the beginning was the Word ... and the Word was God ... and the Word became flesh and dwelt among us....* (John 1:1,14 NKJV)

11. Apostle Paul takes it further by stating that Jesus is equal with God (Philippians 2:6), and in Jesus ... *dwells all the fullness of the Godhead bodily....* (Colossians 2:9 NKJV)

12. These words expressed by the two apostles affirm the unquestionable deity of the Lord Jesus Christ. To seal Christ's deity, the deepest proof of this is declared by Jesus Himself ... *I and my Father are one....* (John 10:30) *Before Abraham was, I am* (John 8:58).

13. Myer Pearlman, in his book *Knowing the Doctrines of the Bible,* states, "Jesus was conscious of two things: a special relationship to God whom He describes as His Father; second, a special mission on earth—His 'Father's business.'

14. "He put Himself side by side with the Divine activity ... *My Father worketh hitherto, and I work....* (John 5:17) *I came forth from the Father....* (John 16:28) *My Father hath sent me....* (John 20:21) He claimed a Divine knowledge and fellowship. (Matthew 11:27; John 17:25) He claimed to unveil the Father's being in Himself. (John 14:9–11) He assumed Divine prerogatives: omnipresence (Matthew 18:20); power to forgive sins (Mark 2:5–10); power to raise the dead, (John 6:39, 40, 54; 11:25; 10:17, 18); He proclaimed Himself Judge and Arbiter of man's destiny, (John 5:22; Matthew 25:31–46).

15. "Christ is that Word, because through Him God has revealed His activity, will, and purpose, and because by Him God contacts the world."

16. The writer in the letter to the Hebrews starts with the announcement *... Has in these last days spoken to us by His Son, whom He has appointed heir of all things, through whom also He made the worlds; who being the brightness of His glory and the express image of His person, and upholding all things by the word of His power, when He had by Himself purged our sins, sat down at the right hand of the Majesty on high....* (Hebrews 1:2–3 NKJV)

17. Myer Pearlman says, "Christ is the Word of God because He not only brings God's message—He is God's message."

18. Spirit-filled believers have no hesitation in testifying about the Person of Jesus Christ because by faith they confess that Jesus Christ is *the Word made flesh*. Jesus took upon Himself human nature and was born of a virgin so that He could reveal the eternal God through a human personality.

19. The Person the Lord Jesus Christ can only be worshipped as God, because He is from God and is the one true God. He is the Person born of a woman, yet conceived by the Holy Spirit and carried the eternal, holy, and incorruptible blood from His Father, the Almighty Ancient of Days.

20. Dr. James Orr seals this aspect of the Person of Jesus Christ when he says, "Doctrinally it must be repeated that the belief in the virgin birth of Christ is of the highest value for the right apprehension of Christ's unique and sinless personality. Here is One, as Paul brings out in Romans 5:12, who, free from sin Himself, and not involved in the Adamic liabilities of the race, reverses the curse of sin and death brought in by the first Adam, and establishes the reign of righteousness and life. Had Christ been naturally born, not one of these things could be affirmed of Him. As one of Adam's race, not an entrant from higher sphere, He would have shared in Adam's corruption and doom, and would Himself have required to be redeemed.

21. "Through God's infinite mercy, He came from above, inherited no guilt, needed no regeneration or sanctification, but became

Himself the Redeemer, Regenerator, Sanctifier for all who receive Him."

22. Jesus was not making a flattering statement of Himself when He prayed to the Father ... *And now, O Father, glorify Me together with Yourself, with the glory which I had with You before the world was....* (John 17:5 NKJV) His eternal existence was before the world began, yet He ... *being in the form of God, did not consider it robbery to be equal with God, but made Himself of no reputation, taking the form of a bondservant, and coming in the likeness of man....* (Philippians 2:6–7 NKJV)

23. His glorious Person is ... *God manifest in the flesh* ... (1 Timothy 3:16), and Jesus is the only One who can share in the Father's glory (John 17:1, 5). God will never give His glory to anyone. (Isaiah 42:8) Thus Jesus is God, and He manifests the glory of God in the flesh on earth.

24. The record in John 5:16–30 is the fitting exaltation by Jesus of Himself, when He astounds His hearers with the greatest explanation of His coequality with His Father. Herein He asserts His deity that He is shown all things the Father does, that He should be honored, and is given the authority to execute judgment.

25. To bring the belief that Jesus is the living Son of God into the twentieth century, the glorious Person of Jesus Christ is never more aptly expounded than when Dr. James Allan Francis wrote in 1926, "Nineteen centuries have come and gone and today Jesus is the central figure of the human race and the leader of mankind's progress.... All the kings that have ever reigned put together have not affected the life of mankind on earth as powerfully as has that one solitary life."

26. The glorious Person of Jesus Christ is heralded throughout the world by Spirit-filled saints who worship and praise Him as Savior, High Priest, and the Son of the living God.

The Divine Person, the LORD Jesus Christ

27. *God has made this Jesus, whom you crucified, both Lord and Christ....* (Acts 2:36 NKJV) Spirit-filled believers have no doubt, neither shame in declaring alongside the first Holy Spirit-anointed message ever preached from a church pulpit that Jesus Christ is Lord.

28. Spirit-filled believers have their faith rooted and grounded in this truth ... *looking unto Jesus, the author and finisher of our faith....* (Hebrews 12:2 NKJV) Their spirit-man seeks an intimate personal relationship with Jesus Christ. He is always exalted as Lord. French Arrington in his book, *Christian Doctrine,* states that the Lord Jesus "Christ is the object of faith, the subject of preaching and teaching, and the hope of everlasting life."

29. From the earliest time, Christian saints reverenced Jesus as Lord of their lives and *the Christ* who was anointed by God to occupy the highest seat of authority at the Father's right hand. The most exquisite statement about Jesus came from the one who doubted Him. Upon recognizing Jesus after His resurrection, Thomas states ... *My Lord and my God....* (John 20:28) In the vernacular, Thomas spoke only two words: *Adonai* (My Lord) and *Elohim* (My God).

30. Thomas' words are echoed by Spirit-filled believers throughout the world who unashamedly proclaim with the same emphasis that Jesus is their Lord personally. Jesus is their *Adonai*—"My Lord." This is personal and reverent acknowledgment that the risen Savior, the Lord Jesus Christ, is not a distant image or instrument carved from an earthly substance by human hands but the intimate and personal Savior sent from the eternal God to impart His peace to everyone who believes. (John 16:33) Christ's deity is never more acknowledged and expressed than when believers declare Him to be their *Adonai* ("my Lord") and their *Elohim* ("my God").

31. *Reach your finger here, and look at My hands; and reach your hand here, and put it into My side. Do not be unbelieving, but believing....* (John 20:27 NKJV) How gracious our Lord is with Thomas. He gives Thomas a greater opportunity than the other disciples to prove that the Lord is the risen Christ. To the other disciples, Jesus only showed His hands and His side (verse 20). However, Thomas is invited to reach his hand and *put it into My side.*

32. Thomas does nothing physical towards the Lord. In his spirit, he realizes that Jesus, the all-knowing omniscient Lord, knows even what is said though He is not there physically. Thomas realizes that Jesus understands his doubt and "hears" his statement in the Spirit. Jesus approaches Thomas with love and compassion and offers him more than the rest of the disciples were offered ... *put it into My side....*

33. Thomas needed no physical proof as he supposed would be necessary. The glorious presence of the risen Lord Jesus Christ (the same witness Thomas had about Jesus before the crucifixion whom Jesus was,) is revealed to Thomas the moment he looked upon the Lord ... *Thomas answered and said to Him Adonai....* A "look" was all he needed. As with the writer's statement to believers today ... *looking unto Jesus* ... (Hebrews 12:2), the focus is on the Lord, *the author and finisher* of one's faith.

34. Absolute capitulation of every self-indulgence, self-satisfaction, and personal desire is the condition Spirit-filled believers find themselves in when they confess Jesus as Lord.

35. They declare Jesus as the vicarious Lord who is their Savior, Hope, and Source of perfect peace.

36. W.A.C. Rowe says, "Christ's Lordship is essentially based upon His own nature. He is divine, nay, we will use the stronger word, about which there can be no shade of misunderstanding, He is deity.

37. "Jesus Christ is God (1 John 5:20). The outstanding distinction of the Christian faith is that Jesus Christ is God and that *God was*

in Christ, reconciling the world unto Himself.... (2 Corinthians 5:19)

38. "Lordship of Christ is also founded upon His mighty and overwhelming victories. He came into the world to defeat Satan and, through death, to destroy the destroyer's power. Christ was expressly manifested to destroy the works of the devil and to deliver the sin-bound sons of men (Colossians 2:15).

39. "Amid the splendor of the clustered jewels of glorious angels and ministering spirits and redeemed men God has set Christ, the Eternal and Lustrous One, in the highest, central place, around Whom all others take their subordinate setting. By nature, by conquest, by appointment, our Savior is Lord of all....

40. "Over every kind of life, every crook and cranny of all God's vast, eternal universe the throne of the Lord Jesus Christ holds its massive dominion. The great Millennium's dawn will soon break when the Coming Lord will reign triumphantly as King over all the nations of the world (John 20:28)."

41. The title Lord vested upon Jesus Christ is the most befitting one because He is Lord of all, and He has, is, and will always be the divine sovereign God of all flesh and creation ... *All authority has been given to Me in heaven and on earth....* (Matthew 28:18 NKJV) There is no one else who can take up the judge's seat at the two forthcoming judgments. The Lord, holy and divine, has the credentials to be the sovereign, just, and fair judge of man. He is God and came in the form of man, remained sinless, and victoriously conquered death thus elevating Him to the highest office of the *Lord Jesus Christ* (Philippians 2:11, Hebrews 2:9).

The Word Made Flesh

42. It is fitting that the Holy Bible contains detailed accounts of *God manifested in the flesh.* Likewise, it is satisfying that the world

has not forgotten the celebration of Jesus' coming in Bethlehem's manger. While the "Christmas story" told to children reverently proclaims the birth of the Savior, Spirit-filled believers hunger for the revelation that surrounds this historic event.

43. This event should start with the visitation by the angel Gabriel to Mary. The place was neither a kingly palace, nor was the handmaid of the Lord a princess. It was a humble home in which a family who upheld spiritual values lived. There was nothing peculiar about the city that made it a special landmark for the world trader. The city was small and populated with humble folk who tilled the soil, did handcrafted work, and were labeled as inferior by the so-called educated upper class in the rest of Israel. This is evidenced by the question ... *Can anything good come out Nazareth?* (John 1:46 NKJV)

44. Into this precious place Gabriel, the messenger of the Lord God, arrived and had a discourse with the Virgin Mary.

45. This was by far the most important message Gabriel ever delivered. God chose the time and the place, and He chose His worthy angel to bring the news to Mary that she was *highly favored* by God (Luke 1:28). No ordinary messenger and no ordinary woman.

46. The angel does not hesitate in announcing that the eternal God is about to perform a miracle that has never happened before. And everything about this miracle is God-ordained and spiritual. Gabriel calms her troubled spirit ... *Fear not,* and then announces that she will *conceive in her womb* the Holy Son of God.

47. Mary's response is truthful and with good reason: she has never been with a man. This gives Gabriel the opportunity to explain the Holy Spirit's intrusion in Mary's life. This was not an immaculate conception; it was a miraculous conception. This was Almighty God performing a miracle within His handmaiden by Himself. Gabriel is only the messenger; Mary is the recipient of the miracle.

48. The event purposed by God from the foundation of the world was announced. *The Lamb of God slain from the foundation of the*

world was to be conceived in human flesh. The need to purge mankind of the sin perpetrated by Adam had to be avenged. Only God could do this, and He had to do it as a human. His highest created being, mankind, had destroyed the perfect union between God and man, and only God could restore it.

49. *That holy thing* ... (Luke 1:35) needed the Godhead's action to bring it to life, and the Holy Spirit impregnated Mary's womb with the *seed*. The seed was none other than the *word*. Mary proclaims ... *Be it unto me according to your word*.... (Luke 1:38)

50. Mary realized that Gabriel was sent by God, and that the words he spoke were from the throne of Almighty God. Herein is the miracle: only God can create something from nothing. God's spoken word exploded the universe into existence. He said ... *Let there be* ... and life sprang forth on the frozen globe, Earth. This same awesome God overshadows Mary, and she miraculously becomes pregnant. There is no physical explanation anyone at any time can render as to how God did it.

51. Gabriel brought the message that was weighed and measured in the scales of God's eternal purposes. The words he uttered that day were Spirit-breathed and Holy Spirit anointed, inspired, and instructed. The sinless seed, the Word, was revealed to Mary, and she was told that her conception would be God-ordained and God-performed (Luke 1:35).

52. Mary received the *word* as she accepted her mission by faith ... *according to your word*.... The Word accepted, and the Word appropriated in Mary's womb infused by the Holy Spirit united the Son of God with human nature ... *the Word was God* ... *the Word became flesh*.... (John 1:1, 14)

53. This is the *seed* spoken of by God to the serpent ... *And I will put enmity between thee and the woman, and between thy seed and her seed; it* (the seed; the Word; the Son of God) *shall bruise thy head, and thou shalt bruise his heel*.... (Genesis 3:15)

54. Martin J Scott gives the following rendition of the Incarnation:

116

"The incarnation means that God (that is, the Son of God) became man. This does not mean that God was turned into man, nor does it mean that God ceased to be God and began to be a man; but that, remaining God, He assumed or took on a new nature, namely, human.... The Incarnation, therefore, means that the Son of God, true God from all eternity, in the course of time became true man also, in one Person, Jesus Christ, consisting of two natures, the human and the Divine...."

55. Apostle Peter gives an exquisite rendering of the holy seed that was conceived in Mary's womb which became flesh: *You were not redeemed with corruptible things ... but with the precious blood of Christ, as of a lamb without blemish and without spot. He indeed was foreordained before the foundation of the world, but was manifest in these last times for you ... having been born again, not of corruptible seed but incorruptible, through the word of God which lives and abides forever....* (1 Peter 1:18–23 NKJV)

56. This seed, which is the Word, is from the eternal God, and it is incorruptible, pure, holy, divine, and became sinless blood. The *lamb slain* was not contaminated with the sin-stained blood of mankind. The Holy Child's veins were infused with the blood that proceeded from the incorruptible Word (seed) that impregnated Mary's womb.

57. Apostle Paul says it best ... *And without controversy great is the mystery of godliness, God was manifested in the flesh....* (1 Timothy 3:16 NKJV)

58. He is absolutely ... *the Christ, the Son of the living God....* (Matthew 16:16)

CHAPTER 12

THE DIVINE PERSON:
JESUS CHRIST'S TWO NATURES

1. The church's rapid growth in the first century reached across cultural, racial, and ethnic differences. The holy message: *Jesus Christ and Him crucified* catapulted thousands of human lives from all walks of life ... *in all Judea, and in Samaria, and unto the uttermost part of the earth* ... (Acts 1:8), converting them to *the faith* that embodied the forgiveness of sin, hope in the promise of eternal life, peace, and faith that moved mountains.

2. It was first revealed and preached to humble folk who, in their poverty, believed that God was the supplier of their every need. However, as church membership grew, countless well-educated and philosophical men also accepted Jesus Christ as Lord of their lives.

3. While there were many educated saints who believed in their heart that Jesus is the Son of God, some were still struggling to relinquish their head-knowledge and exchange it for Holy Spirit-led faith. Added to this, those who opposed Christianity also presented arguments to support their endeavors to disprove the existence of Jesus Christ as the Son of God. Thus followed

questions that were hitherto never asked, let alone considered. One of the very first questions asked in the first century was, "Did Jesus Christ have two natures?" Put another way by the agnostics, "Prove to us that Jesus Christ had two natures."

4. Throughout the centuries that have followed, this question constantly reared its head. There have been many astute theologians who have given great explanations on this subject. However, the Spirit-filled believer relates all these wise men's explanations to their unwavering faith in Jesus Christ as the only begotten Son of God.

The Divine Nature

5. The holy, divine Son of God was born of a virgin, lived a virgin life (sinless life), and died for the sin of the world. He is deity Personified in the flesh, and the divine nature that exists in the Godhead permeated every area of His human frame.

6. W.A.C. Rowe states, "God sent His own Son in the 'Likeness of sinful flesh, and for sin, condemned sin in the flesh.' As a newborn babe, He was ... *that holy thing ... the Son of God*. He commenced His human life what He always was; what He always maintained in His experience; and what He is, and always will be in glory—absolutely holy.

7. "The Savior of the world was crystal-pure in thought, word, and action as flowing from a perfect nature whiter than light. There was no spot or blemish in Him (1 Peter 1:19).

8. "Rather was it the fierce and glowing whiteness of the holy fire of deity (Hebrews 12:29). Christ far outstripped the nature and experience of perfect innocence."

9. Christ's divine nature was the criterion by which He did His Father's will.

10. W.A.C. Rowe continues, "The whole nature and attitude of the

Master was one of sublime perfection: both in the spiritual and practical. Though He moved in this dark world and amongst the sinful multitude doing good (Acts 10:38), He continued living in the heights of pure and intimate fellowship with His holy Father (Matthew 14:23). He ... *was in all points tempted like as we are, yet without sin....* Being free from sin and utterly holy, Christ manifested the scintillating radiance of the divine and the human." (Matthew 17:2, 2 Corinthians 4:6)

11. It is impossible for man to save himself from the penalty caused by his sin-stained blood; neither will a sin-stained blood of another man be good enough to save the whole human race (Romans 3:23). To satisfy the requirements of God's divine ordinance, God needed a sinless person born of human flesh who carried no sin impediment. God's only Son had the qualifications to fulfill the task.

12. Man needed a Savior, and Jesus Christ is the *Savior of the world....*

13. To meet the exact demands of the eternal Holy God's redemption plan, and to execute the shedding of pure, unstained blood, the Savior had to embody the essentials of deity and humanity that were engendered with divine holiness. Jesus Christ's divine nature measured up to every ingredient needed for a perfect salvation.

14. The essential examination of the two natures of Jesus Christ must focus on the eternal purpose of His coming in the form of man. God understood the dilemma of the human race. He was acutely aware of their need to be exonerated from their penalty of sin, and God required sinless blood to achieve perfect salvation.

15. How magnificent is the Holy Writ's explanation of this glorious truth. It gushes forth like a torrential river cascading through the canyons of the human soul and spirit ... *Inasmuch then as the children have partaken of flesh and blood, He Himself likewise shared in the same, that through death He might destroy him who had the power of death, that is, the devil, and release those who through fear of death were all their lifetime subject to bondage.... Therefore, in all things He had to be made like His brethren,*

that He might be a merciful and faithful High Priest in things pertaining to God, to make propitiation for the sins of the people. For in that He Himself has suffered, being tempted, He is able to aid those who are tempted. (Hebrews 2:14–18 NKJV)

16. God seals His purpose for sending His only begotten Son as He brings down the gavel with a thundering declaration that ricochets throughout the world ... *For this purpose the Son of God was manifested, that He might destroy the works of the devil....* (1 John 3:8 NKJV)

17. Sheer divinity, sheer deity, and sheer holiness embodied the Son of God as He *became flesh.*

The Human Nature

18. Without blurring the fact that the holy divine nature of God entered a human life, consideration must now be given to the human nature within everyone born of woman.

19. Returning to W.A.C. Rowe, he states, "As Christ is truly God, so He is truly man. There is a broad, deep stream of sacred instruction concerning the true humanity of our Lord. Our Savior was no mere phantom in human form, with only a show of solidarity before men—He was *bone of our bone and flesh of our flesh.* Yes, Christ took real human nature (Hebrews 2:17) and lived a real human life." (Acts 10:38)

20. "Elements, supernatural and natural, supreme and simple, stand side by side in amazing combination. The star on behalf of the mighty universe royally salutes the wondrous newborn Child.

21. *"The Son of Man* was one of His most outstanding appellations; Christ used it of Himself in a supreme and unique sense—the name carrying an utterly comprehensive and inclusive meaning. He was never 'a' Son of man, but always 'the' Son of man. Truly, *Jesus Christ is come in the flesh....* (1 John 4:2)" He is "the" Son

of Man because His Father is God and He is like no other human born of a woman.

22. As to the fact that Jesus Christ is very God, so is He very man. This does not mean that there are two Persons joined as one. The Son of God is one Person that has two natures, and both these natures in Him are complete and unscathed. They are joined in the glorious Person, the Lord Jesus Christ. Apostle Cyril D. Wilson, an apostle set in the body of Christ, states, "Jesus Christ, begotten of the Father, born of a virgin, human in nature, but absolutely sinless. Christ in Humanity was … a Child born. Christ in His Divinity was … a Son given."

23. Henry Thiessen, in his book, *Introductory Lectures in Systematic Theology,* states, "The Deity of Christ, Christ was conscious of being God incarnate and represented Himself as being such … the constant scriptural representations of the infinite value of Christ's atonement and of the union of the human race with God which has been secured in Him, are intelligible only when Christ is regarded, not as a man of God, but as the God-man…."

24. Thiessen continues, "Christ had an infinite intelligence and will and a finite intelligence and will; He had a divine consciousness and a human consciousness. His divine intelligence was infinite; His human intelligence increased. His divine will was omnipotent; His human will (was limited)." (Mark 13:32)

25. The Bible is filled with the examples of the Lord's human nature. He expressed all the human characteristics of weariness, hunger, and thirstiness. He also labored like all men do and was also tempted in every way all human beings are, yet without succumbing to any sin.

26. The question that needs to be asked is, "What drove the Lord Jesus to abstain from all appearances of sin, and never once entertain the presence of Satan?" Unequivocally, it was His obedience to His heavenly Father's will. He never lost the vision, He never took His eye off the purpose of His coming in the flesh, and He never

veered away from any commission His Father demanded of Him. *Nevertheless, not my will, but thine, be done....* (Luke 22:42)

27. His constant obedience to the Father's will propelled Him to the point of abandonment of everything He desired for Himself. He cast aside every thought and purpose that meandered through His mind that was contrary to His Father's purpose, cut off every personal ambition by surrendering every area of His life to His Father ... *I can of Myself do nothing. As I hear, I judge; and My judgment is righteous, because I do not seek My own will but the will of the Father who sent Me....* (John 5:30 NKJV)

28. It is again emphasized by Jesus when He faces the crowd ... *For I have come down from heaven, not to do My own will, but the will of Him who sent me....* (John 6:38 NKJV)

29. Furthermore, when looking at the answer to this question, the viewpoint should never be from man's perspective, but rather from God's. This compels one's attention to return to the first created human, Adam. Consideration must be given to Adam's nature that was breathed into him by the Spirit; it was sin-free and perfect in its innocence.

30. Adam knew no sin, and he never sinned while he was obedient to God. However, unrighteousness entered Adam's nature when he sinned by disobeying God's command when he ate the fruit from the tree of knowledge of good and evil. Adam's sin-stained nature is passed on to every human thereafter. The same sin-stained "seed" (blood) flows through every human being.

31. Focusing on this subject from God's perspective, it is now clear that Jesus had the same sin-free blood Adam had before Adam sinned because Christ's blood was from the Father and infused by the Holy Spirit. It had the same source Adam's blood had before he sinned. It was/is sin-free. Throughout His earthly ministry, Jesus' blood remained sin-free because Jesus never succumbed to any temptation nor did He disobey His Father's will which Adam did.

32. When comparing the two Adams ... *And so it is written, the first man Adam became a living being. The last Adam became a life-giving spirit. However, the spiritual is not first, but the natural, and afterward the spiritual. The first man was of the earth, made of dust; the second Man is the Lord from heaven.... And as we have borne the image of the man of dust, we shall also bear the image of the heavenly Man....* (1 Corinthians 15:45–49 NKJV)

33. Millard Erickson says, "Rather, His was a personality that in addition to the characteristics of divine nature (He) had all the qualities or attributes of a perfect, sinless human nature as well."

34. Herbert Lockyer says, "What He divested Himself of was the constant, outward, and visible manifestation of His Godhead. Christ did not surrender deity—He gained humanity.

35. "In His Incarnation He became the possessor of a true humanity in union with His eternal deity. As God, He did not enter a human body or join Himself to man. He became Man, that is, He belonged to the stock of humanity when as the Word, He *became flesh.*" (John 1:14)

36. To prevent confusion, it must be clearly understood that Christ's divine nature did not engulf His human nature thus canceling out its existence. They were not fused together to become a different nature: they remained in their distinctive capacities.

37. Millard Erickson continues, "As the image of God, the human is already the creature most like God. The fact that a human did not ascend to divinity, nor did God elevate a human to divinity, but, rather, God condescended to take on humanity, facilitates our ability to conceive the incarnation...."

38. The Lord Jesus Christ was tempted in every way all humans are, yet He never fell into Satan's deceitful trap. He *set His face like a flint* towards His purpose of coming in the flesh.

39. He brought His human nature into subjection to His divine nature and walked in obedience to His Father's will. Even while suffering on the cross, He never lost the purpose of His earthly

visitation. He condemned no one for what they did to Him; rather, He cries to the Father to forgive them (Luke 23:34). As He suffers the worst agony, He speaks words of life to the repentant thief ... *Today you will be with Me in Paradise....* (Luke 23:43 NKJV)

40. He was ... *faithful to Him who appointed Him* ... (Hebrews 3:2 NKJV) and knowing the consequences of disobedience, He never once gave in to it, but instead the Lord Jesus faithfully obeyed His Father (Philippians 2:8).

CHAPTER 13

THE LORD JESUS CHRIST'S
ETERNAL WORK

1. It is appropriate to move into the exact details of this magnificent subject and consider the eternal work Jesus Christ did, is doing, and will still do. It is not only appropriate but is vital to consider Christ's works in this way because the Bible declares that the *unsearchable riches of Christ* have been revealed ... *to make all see what is the fellowship of the mystery, which from the beginning of the ages has been hidden in God who created all things through Jesus Christ; to the intent that now the manifold wisdom of God might be made known by the church to the principalities and powers in the heavenly places, according to the eternal purpose which He accomplished in Christ Jesus our Lord.* (Eph 3:8–11 NKJV)

2. This subject is divided into four parts: Christ's work before He became Son of Man, His work while on earth, His present work since He ascended into heaven, and finally, His future work.

3. To keep the subject in its best format, the work of Christ before He became the Son of Man is discussed in detail under the Doctrine of Creation, and His future work is covered under the chapters of

the end times. The remaining two categories will be covered in this section.

Jesus' Words and Work while on Earth

4. The four gospels are the evidence of Christ's work while He walked this earth. They contain in many cases, not only the works, but also the reason for the works. Christ's many works manifested signs, wonders, and miracles, all of which gave the people the evidence that He was sent from God ... *Rabbi, we know that You are a teacher come from God; for no one can do these signs that You do unless God is with Him....* (John 3:2 NKJV)

5. One of the greatest testimonies that Jesus was sent from God is found when Jesus tells the paralytic that his sins are forgiven him, and the onlookers accuse Jesus of blasphemy. (Matthew 9:1–8)

6. Jesus constantly manifested the works of the Father. The reason for doing this was to give the people the witness and testimony of God's fulfillment of His promise to send them the Messiah and to demonstrate His love.

7. The most profound witness Jesus brought of the presence of the eternal God was the fact that He shone in this dark world as the *light of the world* (John 1:4). Jesus not only spoke the words of love, He demonstrated love. Likewise, He not only showed pity on the lost, He saved the lost through His sacrificial suffering on Calvary's Hill. (Romans 5:8)

8. In all His teaching, He spoke *the words of eternal life* (John 6:68). Never before had the hearers heard such truth uttered from anyone. It sliced through their darkened soul, and His words ploughed deep furrows into their heart, ultimately culminating in a life-changing experience.

9. His words, at times, offended hearers (Matthew 13:57), even though they were the truth. Without doubt, Spirit-filled believers

are assured that every word uttered by Jesus Christ was foreordained by the Father. He never spoke with evil intent, nor did He speak blaspheming the Godhead. There were many who thought He did, yet they were proved wrong every time.

10. Christ's words were so powerful that it had the divine ability to turn men from their daily tasks after they heard ... *Come follow Me* .... (Matthew 4:18–22) They cast aside their occupation and followed Jesus. His words were so powerful that ... *immediately they left the boat and their father, and followed Him* .... (Matthew 4:22 NKJV) Herein is the anointing never more expressed than what was declared in Nazareth ... *The Spirit of the LORD is upon Me, because He has anointed Me to preach* (speak, tell) *the gospel to the poor* .... (Luke 4:18 NKJV)

11. The indwelling power in every word Jesus spoke is beautifully expressed by the two men traveling on the road to Emmaus ... *Did not our heart burn within us while He talked with us on the road, and while He opened the Scriptures to us?* (Luke 24:32 NKJV)

12. The most prolific evidence that Christ's words were life-giving was witnessed when He spoke to Lazarus' dead body ... *Lazarus, come forth!* ... (John 11:43 NKJV)

13. His words were not only life-changing but eternal. They were spoken almost two thousand years ago, and they are still changing lives to this day. Truly, Christ's words have eternal value and influence on people's lives. His own testimony of the origin of His words still resounds in the Spirit-filled believer's spirit ... *Do you not believe that I am in the Father, and the Father in Me? The words that I speak to you I do not speak on My own authority; but the Father who dwells in Me does the works* .... (John 14:10 NKJV)

14. His message not only brought life and hope to the hearer, it contained reconciling utterances that paved the way for the purpose of His coming to be fulfilled, namely saving mankind from their sin.

15. Millard J. Erickson says, "It is important to retain the truths that Jesus reveals God to humanity, reconciles God and humanity to one another, and rules and will rule over the whole of the creation, including humanity." Christ is the Revealer of God, the Ruler both now and to come, and the ever-present Reconciler.

16. Millard Erickson continues, "His preexistence with the Father was a major factor in His ability to reveal the Father, for He had been with Him ... *No one has seen God at any one time. The only begotten Son, who is in the bosom of the Father, He has declared Him....* (John 1:18 NKJV) He told Nicodemus ... *No one has ascended to heaven but He who came down from heaven, that is, the Son of Man who is in heaven....* (John 3:13 NKJV)"

17. Yet, Jesus did not only speak, He also did the works of His Father. His works (while words were part of the work) were always holy and pure. They were accompanied by signs, wonders, and miracles.

18. *Men of Israel, hear these words: Jesus of Nazareth, a Man attested by God to you by miracles, wonders, and signs which God did through Him in your midst, as you yourselves also know....* (Acts 2:22 NKJV)

19. Jesus Christ's presence was like the bright morning summer sun bursting onto earth's surface after a period of darkness. He spoke life-giving encouragement and touched lives with His pure works. Everywhere He went He left evidence that he had been there. No place was too good, too bad, too rich, or too poor for Him to enter ... *God anointed Jesus of Nazareth with the Holy Spirit and with power, who went about doing good and healing all who were oppressed by the devil, for God was with Him....* (Acts 10:38 NKJV)

20. So drastic was the contrast between the works of darkness and Christ's works of life and light that the people were stirred by His actions. The application of the Law had imprisoned their viewpoint, shrouded their common sense, and darkened their

days. They were shackled by the dos and don'ts inflicted on them by the rigid application of the Law drummed into them from the ruling Sanhedrin which caused them to follow in fear.

21. Added to this, the dictatorial Roman rulership enhanced their daily fear as they tried to conform to the Law and simultaneously keep in step with Rome's demands.

22. What they needed was Someone who could show them the way through all this, and God sent His only begotten Son into the world to liberate them. However, He did not obliterate the enemy that enforced its dominance over the people, neither did He bring the peace the people thought the Messiah would. Instead, Jesus Christ intensified many of the Torah's teachings. When He addressed the crowd on the Sermon on the Mount, He said … *You have heard that it was said, you shall love your neighbor and hate your enemy. But I say to you, love your enemies, bless those who curse you, do good to those who hate you, and pray for those who spitefully use you and persecute you….* (Matthew 5:43–44 NKJV)

23. Christ's brief ministry on earth was punctuated by miraculous events that have echoed through the ages. His ability to apprehend any sickness, disease, demonic attack, and even the grave, reinforced His deity and inherent power. His soft gentle touch on blind eyes (Matthew 9:29), His pure hands that were placed on the leper (Matthew 8:3), and His grasp of the dead girl's hand (Matthew 9:23–25) were all filled with His healing touch.

24. Flowing from the Son of God, the anointing of the Holy Spirit streamed forth like a shining light that flooded the body of the sick and the lame (Matthew 15:31). Christ broke the bondage of disease with the touch of His hand, and miracles were performed as He did the works of His Father.

25. Every miracle proved His deity. Every miracle was a sign given to the people that He was the Holy One. How often the people demanded a sign and Jesus gave them many. Yet many still did not believe in Him. The Lord Jesus Christ's miracles and signs

were an invitation to the people to believe in Him. Yet Jesus saw many who still did not believe, and He asked ... *Why do ye not believe me?* (John 8:45–46)

26. While it is important to be knowledgeable of the miracles Jesus wrought, Spirit-filled believers focus on the deeper truths contained in the purpose why the Father allowed His Son to perform them. While on earth, it is apparent that Jesus fulfilled all three offices; after His ascension, He became *the* Prophet, *the* High Priest, and the *King of kings.*

27. Spoken of from the earliest of times, the Son of God was declared as the Prophet who would speak nothing but the words of His Father ... *I will raise up for them a Prophet like you from among their brethren, and will put My words in His mouth, and He shall speak to them all that I command Him....* (Deuteronomy 18:18 NKJV)

28. Prophecy is saturated with spiritual intentions, and Christ's words were spoken from His Father who is Spirit. The depth of meaning to which He took the hearer birthed new life in them. *Blessed are the pure in heart, for they shall see God....* (Matthew 5:8) Jesus spoke prophetical truth as he uttered these words. There were those who heard Him and believed, accepted Him as God, and saw Him as God.

29. Furthermore, He spoke of His death that was to come. He prophesied that in ages to come, God's unbiased judgment would be meted out upon all flesh. The sign of a Prophet is the fulfillment of their prophetical utterances. And to date, the things Jesus prophesied concerning certain events have come to pass. Without doubt, Spirit-filled believers know that those prophetical utterances Jesus spoke concerning future events will come to pass.

30. The Spirit-filled believer clings to the words of Jesus Christ regarding the future prophetical utterances that He spoke of and which have not yet happened. These believers don't only see the event: they see the purpose of the event. In virtually every instance, Jesus prophesied about the reconciling work He was

sent to do ... *I am come that they may have life, and that they might have it more abundantly....* (John 10:10)

31. The very nature of His prophetical statements embraced the reconciling work He was sent to accomplish. (John 16:1–15) Again ... *I go to prepare a place for you....* (John 14:2 NKJV) Jesus spoke of the purpose of His coming into the world, to make way for those who believed in Him, reconciling them to the Father. (2 Corinthians 5:19)

32. His works incorporated His primary role as that of a Priest. Jesus served mankind, He asked for no accolade, and He willingly became the sacrifice for them ... *For even the Son of Man did not come to be served, but to serve, and to give His life a ransom for many. (*Mark 10:45 NKJV) *The thief does not come except to steal, and to kill, and to destroy. I have come that they may have life, and that they may have it more abundantly.... As the Father knows Me, even so I know the Father; and I lay down My life for the sheep....* (John 10:10,15 NKJV)

33. Inasmuch as the office of prophet is evidenced throughout the Old and New Testaments, so too is the God-ordained role of a Priest. Stephen D. Renn says, "An important redemptive-historical element underlies the ministry of priests throughout Scripture ... priests were one of three classes of people (along with prophets and kings) under the old covenant to receive a Spirit anointing from God as a guarantee of their legitimate ministry."

34. The Lord Jesus Christ was anointed by the Holy Spirit (Luke 4:18), a prerequisite for the office of Priest, and took the office of Priest further than the Old Testament priests. While these Old Testament priests offered a sacrificial lamb on behalf of the people, Jesus Himself became the sacrificial Lamb for the people.

35. Furthermore, unlike the annual ritual performed by the priests of the old covenant, Jesus offered Himself once for all. Stephen D. Renn continues ... "The supreme distinction, however, between the old covenant priesthood and that of Christ in the new, is

its eternal unbroken effectiveness. Christ's death on the cross functions as an unrepeatable mediatorial sacrifice that guarantees the certainty of forgiveness of all who put their faith in that action."

36. Spirit-filled believers attest that Jesus was chosen by His Father to occupy this office, and in so doing fulfill all the requirements of Priest. He took His Priesthood further than any earthly priest in that He became the sacrifice when He offered Himself the ransom. Christ, in essence, extended His duties as Priest by becoming the ultimate sacrifice Himself.

37. The result of this action was the pivotal event in the existence of the Levitical priesthood. Because Christ's sacrifice was sufficient for all sin, there is no need for another sacrifice. Thus, Christ, spiritually, met all the requirements the Father had in a sacrifice, and as such, He canceled the priesthood of the Old Testament. The curtain was rent in two; the entrance into the Father's presence was now no longer hidden and reserved for only a high priest. At Jesus' resurrection, He walked out of the tomb not only as Priest but also as the Savior.

38. Once Jesus had completed all the duties of His Priesthood, and more, it is befitting that His Father promoted Him to the highest office in the priesthood to that of High Priest. Spirit-filled believers are persuaded that the glorious Person of the risen Christ ascended to the right hand of the Father and He is seated there for the express purpose of making continuous intercession on behalf of the righteous *holy priesthood* (1 Peter 2:5, Romans 8:34)

39. The writer in the letter to the Hebrews explains the two offices the risen Lord Jesus Christ now holds while He waits for His Father's command to return to the earth ... *Consider the Apostle and High Priest of our profession, Christ Jesus....* (Hebrews 3:1) First the office of Apostle, the One revealing the Father's deep truths through the Holy Spirit to the saints. Second, the High

Priest taking the message from the saints to the Father on their behalf.

40. There are no other words worthy of a higher exaltation of Jesus than those recorded in Hebrews 7:24 ... *But He, because He continues forever,* (He) *has an unchangeable priesthood.* (NKJV)

41. In Jesus' offices of Prophet and Priest, He simultaneously held the office of King of the Jews. The question put to Him by Caiaphas ... *Are you the Christ, the Son of the Blessed?* (Mark 14:61 NKJV) pertains to Christ's spiritual office. Someone had to ask Jesus this question, and it is only befitting that the highest office in the Jewish leadership, the high priest, asked Jesus to confirm His office. (Mark 14:62)

42. While the Jews were primarily concerned with Jesus' confirmation that He was the Messiah, the Son of God, they paid little attention to His office of king. This office, on the other hand, was of more importance to the procurator, Pontius Pilate. He does not concern himself with the Lord's role as the Christ, the Son of God, but focuses on His earthly rulership as King of the Jews (Mark 15:2).

43. Pilate was convinced that Jesus was the King of the Jews, to the extent that he personally wrote the words ... *Jesus of Nazareth, the King of the Jews....* (John 19:19 NKJV) Even when confronted by the angry chief priests, Pilate refused to change his words and stated that he was personally responsible for the declaration of whom he believed Jesus to be ... *What I have written, I have written....* (John 19:22 NKJV)

44. As with the offices of Prophet and Priest, Christ's Kingly office is eternally bestowed on Him ... *Now to the King eternal, immortal, invisible, to God who alone is wise, be honor and glory forever and ever....* (1 Timothy 1:17 NKJV)

45. Spirit-filled believers understand Jesus' kingship to be spiritual. This is the highest office of rulership and authority that can be given to Him. In this instance, Christ's kingship is elevated to more than King of the Jews. After His resurrection, Jesus is

declared the King of the Kingdom of God. (1 Timothy 1:17) This is a spiritual Kingdom into which all born-again believers enter once they accept by faith Jesus Christ's finished work on Calvary, irrespective of their race, religion, or culture. (Luke 1:33, John 3:1–7)

46. The Kingdom of God differs from the Kingdom of Heaven. While both kingdoms are from God, the Kingdom of Heaven is earthly and is the promised kingdom to the Jews. (Isaiah 11:1–9) However, after Christ's resurrection, the spiritual Kingdom of God is now for *whosoever*.... (John 3:16) This kingdom is not ... *eating and drinking, but righteousness and peace and joy in the Holy Spirit*.... (Romans 14:17 NKJV)

47. A king must have a kingdom, and a kingdom a king. A king rules his subjects who are submissive to him in all their ways. Every born-again believer becomes a subject in the Kingdom of God the moment they are born again.

48. From His ascension, all things are now in subjection to Jesus Christ ... *All authority has been given to Me in heaven and on earth*.... (Matthew 28:18 NKJV)

49. Herein begins the announcement of Christ's Kingship over all things. While sent as the King of the Jews, He was rejected by them and therefore He had no subjects. This opened the door for His sacrificial offering to God the Father to now be for *whosoever*. (Acts 10:35) From His resurrection, Jesus was given a more inclusive Kingship that extended beyond the Jews and incorporated everyone who accepts His death and resurrection by faith. (Romans 10:9–10)

50. It embraces more than Jesus' reply to Pilate ... *My kingdom is not of this world*.... (John 18:36) From His resurrection, Jesus can rightfully declare that *all authority* ... is now granted to Him. He who created all things is endowed with the spiritual office of Ruler (King). From the moment He walked out the tomb, Christ became the ultimate authority over all things,

and He was no longer only subjected to His Father's will, but He was endowed with *all power* to rule as the Monarch over both heaven and earth. (Ephesians 1:20–21) From that moment forward, He commissioned the Holy Spirit to minister to the saved and convict the sinner. (John 16:7–14)

51. Matthew's powerful record of Jesus' words must be carefully digested. This one verse ... *And Jesus came and spoke to them, saying, all authority has been given to Me in heaven and on earth* ... (Matthew 28:18 NKJV) is the proclamation of the King affording Him all His credentials. With all His love for His devoted disciples, Christ graciously imparts to them exactly who He is, and thereafter, what their commission is.

52. Herein is the exquisite display of Jesus Christ's love and compassion for His disciples. Even though He is seen by all the disciples, some still doubt that it is the Christ whom they see. *Some doubted....* (verse 17) It is Jesus who *comes and speaks to them.* He does not hold anything against the doubters, but instead approaches them in love and compassion declaring His new status. The befitting action of one who shows compassion: He approaches them. So often Jesus did this (Matthew 9:23, 17:7, Mark 6:34, Luke 14:15, 19:5, John 4:4, 17:16–17, Acts 9:3–5).

53. Throughout His earthly ministry, Jesus demonstrated His power over every force that opposed Him and His disciples. He calmed the raging sea, cast out demons, His words withered the fig tree, He changed water into wine, and He healed and delivered all those who were sick and oppressed. Yet now He declares to the disciples ... *All authority has been given to Me* ... as if they had not already witnessed this!

54. Christ's authority was not taken (snatched) from the hands of human kings on earth. He did not demand His rights and claim (proclaim) His position as king. He did not assume the office, neither did He dethrone anyone so that He could occupy the office of king: It was *given to Me....* What Satan offered Jesus,

and which He refused (Matthew 4:8–9), the Father freely gave and bestowed on Him (Matthew 28:18, Hebrews 1:13).

55. Matthew Henry, in his commentary, states on this subject, "He did not assume it, or usurp it, but it was given Him, He was legally entitled to it, and invested in it, by a grant from Him who is the Fountain of all being, and consequently all power. God ... *set my* (Him) *King* ... (Psalm 2:6) inaugurated and enthroned Him.... He had power before, *power to forgive sins,* but now *all power* (authority) is given to Him." Virtually the entirety of Psalm 2's contents, verse 1–12, references the office of King bestowed upon Jesus by His Father.

56. How unprepared the disciples were for their commission. Jesus calms their doubts by announcing His full authority over all things both in heaven and on earth, and it comes from His Father. This is the first step He takes in showing them their tasks which He had in His heart for them to do. All things that are spiritual, and that pertain to the spiritual Kingdom of God, are from Jesus. His entire charter contained the spiritual endowment of the holy promises of eternal life in Him for everyone who believes.

57. The disciples were transitioning from seeing the physical and material miracles to now being introduced to the spiritual "signs and wonders" they would experience.

58. His words are crisp and forthright ... *Go therefore* ... the first royal command from the King of kings. The *going* is not filled with instructions that an earthly king would give his subjects. Jesus' disciples are not commanded to build huge cities with walls and staked boundaries. They are not told to build mighty armies capable of marching into battle, nor are they given the command to rule with a rod of iron over the enemy.

59. How beautiful are Jesus' instructions ... *(1) make disciples of all nations ... (2) baptizing them in the name of the Father and of the Son and of the Holy Spirit ... (3) teaching them to observe all*

things that I have commanded you.... (Matthew 28:19–20 NKJV)
These are all spiritual things.

60. As with all things from the Godhead, the disciples are not left on their own, comfortless, or powerless and without authority. Jesus leaves them with the most exhilarating promise ... *Lo, I am with you always, even to the end of the age....* (Matthew 28:20 NKJV)

61. The highest office of authority, the most powerful Ruler over heaven and earth, patiently waits for the Day of His return. At that soon coming triumphant event that proceeds from heaven to earth, Jesus will return as *King of Kings and Lord of Lords.* (Revelation 19:16)

CHAPTER 14

JESUS DIED FOR MANKIND

1. So important is the death of Jesus that all four gospels give exhaustive accounts of this. Furthermore, Apostle Paul states that he could not occupy his mind with anything else ... *save Jesus Christ, and him crucified....* (1 Corinthians 2:2)

2. Even the Old Testament prophet, Isaiah, spoke of Jesus' life on earth, and declared that ... *He was wounded for our transgressions.... He was led as a lamb to the slaughter....* (Isaiah 53:1–12 NKJV)

3. While it is never the intention of Spirit-filled believers to ignore, or take lightly the horrible, gruesome physical sacrifice of Jesus on the cross, they focus more fully on the spiritual implications.... *For the message of the cross is foolishness to those who are perishing, but to us who are being saved it is the power* (spiritual power) *of God....* (1 Corinthians 1:18 NKJV)

4. The magnitude of the spiritual message found in Jesus' death is never more eloquently expressed than when Apostle Paul wrote under the anointing of the Holy Spirit ... *But God has revealed them to us through His Spirit. For the Spirit searches all things, yes, the deep things of God. For what man knows the things of a man except the spirit of the man which is in him? Even so no one*

knows the things of God except the Spirit of God. Now we have received, not the spirit of the world, but the Spirit who is from God, that we might know the things that have been freely given to us by God. These things we also speak, not in words which man's wisdom teaches but which the Holy Spirit teaches, comparing spiritual things with spiritual. But the natural man does not receive the things of the Spirit of God, for they are foolishness to him; nor can he know them, because they are spiritually discerned. (1 Corinthians 2:10–14 NKJV)

5. So all-embracing was Jesus' death that it included the heavenly creatures. Their accolade with the twenty-four elders pertaining to Jesus' death is pronounced as a worship anthem ... *And they sang a new song, saying: "You are worthy to take the scroll, and to open its seals; for You were slain, and have redeemed us to God by Your blood out of every tribe and tongue and people and nation, and have made us kings and priests to our God; and we shall reign on the earth."* (Revelation 5:9–10 NKJV)

6. The first glimpse of spiritual insight into Christ's death is found when His human nature is put to the fullest test. It was first the betrayal of one of His disciples, then being *sorrowful unto* death, then the denial of a disciple, Peter, all these even before He began to suffer physically. How horrendous and cruel was the physical punishment, yet he suffered and endured through it. Then worst of all, He faced the worst encounter of the total salvation purpose; sin was thrust upon Him. "The worst kept for the last." Sin and all its consequences were rendered unto the Innocent ... *And the LORD hath laid on him the iniquity of us all....* (Isaiah 53:6)

7. While the sentence of death is pronounced on all human flesh ... *it is appointed unto men once to die ...* (Hebrews 9:27), the Lord Jesus Christ came into the world for the purpose of dying.

8. Jesus Christ's last utterance while on the cross ... *It is finished* ... seals the Old Covenant and its demand of obedience of a sacrificial offering of a one-year old lamb. It points directly to the

142

spiritual application of the New Covenant in His blood (Matthew 26:28) and fulfills an eternal prophecy ... *The Lamb slain from the foundation of the world....* (Revelation 13:8)

9. Jesus Christ, the Son of Man, died physically, and Jesus Christ, the Son of God, was banished into hell spiritually when mankind's sin was thrust onto Him. He drank of the cup (sponge) (John 19:29–30) and immediately when He did that, God placed mankind's sin on Him (2 Corinthians 5:21). The spiritual separation between the Father and the Son had to happen, because there was no other way the Father could justify Christ in the Spirit than to first place mankind's sin on Him on the cross, and then to release Him from hell, the abode of sinners' souls and spirits. (Psalm 16:10, 1 Timothy 3:16)

10. Jesus' death annunciated by His shed precious blood was the required demand God instituted to remove His wrath from being poured out on mankind. God's spiritual punishment on man's sinful state was inducted when Adam sinned. God had no choice but to vindicate His holiness that was violated by man's sin.

11. As gruesome as Christ's death was, so glorious was the result. Jesus took mankind's sin upon Him and paid the price, conquered death and hell so that God could forgive the repentant heart their sin. While sin is as much a physical and mental action, it is also a spiritual schism that created a breach that was impossible for man to repair. God who is Spirit was the only One who could reconcile man to Him.

12. The result was a spiritual victory Jesus gained over hell, death, and the grave. He *destroyed the works of the devil....* He reconciled God and man through His shed blood and removed God's wrath from against a repentant heart.

13. He opened the way for all mankind to enter the holy presence of the Father. The physical tearing of the veil that shrouded the Holy of Holies in the temple signified to the Jew that the shedding of

Christ's blood opened the way for them to spiritually enter His presence.

14. To achieve this spiritual victory, there had to be a moment in time when the holy Son of God was made sin for mankind.

The Cup

15. From the Passover meal until Christ's last breath, there is a spiritual message that pertains to the cup Jesus continually referenced regarding His becoming sin for mankind. Herein is the spiritual application and physical representation used by Jesus to demonstrate the spiritual process He applied to achieve total victory over sin and its penalty.

16. The significance of the cup referenced by Christ is first mentioned when the disciples' mother approached Him and asked that her sons be given the place of honor alongside Jesus in His kingdom. (Matthew 20:20–21)

17. Turning to the two disciples, He asked them ... *Are you able to drink the cup that I am about to drink?* ... (Matthew 20:22 NKJV) It is obvious that the two disciples were not fully aware of the contents of the question they were asked. They willingly answered that they would drink of the cup. They had little understanding of the physical punishment, mental anguish, and spiritual abandonment Jesus was referring to when He referenced the *cup*.

18. Old Testament prophets make mention of the cup of God's wrath and fury (Psalm 75:8, Isaiah 51:17, Jeremiah 25:15). This very same symbol is used in a practical demonstration by Jesus when He was made sin for mankind.

19. When Jesus gathered the disciples around Him in the Upper Room and they had shared the Passover meal, He reached for the bread and told them that it was to be His body that would be broken for them. He then reached for the cup ... *Then He took the cup and*

gave thanks and gave it to them, saying, Drink from it, all of you. For this is My blood of the new covenant, which is shed for many for the remission of sins.... (Matthew 26:27–28 NKJV)

20. This holy instruction is given to all believers to observe it as a reminder of the physical as well as the spiritual sacrifice of Jesus. His body was brutally mutilated, and His Spirit was also separated from the Father's presence.

21. Rising from the table, Jesus and the eleven disciples made their way to the Garden of Gethsemane. Jesus *goes a little farther* ... (Matthew 26:39) into the garden and started praying to the Father ... *O My Father, if it is possible, let this cup pass from Me; nevertheless, not as I will, but as You will....* The Son of God asked the Father three times if there was any way He could remove the "cup" from Him.

22. When He referenced the "cup," Jesus revealed the magnitude of the purpose of the instrument that will be used to demonstrate to the world the moment He became sin. Jesus did not ask the Father to remove the scourging, the false accusations; neither did He ask the Father to find a less punishing way than the crucifixion. He focused on the "cup" asking that this be taken from Him. Herein is the most haunting and worst aspect of Christ's sacrifice: His separation from His Father.

23. Once Jesus has settled in His heart that there was no other way than for Him to be made sin for man, He walked to the disciples, woke them up, and told them the hour had come. When Judas and the palace guards identified Jesus, Peter lunged forward with his sword and sliced off Malchus' ear. Jesus immediately performed a miracle and touched his ear and healed him (Luke 22:50).

24. Jesus then turned to Peter and said ... *Shall I not drink the cup which My Father has given Me?* (John 18:11 NKJV) Jesus did not reference His crucifixion or His physical punishment that was soon to follow. He referenced the cup that He had to drink.

25. It was a usual practice for the Roman soldiers to offer the person who was about to be crucified a drink of wine mingled with gall to lessen the physical pain they were about to inflict on the body. When they offered Jesus a drink, He refused it. (Matthew 27:34) His refusal was not a sign of His bravery to endure pain; He refused to drink of that cup offered Him before He was nailed to the cross, because it was not yet time for Him to be made sin.

26. After Jesus had been on the cross for six hours, He made a profound statement ... *I thirst*.... (John 19:29) To many who witnessed His last six hours, their focus was on His physical suffering. As brutal as it was, there was, however, more happening than the physical suffering.

27. With all the agony and physical suffering Christ's body endured, the last thing on His mind would have been that He was thirsty. His face was bloated from the poisonous crown of thorns that pierced His brow. His torso was ripped to shreds from the scourging, the nails had torn His flesh, and His lungs were being filled with water due to Him not being able to breathe. Yet He says ... *I thirst*....

28. The time had come for Him to drink of the dreaded cup. The Lord Jesus Christ had but a few seconds left before He would give up His Spirit. A diligent Roman soldier heard the two words that proceeded from the Savior's lips. He reached for the closest available instrument he could find that he could use as a "cup."

29. *Now a vessel full of sour wine was sitting there; and they filled a sponge with sour wine, put it on hyssop, and put it to His mouth. So when Jesus had received* (drank of the cup) *the sour wine....* (John 19:29-30 NKJV)

30. Then it happened. The moment Jesus sucked the sour wine from the sponge, God the Father thrust mankind's sin upon Jesus. There was the separation Jesus had begged the Father to take away.

31. It was held back by the Father until the very last few seconds of Jesus' life. The holy Son of God was kept totally sinless until the last breath He breathed. He was made sin a few seconds before

He gave up His Spirit. How precious was the Father's love for His Son that He held back mankind's evil sin until the very last moment … *He said, "It is finished!" and bowing His head, he gave up His Spirit.* The Christ, the Son of the living God *who knew no sin, was made to be sin for us….* (2 Corinthians 5:21 NKJV)

32. It must never be forgotten that Jesus was present as part of the Godhead when the first Adam sinned in the Garden of Eden. He witnessed the cataclysmic rending of the relationship and fellowship Adam had with the Father. The consequences of the sin were so daunting that Christ knew the repercussions that would ricochet throughout mankind's existence.

33. Then, the Lord Jesus Christ (the Last Adam) experienced this same horrific severing from the Father. This was what Jesus had seen as the most difficult part of the entire crucifixion … *Remove this cup from me….* (Luke 22:42)

34. While paying attention to the instrument Jesus referenced, namely *the cup*, it is perhaps the one defining message that pertains to His precious blood. Christ's blood was incorruptible. It was, and still is, *precious*. The Father never allowed His Son's holy blood to see any corruption.

35. It was the most gracious and yet divine command that Jesus' blood remain pure and without sin (the first Adam's blood lost its purity when he sinned).

36. Thus said, the Father had to wait until the very last breath His Son gave, and He had to wait until every last drop of *precious* blood had flowed and was drained from Jesus' body before He made Jesus sin for mankind.

37. The very act of drinking from the sponge (the "cup") signified the "emptiness" of Christ's life of His blood, and it was the declaration that Jesus had no more physical life in Him, because every drop of His *precious blood* was no longer in His body.

38. The cup was the "instrument" the Father used to signify to the world the sin He thrust upon His Son. The effect of drinking from

this cup resulted in sin being placed upon Him and ultimately, separation from His Father.

Christ's Physical and Spiritual Death

39. God's holy record, the Bible, gives details of the activities that took place after Jesus was arrested in the Garden of Gethsemane. His false trial before the Sanhedrin, the appearance before the *fox*, Herod, and the questions posed to Him by Pilate together with the brutal scourging and platted crown of thorns all lead to the ultimate declaration ... *So they took Jesus and led Him away....* (John 19:16 NKJV)

40. It was vital that every prophetic utterance concerning the Son of God's death had to be fulfilled. While the physical and mental experiences that Jesus endured are of utmost importance, Spirit-filled believers desire clarification on the spiritual implications of the purpose of everything that Jesus endured.

41. The Old Covenant demanded that the High Priest laid his hands on the "scapegoat" and it was taken into the "wilderness." He would take the sin-offering bullock and goat ... *whose blood was brought to make atonement in the Holy Place, shall be carried outside the camp....* (Leviticus 16:27 NKJV) So, too, was Jesus led away ... *as a lamb to the slaughter* ... (Isaiah 53:7) and ... *therefore Jesus also, that He might sanctify the people with His own blood, suffered outside the gate....* (Hebrews 13:12 NKJV)

42. The physical journey to outside the city walls spiritually sealed the fulfillment of God's holy demand that the sin offering be removed from the presence of the people and *carried outside the gate.*

43. While the Son of God was being nailed to the cross, there was a long line of Jews carrying a lamb to be sacrificed on the altar in the temple. For the most part they were oblivious of the crucifixion. But more than that, they were totally unaware of the fact that

while they were fulfilling the physical offering of a lamb for the atonement of their sin, God was personally offering the Lamb of God for the spiritual redemption of their sin.

44. Every born-again believer needs to understand the spiritual implications of the physical sacrifice and shedding of Christ's precious blood. To merely analyze the events and understand every detail of the diabolical physical ordeal the Savior endured is only part of the divine message. It has deep spiritual implications that can only be received by revelation.

45. To begin, the relationship Adam severed between him and God was a spiritual relationship. Therefore, the reconciliation of the spiritual relationship is the foremost purpose of Christ being sacrificed. Apostle Paul makes regular reference in his writings to *... Jesus Christ and Him crucified.* He also states that *... it came through the revelation of Jesus Christ....* (Galatians 1:12 NKJV) The full import of the spiritual reason for Calvary is imparted by revelation to believers.

46. The most important point to be remembered is that it was God offering His Son for mankind. This was not an angel or a good person: it was God Himself who sent His only Son to die for mankind. The two parties involved in the severing of the relationship, man and God, had to be involved in the reconciliation of that relationship. Man walked away from God and sinned, and in the sacrifice of His Son, God walked towards man to reunite the relationship.

47. The One who hung on Calvary's cross was none other than God's holy Son. And He suffered the spiritual death of being separated spiritually from His Father.

48. This was not a sacrifice forced upon the Son of God, but rather Jesus Christ surrendered willingly to the act. His own words reveal this ... *I lay down my life that I may take it again. No one takes it from Me, but I lay it down of Myself. I have power to lay it down, and I have power to take it again. This command I have received from My Father....* (John 10:17–18 NKJV)

49. The final three words Jesus uttered from the cross ... *It is finished* ... have such profound spiritual significance that it passes human comprehension ... *Bowing His head, He gave up His Spirit....* (John 19:30 NKJV) Here the divine Son of God signaled His surrender to the awful sin placed upon Him. He knew His Father had just made Him sin for mankind, and He looked down, away from heaven. Now a sinner, he could not look the Father in the eye and bowed His head.

50. Arthur W. Pink in his *Exposition of the Gospel of John* puts it best, "This was not the despairing cry of a helpless martyr. It was not an expression of satisfaction that the end of His suffering was now reached. It was not the last gasp of a worn-out life. No, it was the declaration on the part of the Divine Redeemer that all for which He came from heaven to earth to do, was done...."

51. It is fitting that the Eternal Son of God did not have His Spirit taken from Him. Scripture is clear the He *gave up His Spirit....* (John 19:30 NKJV) When death befalls all of mankind, their spirit is taken from them. Not so with Jesus who gave up His Spirit.

52. Apostle John clearly hears the word from the Savior's lips ... *finished....* In the original tongue, Jesus uttered only one word for the English phrase used ... *It is finished....* This Greek word for "finished'—"teleo"—has a significant meaning. It announces that all the spiritual work Jesus came to do was concluded. There was nothing more He could do, nor was there anything else needed to be done, to accomplish the victory over sin. He was the Lamb of God sacrificed, His precious blood was shed; His sinless, holy life was made sin, and His human body breathed its last breath.

53. Christ spiritually *made an end* (teleo) of all future sacrifices of the one-year-old lambs. His death canceled out the Levitical priesthood, broke down the middle wall of partition, and opened the door to the Father's heart for man's repentant heart to once again be reconciled to Him.

54. Arthur W. Pink says about Jesus' last three words, "This was the

briefest and yet the fullest of His seven cross-utterances. Eternity will be needed to make manifest all that it contains. All things had been done which the Law of God had required; all things established which prophecy predicted; all things brought to pass which the types foreshadowed; all things accomplished which the Father had given Him to do; all things performed which were needed for our redemption."

55. Spirit-filled believers focus on the spiritual implications that followed Jesus' death. Apostle John gives a beautiful account of the laying to rest of both the Son of Man and the Son of God ... *Then they took the body of Jesus* ... (John 19:40); this indicates the physical removal from the cross of Jesus' body, the Son of Man. The human frame had died and was taken from the wretched cross.

56. Apostle John explains how they hurriedly prepared the "body" for burial in a tomb. Then he says ... *There laid they Jesus....* (John 19:42) This signifies the spiritual laying to rest the Son of God. John does not say, "There they laid the body of Jesus." He is telling the reader that in His death, both the Son of Man and the Son of God died. The most precious word in any language throughout the world is "Jesus." The angel declares to Mary ... *You shall call His name JESUS....* (Luke 1:31 NKJV) In this passage, the original tongue emphasizes the name "Jesus" in all capital letters. He is the Son of God born of a woman. Yet He is born of the Father and fully Man, and He died physically and spiritually.

57. The body was taken and laid in the tomb. Likewise, Jesus, the Son of God, was also laid in the tomb. There was a separation from God and man in Christ's death. He died physically and was placed in a tomb separating Him from the living. Added to that, He was separated from the Father and ... *made sin....* Sin broke the relationship between God and man, and the sin-stained Christ was separated from His Father.

58. The spiritual significance of the garden should never be forgotten.

The most sublime place on earth was the Garden of Eden. There Adam sinned and was driven out of the garden from the presence of God. Jesus, the Son of God's dead body, was taken into a garden and placed in a "new tomb." Sin drove man out of the garden, and Jesus' resurrection brought victory over sin from the garden.

CHAPTER 15

THE PRECIOUS BLOOD
OF JESUS

1. *Knowing that you were not redeemed with corruptible things, like silver or gold, from your aimless conduct received by tradition from your fathers, but with the precious blood of Christ, as of a lamb without blemish and without spot* (1 Peter 1:18–19 NKJV).

2. *For it pleased the Father that in Him all the fullness should dwell, and by Him to reconcile all things to Himself, by Him, whether things on earth or things in heaven, having made peace through the blood of His cross. And you, who once were alienated and enemies in your mind by wicked works, yet now He has reconciled in the body of His flesh through death, to present you holy, and blameless, and above reproach in His sight— if indeed you continue in the faith, grounded and steadfast, and are not moved away from the hope of the gospel which you heard, which was preached to every creature under heaven* (Colossians 1:19–23 NKJV).

3. This subject is the central theme of the relationship between God and man. This is the ultimate expression of God's holy, divine love and reconciling work that reunites His relationship and fellowship once again with man.

4. There is no other way mankind can ever be reconciled to God than through the shed precious blood of Jesus Christ.

5. The very essence and power of God's forgiveness of sin is invested in the shed blood of Jesus Christ ... *and the blood of Jesus Christ cleanses us from all sin* (1 John 1:7–9 NKJV).

6. W.A.C. Rowe says, "The precious blood of Christ is the vital heart and indispensable nourishment of the gospel. As good, healthy, rich blood is to the physical frame, so the precious blood of the Lord and Savior Jesus Christ ministers to the eternal salvation of men. Every preacher and believer's testimony that deteriorates in the faith and proclamation of the essential truth concerning the blood of Christ proceeds surely to their death."

7. Throughout the Bible, God has always used blood as a means to atone, cover, and forgive man's sin ... *Without shedding of blood, there is no remission* (Hebrews 9:22 NKJV). It progresses and continues to the final blood sacrifice of His own blood when He sent His only begotten Son to die and shed His blood for many ... *For this is My blood of the new covenant, which is shed for many for the remission of sins* (Matthew 26:28 NKJV). Again, *In Him we have redemption through His blood, the forgiveness of sins, according to the riches of His grace* (Ephesians 1:7 NKJV).

8. God chose blood as the acceptable sacrificial offering for man's sins. God instructed man to use *the life of the flesh* as the means to deal with sin. It was upon His instruction that Moses instituted the Day of Atonement.

9. This was not man's idea; it was entirely God's instruction, and it had God's approval as the means to appease His wrath against men's sin. Jesus instituted the new covenant in His blood which believers accept by faith in His redeeming work on the Cross, namely His death and the shedding of His blood.

10. There is a progression of the significance of the blood in the covenants God made with man to appease His wrath against sin. In the blood, the covenant had its foundation and power. R.A. Torrey references this progression: (Paraphrased) "It is by the blood alone that God and man can be brought into a covenant fellowship with God. That which had been foreshadowed at the gate of Eden, on Mount Ararat, on Mount Moriah, and in Egypt was now confirmed at the foot of Mount Sinai in a most solemn manner. Without blood, there could be no access by sinful man to a holy God.

11. "There is, however, a significant difference between the methodologies of applying the blood in the former cases as compared with the latter. On Mount Moriah, the life was redeemed by the shedding of the blood. In Egypt, it was sprinkled on the doorposts of the houses; but at Sinai, it was sprinkled on the persons themselves. The contract was closer, the application more powerful (Exodus 24:8). When Israel had reached Sinai, God had given His law as the foundation of His covenant. That covenant now had to be established, but as it is expressly stated in Hebrews 9:7, *not without blood*."

12. This crimson flow is evident throughout the Holy Writ. Nothing can dispense with the necessity of the blood. The covenant God made with Israel reflects the sacrifice and shedding of blood by the chosen delegates on behalf of the people, and then the precious blood of Jesus is shed for the total annihilation of the inherent sin in the repentant heart.

Atonement

13. The Old Covenant has the reference of "atonement" as the manner of God's dealing with man's sin.

14. Before Jesus' blood was shed on Calvary, the blood of animals was the means whereby God "covered" the people's sins.

15. The High Priest and, or a priest, took the offering from the people and made atonement for their sins by sacrificing the offering on the altar in the Holy Place on behalf of the people. The High Priest took the blood with him into the Most Holy Place where God dwelt, and he knew he had no access to God's holy presence if he went into it without blood.

16. This sacrifice made as an act of repentance, if accepted by God, was sufficient to temporarily cover the sin of the one who brought the sacrifice. This was the "covering" of the sin through the atoning work in the sacrifice by the High Priest on behalf of himself and the people.

17. The sacrifice was not human blood, but that of an animal. Thus, the offering was an expression of the person's act of repentance. The ritual was designed to make the person "do something" that "cost them" something when they came to the altar. The atonement was the result of the ritual. However, it was the dogma (the belief in the meaning, tenets, and content of the ritual) within the performed ritual that achieved the atoning result.

18. The acceptance of the shed blood was the final step in the covering of the people's sins. Had the person offered himself as the sacrifice and shed his own blood, he would not have survived to live in the atonement for his sins. Thus, a substitute, an animal was sacrificed, and its blood was used on behalf of the person.

Redemption

19. Following the application of blood for the atonement and covering of sin, God perfected the sacrifice and introduced *a better covenant* (Hebrews 8:6).

20. In the sacrifice of His only begotten Son, Jesus, and the shedding of His blood, God sent His own sacrifice and shed His own blood on the altar of the Cross for mankind ... *This is a faithful saying*

and worthy of all acceptance, that Christ Jesus came into the world to save sinners (1 Timothy 1:15 NKJV).

21. Whereas in the Old Covenant man brought a sacrifice to the altar and it was the offering for the *atonement* of his *sins*, God brought Himself as the sacrifice and shed His own blood for the *remission* of *sins* for many (Matthew 26:28, Ephesians 5:2).

22. *Atonement* was the acceptable response God performed when He annually covered the sins of the previous year when the High Priest entered the Holy of Holies and placed the blood on the altar. With Jesus Christ, the eternal High Priest, His one sacrifice, Himself, bought eternal *redemption* of the inherent sin from Adam, and the sins that mankind commits, through His shed precious blood (Hebrews 9:23–28).

23. While atonement covered the sins of the person for a season, redemption remits man's sin (removes it as if it never existed), which brings about reconciliation through the remission of sin. Jesus Christ's shed precious blood is a "continuing remission of sin," "once for all," and "putting it away in the sea of forgetfulness." (1 John 1:7–9) *He entered the Most Holy Place once for all, having obtained eternal redemption* (Hebrews 9:12 NKJV). Oswald Chambers says, "It is an injustice to say that Jesus Christ labored in redemption to make a person a saint. Jesus Christ labored in redemption to redeem the whole world and to place it perfectly whole and restored before the throne of God."

24. Christ's sacrifice did not focus only on the atonement of the people's physical sins of the flesh, but rather it is directed towards and included redeeming the "conscience" of each person. This is the spiritual and soul redemption that is redeemed (cleansed) by His shed blood (Hebrews 9:9, 14 NKJV). That is why man *confesses with the mouth and believes in his heart* (Romans 10:9–10 NKJV) on the Lord Jesus Christ, whose shed precious blood cleanses him from all sin.

25. Jesus' incarnation was for the purpose of death. While humans are born to live, the Lord Jesus Christ was born to die. Jesus Christ's death was not a mere accident or incident of His human life; it was the supreme purpose of it. He became man in order that He might die as Man and for man. He died for a specific purpose, as *a ransom for many* (Matthew 20:28 NKJV).

26. The most glorious accolade that can be given comes from heaven's creatures who proclaim: *And they sang a new song, saying: "You are worthy to take the scroll, and to open its seals; for You were slain, and have redeemed us to God by Your blood out of every tribe and tongue and people and nation, and have made us kings and priests to our God; and we shall reign on the earth ... saying with a loud voice: "Worthy is the Lamb who was slain to receive power and riches and wisdom, and strength and honor and glory and blessing!"* (Revelation 5:9–12 NKJV)

27. Here are the differences summarized.

The Old covered the people's sins, while the New removed them (Romans 3:24–26).

The Old needed a continual annual animal sacrifice, while the New needed only One sacrifice (Hebrews 10:12).

The Old required an animal sacrifice, while the New required God to sacrifice Himself (John 3:16).

The Old needed an act of obedience, while the New is an application of a believer's faith (Ephesians 2:8).

The Old covered the people's physical sins, while the New removes the physical and conscience sin upon repentance (Hebrews 9:9–14).

The Old had numerous High Priests, while the New has one High Priest who continues and is unchangeable (Hebrews 7:22–24).

The Old needed a sacrifice from man, the sinner, towards God, while the New needed God to sacrifice His Sinless Son for many (Matthew 26:28).

Intrinsic Qualities in Christ's blood

28. Within the precious shed blood of Jesus Christ, there are intrinsic qualities that are unique to Him.

29. Throughout the Old Testament, there are numerous accounts of the value God attached to the blood. As oxygen is an integral part of water, so, too, is the blood integral to life (Leviticus 17:11). Even the shedding of a wicked person's blood and the unnecessary shedding of an animal's blood and even to the drinking of blood are specifically addressed in the Bible. Then, to the eternal promise to the martyr whose life was slain, they rest eternally under the altar of God (Revelation 6:9–10). If the blood of animals and mankind is precious to God, how much more precious is His Son's blood— God's very own blood?

30. Andrew Murray says in his book, *The Blood of Christ*, "The blood of Jesus is the greatest mystery of eternity, the deepest mystery of divine wisdom. Within this holy offering of His blood, there is a hidden value of the Spirit of self-sacrifice. The Son yielded up His Spirit and sacrificed Himself for mankind. When this revealed truth is witnessed by faith in the believer's heart, it works out in that heart a similar spirit of self-sacrifice."

Sinless

31. While the blood of fallen man is sin-stained (Romans 3:23), the precious blood of Jesus, God's only begotten Son, is *sinless*. The Bible's declaration that Jesus is conceived by the Holy Spirit is the evidence that the blood from Jesus' Father is God Himself. Therefore, it did not carry the same sin stain that fallen man carries. This fact, in itself, is the most valuable intrinsic quality that separates it from all of humanity's blood. Added to this,

Christ's blood is not only sinless in its origin: it is also sinless in its existence. Jesus was tested and tried by the deceiver, yet Jesus never succumbed to the devil's sinful devices (Hebrews 4:15).

Sin-Free

32. This intrinsic quality is inherent and "built-in" to its source, namely God, the Father of our Lord Jesus Christ. Hence it was from the sinless source and remained sinless throughout Christ's life. Christ's blood needed no justification: it was *sin-free*. His blood needed no forgiveness; it remained sinless and was, therefore, acceptable to His Father.

33. Christ's sinless blood was essential to the Father's purpose. Sin could not be offered for sin. The fundamental principle of the blood sacrifice was the offering of a sacrificial lamb without spot or blemish. Thus, the blood of *the Lamb of God who takes away the sin of the world* was wholly *sinless* and *sin-free*—undefiled (Hebrews 7:26).

34. Herein lies the most effective intrinsic value: Christ's blood was pure and free from sin, and therefore is more powerful than anything man could offer as a self-sacrifice. His blood alone had the ingredient worthy of acceptance by the Father for the redemption of man.

Holy

35. Because Jesus Christ's blood was from a sinless source, the Father, it had the intrinsic value of being *holy*. Not only did God offer through His Son a sinless, acceptable sacrifice and shed His blood, the crimson river that flowed from Christ's life was *holy* blood. The essence of God's nature is His holiness, and it is

manifested in the quality of His blood; for *the life of the flesh is in the blood,* and God offered His Son's life, namely His shed blood. It was holy blood offered to redeem (buy back) sin-stained blood of mankind (Hebrews 7:26).

36. It is biblically correct to state that the *life of the flesh is in the blood,* and to state that *eternal life is in the blood of the Lamb of God.* Christ's blood was from the eternal Holy Father, and Jesus' life is in His blood which is eternal and holy.

Eternal Power

37. The undisputable quality in Jesus' blood is the power it has to remove sin from a repentant heart. This is possible because of the *redemption by the blood* (1 Peter 1:18–19). There must be something in Christ's blood that gives it eternal power. So, what is in it that it possesses an intrinsic power that is unique and found in nothing else?

38. This is Christ's blood placed on the altar for sin. Christ's blood placed on the holy altar of God in heaven had sufficient redemptive power. It has this because the soul of the holy Son of God dwelt in that blood. The eternal life of the Godhead was carried in that blood (Acts 20:28).

39. It is therefore the eternal Spirit that is within the Savior's blood that gives it the power to redeem mankind from his rotten sinful state. The power of that blood in its many effects is nothing less than the eternal power of God because ... *the life of the flesh is in the blood....*

40. This eternal power that can never, and will never, change because it is from the eternal Godhead. It has the unique ability to *redeem, reconcile, reunite, cleanse,* and give *eternal life* to the repentant heart.

Divine

41. Because the source of Christ's blood came from His Father, the eternal God who is divine, so, too, is the life of Jesus divine. This life is in His blood which makes His blood divine. It contains the purest and most holy, righteous, and eternal power that cannot be conquered. Christ's blood was not from His earthly father, Joseph. Jesus was conceived of the Holy Spirit. His blood is from His Father and His Father is divine.

Incorruptible

42. The Lord Jesus Christ was subjected to *all points of temptation* just as mankind is, yet He did not sin (Hebrews 4:15). As Son of Man, He could have relented and fallen into temptation just as Adam did. Because He did not fall, His blood remained uncorrupted. Having succeeded in remaining uncorrupted, Christ's blood remained incorruptible.

43. Therein is the eternal power source; the incorruptible blood can never lose its power. This was the forgotten value the devil never thought of. Had the devil known he could not conquer the incorruptible blood's power and that eternal life resided in Christ's blood, he would never have crucified Jesus.

44. This is the *hidden wisdom* which is in the power of God (1 Corinthians 2:1–8). This is the message within the incorruptible blood: the Lamb of God slain from the foundation of the world (crucified), and the means to redeem mankind was the slain Lamb's incorruptible blood.

45. What made Jesus' blood incorruptible is the question that demands an answer. It is from the Father who is eternal, and the eternal Spirit—Christ's life—is in His blood. This glorious truth

resounds throughout heaven and earth: the blood of Jesus Christ, God's only begotten Son was, and is forever incorruptible.

46. Furthermore, it is in this never changing state because Jesus remained throughout His life on earth *holy, harmless, undefiled,* (and) *separate from sinners* (Hebrews 7:26 NKJV).

The Reason (Purpose) of Christ Shedding His Blood

47. The almighty, eternal, and holy God looked on depraved man and stepped onto the platform of human life and sent His only begotten Son to die for man. His decision was direct and commanding. It was forthright and pitched to deal once and for all with the terrible sin that plagued mankind.

48. God's reasoning was all-encompassing, embracing every area that needed to be taken care of. He gave over His Son to be a sacrifice and, in so doing, broke the power of sin and the works of the devil, shattering them into irreconcilable pieces.

Restoration

49. Flowing from the heart of God, His *agape* (love) for mankind, and the immutable promise God made that He would right man's wrong (Genesis 3:15), God made the way possible for this to happen.

50. Even though Adam willfully transgressed God's command, he could not repair the wrong he did. The eternal damage on mankind that Adam caused when he reached for the fruit of the tree of knowledge of good and evil was the death knell for the entire human race.

51. This spiritual schism created by Adam's disobedience—sin between man and God—now required a blood sacrifice to atone

men's sins before God. Man could not remove sin, only the One against whom sin was perpetrated had the ability to take care of the stain. In the normal course of life, the guilty makes amends to the offended one. Yet in this eternal life, the Offended One paid the price for the wrong of the guilty party.

52. In this "price," it was God who paid. Before God could forgive man's eternal sin, there had to be something before forgiveness in order that it could be applied. That something was a sacrifice.

53. Only once the sacrifice was made could forgiveness flow towards a repentant heart. And God sacrificed His Son and made Him shed His precious blood to right the wrong of sin (1 Corinthians 6:20).

54. Even though the penalty of Adam's sin condemned mankind and separated him from God, the power in the precious shed blood of Jesus removes that sin stain and reunites mankind once again to God.

55. The overriding characteristic that resided in Adam's heart while he was in the garden was *peace* from God. There was no fear, doubt, or unbelief; never a day went by that Adam was not at peace with God and himself. Eden's abode was void of anxiety, nervous tension, and worry. God's peace permeated every area of the garden, until sin entered it. From that moment on, fear rules in the life of every human being. God promised that He would take care of man's fall, and He did when He sent His Son to shed His precious blood and restore that peace ... *having made peace through the blood of His cross....* (Colossians 1:20, Ephesians 2:11–18 NKJV) Now believers have peace even in the midst of their knowledge of good and evil. (John 14:27)

Offering for Sin

56. The Lord Jesus Christ died as an explicit *offering for sin*; that is, that He, a perfect, righteous One who deserved to live, died

in the place of sinful men who deserved to die (1 Peter 3:18). *He bore our iniquities and was wounded for our transgression* (Isaiah 53:5, 1 Peter 2:24 NKJV). The death of Jesus Christ was a specific sacrifice: that is, the just One who deserved to live died in the place of unjust ones who deserved to die. In His death, His blood was the sin offering. Herein is the requirement of God for the remission of sin (Hebrews 9:22).

57. He died as a *sin offering ... He who knew no sin was made (to be) sin for us* (2 Corinthians 5:21 NKJV). It was on the grounds of Christ's death and His shed blood, and on this ground alone, that forgiveness of sin is made possible for sinners.

58. An "offering for sin" or a "guilt offering," which is the exact force of the Hebrew word translated "an offering for sin," was a death of a sacrificial offering from which pardon was offered to sinners.

59. The Word of God declares that apart from the shedding of the blood of Jesus Christ there is absolutely no pardon for sin. There is absolutely no forgiveness outside the redeeming blood of Christ. Without Christ's *blood* being *shed for many*, every member of humanity perishes forever.

A Ransom

60. He died as a *ransom*—that is, His death was the price paid to redeem others from eternal separation from God (spiritual death). His shed blood was the price He paid to redeem mankind. (1 Timothy 2:5–6)

Propitiation

61. Jesus Christ died as the *propitiation* (make amends on behalf of) for mankind's sins. God the Father gave Christ, His Son, to be

the propitiation through His shed blood. Jesus Christ, through the shedding of His blood, is the sacrifice offered and accepted and by which God's holy wrath at sin is appeased (1 John 4:10, Romans 3:25–26).

62. Christ was "a propitiation," "an expiatory sacrifice," on behalf of mankind, and the means of appeasing God's holy wrath at sin. Or, in other words, Jesus, through the shedding of His blood, is the means by which the wrath of God against sinners is appeased.

63. God's holiness and consequent hatred of sin, like every other attribute of His character, is real and must manifest itself. His wrath at sin must strike somewhere, either on the sinner himself or upon a lawful substitute. It struck Jesus Christ, a lawful substitute ... *and the Lord has laid on Him the iniquity of us all...* (Isaiah 53:6 NKJV) The death of Jesus Christ (the shedding of His blood) fulfilled the demands of God's holiness.

Curse

64. Christ died to redeem humanity from *the curse* of the law by bearing that curse Himself (Galatians 3:13). His death by crucifixion redeemed mankind from the curse which they deserved when He took that curse upon Himself.

Substitutionary Sacrifice

65. The Lord Jesus shed His blood as a *substitutionary sacrifice*. He did this in place of mankind shedding their own blood. Any sacrifice mankind made was stained in sin, and God required a Lamb without spot or blemish.

66. The only pure, holy, and worthy blood that has ever existed is His Son's blood. God willingly sent His Son to die. He willingly gave

His Son as a sacrifice that shed His blood on behalf of mankind so that the relationship and fellowship that was severed in the Garden of Eden could once again be restored. (Luke 19:10) Even more ... *it pleased the LORD to bruise Him* ... (Isaiah 53:10 NKJV) because the Father saw the *many* souls who would believe in the risen Christ.

Remission

67. *Without the shedding of blood there is no remission* (Hebrews 9:22 NKJV). The only way God could ever consider pardoning man's sin was if a sacrifice and the shedding of blood was made. Jesus became that sacrifice. In His sinless, shed blood, there is *remission* of sin. His blood had to be shed before any remission could be applied (Ephesians 2:13). He accomplished this when His shed blood was poured out on behalf of mankind. The striking fact is that there was no other blood worthy enough to remit sin.

68. Christ's blood was, in itself, of infinite value because it carried His soul, or life. But the remitting virtue of His blood was also infinite, because of the way it was shed. In holy obedience to the Father's will, He subjected Himself to the penalty of the broken law by pouring out His soul unto death ... *My soul is exceedingly sorrowful, even to death....* (Matthew 26:38 NKJV)

69. It is because of the Person whose blood was shed, and because of the sacrificial way in which it was shed, namely fulfilling the law of God and satisfying its just demands, that the blood of Jesus has such vicarious power.

70. In all these explanations, it must never be forgotten that Jesus did not only die in His flesh, He experienced a spiritual death as well ... *Father, into Your hands I commit My Spirit....* He was spiritually separated from God His Father.

71. Even more profound is the fact that Jesus Christ did not have His Spirit taken from Him; He gave it up. This gives a deep insight to the fullest obedience even unto death ... *Not My will but Yours be done*.... At this moment in His life when the time came for the Word to be fulfilled ... *behold the Lamb of God who takes away the sin of the world* ... Jesus gave up His Spirit and became sin for mankind.

72. The purpose was therefore fulfilled that Jesus shed His blood for the redemption of mankind ... "Redeemed by the blood of the Lamb...." It is because of His redeeming sacrifice that man has remission of his sins. (Matthew 26:28)

73. Jesus entered the heavenly Holy of Holies and presented His blood for Himself, and for all who accept, by faith, His sacrifice of His blood for the remission of their sin. His presentation of His blood asks the Father to allow Him and repentant mankind entrance into the presence of the Holy One ... *That where I am, there you* (they) *may be also*.... (John 14:3 NKJV)

74. Just as Christ's precious shed blood was sufficient to justify Him in the Spirit (1 Timothy 3:16), it has the power to release repentant mankind from their sin. His blood has an almighty cleansing power to forgive those who repent of their sin, as well as releasing them from the kingdom of darkness. (1 John 1:7)

75. The word "redeemed" has a depth of meaning. It particularly indicates deliverance from slavery by emancipation or purchase. The redeeming blood causes the remission of sin when a repentant heart confesses Jesus Christ as Lord. The sinner is enslaved under the hostile power of Satan, the curse of the law, and sin. Now it is proclaimed ... *For You were slain and have redeemed us to God by Your blood*.... (Revelation 5:9 NKJV) It is Christ's shed blood which paid sin's debt and destroyed the power of Satan, the curse, and sin. (1 John 3:8)

76. Redemption includes everything God does for a sinner. Redemption begins from the pardon of sin and the removal of

guilt ... (Ephesians 1:14; 4:30), to the full deliverance of the body by resurrection ... (Romans 8:23–24) and has no end ... *having obtained eternal redemption for us....* (Hebrews 9:12 NKJV) In summary, redemption is the process when Christ shed His blood for sin, and remission is the promise God assures a repentant heart.

77. God's purpose and fullest intentions in offering His Son's life as a sacrifice were fully accomplished.

78. The most precious legacy of Christ's sacrifice, His shed precious blood, still resides in the presence of the Father, on the mercy seat in the heavenly Holy of Holies. The victorious power of the shed precious blood in the presence of God will never lose its ability to redeem mankind.

Reconciliation

79. The crowning achievement of the shed precious blood is the *reconciliation* it brings. The result that flowed in that crimson stream from the Son of God has the power to blot out man's sin and remove it as far as the east is from the west. Based upon this premise, God *forgives* the repentant heart.

80. The removal of man's inherent sin takes place when the repentant heart confesses by faith that the Lord Jesus Christ is the Son of God who died for him and was raised from the dead. (Romans 10:9–10) The repentant heart receives by faith the promise that the shed precious blood of Jesus cleanses him from all sin. This purification from the blood of Christ breaks down the barrier that sin built, and the one who repents is immediately reconciled to God.

81. Sin is disobedience, contempt for the authority of God; it seeks to rob God of His honor as God and Lord. Sin is purposed and

determined opposition to a holy God. It not only can, but it must, awaken His wrath.

82. Although the love of God toward man remains unchanged, sin made it impossible for God to allow man to have fellowship with Him. It has compelled Him to one day pour out upon man His wrath and punishment. Yet, in this immense love that is beyond human comprehension, God sent His Son to die so that He could destroy sin's barrier, remove the schism it created, and breach the gap between Him and man. The shed precious blood was the instrument used, and the effect was redemption that resulted in the perfect reconciliation between God and a repentant man.

Forgiveness

83. When a repentant heart approaches the foot of the cross and pours out self, a gushing river of *forgiveness* flows into the heart. This is made possible because of the shed precious blood's power to remove the inherent sin. The disobedience dating back to Adam that permeates every living soul has no ability to stop the forgiveness that stems from God's heart ... *He is faithful and just to forgive us*.... (1 John 1:9)

84. Nothing can stop that flow. No weapon the devil uses as a blockade to prevent God's forgiveness is powerful enough to stop the flow. The slain Lamb of God is raised from the dead, and the ultimate punishment of sin—death—is destroyed as Jesus openly made a show of the devil, triumphing over him and ... *destroyed the works of the devil*.... (1 John 3:8)

85. Christ's shed precious blood removes the sin stain, and all that resides in sin is eradicated, is forgiven, and removed as far as the east is from the west.

Guilt Removed

86. Man is guilty before God. Guilt is debt. The sinner is guilty. God cannot disregard His own demand that sin must be punished; and His glory, which has been dishonored, must be upheld. If the debt is not discharged and the guilt removed, it is impossible for a holy God to allow the sinner to come into His presence.

87. Can the guilt of sin be removed? Can the effect of sin upon God, in awakening His wrath, be removed? Can sin be blotted out before God? The answer is undoubtedly yes. This can be done and the stronghold of sin is shattered, releasing man from its bondage. Sin's guilty plague is removed when the repentant heart receives Jesus as Lord, and he is embraced in the reconciling arms of his heavenly Father.

88. This is what true reconciliation does. It must so remove the guilt of sin, which plagues the human heart, that man can draw near to God in the blessed assurance that there is no longer the least guilt abiding in him to keep him away from God.

89. Holy Love was unwilling to let man go. Notwithstanding all man's sin, God could not give mankind up. He had to be redeemed. Likewise, His holy wrath could not surrender its demands. The law had been despised; God had been dishonored. God's holiness, rights, and demands had to be upheld. The guilt of sin had to be removed, otherwise the sinner could not be delivered. It was Christ's shed blood that removed man's sin, and the guilt with it, resulting in a reconcilable state accepted by God.

90. Blood of a totally different character was necessary for an effective removal of guilt. Righteousness demanded it; Love offered it.

91. Redemption was the purpose, and the Son's shed blood was the instrument God used to achieve redemption. It was completely achieved and redemption in the shed precious blood of Jesus is continuously available to all who repent.

92. In our Lord's work of redemption, reconciliation is the ultimate and supreme result. It is the highest honor and sublime gift that welcomes the repentant heart as he applies the shed blood of Christ in his life. As he crosses the threshold of salvation, the reconciling effect releases him from his guilt, and he stands blameless before almighty God.

93. The divine shed precious blood was poured out; guilt is removed, and reconciliation is complete; and the message comes to everyone ... *be ye reconciled to God*.... (2 Corinthians 5:20)

Cleansing

94. The union that is once again forged through reconciliation in the shed blood begins the effectual work promised by God. The first result that flows directly from His heart into man's spirit is the *cleansing* flow that the power in the shed blood brings (1 John 1:7).

95. Sin's filth resulting from mankind's disobedience to God's holiness has stained his spirit since Eden. The Lord Jesus Christ's shed blood in the *better covenant* bursts the bonds of sin that shackled man's spirit and *cleansed* his heart by the power in the shed blood. Sin is removed, and the cleansing flow blots out the stain and replaces it with love.

Justification

96. The inconceivable result in human terms evolves from the cleansing flow when the repentant heart confesses Jesus Christ as Lord. Man's spirit and soul, freshly cleansed, is given the right to stand before God and the Lord Jesus Christ as *justified*.

97. Even more inconceivable is the fulfillment of the Word that

a repentant heart can ... *be made the righteousness of God in him*.... (2 Corinthians 5:21)

98. The shed precious blood's cleansing flow breaks the bonds of sin, removes the guilt, reconciles God and man, justifies him to stand in the presence of God again, and allows the Holy Christ ... *who became for us ... righteousness ...* to take up residence in man's heart.

99. The obliteration of the devil's hold over man's spirit is forever removed when God forgives man of his sin. The sign on the door of man's heart heralds the message to the devil in a loud and invincible voice ... *justified.*

100. Justification relates to the believer's standing, while sanctification relates to his state. Justification is the judicial side of salvation. Justification is the verdict and the pronouncement of a judge who declares that he has found the accused person innocent of all guilty charges. How could it be possible for God to declare an unrighteous soul to be righteous and yet retain His holiness, character, and integrity? That is the mystery; yet it has been perfectly done, producing infinite and eternal satisfaction.

101. The declaration of justification can be made because the justice of a holy God has been vindicated fully in the absolute righteousness, utter obedience, and sacrifice of His only-begotten and incarnate Son who shed His divine precious blood. (1 Timothy 3:16)

102. God's sentence of His judgment upon sin utterly spent and buried itself in the fullest measure in the slain *Lamb of God ...* (Revelation 5:6), so that divine justification might minister its vindication, release, and approval. Christ's righteousness is imputed fully and effectually to him ... This *righteousness is the gift of God....* (Romans 5:17) The believer is justified by faith in the blood of Christ.

103. Justification originated in grace (Romans 3:24); was procured by the blood of Christ (Romans 5:9); was ratified by the power

of the resurrection (Romans 4:25); and is appropriated by faith (Romans 5:1).

104. Justification is the article (recognition) of a standing or a falling soul. Justification through the blood of Christ is the wide-open golden gate of grace that leads into the bright and magnificent land of divine favor and fellowship. Everything, literally everything, depends upon the precious shed blood of Christ; but none of this can be man's, unless by faith he lays hold personally of its reality and effectiveness.

Righteousness

105. The filthy, separating, and rotten sin that grinds away in a man's heart before he repents is removed and replaced by *righteousness.* The pure, holy, and divine righteousness that … *Christ is made unto us righteousness* … (1 Corinthians 1:30) *that we might become the righteousness of God in Him* … (2 Corinthians 5:21) now resides in the believer.

106. This righteousness is not of man's doing; it is imparted to him through the forgiveness and cleansing flow in the shed precious blood. It is from God. Matthew Henry says, "The righteousness which is of God by faith, ordained and appointed of God … *surely in the LORD I have righteousness and strength* … (Isaiah 45:24 NKJV), the Lord Jesus Christ is the Lord of our righteousness (Philippians 3:9)."

107. The result that righteousness brings is the marvelous reconciliation man once again has with God. Sin is blotted out and righteousness opens the door to God's heart.

108. Matthew Henry gives the ultimate expression of Christ's righteousness when he says, "Had He not been God, He could not have been our righteousness; the transcendent excellence of the divine nature put such a value upon, and such a virtue into, His

sufferings, that they became sufficient to satisfy for the sins of the world, and to bring in a righteousness which will be effectual to all that believe."

Fellowship Reunited

109. It is God's ultimate desire that man fellowship with Him again like it was in the Garden of Eden. That relationship between God and Adam is what God purposed, and Adam severed it. Only God could heal the breach.

110. That *middle wall of separation* (Ephesians 2:14 NKJV) had to come down, and only God could tear it down. God's holiness was violated, and His wrath had to be poured out to punish the perpetrators. The heavenly Father made the offer and perfected the sacrificial offering. His holy Son would be the vessel used to do it. The deepest gash in the Father's heart, and the most painful agony the Father's soul experienced when He sent His Son to die, was deemed by the Father as sufficient to appease His wrath against sinful man.

111. This divine sacrifice resulted in God opening wide His heart's door, inviting man to *enter in* and fellowship with Him. There is now no need for a veil, there is no need for a High Priest to enter on man's behalf. Neither is any further sacrificial offering necessary, nor a pilgrimage to a holy city, and to stand in a temple made by human hands.

112. Once again, that intimate *fellowship* between Adam and God is restored to everyone who confesses Jesus Christ as Lord ... *for through him we both have access by one Spirit to the Father* (Ephesians 2:18)

113. The forgiven, justified, and righteous believer *enters his closet, shuts the door,* and has the privilege of *mounting up with wings like eagles* and *abides under the shadow of the Almighty,* as the

peace not as the world gives floods his soul in the presence of Almighty God. This is so because of the shed precious blood of His Son and Savior, the Lord Jesus Christ ... *Now in Christ Jesus you who were once afar off have been brought near by the blood of Christ....* (Ephesians 2:13 NKJV)

CHAPTER 16

JESUS' SPIRIT AND SOUL DESCENDED INTO THE PLACE OF THE DEAD

1. The divine Creator who fashioned everything by His almighty power, and the holy testimony to His deity while He was on the earth, also spent three days in the abode of the dead.

2. Clarification on the place of a dead man's soul and spirit is necessary before making a doctrinal statement on Christ's descent into it. The Bible speaks of this place as having "compartments" into which the righteous dead, the unrighteous/wicked dead, and the fallen angels went.

3. The Bible has names for the places of the dead. The Hebrew name for the entire abode of the dead is called *Sheol*. The Greek word that encompasses this word in Hebrew is *hades*. Scripture also speaks of the place of the dead as the *abyss* or *the deep* (Romans 10:7).

4. There are various words that the Bible gives for the compartments. *Paradise* or *Abraham's Bosom* was the place of the righteous dead before Jesus was raised from the dead. *Hell*, or *Gehenna* in

the Greek, is the place of the unrighteous/wicked dead. *Tatarus* is the place of the fallen angels (2 Peter 2:4).

5. When Jesus died, He descended into *hades* and went to the compartments, *paradise* and *gehenna*. At the resurrection of Jesus, He brought with Him the righteous dead out from *paradise*. (Matthew 27:52–53)

6. *Paradise* was emptied when Jesus was raised from the dead, and it is now located in the third heaven (2 Corinthians 12:4). From that time, the righteous dead has their soul and spirit immediately taken from them, and they are present with the Lord (2 Corinthians 5:8).

7. Scripture confirms Spirit-filled believers' understanding that Jesus descended into *hades*. The very first message ever preached from a church platform (on the Day of Pentecost; Acts 2:25–31), Apostle Peter quotes from Psalm 16 referencing Christ's descent into *Sheol/hades*. David, the Psalmist, correctly uses the word *Sheol* because Jesus descended into both compartments of the underworld.

8. Apostle Peter makes a resounding statement that Jesus did not stay in *gehenna, hell,* and that the Father had promised Him this victory from the dawn of time ... *Behold the Lamb of God slain from the foundation of the world....* David declares in his Michtam, Psalm 16:10 ... *For You will not leave my soul in Sheol, nor will You allow Your Holy One to see corruption....* (NKJV) The apostle makes it clear that Jesus descended into *gehenna/hell,* and that the Father's promise was fulfilled when Jesus was raised from the dead (Acts 2:31–32).

9. Christ's purpose for descending into *hades* was twofold. He had to go there because He was made sin, and the place of a sin-stained soul and spirit at death is *gehenna* (hell). He also descended there because ... *for this reason the gospel was preached also to those who are dead....* (1 Peter 4:6 NKJV) Jesus appeared to the souls and spirits of the wicked dead and *preached* to them.

French L. Arrington in his book *Christian Doctrine a Pentecostal Perspective,* says, "In the power of the Holy Spirit, Christ went into hades as a victor not as a victim. As a conqueror, He asserted His lordship and authority. Christ was triumphant even in the domain of the dead."

10. The Lord Jesus Christ went to both compartments in *hades.* His purpose for becoming Son of Man and Son of God was totally fulfilled as He ministered to the living and the dead. Apostle Paul states ... *And without controversy great is the mystery of godliness; God was manifest in the flesh, justified in the Spirit....* (1 Timothy 3:16 NKJV) The only way Jesus could be justified in the Spirit was if His Spirit that was made sin was condemned to the place of a sinful spirit, namely *gehenna.*

11. Jesus foreknew that the Father would not leave His soul in *hades.* Hence, He calls from the cross moments before He dies ... *Into Your hands I commit My Spirit....* (Luke 23:46 NKJV) His call to the Father reaches past the protection of His Spirit. It is the reaffirming cry from the Savior to His Father that Jesus did not forget the promise made to Him that His Father would not leave His soul in *gehenna/hell* (Psalm 16:10, Acts 2:31). This cry from the cross was not merely mouthed from the Son of Man, but it was the Son of God calling from His Spirit to His Father regarding the promise made to Him from the foundation of the world.

12. His purpose for going down into the realm of the dead can be summed up as follows: first, He descended into *gehenna/hell* and announced the wrath of God upon the disobedient unbelievers in Noah's time (1 Peter 3:19–20), and He declared to the rest of the unrighteous their state because they rejected the gospel (1 Peter 4:6). He also suffered as a sinner in *gehenna* (1 Peter 3:18). Second, on the dawn of the third day, and the fulfillment of the Father's promise that He would not leave Jesus in *Sheol/hades,* as Christ took hold of the keys of *hades and death* (Revelation

1:18), He began His resurrection journey. This took Him through the upper compartment of hades, namely *paradise*. He visited *paradise* and emptied it, taking with Him the righteous dead from *paradise* and the grave at His resurrection (Matthew 27:52).

CHAPTER 17

THE RESURRECTION OF
JESUS CHRIST

1. The resurrection of Jesus Christ from the dead is the most powerful declaration the church makes. This undeniable event has drawn sinners to repentance, and it has induced eternal hope in the souls of countless millions. Conversely, the declaration that Jesus was raised from the dead has been shunned by countless millions.

2. As glorious as this fact is to every born-again believer, so distasteful is it to the unbeliever. (Acts 17:31–32)

3. Spirit-filled believers are emphatic about the spiritual implications the resurrection brings to their salvation. The overwhelming victory and inestimable avenue of eternal life to everyone who believes can never be fully comprehended when this subject is contemplated.

4. At the outset, the resurrection demonstrates spiritual power that is unconquerable ... *the power of His resurrection....* (Philippians 3:10) This *power* is a fact that was applied to His being raised from the dead, and the reason for it was to introduce salvation's promise of everlasting life.

5. Apostle Paul's undoubting declaration that he believed in *Jesus Christ and Him crucified* encapsulated the totality of the suffering, crucifixion, His being made to be sin for mankind, and the resurrection of Christ from the dead. The gospel he preached is proclaimed when he says ... *Remember that Jesus Christ of the seed of David, was raised from the dead according to my gospel....* (2 Timothy 2:8, NKJV)

6. Millard J. Erickson, in his book *Christian Theology* says, "The death of Jesus was the low point in His humiliation; the overcoming of death through the resurrection was the first step back in the process of His exaltation. The resurrection is particularly significant, for inflicting death was the worst thing that sin, and the powers of sin could do to Christ. Death's inability to hold Him symbolizes the totality of His victory."

7. To begin with, Spirit-filled believers attest to the fact that the same body that was placed in the tomb was resurrected. It was not another body given to Jesus, but a body that had now been glorified when the Holy Spirit entered the tomb and ... *raised Jesus from the dead by the glory of the Father....* (Romans 6:4 NKJV)

8. Following on after this fact, the subject leads to the consideration of what God did when He resurrected Jesus. As with all unexplainable events that relate to God and His miraculous ways, the Godhead is involved every time ... *but God raised Him from the dead....* (Acts 13:30 NKJV) This declares that God the Father, the Son, and the Holy Spirit were all involved in the resurrection. It was the Father's explicit promise to His Son that He would not let Him see corruption (Psalm 16:10), and the Holy Spirit who ... *raised Jesus from the dead....* (Romans 8:11 NKJV)

9. The Godhead reached into the deepest divine spiritual realm to bring back Jesus from the dead. When the Holy Spirit moved upon the dead body of Jesus, He used spiritual *power* to reunite Christ's soul and spirit with His body. Apostle Paul reflects on this event when he states that he "hungers and thirsts" for this

exquisite and glorious power ... *that I may know him and in the power of his resurrection....* (Philippians 3:10)

10. This resurrection power that stemmed from the highest and deepest recesses of the divine Godhead's source was transfused into Jesus' dead body, and the effectual working of that spiritual power birthed life into Jesus. He is therefore the firstborn from the dead (Colossians 1:18), and Jesus Christ was, in essence, "born again."

11. The Holy Writ further declares ... *And what is the exceeding greatness of His power towards us who believe, according to the working of His mighty power which He worked in Christ when He raised Him from the dead and seated Him at His right hand in the heavenly places....* (Ephesians 1:19–20 NKJV)

12. This magnificent power used to resurrect Jesus was the *glorious splendor of Your* (His) *majesty* (Psalm 145:5 NKJV), and the *excellence* of His *greatness* (Psalm 150:2) that are all found in His *Shekinah* glory. The Father was the Authority who authenticated the glory, and the Holy Spirit was the channel that fused the *glory of the Father* into Jesus' body. (Romans 6:4)

13. In human terms, the human mind cannot comprehend the awesomeness of His *Shekinah* glory. It is ... *spiritually discerned....* (1 Corinthinians 2:14) Apostle Paul yearned for this. (Philippians 3:10)

14. The Savior's first task as the glorified risen Son of God was to enter the heavenly Holy of Holies and present His shed precious blood on the mercy seat as the offering for both His and mankind's sin ... *For Christ has not entered the holy places made with hands, which are copies of the true, but into heaven itself, now to appear in the presence of God for us;* (Hebrews 9:24 NKJV)...*for such a High Priest was fitting for us, who is holy, harmless, undefiled, separate from sinners, and has become higher than the heavens; who does not need daily, as those high priests, to offer up sacrifices, first for His own sins*

and then for the people's, for this He did once for all when He offered up Himself.... (Hebrews 7:26–27 NKJV)

15. The triumphant Christ now glorified was the victor over death (spiritual death), and the conqueror of sin's ultimate penalty, namely death. He *destroyed the works of the devil* (1 John 3:8) and the cataclysmic result of Adam's sin in the Garden of Eden, namely the severing of the spiritual relationship with God, was now annulled by the holy Son of God who reunited this spiritual relationship in His resurrection when He spiritually presented His incorruptible blood on the heavenly mercy seat.

16. It is not a boastful voice, nor is it a self-indulging declaration when Jesus says ... *I am He who lives, and was dead, and behold, I am alive forever more. Amen. And I have the keys of hades and death....* (Revelation 1:18 NKJV) It is from the overwhelming love that the Godhead has for mankind that Jesus achieved this glorious victory. His words are the manifestation of the spiritual reconciliation He achieved which was shattered by Adam.

17. This was achieved through His resurrection by the glory of the Father. The most holy and pure attribute of the Godhead, their glory, was the divine power the holy God used to achieve the resurrection. It broke the chains of death that had bound mankind from the time they were expelled from the Garden of Eden until Christ's resurrection from the Garden Tomb ... *Death is swallowed up in victory. O Death, where is your sting? O Hades, where is your victory....* (1 Corinthians 15:54–55 NKJV)

18. Christ's vicarious resurrection did not only conquer death for mankind, it was the fulfillment of His own words ... *I am the resurrection and the life. He who believes in Me, though he may die, he shall live....* (John 11:25 NKJV) All that Jesus achieved is now available to a repentant heart who by faith confesses Jesus Christ as Lord and believes in his heart that God raised Him from the dead (Romans 10:9). This is a continuous victorious walk in Christ, and should a born-again believer sin, they have the ability

to confess their sin to God and receive forgiveness ... *But if we walk in the light as He is in the light, we have fellowship with one another, and the blood of Jesus Christ His Son cleanses us from all sin....* (1 John 1:7 NKJV) *If we confess our sins, He is faithful and just to forgive us our sins and to cleanse us from all unrighteousness....* (1 John 1:9 NKJV)

19. Jesus Christ's resurrection birthed the New Covenant. This holy event closed the Old Covenant and opened the new. It further postponed the arrival of the physical Kingdom of Heaven and birthed the spiritual Kingdom of God. (Acts 1:1–6)

20. The emergence of the Kingdom of God reached further than the Jew and became the gospel that ... *whoever believes in Him should not perish but shall have everlasting life....* (John 3:16 NKJV) It opened the relationship with God the Father to every human being. The exclusiveness of the Jew bound by the Old Covenant was annulled as Jesus exited the tomb.

21. The application of rituals, the obedience to physical duties and sacrifices, and the adherence to celebrations are all outside of the gospel and the Kingdom of God (Galatians 4:8–10). From that time forward, the application of faith in the finished work of Jesus Christ at Calvary was sufficient for man to enter the presence of the Father. Henceforth ... *there is one God and one Mediator between God and men, the Man Christ Jesus....* (1 Timothy 2:5 NKJV)

22. *For the kingdom of God is not eating and drinking, but righteousness and peace and joy in the Holy Spirit.* (Romans 14:17 NKJV) It is the application of faith that swings open the door to the Father's heart and initiates His mercy (2 Corinthians 4:1). Because of faith, God's mercy enables His grace that forgives the repentant sinner (Ephesians 2:8).

23. The Lord Jesus Christ's resurrection extends beyond His own physical rebirth. It sealed the future of everyone who believes in His finished work. At the appointed time of the Day of the Lord,

at the sound of the voice, the trumpet, and the shout, the righteous dead's bodies will be miraculously released from their graves and be reunited with their soul and spirit. Furthermore: almost simultaneously, the righteous ones living on earth at the time of the trumpet will be taken off the earth and will meet Jesus in the clouds. (1 Thessalonians 4:13–18)

24. While this physical resurrection of the bodies is important, it is the spiritual application of the resurrection that is more important. (1 Corinthians 15:50–58)

25. Jesus Christ's resurrection had three spiritual applications. First, He was raised from the dead when His Spirit and soul returned into His body. Second, He ascended into the heavenly Holy of Holies where He presented His blood on the mercy seat. Only once He had done this was the resurrection complete. Without the acceptance of Christ's sacrifice placed on the heavenly mercy seat, the resurrection would have been spiritually to no avail.

26. Third, once Jesus had completed these two tasks, He could now appear to His disciples and those who believed in Him. Herein is the most profound spiritual application of the resurrection: Jesus' resurrection birthed the Kingdom of God for the *whoever*.

27. The rebirth of a human spirit is only effective when it by faith confesses Jesus Christ as Lord and *believes in their heart that God has raised Him from the dead.* (Romans 10:9 NKJV) Without the confession that Jesus was resurrected, there can be no salvation for the human spirit. The only way it can be born again is for it to have faith in the power of the resurrection. This is a spiritual rebirth and an entry into the spiritual Kingdom of God ... *That which is born of the flesh is flesh, and that which is born of the Spirit is spirit.* (John 3:6 NKJV)

28. Jesus foretold to Nicodemus that the resurrection would be complete once Jesus had presented His shed blood on the mercy seat ... *No one has ascended to heaven but He who came down from heaven, that is, the Son of Man who is in heaven....* (John 3:13 NKJV)

29. The Savior, Jesus Christ, not only fulfilled every requirement of the salvation plan; His resurrection also spiritually accomplished, as the antetype, the final Passover act. On the third day of the Passover celebration, God's people were instructed to bring the "firstfruits" of their harvest and present them in the temple.

30. Apostle Paul gives a convincing explanation concerning Christ's resurrection and the fact that it unequivocally happened in 1 Corinthians 15:12–19.

31. He then continues his discourse and gives the spiritual explanation of Jesus' ultimate purpose for rising from the dead; that He is the *firstfruits of them that slept* (1 Corinthians 15:20). On the third day, the day the people presented their "firstfruits" in the temple, Jesus was the "first" to be raised from the dead. He declares that Christ's resurrection is the first One to be resurrected, and thereafter *those who are Christ's at His coming* (verse 23).

32. In as much as the people returned to their homes and harvested their fields, so Jesus ascended into heaven and will reap a "harvest" of righteous souls worthy to be presented to the Father.

33. Christ's resurrection extends beyond the present and incorporates the entire future events that follow. He is the resurrected One who rules with all power and authority in the Millennium Reign for one thousand years. His judgment at the Great White Throne is the final pronouncement of the penalty upon those who rejected His death and resurrection. It is the holy spiritual presence in the new earth and the New Jerusalem, and once this is accomplished *... Then comes the end, when He delivers the kingdom to God the Father, when He puts an end to all rule and all authority and power. For He must reign till He has put all enemies under His feet. The last enemy that will be destroyed is death. For "He has put all things under His feet." But when He says "all things are put under Him," it is evident that He who put all things under Him is excepted. Now when all things are made subject to Him, then*

the Son Himself will be subject to Him who put all things under Him, that God may be all in all. (1 Corinthians 15:24–28 NKJV)

34. Therein is the full circle complete. What Adam's disobedience inflicted upon the entire human race, so Christ's obedience unto death and His resurrection reconciled humanity to God ... *For as in Adam all die, even so in Christ shall all be made alive....* (1 Corinthians 15:22)

CHAPTER 18

JESUS CHRIST'S ASCENSION
AND PRESENT WORK

1. *To whom He also presented Himself alive after His suffering by many infallible proofs, being seen by them during forty days....* (Acts 1:3 NKJV) Jesus appeared to His disciples and followers over a period of forty days. During this time, He was ... *speaking of the things pertaining to the kingdom of God....*

2. How precious is the thought that the Savior was present amongst the first group of believers who were born again and now in the Kingdom of God. Furthermore, how significant it is that He was physically present during the first forty days of the new covenant in the Kingdom of God. Amongst other teachings, His primary purpose was to lay the foundation of the spiritual Kingdom of God and prepare the born-again believers for the spiritual power that was to be imparted to them (Acts 1:8).

3. Christ's divine presence amongst the believers who not only recognized Him as the risen Christ, but also witnessed that He was the same Jesus whom they knew before His death. This testimony from those believers who saw Him in the flesh is for the believers in this present day sufficient for them to accept by faith

their witness that Christ is alive. Furthermore, it is the witness of the Holy Spirit in man's spirit that Christ is alive.

4. The ascension of Jesus Christ that followed after *many infallible proofs* that He was alive was not only witnessed by His followers but they were also given the promise by heavenly beings that ... *this same Jesus, which is taken up from you into heaven, shall so come in like manner as ye have seen him go into heaven....* (Acts 1:11) The angels' message sealed the hope in the followers' hearts that they were about to start their journey of faith in Christ's finished work, and also that He would return again. The beginning and ending of the Kingdom of God encompasses Jesus Christ, the Savior of the world.

5. French L. Arrington says, "The ascension is the third stage in the exaltation of Christ. He was not only exalted by being raised from the dead, but He also ascended into heaven."

6. The divine and holy Savior, the Lord Jesus Christ, stepped down from the throne room of heaven and humbled Himself, making ... *Himself of no reputation, taking on the form of a bondservant, and coming in the likeness of men. And being found in appearance as a man, He humbled Himself and became obedient to the point of death, even the death of the cross....* (Philippians 2:7–8 NKJV)

7. Into the presence of sinful man, He came, carrying the love of God to everyone who encountered Him. His heavenly throne room was vacated for a period as He endured the humiliation of a false trial that was laced with lies and unprecedented hatred. He suffered at the hands of the Roman procurator and was hoisted against a tree as they crucified Him amongst thieves. While hanging on the cross, He was bombarded by every demon force and sickness that saturated His being. He ultimately felt the heavy load of sin being thrust upon Him as He said, *It is finished.*

8. No one could have been more humiliated. No one could have been more cast down to the lowest level of humanity than Jesus Christ,

who left the highest seat of power, laid aside His full authority, and was catapulted into hell to be a ransom for many.

9. Clinging to the promise of His Father, Jesus waited three days in hell to be resurrected. Thereafter He spent forty days with His beloved followers, teaching them the things pertaining to the Kingdom of God. How patiently He waited for the moment when His allotted time on earth would end. From the Mount of Olives, He was taken up in the cloud of God's *Shekinah* glory.

10. It is without any biblical explanation as to what actually happened as Jesus set foot in heaven. What is told reveals the Father's magnificent exaltation of His only begotten Son ... *God also hath highly exalted him, and given him a name which is above every name....* (Philippians 2:9) Suffice to say that it can be assumed that the angelic host welcomed Him with similar accolades they expressed when He arrived in the manger in Bethlehem.

11. As Jesus Christ returns to the Father's side, He is elevated and honored to occupy the highest seat of authority as the Father proclaims ... *Sit on my right hand, until I make thine enemies thy footstool....* (Hebrews 1:13)

12. Christ's exaltation transcends human comprehension, and can only be spiritually discerned as the Father proclaims ... *Your throne, O God, is forever* and *ever: a scepter of righteousness is the scepter of Your kingdom. You have loved righteousness and hated lawlessness; therefore, God, Your God, has anointed You with the oil of gladness more than Your companions.* (Hebrews 1:8–9 NKJV)

13. It is a breathtaking accolade the Father makes as He annunciates the preexistence, the present existence, and the future existence of His Son, Jesus Christ ... *You, LORD, in the beginning laid the foundation of the earth, and the heavens are the work of Your hands. They will perish, but You remain; and they will all grow old like a garment; like a cloak You will fold them up, and they will be changed. But You are the same, and Your years will not fail.* (Hebrews 1:10–12 NKJV)

14. The exaltation of Jesus is the proclamation of the Father's will fully accomplished. It is from this place that the Eternal Son is forthwith *the Apostle and High Priest of our profession....* (Hebrews 3:1) Spirit-filled believers spiritually praise and worship Jesus in the spirit as the Holy Spirit gives them utterance. They acknowledge the offices of Apostle and High Priest Jesus now fulfills. As Apostle, Jesus imparts the Father's will to Spirit-filled believers; as High Priest, Jesus makes intercession for the saints to the Father.

15. Furthermore, the Lord Jesus Christ baptizes the born-again believer in the baptism with the Holy Spirit (Luke 3:16). Henceforth, the Holy Spirit dwells in the believer's body (1 Corinthians 6:19). This indwelling power flows like a river from the mountain peak of Christ's heart, and is directed by the Holy Spirit into the very existence of a born-again believer. It is then that ... *out of his belly shall flow rivers of living water....* (John 7:38)

16. From the moment Jesus *sat down on the right hand of God* (Hebrews 10:12), and *even now* and until the church is raptured off the earth, He occupies the most exquisite place and highest seat of honor and exaltation from the Most High God. Spirit-filled believers are drenched in the anointing of the Holy Spirit and join the heavenly host's chorus as they release their faith and *mount up on wings as eagles* with praise and worship, exalting their Savior, the Christ, the Resurrected and Ascended Son of the living God.

Christ's Present Work

17. *I will build my church....* (Matthew 16:18) Immediately once Jesus occupied His seat of authority, He began to fulfill His word that He would build *His* church. The Kingdom of God was already established, and from the born-again believers who are subjects to the King of the Kingdom, He baptizes them with the Holy Spirit.

This baptism is the spiritual empowerment and is also the transfer of those who are baptized with the Holy Spirit into the body of Christ, which is His church. (1 Corinthians 12:13)

18. Spirit-filled believers are convinced that the finished work of Christ includes the Father's exaltation of Him and the continuous intercession of Christ who has all authority to do this ... *All authority has been given to Me in heaven and on earth....* (Matthew 28:18 NKJV) The exalted Christ who is seated at the right hand of almighty God holds the scepter of righteousness and from that highest seat, He makes intercession for the believers.

19. He is no longer on earth separating Himself from His disciples ... *and went out into a mountain to pray, and continued all night in prayer to God....* (Luke 6:12, also Mark 1:35) He is now in heaven, no longer on earth, continuously in prayer making intercession for the saints. (Romans 8:34, Hebrews 7:25)

20. The Lord Jesus Christ's state and office in heaven is the full expression of His entire ministry that includes Prophet, Priest, and King. This is the fulfillment of the Old Testament fully achieving their perfection in Him.

21. Jesus gave believers clear instructions on how to enter the presence of the Father. Now in heaven, the Savior occupies a supreme position of *Mediator.* Apostle Paul refers to Jesus' position for mankind regarding their access to the Father in heaven ... *For there is one God, and one mediator between God and men, the man Christ Jesus....* (1 Timothy 2:5)

22. Jesus taught the disciples on the manner in which they must approach the Father when praying ... *I am the way, the truth, and the life: no man cometh unto the Father, but by me....* (John 14:6) On three occasions in John's Gospel, Jesus tells the disciples ... *Whatsoever ye shall ask the Father in my name, he will give it you....* (John 15:16, 16:23)

23. Spirit-filled believers enter the presence of the Father by reverently approaching Him in the name of Jesus. "Father, in the name of

Jesus we come to you...." It is this opening statement that they acknowledge the Father who exalted His Son to His right hand. Furthermore, believers know the only way they can enter the Father's holy presence is in the name of His Son, Jesus. Upon the mention of His name, Jesus, believers can now begin to make ... *supplications, prayers, intercessions, and giving of thanks....* (1 Timothy 2:1)

24. Spirit-filled believers see the deep spiritual achievements of Christ's High Priestly office. His constant intercession for the church is done with the desire that the members of His body are endowed with the spiritual abilities to accomplish the work the Father has for them.

25. As High Priest, Jesus has secured every need of the believer through His death and resurrection. Every earthly, temporal blessing and eternal spiritual blessing is achieved through His redemptive work. Christ can intercede in a manner that no human can comprehend. His mediatorial role is with such depth that the whispering between the Son and the Father on behalf of the saints and the church is uninterrupted communication.

26. The Son seeks the Father's attention to every need the believer has. It is such a close relationship they have that the Son continually lays the petitions before the Father. The believer makes their requests known unto God in *the name of Jesus.* The Son as High Priest has direct access to the Father.

27. Spirit-filled believers know and are assured that when they enter the closet and call upon the name of the Lord, they are entering a Spirit-to-spirit communication and relationship with the Father. Their prayer is therefore not a demand for an earthly, physical need. It is not a request to the Father to perform the impossible to bring about benefit to the one praying. The Spirit-filled believer knows that when approaching the Father in the name of Jesus, they are doing so to enter the deepest spiritual relationship with the Father.

28. They understand that the *High Priest of their confession* is aware

of their petition, need, supplication, or intercession. What the believer is asking the Father for is His spiritual direction and enforcement of the petition ... *Your will be done....*

29. Jesus, as High Priest, perfected the office. He fulfills all the duties ascribed to the office in the Old Testament. Peter C. Craigie, in his commentary on the "priesthood" in *Baker, Encyclopedia of the Bible,* says, "But his position (the High Priest) was more weighty than that of an administrator; just as all priests were servants and guardians of the covenant relationship, the High Priest was 'chief' servant and 'chief' guardian. In his hands rested spiritual responsibility for the entire people of God, and therein lay the true honor and gravity of His position." He continues, "The High Priest entered the Holy of Holies, and standing before the 'mercy seat,' he sought God's forgiveness and mercy for the whole nation of Israel (Leviticus 16:1–9). The High Priest had the great honor and heavy burden of seeking God's mercy for all Israel."

30. So, too, the Savior of the world, the Lord Jesus Christ, is now in the presence of the Father as the saints' High Priest. The exalted Christ, who is the *Head of the church* ... (Ephesians 1:22–23, Colossians 1:18) is ultimately the 'administrator' of the covenant as was the High Priest in the Old Testament. Christ is the presiding authority over everything that takes place in the church ... *And hath put all things under his feet, and gave him to be the head over all things to the church....* (Ephesians 1:22) No human being, no matter how spiritual they may appear to be, can ever instruct the Lord Jesus Christ what to do in and for the church. It is His prerogative, and He said ... *I will build my church; and the gates of hell shall not prevail against it....* (Matthew 16:18) Henceforth, Jesus is Lord of the church and King of the Kingdom of God.

31. One of the worst calamities that has infiltrated the church is the interference of human hands in the divine sculpturing of the church.

32. As was the office of a High Priest in the Old Covenant, Jesus is now fulfilling the 'guardianship' role of the High Priest by ever

making intercession for the saints. He is the Supreme Protector of the New Covenant relationship. He orchestrates this by instructing the Holy Spirit to reveal, guide, and teach believers all truth. (John 16:5–15)

33. In the Lord Jesus Christ's position as Savior, He holds and represents the 'spiritual responsibility' of the New Covenant for the *whosoever*. He secured this when He entered the heavenly Holy of Holies; He placed His blood on the mercy seat, and He gained the Father's acceptance of His sacrifice as sufficient for redemption of man's inherent sin.

34. *Now unto the King eternal, immortal, invisible, the only wise God, be honor and glory for ever and ever. Amen....* (1 Timothy 1:17) Even from the kingship Christ held while in heaven, royalty and kingship were likewise bestowed upon Him at birth. He answered in the affirmative to Pilate that He was the King of the Jews. He still is, and will forevermore, reign as King.

35. As One who has all authority granted to Him, He exercises power in upholding and being in control of all things in the world. Furthermore, He rules as King of the Kingdom of God into which born-again believers enter as subjects when they accept by faith His finished work on Calvary. This sovereign rule as King of the Kingdom of God is immersed in His spiritual vesture of *righteousness, and peace, and joy in the Holy Ghost....* (Romans 14:17)

36. It is in His full authority and power that Jesus allows Satan his time on earth. Christ tolerates the works of the devil. To everyone God gives freewill and, while as King, Jesus understands that not everyone will accept Him as Savior; He suffers the decision of the *many.*

37. While it is fitting to consider the work Christ the King is doing, it is as important to consider the lofty throne from which He rules. First, it is an eternal throne ... *Now to the King eternal....* Second, it is a throne from which unlimited power flows.

38. Such is the office of King the Savior now occupies. Filled with spiritual opulence and glory, Christ rules in this office according to His word. Yet that which awaits Him is even more marvelous.

39. The fulfillment of these three offices of Prophet, High Priest, and King is eclipsed by the role Jesus embraces as Lord of His church. In the organism of His body, the church, Christ as Lord and Savior gathers them as *members in particular.* (1 Corinthians 12:27) No longer are those who are baptized with the Holy Spirit subjects of the King; they are now members of His body.

40. This is the One who lovingly encourages believers ... *whatsoever ye shall ask the Father in my name, he will give it you....* (John 16:23)

Summary

41. The holy, divine Jesus Christ ... *made Himself of no reputation, taking the form of a bond servant and coming in the likeness of men. And being found in the appearance as a man, He humbled Himself and became obedient to the point of death, even the death of the cross. Therefore God has highly exalted Him and given Him the name which is above every name, that at the name of Jesus every knee should bow, of those in heaven, and of those on earth, and of those under the earth, and that every tongue should confess Jesus Christ is Lord, to the glory of God the Father....* (Philippians 2:7–11 NKJV)

42. His work on earth laid the foundation for the saved when He offered Himself as the sacrifice for mankind's sin. His continuing work as the exalted Christ now in heaven solidifies His continuing presence; *I am with you always, even to the end of the age....* (Matthew 28:20 NKJV)

43. The Lord Jesus Christ's ascension invoked the Father's highest honor, elevating Him *to be the head over all things to the*

church, which is his body, the fullness of him that filleth all in all .... (Ephesians 1:22–23) This appointment of the Son of God incorporated His roles as Apostle and High Priest. (Hebrews 3:1) He gave gifts unto men ... *some, apostles; and some, prophets; and some, evangelists; and some, pastors and teachers* ... (Ephesians 4:11) for the fulfillment of His mission to *build* His *church* (Matthew 16:18)

44. Furthermore, Jesus is now the intercessor who ... *ever liveth to make intercession for them* (Hebrews 7:25). He is ever mindful of the believer's plight as they *earnestly contend for the faith which was once delivered unto the saints* (Jude 3). Even though the believer stumbles during his pilgrimage, the Lord Jesus appeals to the Father's mercy as He fulfills His role as Advocate on behalf of the believer. (1 John 2:1) Confession and repentance in a believer's heart is secured and his sins are forgiven him because of the Advocate, Jesus, presenting the sincerity of the repentant heart to the Father.

PART 4

The Doctrine of the Holy Spirit

CHAPTER 19

THE DOCTRINE OF THE HOLY SPIRIT

1. Spirit-filled believers are ever seeking for more of God. They are aware that all they are taught, revealed, and led to believe are from the Holy Spirit. There can be no other source of teaching than from the Holy Spirit. He is the only teacher, instructor, and guide believers need when seeking a deeper walk with God.

2. French L. Arrington launches his chapter on the Holy Spirit with these words, "The Holy Spirit in the One who applies the saving benefit of the cross to us. However, in the scriptures the work of the Holy Spirit is seen as manifold. Creation and new creation, the resurrection of the dead, eternal life, the Kingdom, and the final consummation of history are all the works of the Spirit. The story of Jesus Christ is an account of the works of the Holy Spirit. Christ's incarnation, mission, anointing, ministry, death, and resurrection were by the Holy Spirit ... *For the law of the Spirit of life in Christ Jesus hath made me free from the law of sin and death...."* (Romans 8:2)

3. Spirit-filled believers have an acute awareness that the Holy Spirit is not merely an agent of the Godhead: He is God Himself. It is

God, the Holy Spirit, that is active in their lives, and the operation of all they do is God-invested and God-infested. He is not a whimsical fantasy that is only occasionally apparent. The Holy Spirit is omniscient, omnipresent, and omnipotent. He is there all the time, always present to guide, always fully operational in all His power, and all-knowing in every circumstance.

4. While the Holy Spirit is doing the bidding of Jesus Christ, He is not a representative chosen by Jesus, but is in fact an equal part of the Godhead fulfilling the operational procedures of the Godhead through believers. The combined unity of the Three-in-One is never more evident than when the Holy Spirit manifests Himself in the relationship with the Father and the Son by fulfilling their promises.

5. The biblical reference to the Holy Spirit's involvement in all that the Godhead does is inaugurated when in the very first two verses of the Holy Writ it states ... *The Spirit of God was hovering over the face of the waters....* (Genesis 1:2 NKJV)

6. No subject is more difficult to summarize than the Godhead. More so the evidence, existence, and work of the Holy Spirit. At best, it can be said of the Holy Spirit: He created the world mankind inhabits (Psalm 33:6), He is the creator of man (Job 33:4, Psalm 104:30), He adorned the heavens (Job 26:13), and He is the One who takes the eternal spirit from man (Isaiah 40:6–8). None of these statements can be reasoned in man's puny mind. They are spiritually discerned. Richard D. Paterson in his commentary on Job says: "Mankind catches a glimpse and a whisper of God's workings. Full knowledge is beyond human understanding." (Job 5:9, 11:7–8, 42:1–3)

7. As an opening salvo on this vast subject of the doctrine of the Holy Spirit, here is a quote from the pages of Prof. Charles Erdman's book, *The Holy Spirit and Christian Experience:* "The (Holy) Spirit cannot be (active) where Christ is denied as Redeemer, Life, and Lord of all. Christ is 'The Truth' and the Spirit is 'The Spirit of

Truth'; all is personal, not abstract, ideal, and the sum and substance of material wherewith the (Holy) Spirit works in Christ....

8. "In brief, the (Holy) Spirit must be silent altogether in pulpits and churches where 'a different gospel which is not another gospel' is preached, and where unrebuked and unchecked prevail, although in a form of Godliness, 'the lust of the flesh, and the lust of the eyes, and the pride of life' and the things which are 'not of the Father, but ... of the world'; things which are not of the new nature and spirit in which the Holy Spirit dwells and through which alone He can work and testify....

9. "We should be warned by the history of the apostolic churches, once so full of the (Holy) Spirit, but which perished from their places long ago. The same denial of Christ, the same worldliness is our danger today...."

10. In order that the operational procedures of the Holy Spirit be clearly understood, there needs to be an explanation of His working with believers and Spirit-filled believers. The ever-presence of the Holy Spirit is constantly upon born-again believers while the Holy Spirit is constantly residing within the Spirit-filled believer's body. (1 Corinthians 6:19)

11. When the Holy Spirit takes up residence in a believer's body (at the baptism with the Holy Spirit), the believer becomes the conduit the Holy Spirit uses to bring about the works He is instructed to do by Jesus Christ. (John 16:7–15) Spirit-filled believers don't anticipate the Holy Spirit coming upon them; they live by the Holy Spirit that is within them.

12. The Holy Spirit is constantly at work with the born-again believer, revealing to him the necessity of a spiritual relationship with the Godhead, namely spirit to Spirit. In the Spirit-filled believer's life, the Holy Spirit leads their spirit to accompany Him into the holy spiritual presence of the Godhead and reveals and guides the Spirit-filled believer into all Truth what things pertain to the effective working of the church. (Ephesians 2:18–23, 3:1–21)

The Purpose of the Holy Spirit

13. Scripture is clear, and the eternal words of Jesus Christ personally proclaim the Holy Spirit's purpose in the world after Jesus ascended to heaven ... *Nevertheless I tell you the truth. It is to your advantage that I go away; for if I do not go away, the Helper will not come to you; but if I depart, I will send Him to you. And when He has come, He will convict the world of sin, and of righteousness, and of judgment: of sin because they do not believe in Me; of righteousness, because I go to My Father and you see Me no more; of judgment, because the ruler of this world is judged. I still have many things to say to you, but you cannot bear them now. However, when He, the Spirit of truth has come, He will guide you into all truth; for He will not speak on His own authority, but whatever He hears He will speak; and He will tell you things to come. He will glorify Me, for He will take of what is Mine and declare it to you. All things that the Father has are Mine. Therefore I said that He will take of Mine and declare it to you....* (John 16:7–15 NKJV)

14. Such a manifold task and application of these huge responsibilities Jesus speaks of can only be entrusted into the hands of the Holy Spirit who is the only One capable of accomplishing and fulfilling this enormous task.

15. Furthermore, it is only God the Holy Spirit who has the spiritual ability to achieve the Godhead's desired results. Ultimately, the desired result of the Godhead is the continuous revelation of the existence of God in the midst of mankind. God's eternal purpose is manifested through the Holy Spirit in every age and dispensation.

16. What Jesus Christ accomplished as Son of God and Son of Man is now continued through the Holy Spirit who testifies of Christ's glorious victory over death, and of the eternal presence of God to everyone who believes in Him ... *But when the Helper comes, whom I shall send to you from the Father, the Spirit of*

truth who proceeds from the Father, He will testify of Me.... (John 15:26 NKJV)

17. Dr. Norman Geisler, in his book *Systematic Theology Volume Two*, says, "The Father is the Planner, the Son is the Accomplisher, and the Holy Spirit is the Applier of salvation to believers. The Father is the Source, the Son is the Means, and the Holy Spirit is the Effector of salvation—it is He who convicts, convinces, and converts."

18. The Holy Spirit is fully capable and can achieve all that is required of Him because He is God, equal in power, attributes, and glory with the Father and the Son.

19. Spirit-filled believers stand fast on the foundation of the Word that declares what the Holy Spirit's purpose is in the church age. The Holy Spirit is the *power* source that empowers believers to walk victoriously. He is the Supplier of their ability to witness to a lost and dying world ... *But ye shall receive power, after that the Holy Ghost is come upon you: and ye shall be witnesses unto me both in Jerusalem, and in all Judea, and in Samaria, and unto the uttermost part of the earth....* (Acts 1:8)

20. In addition to the Holy Spirit being the power source for the Spirit-filled believer, He is the Member of the Godhead who reveals their purposes from God's throne in heaven to this church age on earth. (1 Corinthians 2:10) Revealed truth is not a natural conviction; it is the total acceptance of God's uttered purpose into man's spirit. (1 Corinthians 2:11–13)

21. Apostle Paul emphatically states that human comprehension cannot receive the things of God because they are revealed truths that can only be spiritually discerned ... *But the natural man receiveth not the things of the Spirit of God: for they are foolishness unto him: neither can he know them, because they are spiritually discerned....* (1 Corinthians 2:14)

22. The Holy Spirit's purposes are spiritually numerous and untethered; He is the "plumb line" that exposes unrighteousness

from righteousness; He is the "lighthouse" that beams the path of truth and life to all who seek it. He directs the believer towards Jesus Christ and what He accomplished for mankind. He is the omnipresent reminder of the omniscient presence of the Holy God amid a perverse society. He is, in fact, the Person of the Godhead who ... *shall never leave thee nor forsake thee....*

The Works of the Holy Spirit

23. At the outset, the Holy Spirit's works, instructions, and duties do not come from man; they are conceived and agreed upon by the Godhead for man. It is important to know the works of the Holy Spirit in the Old Testament. However, for the church age it is vital to know His current workings.

24. In the Old Testament, amongst God's people the Jews, He directed them to the demands of the Law. He revealed the people's condition through the mouth of prophets and in the written word.

25. The Old Testament prophet, Isaiah, and the gospel of Luke, record the foretelling of the One who was sent by the Father, and was in the midst of His people to do the works of the Father: *The Spirit of the Lord is upon Me, because He has anointed Me to preach the gospel to the poor; He has sent Me to heal the broken hearted, to proclaim liberty to the captives and recovery of sight to the blind. To set at liberty those who are oppressed; to proclaim the acceptable year of the Lord....* (Luke 4:18–19 NKJV) Jesus did all these marvelous works while He was on earth.

26. The Lord Jesus enlightens the disciples that there will be One after Him who will *guide them into all truth.* All that Jesus did was local, while that of the Holy Spirit's work is universal. Jesus' personal ministry was appropriated physically through word and voice to man and their senses, while the Holy Spirit's ministry is Spirit to spirit, reaching man's heart and will. Added to this

miraculous works of revealing the state of man's inherent sin, the Holy Spirit also continues the work of Jesus Christ through believers who are still today saved, healed, delivered, and liberated from oppression.

27. A commentator in the *Pulpit Commentary on John* says, "While He (Jesus Christ) remained with His disciples, they tenaciously clung to the idea of a temporal king and a temporal kingdom, and this idea would last as long as His personal presence; but His departure by death had a direct tendency to destroy this notion and blast this hope for ever, and prepare them for the advent of the Holy Spirit, who would, on the ruins of the temporal kingdom, establish a spiritual one, a *kingdom of God within.*

28. "The personal ministry of Jesus was essentially temporary; that of the Spirit is permanent. Jesus came only for a time, and under human conditions was subject to persecutions and death... but the Spirit came to remain with and in His people forever and was personally above any physical injury from the wicked world."

29. How magnificent is His work amplified in the age of grace (the church age)! Now He, the Member of the Godhead, proclaims Christ's finished work on Calvary to the entire world. From Jesus Christ's ascension, the Holy Spirit has been *sent* to proclaim the message of salvation.

30. It is appropriate to study this holy subject in three parts: the Holy Spirit's work in the world, the Holy Spirit's work in the believer's life, and the Holy Spirit's work in the church.

31. To expound on the words of Jesus regarding the work of the Holy Spirit, it is important to fully comprehend who it is that is referred to as the *Comforter/Helper* in John 16:7. Herein is the guidepost that illuminates the work of the Holy Spirit more clearly. The Greek word for *Comforter/Helper* is "parakletos." A more definite translation that expresses the effective working Jesus mentions the Holy Spirit will do is *advocate.*

32. W.A.C Rowe says, "His first move in this direction is towards the world. He must begin here in order that they may be saved. In John 16:8 we see that *He will convict the world of sin, and of righteousness, and of judgement.* These are warning notes. They are decisive and sharp. This 'pointedness' was evident in the experience of Saul of Tarsus: *It is hard for thee to kick against the pricks.* (Acts 9:5) This is the Bible doctrine of conviction."

33. The work of the Holy Spirit in *the world* is His revealing to man of their state of sin and the consequences thereof. His work is a continuing work of the Lord Jesus Christ who came into *the world.*

34. It is into this same *world* that the Holy Spirit continues to expose man's sinful state. Jesus ... *was in the world, and the world was made by him, and the world knew him not....* (John 1:10) This is nothing less than "unbelief" in Jesus Christ because they did not "know/love" Him. Arthur Pink says, "Unbelief is far more than an error of judgment, or nonconsent of the mind, it is aversion of heart (1 Corinthians 2:8)."

35. The tragic words of Jesus to His disciples echoes throughout the world like a never-ending ringing in their ears ... *of sin, because they believe not in me....* (John 16:9) Unbelief is the seed that germinates into evil.

36. The presentation of the love of God to a lost and dying soul can only be presented by the Holy Spirit. Salvation deals with eternal life, and the Author of this eternal life is God. Hence, the Holy Spirit's work in the sinner's life is divine in its origin and holy in its presentation. This is the Holy God (Holy Spirit) dealing with the eternal destiny of a human spirit.

37. He will of necessity present Christ's finished work of salvation with a sharp "piercing" effect that exposes the state of the sinner's evil nature who has a *hardness of heart* (Romans 2:5). This sharp pointedness reveals to the sinner how far they have strayed from the truth. Every time they reject the Holy Spirit's call to repentance, they, in essence, *kick against* the *sharp two-edged sword.*

38. The variance in presentation of God's eternal love for man by the Holy Spirit is also marked by the discernment within a man's heart and soul when they hunger for salvation. The Holy Spirit does at times reach into the human spirit by gently exposing the divine love God has for him. This love reveals the purpose of God's sacrifice of His Son as He convicts the lost. The Holy Spirit's gentle wooing will *whose heart the Lord opened, that she attended unto the things which were spoken....* (Acts 16:14)

39. In every method the same message is presented, and the same conviction of sin is evidenced. This is the purpose of the Holy Spirit's work in the world: to convict the sinner. Rowe continues, "Warning or wooing, the purpose is the same; to snatch brands from the burning. He convicts, convinces, and constrains."

40. Spirit-filled believers are aware that the "convicting," "reproving" of the Holy Spirit of a sinner's spiritual condition and state is absolutely conclusive. When the Holy Spirit declares the truth, the sinner has no argument, reason, or justification that can acquit them from the *wages of sin.* (Romans 6:23)

41. The Holy Spirit, having convicted the sinner of his state, will *reprove* the sinner of righteousness which the Lord Jesus Christ fulfilled to perfection in His life and His death. Christ ... *became for us ... righteousness....* (1 Corinthinas 1:30) Christ's righteousness is not done only for Himself (1 John 2:1), but for all mankind who believes in Him. (2 Corinthians 5:21)

42. With the presentation that Jesus Christ is the Righteous One, the Holy Spirit then exposes the only remedy for the sinner's unrighteousness—the righteous Lord Jesus Christ. His work in the life of the sinner reveals the necessity of repentance of sin and the confession by faith in a risen Savior who is all righteousness and has achieved the victory over death and the grave, thus opening the way to forgiveness.

43. Arthur Pink continues, "It is the Spirit's presence on earth which establishes Christ's righteousness, and the evidence is that He has

gone to the Father.... The fact that the Father did exalt Him to His own right hand demonstrates that He was completely innocent of the charges laid against Him.... The world was unrighteous in casting Him out; the Father righteous in glorifying Him, and this is what the Spirit's presence here established."

44. This striking contrast between righteousness and unrighteousness revealed by the Holy Spirit to the sinner is the convincing element that enlightens the sinner's heart to realize their guilty state. They discern that the work of Jesus Christ's death and resurrection proved Christ's righteousness which elevated Him to the right hand of the Father, and is, by contrast, unavailable to them in their unrighteous, guilty state.

45. *Of judgment, because the prince of this world is judged....* (John 16:11) Let it be declared as vociferous as possible: *Christ has destroyed the works of the devil. He has conquered death and the grave.* The gavel has fallen on the judgment of Satan, he is judged and found guilty, hence his judgment is over ... *the ruler of this world is judged....*

46. What is now important for mankind is that the Holy Spirit produces evidence in the heart of those who do not love Christ, and the consequences of their refusal to love Him. The world is guilty for refusing to believe on Jesus Christ and His finished work at Calvary. They are condemned through the evidence of Christ's righteous exaltation to the right hand of the Father. Now judgment can be the only concluding action ... *He who believes in the Son has everlasting life, and he who does not believe the Son shall not see life; but the wrath of God abides on him....* (John 3:36 NKJV)

47. There is no refuting argument or defense that can be presented which will allow the unrepentant heart to escape God's judgment. Sin's conceiver, Satan, the devil, is judged, and sentence is passed on him. So, too, does the Holy Spirit reveal to the *world* the judgment that awaits them if they refuse to accept the Savior of the world.

CHAPTER 20

THE DOCTRINE OF THE
HOLY SPIRIT – CONTINUED

1. *He shall glorify me: for he shall receive of mine, and shew it unto you*.... (John 16:14) Perhaps the most precious work the Holy Spirit does from the moment Jesus ascended into heaven is the *glorification* and exaltation of the Lord Jesus Christ.

2. Herein is the Godhead once again fully operational. The Father *has highly exalted Him (Jesus)* and given Him a name which *is above every other name;* Jesus has completed the work of salvation on earth, and into this *world* the Holy Spirit exuberantly glorifies Jesus Christ as Lord and Savior.

3. The magnificence of the Holy Spirit's work has always been the same towards the exposition of Jesus. His miraculous work with Jesus begins at His conception; He anoints the Son of God to *preach the gospel*.... He raises Him from the dead by the glory of the Father, and now He invokes the glory as He *glorifies Me* on earth.

4. The spiritual work and mighty accomplishments the church did in the first century were so impactful that thousands of new converts turned from their wicked ways and walked in spiritual newness of

life. In all their affairs, the early believers were *led of the Spirit....* They had no claim to any of their achievements: it was wrought through the indwelling power of the Holy Spirit.

5. These men *preached Jesus Christ and Him crucified,* they were anointed by the Holy Spirit to speak boldly to kings, the rich, and the poor. They manifested the indwelling presence of the Holy Spirit by willingly sharing all they had with each other as the fruit of the Spirit flowed like a river in their lives.

6. How tragic that as the centuries passed on, the church meandered from its roots of spiritual exaltation of Jesus Christ to an institution of profit and personal glorification instead of continuing in prophetical utterances and glorification of the Lord Jesus Christ. Clearly, this is the work of the adversary, the devil, to turn the church away from the power source that glorifies the risen Christ.

7. Thanks be to God, the Holy Spirit, for the return of those who seek the *deep things of God* (1 Corinthians 2:10), and now Spirit-filled believers are *led of the Spirit* (Romans 8:14) and are the channel through which the Holy Spirit once again glorifies Jesus in the church.

8. As the Lord Jesus Christ is seated in His exalted position at the right hand of the Father, now the body of Christ, the church, has a Divine Person continually with them, in them, and glorifying Christ through them. The Holy Spirit *quickens* (John 5:21, Romans 8:11), He *guides into all truth* (John 16:13). He confirms *the sonship bestowed* on believers (Romans 8:16), He is the Helper who *helps their weaknesses* (Romans 8:26), and *has sealed* them *unto the day of redemption* (Ephesians 4:30). All this is done to the glory of the Son of God, Jesus Christ.

9. *Most assuredly, I say to you, he who believes in Me, the works that I do he will do also; and greater works than these he will do, because I go to My Father....* (John 14:12 NKJV) This statement from Jesus to the disciples must have startled them. Their last three years with Him could never have been greater. Christ's ministry,

His teaching, and His holy walk mystified them. Consequently, they could not perceive anything *greater.*

10. Jesus speaks of the unification of the Godhead and the Oneness that exists between them ... *I am in the Father, and the Father in Me. The words that I speak to you I do not speak on My own authority; but the Father who dwells in Me does the works. Believe Me that I am in the Father and the Father in Me, or else believe Me for the sake of the works themselves....* (John 14:10–11 NKJV)

11. Apostle Philip, lingering in the tradition and his attachment to the Law, asks that they be shown the Father. Arthur Pink's comment on Jesus' reply is, "The corporal representation of God, such as Philip desired, was unnecessary; unnecessary because a far more glorious revelation of Deity was right there before him."

12. Not only was there unity of thought and application in their words and works, their Oneness is so intimate that all that the Godhead is and does is sublime and glorious. Spirit-filled believers immerse themselves in the anointing of the Holy Spirit who directs their attention to the Son of God who declares ... *At that day ye shall know that I am in my Father, and ye in me, and I in you....* (John 14:20)

13. The Holy Spirit's constant reminder to Spirit-filled believers is therefore Jesus Christ's glorious work, vicarious death and resurrection, thus conquering the devil's hold on mankind. Believers cannot, and must not, lose sight of the ascended Christ who is seated at the right hand of the Father, magnified and highly exalted. This exaltation and revelation is given by the Holy Spirit into the believer's spirit.

14. In the *Pulpit Commentary on John*, a commentator states, "It is important to observe the order, so to say, of the Spirit's revelation concerning Christ. The great outstanding facts of our Lord's manifestation to men are His incarnation, His cross, His crown. It is around these that all the doctrines of faith are clustered.

15. "Out of these facts they are set to grow. From the very first—that is to say from Pentecost—the Holy Spirit bore a certain witness concerning them all. The words of Apostle Peter, *God hath made that same Jesus, whom ye have crucified, both Lord and Christ....* (Acts 2:36) These words were the beginning of the ministry of the Holy Spirit. And then, as time went on, the full meaning of the cross was unfolded, and the Apostle Paul, who, above all things, preached *Jesus Christ and Him crucified."*

16. The question asked is what then does the Holy Spirit do to glorify Jesus. Walter A. Elwell's exposition in *Baker's Encyclopedia of the Bible* says, "The singular splendor of God and its consequences for mankind, (are) the glory of God (that) can be described as an attribute and a category referring to the historical manifestation of His presence.... As an attribute, God's glory refers primarily to His majestic beauty and splendor and the recognition of it by mankind.... It is also an ethical concept and embraces His holiness, for to sin is to *fall short of the glory of God."*

17. The Holy Spirit perpetuates this manifestation of God's glory by constantly glorifying Christ to the world, the believer, and the church. It is humanly impossible for the natural man to grasp the concept that a virgin woman could conceive a Son in her womb. It is beyond human comprehension that a Man can be raised from the dead, ascend into heaven (a place unknown in human thinking), and who will in the future return to this earth.

18. Contrary to their unbelief, the Holy Spirit ministers to the sinner's spirit and soul and is able to reach past their unbelief and open the tomb that encases his spirit, thereby revealing to him the truth. The repentant heart confesses by faith all that he receives regarding Christ's glorious work and is thus born again. The work of the Holy Spirit does not direct the born-again believer to the revelation that He, the Holy Spirit, imparts to him, but rather to the glorious work Christ wrought in His ministry on earth; *He will glorify Me.*

19. Christ did not come in a *pillar of fire*; but after His ascension, the Holy Spirit was poured out as *tongues like as of fire* (Acts 2:3) as they were baptized with the Holy Spirit. *The Spirit of truth* reveals the majesty and splendor of Jesus Christ to the church by continuing Christ's ministry through the believers' lives. The glorifying of Christ by the Father is when He was elevated and seated at the Father's right hand. Now on earth, Christ is continually glorified by the Holy Spirit through revelation to man.

20. Spirit-filled believers realize that the manifestation of the Godhead's presence, and evidence of their works amongst men, are all made known to them by the Holy Spirit. Yet, they immerse themselves in an even greater truth. The infinite, omniscient, and omnipresent eternal *God is a Spirit: and they that worship him must worship him in spirit and in truth* (John 4:24); enables them to grasp the fact that all the deep truths hidden in the *secret place of the Most High* and all the hidden things of the divine Godhead's counsels are exposed in the truths the Holy Spirit reveals to the Spirit-filled believer.

21. The intimate fellowship that the Holy Spirit has with the Father and Jesus is never compromised by Him. He is in absolute harmony with the intent of the Godhead's spiritual motivation for mankind. In all this, the Holy Spirit indwells the Spirit-filled believer and glorifies Jesus Christ by exalting Him through the believer. The works that the Holy Spirit does, even to the extent that they exceed the works of Jesus, are never placed as a crown of glory upon the Holy Spirit; they are all done and achieved reverencing the ascended and exalted *Jesus Christ and Him crucified.*

22. Henceforth, Spirit-filled churches are intent on proclaiming *the apostles' doctrine, fellowship, breaking of bread and prayers....* (Acts 2:42) How exquisite is the fact that they never forget the *breaking of bread* which is the direct application of the Holy Spirit's constant reference to *Jesus Christ and Him crucified.* They cannot, and dare not to their peril, ever forget the Holy

Spirit's counsel that glorifies Christ in His death, resurrection, and ascension.

23. The Holy Spirit's dynamic task amongst believers initially focuses on the vital work of sanctification. W.A.C. Rowe says, "Regeneration gives place to the further work of sanctification. Believers are the purpose of the Father (Galatians 1:15), the purchase of the Son (1 Timothy 2:6). Sanctification is preparation: it is to make the believer separate, clean, and beautiful (1 Corinthians 6:11).

24. "The sequence of the Holy Spirit's work and experience would seem to be (1) 'Sealed with (the) Spirit' (Ephesians 1:13); (2) 'Earnest of the Spirit' (2 Corinthians 1:22); (3) 'Filled with the (Spirit)' (Acts 2:4 and 2:38–39), which is the baptism with the (Holy) Spirit.

25. "The believer is the *temple of the Holy Ghost* (1 Corinthians 6:19). In possessing the believer, He controls the life for God. As in the Godhead so in the body of Christ He is the communion between the member and the Head and member with member ... *the communion of the Holy Ghost."* (2 Corinthians 13:14)

26. Then there is the work of the Holy Spirit in the church. Rowe continues, "He (the Holy Spirit) is the great Uniter. It is the spirit which gives life to a natural body. It is the spirit that holds the members together in vital union. When the spirit leaves the mortal body (in its death) it quickly passes into complete disintegration, returning to its original constituent element of dust. Thus, it would appear that it is the baptism with the Holy Spirit (1 Corinthians 12:13) that is a decisive act in initiating and joining the members to the body of Christ. The importance of a great act of the Holy Spirit in bringing together a body is seen in Ezekiel 37:1–10. It was the breath, the Spirit of God, that brought the dry bones together as a new body and made them live.

27. "The Holy Spirit is the great Administrator in the Church of Jesus Christ (1 Corinthians 12:11). He presides and governs on

behalf of the Ascended Head. This hallmark is seen in Acts 15:28, *It seemed good to the Holy Ghost, and to us....* His stamp or authority is clearly marked in Acts 20:28 ... *The Holy Ghost hath made you overseers ... (over) ... the church of God....*"

28. This magnificent work of the Holy Spirit is evidenced when the members of the body of Christ are unified in *one faith* and follow the teachings of the Holy Spirit. It is not the teachings of man to man but the holy, divine teaching from the divine, Holy Spirit to man. The tragedy in the modern-day church revolves around the gimmicks of man who hooks the members by offering them rewards for "sowing financial seeds" into their church's ministry, omitting the preaching of sin and the shedding of Christ's precious blood.

29. There is never any compromise when the Holy Spirit reaches deep into the heart of an ordained minister of Jesus Christ. W.A.C. Rowe continues on the work of the Holy Spirit in the church, "He is the great Teacher. It is His work first of all to reveal the truth of God to the apostleship, so that, under His anointing, it can truly go forth as the 'Apostles' doctrine' (Acts 2:42).

30. "Moving in oneness with the Head, which is Christ, He breaks forth to the apostles and prophets with marked revelation (Ephesians 3:5). The Lord spoke of Him that ... *He shall teach you all things* ... (John 14:26), and that ... *He will show you things to come....* (John 16:13) It is His divine business to do this through all the ministerial functions in the church. It is also His business to work inwardly in the hearts of believers that ... *the eyes of (their) understanding (be) enlightened....* (Ephesians 1:18) To experience these two operations is to enjoy the privilege of real discipleship in the school of the Master."

31. To conclude the exposition of Jesus' words on the work of the Holy Spirit taken from John's gospel, a commentator in the *Pulpit Commentary* says, "His teaching is not self-originated, like that of Satan (John 8:44). He shares in the intellectual fellowship

of the Father and the Son, is initiated into the Divine scheme of salvation, and is thus enabled to make known the revelation which God gave to Jesus Christ (Revelation 1:1).

32. "His teaching lifts apostolic inspiration above the region of mere spiritual illumination enjoyed by all saints. It was an instruction as to things not yet disclosed or known on earth.

33. "His teaching lifts the veil of the future. (a) The things to come are the destiny of the Church till its final consummation. (b) The Holy Spirit thus declares beforehand the inspiration of the Epistles and the Apocalypse.

34. "The Lord has a full consciousness of the greatness of His Person and His truth … *All things that the Father hath are mine: therefore, said I, he shall take of mine, and shall show it unto you….* (John 16:15)"

35. There was, is, and will never be any doubt in the Father and the Son's hearts about the effectiveness of the divine work of the Holy Spirit in the world. He is the perfect One and the only One who is able to reach into the spirit of a lost sinner and mature a believer's life.

The Holy Spirit's Role in the Work of Sanctification

36. Once the repentant heart is washed in the blood of the Lamb, regeneration is instantaneously completed. Because their sin is blotted out, the forgiven man stands justified before God. It is now the Holy Spirit who begins the process of sanctification in the believer.

37. Let it be clearly stated that this vital work in a believer's life involves the entire Godhead. They are … *sanctified by God the Father….* (Jude 1) The intrinsic holiness of the Father lays the foundation for the process to begin. Christ's glorious achievement

at Calvary procures the guarantee of sanctification when He was ... *made unto us sanctification* ... (1 Corinthians 1:30), and ultimately, the Holy Spirit preens the believer's body, soul, and spirit unto cleanliness ... *through sanctification of the Spirit*.... (1 Peter 1:2)

38. It must be clearly understood that sinners are instantly forgiven, but the cleansing process of being sanctified is a progression in their life. W.A.C. Rowe explains, "There is a twofold relationship in the ministry of Christ to man: in reconciliation, His work was for us, but in sanctification His work is in us. Salvation makes us safe, whereas sanctification makes us sound. Regeneration is an instantaneous act, whereas sanctification comprehends the instantaneous act and a continual process."

39. It is again only right that the focus is on Jesus Christ and His plea to His Father ... *Sanctify them by Your truth. Your word is truth. As You sent Me into the world, I also have sent them into the world. And for their sakes I sanctify Myself, that they also may be sanctified by the truth. I do not pray for these alone, but also for those who will believe in Me through their word....* (John 17:17–20 NKJV)

40. The Lord Jesus does not ask the Father to give them wisdom, power, or riches; He asks the Father to separate them, cleanse them, and make them worthy for their task ahead of them. Jesus asked His Father to separate them and seal them from all impurities in their spirit, soul, and body; namely *sanctify them*. Jesus' desire was that His disciples be holy, righteous vessels of honor. (1 Thessalonians 5:23)

41. While it is observed in so many humanistic methods that apply force, dogmatic persuasion, and dictatorial demands compelling a person to become an instrument in the hands of others, how beautiful it is to follow the steps of the Godhead as they are involved with the sanctifying process of the believer. If the believer is desirous of a deeper walk in Christ, then there needs

to be a progressive growth from the natural man (1 Corinthians 2:14) to the carnal man (1 Corinthians 3:1–4), and finally, to the spiritual man (1 Corinthians 2:15).

42. Even more reassuring is the comfort and peace within a believer who knows that they are in the hands of the Master Surgeon who operates with skilled precision and perfection. In order that the central focus is never lost, it is appropriate that reference is made again and again to Jesus Christ and His finished work on Calvary. In this divine sacrifice of the Son of God sin was taken care of, as well as the sanctification of every born-again believer.

43. W.A.C. Rowe says, "Christ and the cross are the only and sufficient grounds for sanctification. The cross is the focal point of all divine dealings as it is the fixed place for sanctification, as it is for justification. Sanctification entails absolute oneness with the crucified, *He that sanctifieth and they who are sanctified are ... one* (Hebrews 2:11). Calvary is a perfect sacrifice for justification and a perfecting sacrifice for sanctification. Calvary is the Savior's cross, the sinner's cross, and the cross of the sanctified."

44. "Sanctification" is the biblical word for the "spiritual separation" and "anointing" to do the bidding of God. The foundation principle of sanctification is to set apart for special divine ownership. The standard against which sanctification is measured is none other than the holiness (sanctified life) of the Lord Jesus Christ (Romans 8:29). It is the requirement a believer must adhere to in becoming Christlike.

45. As previously stated that believers are subjected to the Master Surgeon's touch as they are sanctified, it is appropriate that consideration be given to the Godhead's involvement in this vital process. None of the sanctifying process is achieved by human, fleshy means or the bringing down of sin's stronghold: it is wrought by God. (John 17:19, Jude 1) God alone justifies the repentant heart, and He sanctifies their unclean state.

46. Believers are to *grow in grace, and in the knowledge of our Lord*

and Savior Jesus Christ (2 Peter 3:18); they are transformed into the *same image from glory to glory* (2 Corinthians 3:18). Thus said, this implies a constant progressive growth, cleansing and going *on unto perfection* (Hebrews 6:1), which is finally achieved on that great Day of the Lord.

47. The Holy Spirit is constantly at work in believers' lives, as should the believer adhere to the Holy Spirit's leading into a purer life. It is the Holy Spirit who leads, and the believer who turns from their uncleanness and impurities by the power and help of the Holy Spirit ... *The horse is prepared against the day of battle: but safety is of the Lord....* (Proverbs 21:31)

48. Rowe continues, "It has the deep purpose of thorough cleansing. The Lord commanded the Levites to ... *sanctify the house of the LORD God ... carry forth the filthiness out of the holy place* (2 Chronicles 29:5). There must be a removal of iniquity to make possible an inflow of purity. As a divine habitation, we must be made meet for our royal guest in inward condition and outward action.

49. "Sanctification is a Person; it is absolutely, wholly, and utterly the glorious Person of Christ. (*ye in Christ Jesus who of God is made unto us ... sanctification ...* 1 Corinthians 1:30) Christ is as much the totality of our sanctification as He is of our justification. Just as salvation is not self-reformation, so sanctification is not self-culture. It is taking Christ as our life and making Him in very truth our *All-in all* (Colossians 3:11)."

50. The complete, finished work Christ accomplished for mankind, as the crucified One, exalted to the right hand of the Father, Jesus Christ is the Object presented to the soul. Therefore, it is biblically correct to state that sanctification is not something, but Someone.

51. At the outset, there must be a purifying of the born-again believer's spirit which can only be cleansed (purified) by the Holy Spirit. Rowe states, "There is a vast amount of work to be done in the spirit of man between conversion and perfection, in the realms of

sanctity, humility, love, and deep desire for the life of fellowship with God. It is possible to be outwardly exemplary but to have wrong things abiding in the spirit."

52. This sanctifying process is only possible when the believer obediently submits his spirit to the Holy Spirit's witness that He must purify the spirit within. The "crooked spirit" needs to be straightened, and the lingering impurities need to be purged so that man's born-again spirit can become a sanctified tabernacle for the Lord to inhabit. This work is a divine work purposed in God's heart for believers ... *who gave Himself for us ... and purify for Himself His own special people, zealous for good works....* (Titus 2:14 NKJV)

53. The purifying of the spirit is a holy work. *The Spirit itself beareth witness with our spirit, that we are the children of God....* (Romans 8:16) The constant reassurance from the Holy Spirit to the born-again believer is that their salvation is wrought through Jesus Christ, and all they now encounter on their journey through life is Spirit-led and taught. This is not found in textbooks, nor in the manifestation of good works; it is the Holy Spirit Himself who *bears witness.*

54. The highest call and most important decision any human being can make is the surrender of their life to Jesus Christ. The new birth is an awakening of the spirit within that comes from the heart of God to the heart (spirit) of man. (John 3:5–7) Henceforth, the work of the Most High God is continued through the Holy Spirit's sanctifying process of purifying the born-again believer's spirit.

55. While the Holy Spirit purifies the spirit, He also purges man's soul. Rowe says, "There is a work of sanctification for the soul which touches self and personal relationships. It involves deliverance from selfishness and is connected with soulish affections." Such affections are personal desires that can be contrary to God's will, and therefore need to be purged and eradicated from the soul.

56. Again, as with man's spirit, the born-again believer must willingly submit in absolute obedience to the Holy Spirit's purging. The control that the devil has over many peoples' mind is one of the greatest hindrances man has in submitting to the perfect will of God. It is here that the battle is at its fiercest. Man must surrender his *carnal* thoughts and relinquish his control of every decision into the hands of the Holy Spirit so that he can be led *into all truth. Come let us reason together* ... man with God, the Holy Spirit, who can expose that which is contrary to God's will.

57. To continue with Rowe who emphasizes the work the Holy Spirit undertakes with man in his body, "The body of the believer is an object of sanctifying ministry. The Lord Jesus, in becoming incarnate and taking a physical, human body, raised it to a place of reverence and made it a sanctified temple in which to dwell, an honored instrument through which He could express His life ... *A body hast thou prepared me* (Hebrews 10:5).

58. "The Lord is the Savior of the body (Ephesians 5:23). The whole of creation is waiting for the redemption of the body (Romans 8:22–23). We are taught emphatically that the body is for the Lord (1 Corinthians 6:13) and that we must present it to God as a living sacrifice (Romans 12:1) ... *Let not sin ... reign is your mortal body* (Romans 6:12). Set the body apart for the Lord, yield it to the ministry of sanctification and, whatever happens, it must never be allowed to dominate life (1 Corinthians 9:27)."

59. The lust and works of the flesh are the result of the soul's intentions and decisions. The *old man* must die, and the *new man* must *put on the Lord Jesus* and *grow in grace and knowledge of the Lord Jesus Christ*.... This happens when the born-again believer totally surrenders and submits to the Master Sculptor, the Holy Spirit.

60. The sanctification of believers is never more apparent than when they gather together as the church. It is a desire of Jesus that the believers be one and in one accord (John 17:17–21). In His

prayerful request, Jesus asks the Father to sanctify them as He sanctified Himself for the church (John 17:19), and ... *Christ also loved the church, and gave himself for it; that he might sanctify and cleanse it....* (Ephesians 5:25–26)

61. The sanctified state of believers is the blending of their spirits into one accord as they gather together as a body of believers, the church. Herein is the spiritual unity exercised and manifested when corporately, the members are fused together through their sanctification and enter into unified praise, worship, celebration of the Lord's Supper, and feasting on the Word.

62. It is when the church gathers together in unity of Spirit and are sanctified by the Holy Spirit, their righteousness is of Jesus Christ, and their expectations are the promises of the Father, that their fervent prayers and worship are as a united firebrand reaching the heart of the Father. This lofty height raises them above the world and its trappings, and they focus on the anticipated rapture of the saints.

CHAPTER 21

THE DOCTRINE OF THE HOLY SPIRIT – CONTINUED

The Baptism with the Holy Spirit

1. *He shall baptize you with the Holy Ghost and with fire....* (Luke 3:16) John the Baptist declared that while his baptism was an instruction from God, man being used by God to bring the people to repentance, there was coming One after him who would be God manifest in the flesh, who would divinely baptize believers with the Holy Spirit; the Godhead is thus involved in this spiritual blessing made available to believers.

2. Herein is the experience born-again believers undergo that immerses them into the body of Christ (1 Corinthians 12:13), empowers them for a more Spirit-led witnessing of Jesus Christ (Acts 1:8), and endows them with spiritual gifts, which the Holy Spirit distributes to each one as He wills. (1 Corinthians 12:11)

3. This beautiful, divine experience of which all believers can and should partake has enormous benefits for the one who is baptized with the Holy Spirit. These precious benefits need to be studied

in detail to help all understand the promises spoken of in the Holy Writ.

4. To begin this all-important doctrine, it is worthy to note that the Word is, where the translators found it necessary, translated from the original Greek that never used prepositions, to include a preposition to better clarify the Greek meaning. Hence, some translations state that the baptism is "in" the Holy Spirit, while others state it is the baptism "of" the Holy Spirit. To ensure the perfect will of God is fulfilled, it is only right that the correct emphasis is placed on the fact that Jesus baptizes believers "with" the Holy Spirit.

5. As with all doctrinal tenets, the baptism with the Holy Spirit involves the entire Godhead. It is the Father's will that the relationship between Him and man be fully restored. It is the Lord Jesus Christ who opened the door to this restoration, and it is Jesus Himself who baptizes the believer with the Holy Spirit.

6. The Bible gives clear accounts of the fundamental doctrine that there are two experiences that are essential to fully equip and empower believers to be witnesses ... *unto the uttermost part of the earth*.... (Acts 1:8) The first experience is the new birth (born-again) for those who repent, and the second is the baptism with the Holy Spirit. These two experiences were the norm in the early church, and that they were an essential part of their *going on unto perfection* was never doubted by anyone who walked through redemption's holy entrance into the glorious light of the gospel.

7. The Lord Jesus Christ's accomplishment at Calvary tore down the middle partition of sin, made a complete provision for redemption that reached deep into the heart of the person lying in the miry clay, and gave him access to the holy presence of God. The pardon from sin was, and is, fully accomplished; and now the indwelling spiritual power to walk circumspectly in His presence is imparted to those who are baptized with the Holy Spirit. It is the glorious

progression from Calvary to Pentecost, the provision of pardon to the promise of power.

8. The Word has various accounts of this experience believers had. It is found throughout the church's growth in the book of Acts and in the New Testament Epistles. To clarify any misgivings, when a person is born-again, they accept Jesus Christ, and the Spirit of Christ dwells in their heart (Romans 8:9, Galatians 4:6). The Holy Spirit (the Spirit of Truth) reigns with Christ in the believer's heart.

9. What now follows is the Holy Spirit's empowerment promised by Jesus (Acts 1:8). This divine process is none other than the baptism with the Holy Spirit at which moment the Holy Spirit takes up residence in the believer's body (1 Corinthians 6:19). An example of this process is found in Acts 19:1–8.

10. Apostle Paul is in Ephesus preaching and twelve men, disciples of Christ, approached him. These were men who had accepted Jesus Christ as their Savior, yet they had no knowledge of the Holy Spirit and the work He could do in their lives. *Have ye received the Holy Ghost since ye believed...?* (Acts 19:2) This is a perfect example of a humble and obedient listener who hears the gospel and responds to the message of salvation but is not aware of the power Jesus promised which would follow them that believe ... *He that believeth and is baptized* (in water) *shall be saved....* (Mark 16:16) These twelve men believed and were saved. They needed to continue through the waters of baptism and the baptism with the Holy Spirit.

11. God's servant explains the fullness of being baptized by immersion in water, and they willingly accept his teaching and are baptized. He then lays hands on them to receive the baptism with the Holy Spirit, and they are baptized as was evidenced by their speaking with tongues and prophesying. (Acts 19:6)

12. In all the examples found in the book of Acts, the initial evidence of the baptism with the Holy Spirit is the speaking with tongues.

This powerful witness that the Holy Spirit is now in the believer's body is the assurance that they have been endued *with power from on high*. (Luke 24:49)

13. It is important to study in detail the spiritual experience of speaking in tongues. Thus so, because it is the great controversy that exists between Spirit-filled believers and believers. It must be remembered that the baptism with the Holy Spirit was the norm for the church. There was never any doubt about this divine endowment upon believers; it was the expected and anticipated blessing from God for them.

14. Scripture speaks of "tongues," "other tongues," "tongues of angels," and the "gift of different kinds of tongues." Apart from the "gift of different kinds of tongues," the initial sign that a believer is baptized with the Holy Spirit is expressed in one of these three ways. This is a divine and spiritual impartation into the believer.

15. On the Day of Pentecost, the disciples in the Upper Room spoke with "other tongues." (Acts 2:4) They were baptized with the Holy Spirit and spoke with other tongues (in languages) they had never learned at any time. This manifestation has occurred many times since the Day of Pentecost, when believers who are baptized with the Holy Spirit will speak in a language they have never learned, or perhaps even heard.

16. The same evidence is also witnessed, as in Acts 19:1–6, when Apostle Paul laid his hands upon them, the men spoke with tongues. Here they did not speak in languages known to man but *with tongues*. Scripture is silent on the origin of *tongues* other than to unequivocally state that it is from the indwelling Holy Spirit.

17. Apostle Paul speaks of "tongues of angels" (1 Corinthians 13:1). This heavenly language can be imparted to the believer who speaks in a language no human has ever heard. It is the language of the heavenly host who constantly praise God in heaven.

18. The Bible declares that there are *different kinds of tongues* (1 Corinthians 12:10), thus confirming and emphasizing the

explanation above. One of these three renderings of *tongues* will occur when a believer is baptized with the Holy Spirit. The evidence for the believer that they are baptized with the Holy Spirit takes place when he surrenders his spirit to the Holy Spirit and receives the Holy Spirit into his very being.

19. The empowering of the believer is the result of his "surrendering" of his body, soul, and spirit to the Holy Spirit. There will be no baptism if the believer refuses to submit to the Holy Spirit. There will be no baptism if the believer does not exercise his faith in God. The baptism with the Holy Spirit is not a calculated, planned, and humanly designed step the believer must take. It is a God-ordained and God-imprinted impartation of the Holy Spirit who takes up residence in the believer's body, because the believer exercises his faith and surrenders to the Holy Spirit's bidding.

20. This divine and holy spiritual experience, as is the born-again experience a believer goes through, should never be tarnished by involving the human explanation for such a divine spiritual experience. This is God's holy business, and it is freely offered to God's children—believers.

21. The spiritual utterances, tongues, that flow from a Spirit-filled believer's heart as he speaks is the Holy Spirit's "language" that the Holy Spirit uses through the person: the Holy Spirit within the person to *God who is Spirit.* This is the personal usage given to those who are baptized with the Holy Spirit. It is the private and individual interlude that is available to the person who submits his vocal chords and tongue to the Holy Spirit ... *Likewise the Spirit also helps in our weaknesses. For we do not know what we should pray for as we ought, but the Spirit Himself makes intercession for us with groanings which cannot be uttered....* (Romans 8:26, Ephesians 6:18 NKJV)

22. This usage is available to all who are baptized with the Holy Spirit and is also used as the individual praises and worships God in the Spirit. The hearers on the Day of Pentecost said ... *We do hear*

them speak in our own tongues the wonderful works of God.... (Acts 2:11)

23. Apostle Paul clarifies this application as he says ... *For he that speaketh in an unknown tongue speaketh not unto men, but unto God....* (1 Corinthians 14:2) Thus, the person who worships God in the Spirit is inspired by the Holy Spirit who sets him in direct communion with God.

24. *For if I pray in a tongue, my spirit prays, but my understanding is unfruitful. What is the conclusion then? I will pray with the spirit, and I will also pray with the understanding. I will sing with the spirit, and I will sing also with the understanding....* (1 Corinthians 14:14–15 NKJV)

25. When there is a gathering of believers, and some are baptized with the Holy Spirit and some are not, tongues become the sign to them who are not baptized with the Holy Spirit of the indwelling Holy Spirit in those who are baptized. The word says ... *With men of other tongues and with other lips I will speak to this people: and yet, for all that, they will not hear Me, says the Lord. Therefore tongues are for a sign, not to those who believe but to unbelievers....* (1 Corinthians 14:21–22 NKJV)

The Gifts of the Holy Spirit

26. The glorious work of the Holy Spirit in Spirit-filled believers is manifested in many ways. At the outset, the fruit of the Spirit is the ultimate sign of the indwelling Holy Spirit in the life of a believer as they walk *in His steps.* The basis of everything a believer and a Spirit-filled believer is and does is always rooted in the operation of faith. Thus, all glory and honor is bestowed upon the Godhead when any spiritual fruit or gift is exhibited, simply because the individual is not the author of the gift or fruit

but the channel through which the Holy Spirit operates. The Lord is sovereign in the realm of these gifts.

27. Rowe introduces this important doctrinal tenet by stating, "The Holy Spirit proceeding from the Father (John 14:26) and from the Son (John 16:7) is the glorious divine Agent. *There are diversities of gifts, but the same Spirit* (1 Corinthians 12:4). Every divine activity and particularly the nature and operation of the Gifts of the Spirit are but manifestations of the blessed third Person, God, the Holy Spirit. Every true gift is of the actual nature of the Holy Spirit, and every anointed manifestation is His actual operation."

28. Rowe continues, "These gifts are of Himself divine, supernatural, powerful, and consisting of the nature and ability of their individual designations. They are impartations by the Holy Spirit and of the Holy Spirit, and they are designed for a special channeling of the working of the divine attributes, from the glory of the Godhead, and concentrating them upon the needs in the region of the experience of men."

29. The gifts of the Holy Spirit are in their most exquisite operation when used amongst believers. Their operation brings enlightenment and comfort as they reveal the truth and beam light into the lives of the Spirit-filled believers gathered in worship.

30. The Bible records nine Gifts of the Holy Spirit that are given to certain individuals in the body of Christ. These are given *individually as He* (the Holy Spirit) *wills.* (1 Corinthians 12:11 NKJV) Even more importantly, these diverse nine gifts are given to ... *to every man to profit withal....* (1 Corinthians 12:7)

31. The nine gifts recorded in 1 Corinthians 12:3–11 can be categorized into three dimensions: the revelation gifts, the power gifts, and the voice gifts. For greater clarity, it is appropriate that they be studied in each category.

32. *For to one is given the word of wisdom....* (vs. 8) What the world needs in this modern age is not more knowledge, more gadgets, or more power; its greatest need is wisdom to perform all their being

with integrity and upright character. The lack of wisdom is often the demise of perfect application. Rowe states, "A person may have great knowledge and yet be crippled for a lack of wisdom to apply it. Wisdom is the instrument and handmaid of knowledge.

33. "The manifestation of the Gift of the Word of Wisdom is something extraordinary and intense. It is supernatural and brings a flood of light on the solution of a special problem or need, particularly in the services and affairs of the church."

34. This gift resides in any person in whom the Holy Spirit chooses to impart it. They are not chosen because of their extensive education, wide-ranging worldly experience, or charismatic eloquence, but *as the He* (the Holy Spirit) *wills.* The person has a humble heart, submissive to the Holy Spirit's bidding, and often their words astound the hearers because the word of wisdom that flows from them far exceeds the gifted person's human comprehension.

35. Such is the example Jesus explains to His disciples. He is foretelling them about the end times and how they should respond when facing those of education and authority ... *Therefore settle it in your hearts not to meditate beforehand on what you will answer; for I will give you a mouth and wisdom which all your adversaries will not be able to contradict or resist....* (Luke 21:14–15 NKJV) Jesus reassures the humble men of Galilee (fishermen) that they need not concern themselves because they are unlearned (Acts 4:13). They will receive wisdom at the right time and answer their adversaries with astonishing wisdom.

36. This gift's use is for "the understanding and application of truth or principle; or in the right counsel and attitude for a truly divine course of action." (Rowe)

37. This "revelation" gift is not the result of human knowledge, but rather revelation from the Holy Spirit that explains the essence and necessary action required to fulfill a task.

38. *To another the word of knowledge through the same Spirit....* (vs.8) Rowe explains it in the following way, "In the operation of

this gift the blaze of illumination wrought by the Holy Spirit is a flash of knowledge which is not the product of reasoning, nor the reflection of the natural mind. It does not originate in the natural man. This knowledge is higher than the powers of self-education or attained through personal experience: it is even higher than knowledge ordinarily attained by a sanctified believer through devotional Bible study and Christian experience though that may be rich and good. Knowledge of this kind is completely divine in its origin and supernatural in its character. It is imparted and not acquired, revelation and not education."

39. The gift is extraordinary in that the one being used brings forth light onto a subject hitherto not known by anyone. It is used to direct, explain, or reprove error by exposing the true intent of a proposed action. In this world that is saturated with deceit and corruption, the truth needs to be presented, and this gift has often been used to throw light onto a path taken through lack of knowledge and which needs to be corrected.

40. *To another the discerning of spirits....* (vs. 10) The ever-present spiritual satanic attack on believers and the false antitype of spiritual information when Satan interrupts the life of a believer as he comes *as an angel of light* (2 Corinthians 11:14) and sows confusion must be checked and corrected every time. Furthermore, Spirit-filled believers are taught to *try the spirits whether they are of God.* (1 John 4:1) The most exquisite demonstration of God's presence is when the Holy Spirit is manifested through the gifts of the Spirit; yet how harmful and destructive the devil is when believers are led astray by a false spirit.

41. This gift is supernaturally in operation when it shines light into the lives of Spirit-filled believers, enabling them to distinguish between the Spirit of God (Acts 14:9–10), the spirit of man (Acts 5:3–5), and things instigated by evil spirits (Acts 16:16–18). "It is impossible for the natural man to do this for himself, because he cannot understand the mind and workings of God

(1 Corinthians 2:14). Neither can he understand the strategies and activities of Satan and evil spirits, but the Holy Spirit reveals these (Acts 13:8–10)." (Rowe)

42. This gift's ultimate effect on the gathering of Spirit-filled believers is the confirmation that at the time true spiritual revelation is presented to the believers, comfort and upliftment is assured because the use of this gift confirms the source of the revelation. It is the rudder that steadies the believer on his spiritual course, enabling him to stay away from false teaching and confusion.

43. *To another faith....* (vs. 9) To understand the operation of this gift, it is paramount that the subject of faith be clearly understood. There is *the measure of faith* (Romans 12:3) that every person is given to receive Jesus Christ as their Savior, there is faith everyone has enabling them to walk believing *in the things hoped for* (Hebrews 11:1), and then there is the *gift of faith* which effectually brings about the exposition of spiritual and supernatural miracles.

44. The Holy Spirit will give this gift to anyone He wills. Those so gifted are not necessarily the highly educated, most prominent, or influential members of the body of Christ. They are the vessels the Holy Spirit chooses that are *full of the Holy Ghost and of faith* (Acts 11:24) and ready and able to be used in this potent measure. The evidence that the gift has been operational is the miraculous results that are witnessed. It is clearly the cause of supernatural faith that presents the result; for the result could never have been conceived in the natural mind.

45. *To another gifts of healings by the same Spirit....* (vs. 9) The Bible clearly states that when a member is sick, they call for the elders to anoint the sick with oil and pray the prayer of faith (James 5:13–15). This is the role an elder performs in the course of their spiritual duty. It is incumbent on them to visit the sick and pray for them, even if they do not have the gifts of healings. God's holy Word promises *the Lord will raise him up.*

46. Rowe explains it in the following way, "There are manifold modes of operation in obtaining healing: by prayer (John 15:16), by agreement of believers (Matthew 18:19), by the laying on of hands of believers (Mark 16:18), by the anointing of oil by elders, together with the prayer of faith (James 5:14–15), by the application of the Word of God (Psalm 107:20), by inspired command (Acts 14:9–10)."

47. It is not a self-claimed gift a believer has but rather the Holy Spirit who will impart to a believer this supernatural gift that is used in various ways. "The gifts of healing compose that supernatural function through which the stream of healing virtue passes from the Holy Spirit to the person to whom it is to be applied." (Rowe)

48. It is the only gift the Holy Spirit imparts that is plural. There are many diseases, different types of bodily sicknesses, and needs that this gift covers. There are believers who receive the ability through the Holy Spirit to heal certain sicknesses and are used in that sphere, while others are gifted and used to heal certain other sicknesses.

49. "The exercise of the Gifts of Healing is purely the power of God, and the healing that results is exclusively divine healing. It is solely the work of the Holy Spirit and has no relationship in any way with the operation of so-called psychic powers, physical magnetism, mental exercises, autosuggestion, or other attempts of mind-over-matter control." (Rowe)

50. *To another the working of miracles....* (vs. 10) A miracle is an exceptional event that has no human explanation. It defies human comprehension and rational thinking. It is the fullest demonstration of the presence of God, the Holy Spirit, who brings about a result that benefits believers.

51. This gift is also a sign to the lost or those still seeking salvation of the promise of God's presence to everyone who believes. Sound preaching is required when such a demonstration is evident, so that the sinner desires the Giver of the gift and not merely the gift.

52. French Arrington, in his book *Christian Doctrine: A Pentecostal Perspective,* says, "The gift of miracles was never done by Jesus or by the apostles simply to display power, but to bring glory to God. Miracles are not to magnify those seeking to demonstrate their own greatness."

53. *To another prophecy....* (vs. 10) This gift is the audible announcement of the Spirit's intentions to believers gathered together. Its entire reason for being used by the Holy Spirit is for the edification, exhortation, and comfort of believers. (1 Corinthians 14:3–4)

54. It is different in its operation from the Spirit of Prophecy and the office of a Prophet. It is God revealing His deepest intentions to the heart of believers. The hearer is uplifted and encouraged as the Holy Spirit uses a human channel to impart words of edification, exhortation and comfort. Furthermore, the person who has this gift imparted to them by the Holy Spirit never loses control of their human consciousness and enters into a trance or an unnatural spirit-world. The Holy Spirit does not sow confusion but requires that all things be done decently and in order (1 Corinthians 14:40).

55. Prophesy differs from a sermon a preacher delivers. Sermons are prepared messages a preacher has for the congregation, while the gift of prophesy is a Holy Spirit-inspired revelation given through a chosen vessel in a spontaneous manner. The verification that the prophetic utterance is from God is none other than the eternal Word of God. The gift of prophecy, like all the gifts of the Holy Spirit, aligns itself with the Holy Writ.

56. *To another different kinds of tongues....* (vs. 10) The Holy Spirit is responsible for gifting some Spirit-filled believers with the *gift of different kinds of tongues* as well as, to others, the *interpretation of tongues* (vs. 10). These gifts are verbally expressed in a gathering of Spirit-filled believers and are done by the same Holy Spirit through them. It is the Holy Spirit who

uses the gift through the Spirit-filled believer for the edification of those present. (1 Corinthians 14:26)

57. While all Spirit-filled believers have the initial evidence of the baptism with the Holy Spirit, which is the spiritual utterance of other tongues, or the tongues of angels, the *gift of tongues* is a unique gift imparted to only some, and therefore differs from the initial manifestation a believer has when they are baptized with the Holy Spirit.

58. The gift is used to edify those gathered in Jesus' name, not for an individual in their private prayer time when they are alone with God. *He that speaketh in an unknown tongue edifieth himself....* (1 Corinthians 14:4) The Holy Spirit, through Apostle Paul, gives a detailed teaching on the use of the gift of tongues ... *for he who prophesies is greater than he who speaks with tongues, unless indeed he interprets, that the church may receive edification.* (1 Corinthians 14:5 NKJV)

59. *Even so you, since you are zealous for spiritual gifts, let it be for the edification of the church that you seek to excel. Therefore let him who speaks in a tongue pray that he may interpret. For if I pray in a tongue, my spirit prays, but my understanding is unfruitful. What is the conclusion then? I will pray with the spirit, and I will also pray with the understanding. I will sing with the spirit, and I will also sing with the understanding. Otherwise, if you bless with the spirit, how will he who occupies the place of the uninformed say "Amen" at your giving of thanks, since he does not understand what you say? For you indeed give thanks well, but the other is not edified. I thank my God I speak with tongues more than you all....* (1 Corinthians 14:12–18 NKJV)

60. The apostle goes further regarding the usage of the gift of tongues. *How is it then, brethren? Whenever you come together, each of you has a psalm, has a teaching, has a tongue, has a revelation, has an interpretation. Let all things be done for edification. If anyone speaks in a tongue, let there be two or at the most three,*

each in turn, and let one interpret. But if there is no interpreter, let him keep silent in church, and let him speak to himself and to God. (1 Corinthians 14:26–28 NKJV) The use of the gift of tongues is used to edify the believers and can only be so if there is an interpretation of that tongue. This is either done by someone else in the meeting, or by the person who uses the gift of tongues.

61. *To another the interpretation of tongues....* (vs. 10) This gift is imparted by the Holy Spirit to those of His choosing, and it can never be assumed by a person that they have the gift. These are spiritual gifts, and as such, spiritually endowed. It is never applied from the person's intellect, but rather it is the Holy Spirit who enables the interpretation to be uttered from the person's spirit.

62. Clarification regarding this gift is needed. It is the "interpretation" of tongues and not the "translation" of tongues. Translation will necessitate the verbal conversion of the words spoken in tongues, while interpretation will allow the gifted believer to interpret the message of the tongue. Hence, the believer who brings forth the utterance of the gift of tongues might have a short message, and the interpreter could have a longer explanation of the interpretation.

63. The application of the gift of tongues and the interpretation of the tongues is often not used in accordance with the word of God. There are definite parameters measured for the use of these gifts.

64. At the outset, there should never be less than two utterances, or more than three utterances, of the gift of tongues in a meeting. These two, at the most three, utterances, can be delivered by one person, or there could be more than one person who uses the gift of tongues, yet there should be only one interpreter. (1 Corinthians 14:27)

65. Furthermore, the gifts are used in a specific order. The person who is led by the Holy Spirit to be used in bringing the first utterance of the gift of tongues will speak while the assembly remains silent. Thereafter, the interpreter will interpret the gift. Once the message is interpreted, the next use of the gift of tongues

is brought forth. Thereafter, the interpreter will continue with the interpretation. The gift of tongues could be used a third time with the same person interpreting the message.

66. It is tragic to learn that many denominations emphatically decree that the gifts of tongues and interpretation are literally banned in their meetings, while the Bible declares ... *Wherefore, brethren, covet to prophesy, and forbid not to speak with tongues....* (1 Corinthians 14:39)

CHAPTER 22

THE DOCTRINE OF THE
HOLY SPIRIT – CONTINUED

The Fruit of the Spirit

1. The demonstration of the fruit of the Spirit is the most definitive explanation of the extent of a believer's *knowledge of our Lord and Savior Jesus Christ*. (2 Peter 3:18) When the fruit of the Spirit is manifested in the believer's life, it speaks volumes of their relationship with Jesus Christ.

2. Nothing should ever precede their relationship with Jesus Christ. All that a born-again believer is, and will be, is surrounded by his knowledge and intimate commitment to his Savior. The ever-present desire within propels him towards being in the likeness of Christ. The perfect demonstration of Christ's indwelling presence in a believer is never more apt than when the fruit of the Spirit radiate from the believer.

3. *I am the (true) vine, you are the branches. He who abides in Me, and I in him, bears much fruit; for without Me you can do nothing.* (John 15:5 NKJV) The pure, holy, and divine clusters of fruit that are produced from the holy Source and meticulously dressed by

the *vinedresser* are freely available to all who *diligently seek Him.* (Hebrews 11:6)

4. The *true vine* is perfect; the *vinedresser* is perfect: thus, enabling believers to freely partake of the fruit and become Christlike to the fullest extent. It is the responsibility of the believer to *build up their most holy faith, stand fast in the liberty wherewith Christ has made you* (him) *free,* and *launch out into the deep,* as he *draws nigh unto God.*

5. The fruit of the Spirit must be evidenced in every word and action a believer says and does. The level of their spiritual maturity and their knowledge of the Lord Jesus Christ is assessed by the quality of the fruit they produce. Their words and actions, if they are enriched by the lush fruit of the Spirit, will mirror Jesus' words and actions. However, when there is a distant relationship with the Savior and the believer is *unskillful in the word of righteousness ... he is a babe* (Hebrews 5:13), and there is little evidence that he truly knows the Lord (Acts 4:13, Philippians 3:10).

6. When the fruit of the Spirit beams forth from a radiant heart, the believer immediately detects that the indwelling Holy Spirit's intentions are far more important than the works of the flesh.

7. As mentioned above, the *true vine* and the *vinedresser* are the handiwork of holy God. Therefore, the fruit is entirely God's work and not man's. It is God who producers the fruit, and man who shows it forth to the world.

8. The fruit of the Spirit is one fruit with nine parts/aspects. The vine's produce glistens in the sun as the skin shines absorbing the nourishment of the heat; the flesh of the grape is enriched by the chemicals in the soil; the seeds feed the whole fruit as it takes shape around them; and the brightness of the radiant color of the grape draws the onlooker to partake of it. All these attributes make up the fruit. So, too, the fruit of the Spirit possesses all the qualities that enable a believer to become fully Christlike.

9. Bringing the explanation into a clearer view, Evan Hopkins

dissects the biblical passage on the fruit of the Spirit into three parts: "Condition that embraces *love, joy,* and *peace* which explain the condition of the spirit and soul. Conduct, which includes *long-suffering, gentleness,* and *goodness* which demonstrate the external evidences of the indwelling Spirit. Character, which includes *faith, meekness,* and *temperance* that produce personal results in the believer's life."

10. *Love.* This aspect is the distinctive quality that attracts the observer to the believer. It exceeds charity, caring, and helpfulness. This quality is immersed in *agape* that is from the root Source of the entire fruit.

11. Love is the light that shines in the sinner's dark world, displaying the sincere, righteous Holy Spirit that resides in the believer. Furthermore, it is the identification of the Christlikeness believers discern in each other when they gather together. It is the quality that resides in the believer's heart which embraces every deed. The believer is filled with unprecedented appreciation for their salvation, which is expressed in their love for God.

12. The extent and depth of love in a believer's heart is the testimony of their relationship with Jesus Christ. *You shall love the LORD your God with all your heart, with all your soul, with all your strength, and with all your mind, and your neighbor as yourself.* (Luke 10:27 NKJV) These words of Jesus encompass the whole fruit. It is the love the believer has for God that radiates in them and is expressed towards their neighbor.

13. Jesus' teaching goes further than loving the loveable. He says, *But I say to you, love your enemies, bless those who curse you, do good to those who hate you, and pray for those who spitefully use you and persecute you....* (Matthew 5:44 NKJV) The *enemies* of the gospel of Jesus Christ have their *heart pricked* when believers demonstrate the fruit of love. Their love shines as a beacon into the darkened heart and draws the sinner towards the truth.

14. *Joy.* W.A.C. Rowe says, "Joy, as the fruit of the Spirit, is an

enlarged capacity for the impression and expression of this experienced quality of the divine life." It echoes the Psalmist's phrase ... *In thy presence is fullness of joy; at thy right hand there are pleasures for evermore....* (Psalm 16:11)

15. The joy that flows through the Spirit-filled believer's heart comes from the *river of life* that has its source in the heart of almighty God. The rejoicing spirit is elated because the witness of the Holy Spirit within constantly testifies about abundant life. The knowledge that God whom the believer serves is the Way, the Truth, and the Life (John 14:6) assures him that God cannot lie and will always be truthful. Mankind can never be fully trustworthy, but God is beyond any doubt that He is faithful and true.

16. Spiritual joy at His right hand at times brings vociferous praise to God as it expresses the intent of a rejoicing heart. Then, there is the quiet calming satisfaction of a Spirit-filled heart that is amazed at the work the Holy Spirit has done in his life. This joy provides the believer with the contentment that God's word is *yea and amen*.

17. The spiritual fruit of joy is not dependent on any achievement or deed; it is out of a grateful heart that grasps the fullest assurance of God's forgiveness. It does not bring emotional exuberance to the soul, but rather an inner joy in the spirit that is Spirit-led and Spirit filled. It is the "overflowing" expression of spiritual things that brings joy to the believer.

18. *Peace.* The first emotional exhibition Adam and Eve experienced in the Garden of Eden after they sinned was the evaporation of the peace of God they had enjoyed. It was replaced by fear. This evil emotion, fear, has dwelt with mankind since that day. However, into the heart of the believer the Holy Spirit imparts again spiritual peace which the devil had robbed mankind of when they succumbed to his deceit.

19. This divine impartation is not only present in times of refreshing and comfort; it is also present in times of discomfort and trouble.

Apostle Paul declares that the church is to continue in *the bond of peace* (Ephesians 4:3). This spiritual peace flows like a river from the Source, and is, first, the reconciling peace with God; second, the peace in God, and third, it is the bountiful supply of peace from God that overthrows fear. *My peace I give to you; not as the world gives do I give to you. Let not your heart be troubled, neither let it be afraid....* (John 14:27 NKJV)

20. How magnificent is the precious characteristic of peace Jesus leaves for believers to bask in. In this world of turmoil and strife, Christ, who is our peace, tells His followers that He will leave ... *My peace* to all who walk in His light.

21. Spiritual peace flows throughout man's body, soul, and spirit. It is an abiding protector that conquers carnage, serenely settles a disturbed soul, and calms the troubled emotions ... *And the peace of God, which surpasses all understanding, will guard your hearts and minds through Christ Jesus.* (Philippians 4:7 NKJV)

22. W.A.C. Rowe says it best, "It is the whole redeemed nature of man in perfect harmony within itself, as well as the complete harmony of the whole man with his Maker and Redeemer."

23. *Longsuffering.* How appropriate the translation in this instance is regarding the Greek word "makrothymia." It is correctly translated "longsuffering" and not "patience" which is in Greek, "hypomone." Mankind must exercise "patience" with things over which he has no control. He cannot hasten the hours in a day; he cannot speed up the orbit of planet earth; he has no control over the events of nature and must therefore exercise patience as he waits for them to take their course. On the other hand, he has influence over mankind. He can encourage, force, or compel another person to act more hastily. Conversely, he can wait or exercise longsuffering with the person. Mankind suffers mankind; he is to be longsuffering with his counterpart, while he must be patient with things in life over which he has no control.

24. This fruit flows constantly from God's heart towards mankind ...

the riches of His longsuffering.... (Romans 2:4) Jesus shows this fruit with the lost. (1 Timothy 1:16) God's longsuffering is best expressed by Apostle Peter... *The Lord is not slack concerning His promise, as some count slackness, but is longsuffering toward us, not willing that any should perish but that all should come to repentance....* (2 Peter 3:9 NKJV)

25. As the Source expresses the highest quality of the fruit of longsuffering, so ought His children to abundantly yield and exercise the fruit towards each other. (Ephesians 4:2) It is only the Holy Spirit that can manifest such a fruit in mankind. This fruit has the unquenchable and conquering power to overcome any devilish influence such as hatred, bitterness, and strife.

26. Believers are to bear the fruit of the Spirit in both good and evil circumstances. Longsuffering allows the believer to go beyond attacking the enemy, showing hatred when hatred is shown towards him, expressing frustration towards another, and being critical of another's incompetence; it calms the emotional intentions of a frustrated reaction, and responds with temperate endurance.

27. If Spirit-filled believers are to walk *circumspectly in Him,* then they are to resist the emotional discharge of taking offense, rendering evil for evil, and leveraging due recompense towards a carnal infraction against them. This is God's fruit from the Holy Spirit. It is only right that Spirit-filled believers earnestly seek to be more Christlike, and with disciplinary accord, express longsuffering towards his fellow man.

28. *Kindness.* This fruit is the quality that demonstrates the way believers treat others. Their meekness is a quality that brings others to a closer understanding of the Christ within them. This quality is evidenced because the Source of the fruit is from a gracious heart that loves others with all kindness and meekness. (Matthew 11:29)

29. It is never abrasive or filled with harmful intent but is rather apt to showing grace and kindness. It is a moral discipline that links

self-control in every word and deed. This is particularly the case when dealing with those who are intolerant and unforgiving. The way believers express their *love for the enemy* is manifested when they *bless them that curse you, do good to them that hate you ...* (Matthew 5:44) which is chiefly expressed as showing kindness by the believer to those less fortunate than they are.

30. When kindness is shown to others, it never seeks a reward. It is done unselfishly and with the single purpose of drawing a person closer to Jesus Christ. How enlightening is the fact that those showing kindness (or meekness) towards others are highly blessed of God and *inherit the earth.* (Matthew 5:5)

31. *Goodness.* The aptitude with which every activity must be approached is with the desire to be regarded by God as "well-being." Yes, the motive must always be with "well-doing," but it is of little emphasis if the heart is inflicted with wrong intentions. A "well-being" believer is driven by the desire to constantly fill others with God's goodness. It is a generous heart that produces goodness. (Ephesians 5:9)

32. The manifestation of the active grace of goodness depends upon the rightness of heart. Evan H. Hopkins says, "Character and conduct; creed and deed; word and work should always be united."

33. This fruit is the antibiotic the world so desperately needs to heal its disease of hatefulness. The indwelling Holy Spirit's character trait is the only means that can heal the crooked and perverse world's rampant hatred. *How great is thy goodness....* (Psalm 31:19) It contains a power that defuses a hateful approach ... *and fulfil all the good pleasure of his goodness, and the work of faith with power....* (2 Thessalonians 1:11)

34. Every attribute of God's nature is good; He alone is *good.* (Matthew 19:17) It manifests the fullness of the Holy Spirit residing in believers, and it draws them ever closer to God as they

grow in the grace, and in the knowledge of our Lord and Savior Jesus Christ.... (2 Peter 3:18)

35. *Faithfulness.* The ultimate purpose of the fruit of the Spirit is the outpouring of the indwelling Holy Spirit that flows like a river from the believer towards the world. This fruit demonstrates the faithfulness of a believer. First, it is the commitment in the believer's heart to be faithful to his Redeemer. Second, he is faithful to his fellow believers, and third, it is to the lost in the world where there is no trust.

36. The unwavering obedience Jesus showed towards His Father is rewarded by the Father when He crowns His Son with the title: *Faithful and True....* (Revelation 19:11 NKJV) Hasten the day when believers are elevated to this gracious position and *be like Him.* (1 John 3:2)

37. Believers are called to *finish the race* (2 Timothy 4:7), remain faithful to God in all their ways. This race need not be seen as the person crossing the finish line first, but rather that they have run the race faithfully to the end. Life is not only about winning; it is about faithfully contending throughout the entire journey. Rowe says, "God allows circumstances in our life, even of darkness and disappointment, in order to nurture and develop faith or faithfulness."

38. It is the Word that seals this reward for those who are faithful ... *Be thou faithful unto death, and I will give thee a crown of life."* (Revelation 2:10)

39. *Gentleness.* This is the fruit that displays the divine all-powerful God ministering every moment of the day as He handles the repentant heart. The analogy of the lioness in the wilderness is a perfect example. This ferocious beast attacks its prey, and with her powerful jaws snaps the neck of a large catch. It deals swiftly and decisively as the jaws inflict a deathly grip. Yet, these same jaws can pick up her cubs and, with gentleness, carry them from one place to the next without so much as a scar on the young cub's

neck. How apt, the *lion of Judah* inclines His ear to the need of a believer, and with gentleness carries them through their ordeal.

40. "Gentleness is power ... greatness depends upon gentleness, and not upon mightiness! Worldly axioms have it that knowledge is power; money is power. The Scriptures say gentleness is power.

41. "True followers of the 'gentle Jesus, meek and mild,' must exhibit the excellent quality of gentleness if others are to be won as they hear us speak about the kindness and love of God, our Savior...." (Rowe paraphrased)

42. This is in total contrast to the natural or carnal man's thinking. However, when the Holy Spirit is in residence, the majestic fruit of gentleness transforms the Spirit-filled believer into someone who is understanding, caring, and compassionate for the wayward one.

43. The Savior Jesus Christ is the most exquisite pattern to follow. Gentleness is the tender and experienced touch of the loving Shepherd in dealing with His flock, and Christ has been set before the church as the *good Shepherd ... of the sheep.* (John 10:11, Psalm 79:13) It is within the framework of a gentle spirit that believers approach their everyday activities and conversation. Guidance by force creates a reaction, whereas guidance from a gentle spirit creates a response.

44. *Self-control.* A writer has said, "Self-control (temperance) is the right handling of one's soul." W.A.C. Rowe says, "Self-control (temperance) is the throne of man's will, under the sweet influences and direction of the Holy Spirit, bringing every power and possibility into its fullest and best harmony and use...."

45. It is the ultimate exhibition of the born-again spirit that is no longer freewheeling along life's broad way but is carefully harnessed by the loving Spirit of Christ that guides them along the *straight and the narrow way.*

46. The Holy Spirit imparts this fruit that strengthens the believer's moral code of conduct, enabling him to bring into subjection every action. (1 Corinthians 9:27)

47. Furthermore, there is no variance in the believer's conduct regarding similar tasks or teaching they are required to share. There is an "even-keel" that keeps them ever the same throughout every word or deed. They do not *stray* (1 Timothy 1:6 NKJV) or sway like a reed in the wind, but they are stable and able to be entreated with respect because of the temperate spirit they manifest.

48. The Word is filled with beautiful examples of how Jesus remained temperate and demonstrated self-control throughout His many difficult encounters with those who misunderstood Him. His quiet reply to the self-righteous and indignant Jewish leaders when they brought the woman caught in the act of adultery stunned them and brought their high-mindedness down to self-examination. *He that is without sin among you, let him first cast a stone at her....* (John 8:7)

49. In conclusion, this divine fruit of the Holy Spirit is the purest evidence of the indwelling Christ residing in the believer's heart. Love is the ultimate motivator for the remaining eight parts of the fruit to be engaged in all that believers do and say.

50. Spirit-filled believers strive to uphold the perfect will of God (Romans 12:2). If there are any deficiencies and poor application of any one of the parts of the fruit of the Spirit, then the Spirit-filled believer's life is not perfect. It can be likened to the musical instrument that is hindered by missing parts; the harmony and function will be marred. The Spirit-filled believer's conduct is tarnished by a lack of, or weak display, of any of these divine qualities. Hence, they are encouraged to *earnestly contend for the faith which was once delivered unto the saints....* (Jude 3)

PART 5

The Doctrine of Creation

23. DOCTRINE – The Creation of Physical and Things seen
    a. The Original Earth. This part emphasizes the original created earth and what took place during that time.
    b. The Frozen Earth. This explains the expulsion of Lucifer from heaven and the state the earth was placed in by God.
    c. The Present Earth. This introduces the passage of Scripture in the opening chapters of Genesis. It explains that God "spoke" and it was done and then also "made/created" certain things to once again populate the earth. It references the "ages" and "dispensations." It does not pay any particular attention to the seven days of creation; the Bible is explicit enough on what happened and easy to be read and entreated.
24. DOCTRINE – The Creation of Spiritual and Unseen Things
    a. Invisible Creation. This details those invisible created things such as man's soul and spirit, and angels who are spirit beings.
    b. Angels are studied in detail—their personal attributes, everlasting state, and their purpose and mission.
    c. Lucifer (Satan, the devil), and the fallen angels. This section studies the work of Lucifer, his demise, and the result of the

decision the fallen angels made when they chose to follow Lucifer and deny God.

d. The Heavens. These places are examined and where Scripture permits, the reason and evidence for the creation of the three heavens.

CHAPTER 23

THE DOCTRINE OF CREATION

1. *In the beginning God created....* (Genesis 1:1) At the outset, this doctrinal tenet emphatically declares there is only One Creator, *Almighty God.* (Genesis 17:1)
2. To encapsulate this verse in a clearer understanding, be it known that Almighty God is *eternal* and as such existed, and has always existed, before He created anything. (Revelation 11:17)
3. God's creation consisted of two basic forms: the material and the spiritual. The cosmos and its contents are the material visible creation, while the angelic host and man's soul and spirit are invisible creations. (Colossians 1:16)
4. It is of great importance that the doctrine of the Spirit-filled church focuses on the eternal creation of soul and spirit and the invisible things. The soul and spirit are eternal from their creation, and their destiny is determined by the individual's own decision. However, there is a need to establish the fact that God created all things material, and that there is no biblical evidence for the theory of evolution of Gods' created humankind.

Visible/Material Creation

5. *In the beginning* ... a "period" of existence unknown to mankind. Because God is eternal, He has no beginning. He "is" always "now." What God did before He created anything is unknown to mankind. In fact, it does not concern those He created; it is His concern and it belongs to Him. (John 17:5)

6. In eternity, there are no measurements of time, space, or distance. God ... *I Am* existed eternally without any of these dimensions. Thus, this doctrinal tenet is the springboard to faith in God. Faith in the living eternal God is the only means by which humans can comprehend the vastness of the statement, "God has no beginning or end."

7. Consequently, the opening verse to the Holy Writ introduces the "period" when God created the heavens and the earth. This is the dawning of the introduction of measurement. Norman Geisler says, "The world did not begin in time; the world was the beginning of time. Time did not exist before creation; it was not a creation in time but a creation of time."

8. The Bible states that God created the world and manifests Himself in it. (Psalm 19:1) The expository explanation on Genesis 1:1 in the *Holman Study Bible* states that God does not "modify preexisting matter but calls matter into being out of nothing." (Psalm 33:6, 9; Hebrews 1:3) It is therefore correct to state that *in the beginning* ... the "moment" God began to create—references the eternal God creating something out of nothing. Augustine explains that there was no time before time, only eternity. The distinguishing mark between time and eternity is that the former does not exist without some movement and change, while in the latter there is no change at all.

9. This introduces the discourse on the subject *created*. Spirit-filled believers stand fast on the declaration that God created the world out of nothing—"ex nihilo."

10. Nothing cannot create something, but something can be created from nothing. This is what Almighty God did. God is the cause of creation, while the created heavens and the earth are the result, or effect. It was at this juncture that God introduced the measurements of "time," "distance," and "space." This was the *beginning* of the creation of time, and not a creation in time, for God is outside of time, namely, eternal.

11. To conclude, "It is not impossible for an infinite Creator to produce a finite creature. Thus, God, who is Existence, brought all else into existence. God created not only by His power but also by His will." (Geisler) Spirit-filled believers drench their soul in this fundamental belief that God willed creation, and God created it from nothing. As Creator, God is eternally self-existing, while all of creation is wholly dependent on its Creator.

12. Creation of everything: the heavens, the earth, angels, and man are all by the will of God. Nothing has ever been created that was not by God's will. His will is the cause of all things created, and He alone is the reason why all things created exist. It is by faith alone that believers accept this doctrinal tenet ... *By faith we understand that the worlds were framed by the word of God, so that the things which are seen were not made of things which are visible....* (Hebrews 11:3 NKJV)

13. Apostle Paul gives an even clearer explanation that it was Jesus, the Word (John 1:1–3) within the Godhead, who spoke creation into existence ... *For by Him all things were created that are in heaven and that are on earth, visible and invisible, whether thrones or dominions or principalities or powers. All things were created through Him and for Him. And He is before all things, and in Him all things consist....* (Colossians 1:16–17 NKJV)

14. This Scripture gives insight into the reason why all things were created. Prior to things being created, the Godhead was all that existed, and there was, as it still is, perfect unity and harmony

within the Godhead. They were complete in their uniformity and needed nothing else.

15. In this harmonious state, the Word, Christ Jesus (John 1:1), was favored with the gift of creation from the Father and the Holy Spirit ... *All things were created for Him.... Whom He has appointed heir of all things, through whom He also made the worlds....* (Hebrews 1:2 NKJV)

16. Jonathan Black, in his book, *Apostolic Theology*, says, "Christ is not simply a rescue plan for creation. Christ is the true purpose of creation."

17. The eternal God's Word had the power to call that which had no existence into being. His word has both authority and power to perform the impossible. The original creation of the heavens and the earth, together with all things that were created, came about by His word ... *For he spake, and it was done; he commanded, and it stood fast....* (Psalm 33:9)

18. That same Word which created all things and brought that which was nothing into existence is the same Word residing in the present age. It is none other than the eternal Word of God, the Holy Bible available to all nations in every tongue; *All Scripture is given by inspiration of God,* (God-breathed) *and is profitable for doctrine, for reproof, for correction, for instruction in righteousness, that the man of God may be complete, thoroughly equipped for every good work.* (2 Timothy 3:16–17 NKJV)

19. Eternal God, ever existing and ever present, who by the power of His word created all things, is within His spoken word that is now recorded in the Holy Bible. This Holy Writ contains every spiritual need, desire, instruction, and is the entrance into who God is, who created all things by the word of His mouth.

20. This doctrinal tenet is important to Spirit-filled believers because it gives clarity to the existence of earth and its state at various times. Spirit-filled believers accept the Bible as the proof and evidence that God created all things: they do not need any human discovery

or explanation via science or anthropology. Scientific evidence always proves the contents of the Bible regarding creation. God's Word does not have to prove science's discoveries; science merely proves its discoveries about God's Word on creation.

The Original Earth

21. To begin, the focus is placed on earth as a created planet. Its original creation is in the dateless past, making it in mankind's measurement millions of years old. Scripture speaks of the *world that then was....* (2 Peter 3:5–7) This references the period before Genesis 1:3. This is described as the "Original Earth" found in Genesis 1:1.

22. This original earth is in a "time" known as the Pre-Adamite Earth. The Bible declares that it was entirely "Eden," a garden of beauty, splendor, and harmony. The custodian of earth was a covering cherub appointed by God, whose name was Lucifer. (Isaiah 14:12, Ezekiel 28:16) Ezekiel's reference to Lucifer's operations describes Lucifer as the king of Tyrus who developed a method of trading that brought great wealth and pleasures to the inhabitants. There has never been a king of Tyrus, and biblical scholars agree that this reference is made of Lucifer which explains his activities through those on earth.

23. Lucifer's success caused him to lust after more power than was already given to him. He was privileged to walk upon the holy mountain of God and was perfect in all his ways from the day that he was created, until iniquity was found in him ... his heart was lifted up because of his beauty, which distorted his wisdom as he became more corrupt. (Ezekiel 28:14–15 NKJV)

24. His pride, lust for power, and control of the inhabitants on earth drove him to desire to be like God, and he wanted to ascend to the throne of Almighty God. It was at that moment that God dealt to

Lucifer the declaration that ended his angelic rule. (Isaiah 14:12–21, Ezekiel 28:11–19)

The Frozen Earth

25. Lucifer was banished from heaven and *cast down to the ground.* His punishment was such that he was sent to earth from where he orchestrated his lust. God did not leave earth in its "Eden" state but reduced it to a wasteland of ice ... *the world that then was, being overflowed with water....* (2 Peter 3:6) Lucifer/Satan now roamed this earth that was without *form and void.*

26. The inhabitants, or "human form," that existed on earth at that time also perished. Anthropologists are discovering evidence of the "human form" that dates back millions of years, proving their existence. Lucifer/Satan was a created spirit being. The population on earth were "human-form" that had a spirit and a body which he corrupted and lured away to become his followers. He corrupted these people through the *abundance of his trading.* (Ezekiel 28:16) This "human form" over which Lucifer had custody followed him and he became their god. God did not instruct Lucifer to do this—Lucifer was merely the custodian of God's created beings. Hence, everything on earth that God had created, including the population, perished when He froze the earth. (Jeremiah 4:23–26) The Scofield reference edition of the Bible comments that the Bible "clearly indicates that the earth had undergone a cataclysmic change as the result of a divine judgment."

27. The "human form" that inhabited the earth during that time perished. However, with all things God has created that has a spirit, the spirit is eternal in existence. As with Lucifer, who is a created angelic spirit being, his spirit lives eternally. Likewise, the spirits that were within this "human form" live eternally. The

moment God cast Lucifer out of heaven onto the earth, He froze the earth, and, consequently, the spirit that was in the "human form" remained on the frozen earth after their bodies perished. These ungodly spirits were incarcerated in the frozen earth together with Lucifer/Satan.

28. Once God restored the earth to a habitable state (Genesis 1:3–31), these spirits began to roam the earth. These are the demon spirits that are present on earth today. They constantly seek to once again inhabit a human body and return to a habitation like they originally had, and from which they were cast out when God froze the earth. They are under Satan's evil command and instruction as they endeavor to enter the present population on earth.

The Present Earth

29. The Bible begins in Genesis 1:1 with the original creation of the heavens and the earth. The Hebrew word used for "create" is "bara." Verse 2 explains the condition of the original earth after God had frozen it. Thereafter, from verse 3, the Bible begins to explain the restoration of the earth as it is known today. Clarence Larkin in his book, *Dispensational Truth*, states, "The six days' work as described in Genesis 1:3–31 is not a description of how God made the Original earth, but how He restored it from its 'formless and void' condition to its present state."

30. The restoration process did not need many natural things to be created. They were already present on the frozen earth. Hence the Bible states that … *God said….* God did not create *light, atmosphere,* and *waters,* He merely spoke them into existence again. (Genesis 1:3–8) The Hebrew word used for "make" is "asah" which is different from "create," which is "bara" in Hebrew.

31. In the passage of Scripture, Genesis 1:9–5, Larkin says, "This is

simply a reversal of the cataclysmic convulsions that submerged the Pre-Adamite Earth, and by upheaval caused the earth to emerge from its 'Watery Grave.' (Genesis 1:11–13) This was not a new creation but a resurrection. The earth rises up out of the 'Waters of Death,' and seeds, and the roots of plants and herbs and trees are called upon to germinate and sprout and grow as they did before the catastrophe that submerged the Pre-Adamite Earth."

32. Once God had restored the natural habitat on earth, He *made* the sun and the moon to shine during the day and the night (verse 16), indicating that God fashioned existing created things (sun and moon) into a condition that provided light. A practical analogy that can be used for "asah" (made) is that of a carpenter who takes a hewn tree and, from it, makes a useful instrument (a table).

33. God also created ("bara") things that had never existed. The first "created" ("bara") forms that God placed on earth after its restoration were the *great sea creatures and every living thing that moves, with which the waters abounded, according to their kind, and every winged bird according to its kind.* (verse 21 NKJV)

34. Once all was made and created, God then focused on His most perfect creation, man. It was out of the dust of this earth that God created man and gave him full custodianship over the earth ... *So God created man in His own image; in the image of God He created him; male and female He created them.... Have dominion over the fish of the sea, over the birds of the air, and over every living thing that moves on the earth....* (verse 27–28 NKJV)

35. On the restored earth, God planted a garden eastward of Eden, and into the garden He placed created man (Genesis 2:8). This was the abode God prepared for His created humans, Adam and Eve.

36. During the time of their innocence in the Garden of Eden, Adam and Eve were led by their spirit that was in constant communion with God, Spirit to spirit. After succumbing to the sin of

disobedience, their soul acquired *knowledge of good and evil* which turned their life upside down. Because of their terrible sin, their soul (reason and intelligence) began commanding their body and spirit. This inherent sin state is within all who are born of man. (Romans 3:23) God did not leave them in the idyllic Garden of Eden but drove them out into the world from where they had to fend for themselves.

37. Adam and Eve worked the earth for their survival. They planted, reaped, and made their abode outside of Eden. God sealed this place and never permitted anyone else to enter it.

38. To better understand the depth of Scripture, Spirit-filled believers follow the biblical explanation of the periods that have brought man from the creation of Adam to the ultimate fulfilment of God's purpose for him. These periods throughout the Word are best described as they relate to the overall changes in earth's condition, termed "ages," and the moral state of mankind, termed "dispensations."

39. The Bible's message can be separated into three "ages." These ages are periods of time, space, and distance that change when a cataclysmic event on earth takes place. Within these ages are "dispensations" that refer to the moral standing and changes that mankind undergoes during an age.

40. The first "age" is called the Antediluvian Age. This is the period from Adam and Eve's fall in the Garden of Eden until the flood in Noah's day. The moral standing of man during the initial stages of the age was that of innocence until man ate of the tree of knowledge of good and evil. God banished them from the Garden of Eden and cursed the ground which man had to work to survive. (Genesis 3:17–19) With this change, moral decay began to infiltrate man's soul.

41. *The earth also was corrupt before God, and the earth was filled with violence. So God looked upon the earth, and indeed it*

was corrupt; for all flesh had corrupted their way on the earth. (Genesis 6:11–12 NKJV)

42. Because of this moral decay and corruption, God purged the earth in Noah's day with devastating floods. The rain (waters) were poured out for forty days and covered the entire earth (Genesis 7:12), destroying all living things that were not in the ark. This was a cataclysmic event that closed the Antediluvian Age.

43. After more than six months' stay in the ark, Noah, his family, and the animals left the ark and once again worked the earth. This was the beginning of the Present Age. (Genesis 9:1–7) God establishes a new covenant ... *Thus I establish My covenant with you: never again shall all flesh be cut off by the waters of the flood; never again shall there be a flood to destroy the earth. And God said: This is the sign of the covenant which I make between Me and you, and every living creature that is with you, for perpetual generations: I set My rainbow in the cloud, and it shall be for the sign of the covenant between Me and the earth....* (Genesis 9:11–13 NKJV)

44. To summarize this Antediluvian Age, it encompassed two "Dispensations." The first was the moral innocence of Adam and Eve, and second, it was the moral decay and corruption of mankind. This caused God to destroy all living things except for those He shut in the ark. (Genesis 7:16)

45. From Noah until the Second Coming of Jesus, the Present Age exists. Even though God demonstrates His presence in their midst, mankind continues along their path of wayward destruction.

46. This age can be divided into four "Dispensations." The first dispensation is the period when human government was established and ended at the Tower of Babel. (Genesis 11:1–9) It began when Noah and his son, Shem, led the people in the way of the Lord and reestablished the worship of God who delivered them from the flood by reintroducing the sacrificial altar. (Genesis 8:20–22) However, amongst mankind, corruption and the lust for

power again reared its head. In this dispensation, man became a unified and powerful force that was tempted to *make a name for* (themselves) *ourselves* (Genesis 11:4 NKJV). God intervened and scattered them throughout the earth and confused their languages (Genesis 11:6–8).

47. The second dispensation in the present age began with the patriarchs. It was the time when mankind turned from their worship of God to the establishment of idolatry and the overwhelming increase of idol worship. It was from amongst the idol worshippers that God chose a patriarch, Abram. This dispensation began with a journey from the Ur of the Chaldeans into Canaan. God made a covenant with Abram, changed his name to Abraham, and promised him and his generations the land to which He had led him.

48. Abraham's son, Isaac, and the next generations from Jacob to Joseph are considered the patriarchs of this dispensation who followed the Law of God. This law encompassed two commands: love the Lord your God and your neighbor. (Matthew 22:37–40) By these two commandments the patriarchs lived and established their race. The tragic end of this dispensation was the captivity of the Israelites in Egypt.

49. The third dispensation started when God called Moses to deliver His people, Israel, from the bondages of slavery in Egypt, and led them into Canaan, the land He promised to Abraham. (Exodus 3:6–10) This dispensation, as with the preceding dispensations, began with a miraculous God-given experience. God delivered them from their bondage and allowed them to return to Canaan.

50. During their journey to Canaan, God presented them with His theocratic rulership. He introduced the Law of Moses, the Ten Commandments, that His people were to follow. By contrast, this "governmental rule" was God to man, whereas the governmental rule in the first dispensation was a humanistic form of government,

namely man to man. Clarence Larkin says, "This dispensation extended from the Exodus to the birth of Christ."

51. This third dispensation continued until Jesus was crucified, raised from the dead, and ascended into heaven. His victory over death and the grave closed the dispensation and covenant of Law and opened a third dispensation of Grace. This is the dispensation of the church and the establishment of *a new covenant* in Christ's *blood* (Matthew 26:28 NKJV). It begins at the cross and ends at the rapture of the saints.

52. At the rapture of the saints, the fourth dispensation begins—that of judgment. The saints are before Jesus at the Judgment Seat of Christ in heaven, and the remaining unbelievers and the Jews on earth come under the horrific judgment of the Antichrist during the Great Tribulation.

53. What follows the Present Age is the introduction of the "Age to come" (Ephesians 2:7). This age starts at the return of Jesus to earth until the new heaven and the new earth are ushered in. During this age, two dispensations occur. The first dispensation in the age to come is the one thousand years' reign Jesus has on earth (Millennium Reign). Jesus rules this period in righteousness. Once the Millennium period is concluded, a new heaven and a new earth are introduced, and the fourth and perfect dispensation starts. This is the time when God introduces a new heaven and a new earth, and mankind lives in the holiness of God forever. (Revelation 22:5)

CHAPTER 24

THE DOCTRINE OF CREATION –

CONTINUED

Invisible Creation

1. God, in His infinite wisdom, created spirit beings called angels, and He created within man an invisible spirit and soul. Unlike all other things created, these two invisible creations live eternally.

2. There are some similarities between the angelic host and man's created soul and spirit.

   Both are an eternal spirit from the day of their creation.

   Both angels and man have free will to accept or reject their Creator.

   They are created to worship and bring pleasure to God.

   They are the messengers of God's will and purpose, angels from Heaven and man on earth who does God's bidding.

   They have intellect and emotions.

   They are both exposed to evil temptations. While righteous angels have already been freed from their temptation and judgment, and the unrighteous angels have been incarcerated until their judgment, man undergoes this trial from the time he is born until his spirit and soul are separated from his body when he dies.

Angels

3. Angels are not eternal in existence. They were created by God (Psalm 148:2, 5, Col. 1:16). They were created before Earth was created (Job 38:6–7). However, from their creation, they live eternally (Luke 20:35–36).

4. Angels are "spirit beings" created by God for specific purposes. They worship and serve God (Psalm 19:1), and they are protectors of God's temporary creation. They destroy, build, and change God's creation at His command.

5. They are the protectors of God's supreme creation, mankind. (Hebrews 1:14) They have destroyed the wicked, saved the righteous from wicked onslaughts, brought messages of encouragement, and warnings of impending grief and doom.

6. They never marry or procreate. (Matthew 22:30) Neither do they die or must be separated from a physical form such as a body when man's soul and spirit is taken at his death.

7. These spirit beings have intellect, emotions, and possess a will of their own. They are created "above" man; i.e. they have greater powers. They are spiritually created, indivisible, and have no matter (bodies) until called upon by their Creator to assume a body for a purpose.

8. They have no mortal body that must die and decay. They are wiser and stronger than man. They are not bound by limiting capacities that man has (time and distance).

9. As to the number of angels God has created, there is no definitive count in the Bible other than to quote that there are many thousands. (Hebrews 12:22, Revelation 5:11)

10. God's created place for the angelic host is heaven. They serve

God from the moment they were created and constantly worship Him. The Bible states that there are *heavens*. The place where angels dwell is in the heaven known biblically as the *third heaven* (2 Corinthians 12:2) where God has His throne (Revelation 4:1–2), which is also the place where a righteous man's soul and spirit is destined after his death.

11. The *third heaven* is a place of spiritual harmony and reverencing God. From this place, God dispatches His angels to fulfill specific tasks and functions. The place created for angels is in the eternal presence of God. It is outside the measurement of time and distance. It is a *place*, not a figment of man's imagination. It is in existence today. It is a spiritual place where spirits live in the presence of God. The spiritual inhabitants constantly worship the Creator. (Psalm 148:2–6)

12. The angelic host is structured in heaven. Each of the separate created angelic hierarchy (seraphim, cherubim, archangels, and angels) resides in a God-created place.

13. Heaven has a *spiritual "heavenly Holy of Holies"* not created by man, but God. (Hebrews 9:23–28) Around this "throne room" (Psalm 45:6, Isaiah 6:1–6) seraphim worship God. This is the highest seat of authority and "innermost" part of Heaven. Here exists a seat at the *right hand of God*, the place of honor and power to which Jesus Christ was elevated and now resides. (Acts 2:30–33, Hebrews 1:13)

14. This is the place of the *spiritual altar* where Jesus constantly makes intercession for the righteous saints (Hebrews 7:25, 13:8–17). Jesus placed His own blood on the *spiritual mercy seat* which is the blood offering God, the Father, accepted for the forgiveness of sin (Hebrews 9:11–15).

15. The born-again believer approaches the Father in the Name of Jesus. (John 16:23) His Name gives access to the Father while believers are on the earth. Furthermore, Jesus ... *who is even at*

the right hand of God, who also maketh intercession for us....
(Romans 8:34)

16. In this divinely created place, the angelic host fulfills their ultimate mission of worshipping God. Surrounding the highest seat of honor, the holy throne of God, seraphim are constantly present saying ... *Holy, holy, holy, is the LORD of hosts: the whole earth is full of his glory....* (Isaiah 6:3) Likewise, Apostle John gives the account that was revealed to him about the holy throne ... *Then I looked, and I heard the voice of many angels around the throne, the living creatures, and the elders; and the number of them was ten thousand times ten thousand, and thousands of thousands saying with a loud voice: Worthy is the Lamb who was slain to receive power and riches and wisdom and strength and honor and glory and blessing....* (Revelation 5:11–12 NKJV)

17. Cherubim are instructed by God to protect and seal His creation. They were *placed ... at the east of the garden of Eden, and a flaming sword which turned every way, to guard the way to the tree of life....* (Genesis 3:24 NKJV) They "covered" the Ark of the Covenant (1 Samuel 4:4, Psalm 99:1).

18. Scripture speaks of one archangel, Michael. (Jude 9) His tasks are that of a mighty warrior. He is the archangel designated to war against the devil (Revelation 12:7–12) and cast him out of heaven (the second heaven).

19. The tasks of the remainder of the angelic host are varied. They communicate God's message to humans. Gabriel, a named angel, brought messages to God's servants, Zechariah and Mary (Luke 1:13–38). They also minister to man's needs and rejoice when a lost sinner repents (Luke 15:10).

20. They possess the ability to execute the judgment of God on His enemies. They have great strength and can protect believers from evil onslaughts (Exodus 14:19, 2 Kings 19:35, Acts 12:23). They stand ready to accompany Jesus at His return to earth (Matthew 25:31). They are available and are instantly dispatched by their

Supreme Commander, Jesus Christ, who will ... *send His angels with a great sound of a trumpet, and they will gather together His elect from the four winds, from one end of heaven to the other....* (Matthew 24:31 NKJV)

Lucifer (Satan, the Devil), and the Fallen Angels

21. Per the Bible, a *covering cherub*, Lucifer, became possessed with his beauty and his power over the created "human form" on the Pre-Adamite earth, and desired to replace God on His throne. In his attempt, he gained support of a third of the angelic host who acknowledged him as their god.

22. God dealt with Lucifer and cast him out of heaven. (Isaiah 14:12–21, Ezekiel 28:11–19) Simultaneously, God cast from His presence in heaven those fallen angels who chose Lucifer above God ... *For ... God did not spare the angels who sinned, but cast them down to hell and delivered them into chains of darkness to be reserved for judgment....* (2 Peter 2:4, Jude 6 NKJV)

23. Fallen angels are not demon forces that roam the earth. These angels, who were succumbed to follow Lucifer, are to never populate the earth after their expulsion from heaven.

24. These fallen angels are held in their own place, Tartarus, *in chains of darkness*. For them, the contrast between heaven and Tartarus is their torment and punishment. They were in the presence of God's Shekinah glory, the perfect light of God, whereas now they are in total *darkness*. This is spiritual darkness that separates them from the presence of God. These chains are equally tormenting to them because there was a time when they could be dispatched anywhere at any time, but now they are bound and locked up, preventing them from going anywhere.

25. Tartarus will be opened at the Great White Throne Judgment, and these angels will be judged and cast into the Lake of Fire (2 Peter

2:4, Jude 6). This is the final act of separation from God for the fallen angels. Their abode will then be with the wicked in the Lake of Fire.

26. It is important to study the existence of Lucifer/Satan, whom God cast out of heaven. To begin, this adversary was a beautifully created angel who was given custodianship of some of God's creation. He possesses unbelievable wisdom and both spiritual and physical strength. Ezekiel 28:11–19 gives a full description of the countenance and abilities of Lucifer.

27. His pride, lust, and desire for total control of all things created was his demise. God dealt to him the act of expulsion from His presence when He cast him from heaven onto the earth. (Isaiah 14:12–20)

28. Satan is the adversary of mankind. He is relentless in his pursuits to *steal, and to kill, and to destroy....* (John 10:10) He has knowledge of the Godhead and of the Holy Spirit's power imparted to Spirit-filled believers. (Acts 1:8) Even so, Satan unleashes enormous attacks and enticement on Spirit-filled believers who constantly ... *Do not wrestle against flesh and blood, but principalities, against powers, against the rulers of darkness of this age, against spiritual hosts of wickedness in the heavenly places....* (Ephesians 6:12 NKJV)

29. The extent of his wisdom and capabilities as a covering cherub are above that of man who has never been born-again. He has extreme influences over man's flesh and soul. The enticements and lusts of the flesh are part of his arsenal that lures mankind into sinful acts.

30. God banished Lucifer/Satan from His presence in heaven to earth where he roamed for countless years. At the restoration of earth and the creation of man, Satan again began his relentless attack on mankind to turn them against God. He was personally and spiritually present on earth from where he orchestrated the demon forces to corrupt mankind.

31. When Jesus was raised from the dead, He destroyed the works of the devil (1 John 3:8), and Jesus proclaimed ... *Now shall the prince of this world be cast out....* (John 12:31) It was at the time of Jesus' resurrection that Satan was cast off the earth into what is called the "second heaven." From this place, he commands his demonic cohorts and indoctrinates human followers to sow deceit and evil amongst the people on earth.

32. The ultimate victory and destruction of the devil's work by Jesus is the victory over death (eternal separation from God) to everyone who believes in Him (Romans 6:23, 10:9–10). Following Jesus' ascension to heaven, the Holy Spirit's omnipresence amongst the people on earth presents *Jesus Christ and Him crucified,* which is salvation. (John 16:7–15) Satan, as ruler of the earth, has been *judged* (John 16:11) and launches his attacks from the second heaven by commanding the demonic forces and deception towards mankind.

33. Satan's foremost weapon on mankind is his deception. He is the deceiver who has a sin-infested counterfeit operation that mirrors God's holy ordinances and the divine grace that flows from a merciful God. (Galatians 1:6–9, 1 Timothy 4:1–2) He *blinds* the minds (2 Corinthians 4:4), sows confusion that deceives man into believing a lie (John 8:44, 2 Thessalonians 2:9–12).

34. His deception is infested in people who proclaim a false doctrine that deceives believers into adopting counterfeit and false teachings ... *But there were false prophets among the people, even as there will be false teachers among you, who will secretly bring in destructive heresies, even denying the Lord who bought them, and bring on themselves swift destruction... by covetousness they will exploit you with deceptive words....* (2 Peter 2:1,3 NKJV)

35. His first attack on created man was none other than deception. He tempted Eve to partake of the fruit of the tree of knowledge of good and evil by deceiving her with the deceptive question

... *hath God said*.... (Genesis 3:1) He seals his deceit when he affirms to Eve in a lie ... *Ye shall not surely die*.... (Genesis 3:4)

36. The carnal man who has never accepted Jesus Christ as his Savior is not a real threat to the devil. This person is the easiest and most vulnerable instrument he has at his disposal. Satan is aware of the greatness and holiness of God, and he *blinds* and *confuses* the minds of lost sinners, keeping them in the way of sin's darkness. These people are disposable fodder in his methods of destruction. His real concern is the attack he relentlessly launches on the saved.

37. Born-again believers are his primary target. The devil knows the glorious presence of Almighty God and the extent of His love. He observes the transformation that takes place when a man's spirit is born again, and he knows it is the result of the victory Jesus won at Calvary. Satan is not oblivious to the glorious rebirth of a man who accepts Jesus Christ as his Savior. It fuels the devil's wrath and hatred as he experiences the *bruise* (on) *thy head*.... (Genesis 3:15)

38. God's purging of heaven during the seven years of the Great Tribulation begins in the middle of that period. Satan and his angels war with the archangel, Michael, and his angels. This is the final expulsion of Satan from the second heaven. He is cast from this place back onto earth. This is the time when he unleashes a horrific attack as an anti-type of all that God is.

39. Satan sets up an anti-Godhead comprising of the dragon (anti-Father), the beast (Antichrist), and the false prophet (anti-Holy Spirit). From this platform, he infiltrates every area of man's existence for *a short time*. (Revelation 12:12)

40. The heavens are rid of the satanic presence, and God pours out His wrath on earth through an abundance of plagues, as well as redeeming a chosen remnant of His people, the Jews.

41. At the conclusion of the seven years Great Tribulation, God

casts Satan into the bottomless pit for one thousand years. (Revelation 20:1–3)

42. To conclude, God's first invisible creation were the spirit-beings, angels. Their place of residence is heaven, and they are constant worshippers of God as well as do His bidding. The fallen angels and Lucifer were banished from this heavenly residence. The fallen angels are *in chains* incarcerated until the Great White Throne Judgment, while Lucifer is the enemy of mankind on earth. His current place is the second heaven.

43. The second invisible creation, man's soul and spirit, is discussed under the Doctrine of Man.

The Heavens

44. Scripture gives limited details about the heavens. At the outset, the *third* heaven, as mentioned above, is the place where angels reside. However, in this place there are other beings who have been taken there and reside in the presence of God.

45. To begin, Jesus is seated at the right hand of God in heaven. He is in His resurrected body that consists of flesh and bone. (Luke 24:39)

46. Second, in a place in heaven, there are resurrected people who have a body (flesh and bone), a soul, and a spirit. These are the ones who were resurrected after Jesus was raised from the dead. All these resurrected beings died before Jesus was crucified. When their bodies were returned to the ground, their spirits were taken to a place the Bible calls *Paradise*. At Jesus' resurrection they were raised from the dead, released from *paradise*, and *appeared* to man on earth, testifying to God's Word. (Matthew 27:52–53) There are no resurrected people on earth, and from this it is accepted that they were taken into heaven to be with Jesus. What they are doing in heaven while they wait for the return of Jesus to the earth is unknown to the inhabitants on earth.

47. Third, there are *two* human beings in a place in heaven who have never seen death: Enoch and Elijah. The Bible records that Elijah *went up* in a chariot of fire (2 Kings 2:11), while Enoch was *taken* by God as he *walked with God.* (Genesis 5:24)

48. Their righteousness and obedience to God while in human flesh, bone, and blood are the absolute testimony of man's ability to walk in perfectness before God while on earth. Because of this holy walk while on earth, God *took* them (raptured them) off earth to be in His presence in human form.

49. God has kept Enoch and Elijah in this human form for a specific purpose; they are to testify to the world in the Great Tribulation about God. (Revelation 11:1–14) The human body must always die before it can be resurrected as a glorified body for man's soul and spirit to live eternally. These two witnesses will be killed, and God will raise them up after three days and call them to heaven. They will return to heaven and live with the resurrected saints in the place God has prepared for all the resurrected ones who ascended to heaven with Jesus at His ascension.

50. Fourth, heaven has a place for the *dead in Christ.* (1 Thessalonians 4:16) This is the place where the righteous *souls and spirits* go immediately their body dies. (2 Corinthians 5:8)

51. This is a place where souls and spirits of the righteous dead reside. They do not have bodies.

52. Regarding the first two heavens, the Bible does not give as much detail about them as it does about the *third heaven.* Suffice to say that the firmament is the natural first heaven restored by God ... *and God called the firmament heaven....* (Genesis 1:6–8)

53. Regarding the second heaven, Scripture declares that Satan resides in a place referred to as *heaven* from where he is cast out back onto *the earth.* (Revelation 12:7–9) Little is known about the second heaven other than it is Satan's abode, and it is cleansed when Michael and his angels do battle with the devil and his angels and remove him from it.

54. To summarize the subject of the heavens, it is important to accept by faith that God created the heavens where spirit beings dwell as they wait for the Judgment Seat of Christ and the Marriage Supper of the Lamb in heaven. At this juncture, the spirits and souls in heaven receive a glorified body and stand alongside those currently in heaven in a glorified body.

55. The heavens will be cleansed, and the first heaven, the firmament, also undergoes a restoration as God renovates the earth with fire and creates a new heaven, a new earth, and a New Jerusalem.

PART 6

The Doctrine of Man

CHAPTER 25

THE DOCTRINE OF MAN

1. *So God created man in his own image, in the image of God created he him; male and female created he them....* (Genesis 1:27) Spirit-filled believers know and attest to the fact that man is not an evolved specimen that grew out of some other creation: they are explicitly and uniquely created by God.

2. The Bible says that mankind is created in God's *image and likeness.* (Genesis 1:26) The resemblance of *image* has been said to mean that man is created as God imaged (imagined) how he should be created. It is God's creation, and God created him with mental capacity and the ability to function on His earth, as God imaged man to be.

3. Mankind is not a useless form with no intentions or aptitude of existing independently. He is endowed with much more than every other created animal, bird, or fish. God desired that His created being be endowed with these traits, and as such, man is gifted with abilities above any other creation.

4. These intrinsic traits are encased in an incredible gift from God, namely, self-will. These God-given abilities can be used by mankind to focus on their Source, or mankind can channel them into a destructive and self-destructive avenue. Adam chose the

latter path and submerged the entire unrepentant human race into a state of sin ... *for all have sinned, and come short of the glory of God....* (Romans 3:23)

5. Before Adam sinned, the divine image was perfect and innocent. He walked in the presence of God and fulfilled God's pleasure, exactly as God had imaged he should. Every aspect of man was pure and clean, enabling him to walk in uprightness before his Creator. These attributes are who God is ... *His own image.*

6. It was man's self-willed decision to turn from God and disobediently fulfill his desire to eat of the forbidden fruit that severed the relationship between man and God. Sin permeated every area of man, and the image God purposed was tarnished forever.

7. *God's likeness* is the definition of man's inner being that involves moral and spiritual likeness to God. God is holy, pure, divine, righteous, and altogether love. These are God's gifts imparted to His created humankind. God created them in His *likeness*, as He is. Mankind is able to follow after this likeness or turn away from it, which he regrettably did, allowing sin to enter his being.

8. In essence, Adam rejected the divine way and followed his own destructive path. God in His abundant love, mercy, and grace restored this relationship at Calvary's Cross.

9. God's love is beyond human comprehension. He observed how man willfully disobeyed His command, and yet He never banished him to a lost eternity without making a way of escape for man to be reconciled to Him.

Man Is the Tri-Part Creation of God

10. Spirit-filled believers trust the Scripture that states created man is spirit, soul, and body. (1 Thessalonians 5:23) This is the imaged creation of God who created mankind after His likeness.

11. God's tri-part creation of man began when He *formed man of the dust of the ground.* (Genesis 2:7) The *form* is the translation for "shaped" man out of the dust. The dust (shaped body) had no life in it until God *breathed into his nostrils the breath of life.* This *breath* was the "life-giving" spirit God created in mankind. From the moment the body had a spirit, man became *a living soul.* The fusing of the two parts, body and spirit, produced the third part, namely the soul. Watchman Nee, in his book *The Spiritual Man,* gives this illustration, "Drop some dye into a cup of water. The dye and water will blend into a third substance called ink. In like manner, the two independent elements of spirit and body combine to become a living soul."

12. In the state of innocence, when God created Adam, his spirit controlled his body and soul. Man's spirit was in constant contact with his creator, God. His spirit received directions from God, who is Spirit. Man's spirit directed his soul. The soul directed the body to perform its will.

13. The spirit is a God-created part of the human being. This is where the relationship between man and his Creator exists. In its purity, Adam's spirit communed with God until he sinned. God cannot accommodate sin. Adam broke the relationship and communication between him and God, and it caused his spirit to no longer be pure but stained by sin.

14. Adam's spirit was the ruling part over his soul and body. It was from the guidance of God, Spirit to spirit, that he functioned in the Garden of Eden. The instant he sinned he acquired the knowledge of good and evil, and his soul was now the ruler of his spirit and body. Adam's spirit *died.* This is the first stage God said would happen to him if he ate of the tree of knowledge of good and evil ... *for in the day that thou eatest thereof thou shalt surely die....* (Genesis 2:17)

15. Adam's *death* began when he lost the relationship with God. His physical death happened much later. Suffice to say that his spirit's

death was the losing of control of the body and soul, resulting in the spirit becoming dormant in him and literally of no use until it is born again.

16. Watchman Nee says it best, "Every human being still has in his possession a spirit, although it is darkened by sin and impotent to hold communion with God." This is unregenerate man who lives according to his sin nature with which he is born. The resultant sin Adam did has poisoned every human being born on earth until they are born again. Lockyer categorically states, "The results of Adam's sin are terrible to contemplate. Sin became universal." (Romans 5:12, 19)

17. The moment Adam sinned, the soul became the ruler of the body and the spirit. The soul is the seat of man's free will, intelligence, emotion, and reasoning. It was elevated to the position of controller when Adam became knowledgeable of what is good and evil. No human being can ever declare they don't know what is good or evil; all are born with this inherent ability to discern the difference.

18. The soul's desires are fed by the senses the flesh observes as well as the intuitive thoughts it conjures in dealing with every decision it reasons and ultimately makes. The flesh (body) is stimulated by touch, taste, smell, sound, and sight, transmitting its desires to the soul. The soul is influenced by these impulses that cause it to decide on an action. In unregenerate man, their spirit has no part in this process. The sin nature is the manual the soul references when making every decision ... *among whom also we all once conducted ourselves in the lusts of our flesh, fulfilling the desires of the flesh and of the mind, and were by nature children of wrath....* (Ephesians 2:3 NKJV)

19. The restoration of the relationship and fellowship between God and man could never be restored by man; his sin made him incapable of this reunification. Only the offended and rejected party in the relationship, namely God, had the holy, pure, righteous, and

divine ability to do this. God offered Himself, through His Son, Jesus Christ, as a sacrifice to remove the stain of sin perpetrated in the Garden of Eden, and which is inherent in all mankind. (John 3:16, Hebrews 9:12, 14–15) ... *But this man, after he had offered one sacrifice for sins forever, sat down on the right hand of God....* (Hebrews 10:12) The death and resurrection of Jesus opened the pathway to the *throne of grace* (Hebrews 4:16) ... *I am the way ...* (John 14:6); and upon man's confession and repentance of sin, he accepts Jesus Christ as his Savior and is born again ... *That which is born of the Spirit is spirit....* (John 3:6) This is the awakening of man's spirit that is dominated by his soul to once again be the ruling part of his soul and body.

20. What was originally purposed by God—that man's spirit be the essential part of his nature—was, through sin, made subject to his soul. God's creation of man was not purposed this way, but man's decision (self-will) to sin forfeited this Spirit-to-spirit relationship, causing the separation of his spirit from God. The victory Jesus accomplished on the Cross was the restoration of the relationship between God and man.

21. The instant the person confesses Jesus Christ as Lord and he repents of his inherent sin, he is born again. This takes place at the Cross, and his spirit is filled with the Spirit of Christ.

22. From that moment the work of the Holy Spirit begins, which is the separating of the soul from the spirit (dividing asunder the control the soul has over the spirit). The liberation of the spirit is performed by the Holy Spirit's skillful application of the two-edged sword, the Word, which the Holy Spirit uses as He matures the believer. (Hebrews 4:12)

23. The Holy Spirit's severing of man's soul and spirit that is performed with the instrument of the Word of God is not an instantaneous slice that divides them apart. It is a slow and convincing revelation into the spirit. The clinging jaws of the soul that have engulfed the spirit are reluctant to release its grip on the spirit, thus making the

Holy Spirit's dividing work a delicate and purposeful activity that separates the two vital components of man while at the same time not destroying either of their abilities and importance.

24. Man's soul and spirit live forever, and neither must be bruised or damaged while the Holy Spirit surgically uses the power in the Word of God to separate them. The speed of the process is however not up to the Holy Spirit, but rather in man's hands as to how quickly he wants to be entirely Holy Spirit and spirit-led.

25. It cannot be stressed enough that the realignment of control from soul to spirit in a man is achieved through only one measure, faith. Faith applied lets the Holy Spirit have His way as He takes the Word of God and expertly performs the separation of man's two invisible parts from each other. (Romans 10:17)

26. The *image* and *likeness* that was indelibly stained by sin is cleansed by Jesus Christ's sacrifice. Jesus, the perfect Man, the sinless Man, the holy Man is ... *the image of the invisible God ...* (Colossians 1:15) and ... *who being the brightness of His glory and the express image of His person, and upholding all things by the word of His power, when He had by Himself purged our sins....* (Hebrews 1:3 NKJV)

Man's Privilege, Purpose, and Promise

27. Ultimately, the question needs to be asked: why did God create man in His own image and likeness? The biblical answer is the only explanation needed.

28. First, man is a Privileged Creation. Scripture speaks of the status man has in the order of God's creation ... *What is man that You are mindful of him, and the son of man that You visit him? For You have made him a little lower than the angels, and You have crowned him with glory and honor....* (Psalm 8:4–5 NKJV)

Without doubt, man is God's highest and most perfect creation in which He, by His Spirit, also dwells.

29. This Scripture states that man is created *a little lower than the angels*. The correct translation of the word *angels* is *God*. However, to give the rightful status of created man who has authority and dominion over God's creation (Psalm 8:6–8), the word *angels* is used because of the bodily form man has, and which must die and return to the earth's dust. Angels have no bodily form and never die. Hence the clarification of man's status as created a little lower than the angels.

30. To extrapolate it further, once man's spirit is born again, he enters the promise of eternal life in the presence of Almighty God forever even as the angels are eternally present. Henceforth, man is higher than angels and will judge them. (1 Corinthians 6:1–3) Thus, the correct translation can be stated that man, once born again, is higher than angels yet a *little lower than God*.

31. In this privileged state, man can communicate with his Creator. There is no distance between man's born-again spirit and God. The *way, the truth and the life* ... is abundantly opened by Jesus Christ' death and resurrection, and now His name affords mankind access to the spiritual presence of Almighty God, the Father. Prayer unlocks the door to the Father's heart and, in His holy presence, man is privileged to pray in the spirit with his Creator.

32. Furthermore, this privilege enables man to worship and praise his Creator. In like manner, as the angels do, man can enter the *closet ... abide under the shadow of the Almighty ... mount up on wings as eagles* and pour out adoration, adulation, and utterances *in tongues of angels* in the very presence of Almighty God. This privilege is given to no other living creature.

33. How utterly sad and disappointing to God is the dearth of both prayer and adoration man makes to God. The overwhelming anarchy, hatred, and lust of the flesh is entirely unnecessary, and would pale into insignificance if man would avail himself of the

privilege and focus his energies on entering God's presence with fervor and a righteous hunger to commune with Him.

34. Ultimately, man is privileged to have fellowship with God. The wall of separation is brought down at the Cross, and the intimate *knowing God* in perfect fellowship where no sin or discord exists is the absolute privilege every born-again believer enjoys. There is no debt hanging over the repentant heart, neither is there guilt that gnaws at his soul. It is fellowship sublime, and pure sweet love that flows both from God to man and from man to God.

35. The awful separation that was the result of sin, and which banished man into isolation from his Creator, is eradicated at the Cross. The nail-scarred hand reaches down and lifts the repentant heart out of the miry clay, cleanses its sin stain, and brings it into the presence of the Holy Father to fellowship in pure undefiled righteousness.

36. Second, man is a Purposed Creation. The Bible declares that the purpose for which man is created is for God's glory ... *for I have created him for my glory....* (Isaiah 43:7) This divine creation by Almighty God is the manifestation of His glory on earth. Nothing compares to this creation. The loftiest mountain peaks and the deepest ravines arrayed in the splendor of God's colors doesn't come near the magnificence of created man. And this unmatched creation God purposes that man manifests His glory.

37. Furthermore, it is by God's own will (desire) and for His pleasure that man is created ... *For thou hast created all things, and for thy pleasure they are and were created....* (Revelation 4:11) The ultimate expression of God's pleasure occurs when the Spirit-filled believer *mounts up with wings like eagles, hungers and thirsts after righteousness,* and *meditates day and night on the Lord.* It is in holy convocation, Spirit-led worship in unknown tongues, songs of praise erupting from a pure heart that reaches Almighty God as a *sweet savor.*

38. Mankind is purposed to serve the Lord God ... *serve the LORD*

thy God with all thy heart and with all thy soul.... (Deuteronomy 10:12) Incredible as it may seem, man is called upon to serve God, yet God gives man the ability and wherewithal to serve Him *... my God shall supply all your need....* (Philippians 4:19)

39. Mankind is commanded to *... go ye into all the world, and preach the gospel to every creature ....* (Mark 16:15) Spirit-filled believers don't take this command lightly. They understand that their task is to be a light in the dark world, a testimony and witness of the saving grace of God, and an example of the indwelling righteousness as they no longer walk in their old ways but now *walk in the Spirit.* (Galatians 5:25) This is the purpose of the church throughout all its existence.

40. The Christian's command is from heaven's most glorious Citizen, Jesus Christ. His power to perform his tasks is from the most glorious Holy Spirit, and his workmanship is entirely drenched in the anointing from the Most High God. Lewis Chafer says it best, "The Christian is a citizen of heaven and after he is saved is detained here in this world in the capacity of a witness. He is a pilgrim and stranger, an ambassador from the court of heaven."

41. This grandiose creation, mankind, that was purposed by God to *have dominion* (Genesis 1:26) over every living thing on earth, is once again reconciled to the Father, and is now licensed to share with the lost sinner the greatest gift from God—forgiveness of sin and eternal life through Christ Jesus.

42. Third, Man is Promised Everlasting Life *... Let God be true, but every man a liar....* (Romans 3:4) God has given mankind the promise *... whosoever believeth in him should not perish, but have everlasting life....* (John 3:16) His promises are unchanging, and He will honor His word to the redeemed. Everlasting life will not be given to the redeemed because they hold God accountable to His Word; it will happen because God has promised He will give mankind everlasting life. (1 John 2:25)

43. Faith in Calvary's finished work is all God requires a repentant heart to have to be an heir of His promise. Faith reaches into the unseen and hopes for the fulfillment of God's promise (Hebrews 11:1). It is through the application of faith that the believer becomes determined to cling to the promise that he is redeemed. It is by faith that he confesses Jesus Christ as Lord, and in faith walks according to the precepts of God's Word.

44. Closely allied to the Doctrine of Man are the Doctrine of Predestination, the Doctrine of Sin, and the Doctrine of Salvation.

Predestination

45. The omniscient, omnipresent, and omnipotent God, who has all things under His control, can purpose every action man has, is, and in his future, will do. In His infinite wisdom and knowledge, God has full comprehension of every aspect of man's thinking and doing long before he ever says or does anything. It is because God has this *foreknowledge* that He can *predestine* man's existence. These are vital prerequisites in this difficult subject.

46. To expand the biblical explanation, Scripture further teaches that it is God who *elects* from mankind those He chooses to fulfill certain functions on His behalf. It is, therefore, vital that these three words, *foreknowledge, election,* and *predestination* be kept together as the subject is studied. Dr. C.I. Scofield says, "The divine order is *foreknowledge, election, predestination.* That foreknowledge determines the election or choice is clear from 1 Peter 1:2, and predestination is the bringing to pass of the election. Election looks back to foreknowledge: predestination forward to the destiny."

47. It cannot be overstated that God is altogether sovereign, supreme, and almighty. He alone is the omniscient Being who has full comprehension of all that man is. God has full knowledge of

every fiber of man's being. There is nothing man does or says that takes God by surprise; He knows it before man speaks or does it (*foreknowledge*). Furthermore, God predestined the church even before the creation of time. It was always within the Godhead to establish the body of Christ, and have believers enter into a divine relationship again after the fall.

48. If this is the case, and it is, then surely God's *foreknowledge* of man's utterances and deeds predestine him to the place of his choosing, and not God's choosing. God knows what decision man will make, and therefore God can predestine him to that end.

49. Mankind's puny mind cannot fully comprehend the fact that God knows everything long before it will ever happen. His mind can only assume future events. All the planning and rules mankind lays to perfect a future incident does not assure him of the result he imagines it to be. It is only hindsight that allows mankind to view the incident in its fullest extent.

50. Even though mankind can draw on previous events of the same incident, they will never be the same as the proposed future event. This is a simple fact based on the premise that mankind does not have foreknowledge of anything. God is well aware of man's intention and proposed action, and God knows every detail, statistic, and minute activity associated with an event that has not yet happened. God's *foreknowledge* is unique to Him and outside of man's capabilities.

51. Because God has *foreknowledge,* He knows the ability a man has that enables him to fulfill His good pleasure. God will *elect* a person because He knows what the result will be ... *elect according to the foreknowledge of God the Father...* (1 Peter 1:2). Hence, God's *foreknowledge* of a person enables Him to *elect* him and thus predestine the person's future ... *For whom He foreknew, He also predestined to be conformed to the image of His Son ... Moreover whom He predestined, these He also called....* (Romans 8:29–30 NKJV)

52. God is *not willing that any should perish, but that all should come to repentance....* (2 Peter 3:9) Because of God's love, mercy, and grace, it is His desire that all mankind should be saved. However, the decision to accept the *gift* of salvation is man's. Those who receive Jesus Christ as their Lord and Savior are the *elect ... vessels of mercy, which he had afore prepared unto glory* (Romans 9:23).

53. The continuous life as the *elect* is determined by man. It requires a diligent attention to the Holy Spirit's leading and guidance into all truth. Apostle Peter reminds believers of this path they must walk (2 Peter 1:5–9), as it assures them of being steadfast and unmovable ... *Brethren, be even more diligent to make your call and election sure, for if you do these things you will never stumble....* (2 Peter 1:10 NKJV)

54. There is no truth in the statement that God chooses those He wants to grant eternal life and those He banishes to a lost eternity. It is mankind's individual choice to accept the gift of God, and because God has foreknowledge of what man's decision is going to be, He can predestine him according to this end.

PART 7

The Doctrine of Sin and the Doctrine of Salvation

The Doctrine of Sin

26. DOCTRINE - Original Sin
    a. The origin of sin
    b. Soulish sins
    c. The sins of the flesh
    d. Spiritual sin
    e. Degrees of sin
    f. The unforgivable sin
    g. God's remedy for man's sin
    h. The Doctrine of Hell. This subject is covered in detail as to the created places of the underworld and the various destinations of the dead.

The Doctrine of Salvation

27. DOCTRINE – Of Salvation: The Purpose of Christ's Earthly Mission.

a. Salvation: "Atonement" and "Redemption"
b. Repentance:
c. Justification:
d. The Possibility of Falling from Grace

CHAPTER 26

THE DOCTRINE OF SIN

1. *For all have sinned, and come short of the glory of God* ... (Romans 3:23) ... *for the wages of sin is death* ... (Romans 6:23) ... *If we confess our sins, he is faithful and just to forgive us our sins....* (1 John 1:9) The Bible is very clear about sin, the consequences of sin, and the love, mercy, and grace God has towards those who repent of their sin.

2. In this contemporary world, Satan is blinding, deceiving, and convincing mankind to believe that sin has no real death, namely, separation from God. What mankind interprets as sin today is measured against philosophical and social standards. These standards are based on humanistic and legal declarations that govern human conduct thoroughly void of the true meaning of sin.

3. Furthermore, because of a humanistic view, what one man views as sin another does not. The biblical rendition of sin and its consequences also provides the answer of salvation. If there is no biblical reference to sin, then there is no victory over sin.

The Origin of Sin

4. Spirit-filled believers know and affirm that sin originated in the time when Lucifer (Satan) elevated himself to a prideful and arrogant position. It was his selfish and evil intent to overthrow God and become as God. This evil intent was, and still is, so aggreging that he was banished from heaven. Far too many preachers avoid declaring the fact that sin is from the devil, and they veer away from proclaiming ... *the soul that sins shall surely die, ... the wages of sin is death ... the blood of Jesus Christ His Son cleanses us from all sin.* These words appear hollow in a contemporary world, having no impact on a socialistic and humanistic adoption of the consequences of sin.

5. Deception has, is, and will be the weapon Satan uses against the righteous. Yet the Bible is clear ... *Be not deceived; God is not mocked: for whatsoever a man soweth, that shall he also reap* .... (Galatians 6:7) Spirit-filled believers are adamant that their enemy, the devil, is out to ... *steal, and to kill, and to destroy....* (John 10:10)

6. When contemplating the subject of sin, Spirit-filled believers know, and are abundantly aware, of the seriousness God places on sin and the sinner.

7. Throughout the Holy Writ, there is constant reference to man's sin and the seriousness with which God views it. This is not a subject that is open to human interpretation or socialist and legal governance; sin and its consequences are between man and God. The plumb line that is the only true standard that measures sin is the eternal Word of God. He alone is *the way, the truth, and the life.* (John 14:6)

8. Sin is defined in the *Bible Encyclopedia* as, "Sin is to be defined primarily in relation to God. It is disobedience, unbelief, ignorance, the positive assertion of usurped autonomy, and the wicked deviation from, or violation of, God's righteous will and

law. The breach of a right relationship with God carries with it the disruption of a right relationship with others and the disintegration of self. But this is derivative (result) for it is because of sin against God, there is sin against others."

9. It is worth studying the definition as it has been portrayed through the church age. The first apostles declared the depravity of man's soul ...*All have sinned and come short of the glory of God* .... Then to Augustine who, centuries later, stated, "Sin is turning away from the Creator, and turning toward inferior, created things." Martin Luther declared in the sixteenth century, "Our nature has been so deeply curved in upon itself because of the viciousness of original sin that it not only turns the finest gifts in upon itself ... it even uses God Himself to achieve these aims ... for its own sake."

10. More aptly put, the first chief apostle of the Apostolic Church of Great Britain, D.P. Williams, said in the early twentieth century, sin is "turning toward everything that is evil and devilish, and away from God and all that is good and true. It is a deficiency of love to God and man, (and as well as) a preference of self to God."

11. Spirit-filled believers take it to a logical conclusion: sin is not only a transgression of God's holiness, it is the lack of obedience to abide in His holiness. Further, it pertains to acts of ignorance that—because the person is unaware or not willing to follow God's righteousness and holiness—they substitute it with falsehood.

12. A perfect example of this tragedy is the present denominational diversity within the church. The blueprint for the church's structure is carefully outlined in the Holy Writ. Yet there are many deviations from it, and Jesus' divine impartation of apostles, prophets, evangelists, pastors, and teachers to the church have been cast aside and replaced with man's humanistic inventions of every conceivable title and function other than what Jesus gave to the church.

13. Apostle Peter proclaims that there will be *false apostles and false teachers* (2 Peter 2:1) that will creep into the church, so believers are reminded to *...be sober, be vigilant; because your adversary the devil walks about like a roaring lion, seeking whom he may devour....* (1 Peter 5:8 NKJV)

14. Apostle Paul says ... *But what I do, I will also continue to do, that I may cut off the opportunity from those who desire an opportunity to be regarded just as we are in the things of which they boast. For such are false apostles, deceitful workers, transforming themselves into apostles of Christ. And no wonder! For Satan himself transforms himself into an angel of light. Therefore it is no great thing if his ministers also transform themselves into ministers of righteousness, whose end will be according to their works....* (2 Corinthians 11:12–15 NKJV)

15. The biblical account of the existence of sin and its consequences that drive it to deplorable acts is never more clearly explained than from the conduct the Jews and Romans enacted with Jesus. The divine, holy Christ faced the world that was filled with seething hatred towards Him. They despised Him and abhorred the Father and Jesus to such an extent that in their despicable hatred, they sinned by murdering the pure and righteous One. (John 15:22–25)

16. What a remarkable thought: the holy God who is totally without sin and is the only One who can truthfully unmask the intention of sinners, faces sinners who, in their hatred, put to death the only One who can forgive their sins.

17. It is summed up by a twenty-first century preacher, "Sin is any thought, intention, deed or persuasion that is contrary to God's will and purpose for mankind."

18. With this understanding that Satan is the one who first sinned and deceives mankind, it is vital that Spirit-filled believers know the mind of God regarding sin. They view this subject from God's standpoint and not man's interpretation.

19. Delving into the intentions of sinners and the acts of sin, it must be

clearly understood that "sin is not merely wrong acts and thoughts, but sinfulness as well, an inherent inner disposition inclining us to wrong acts and thoughts. We are not simply sinners because we sin; we sin because we are sinners. Sin is simply failure to let God be God and acknowledge God as God." (Millard Erickson)

20. Sin and its consequences are entirely the responsibility and accountability of mankind. It is mankind who sins and permits the growth of this evil to its ultimate destination ... *Let no one say when he is tempted, I am tempted by God; for God cannot be tempted by evil, nor does He Himself tempt anyone. But each one is tempted when he is drawn away by his own desires and enticed. Then, when desire has conceived, it gives birth to sin; and sin, when it is full-grown, brings forth death....* (James 1:13–15 NKJV)

21. The Bible gives numerous accounts of certain cataclysmic sins. The first is unbelief: Jesus said, *He who believes in Him is not condemned; but he who does not believe is condemned already, because he has not believed in the name of the only begotten Son of God....* (John 3:18 NKJV) An example of this sin is found when Jesus was crucified. One of the two thieves did not believe Jesus was the Savior while the other did, and he was saved.

22. The second and third are rebellion and stubbornness ... *Rebellion is as the sin of witchcraft, and stubbornness is as iniquity and idolatry ....* (1 Samuel 15:23) Rebellion is clearly witnessed in Judas Iscariot who rebelled against all he knew of Jesus and who He was. The rich young ruler is the example in the Word of stubbornness. He refused to give up what he had acquired and follow Jesus.

23. Fourth, the root of all sin is pride: *For all that is in the world, the lust of the flesh, and the lust of the eyes, and the pride of life, is not of the Father, but is of the world....* (1 John 2:16) Jesus gave the example of the Pharisee and the publican and how opposite they

were, one filled with pride and self-indignation, while the other humbly confessed his sinful state.

24. Fifth, undoubtedly, the most expressive sin towards God's goodness and love is hatred. The devil is pouring out immeasurable and violent hatred on all who confess God to be holy and righteous. His indoctrination of hatred into the souls of wicked and sinful men has always been evidenced throughout all generations. It is appalling that those who encourage hatred towards others shroud this belief and action under the disguise of religion, promising the perpetrators a heavenly reward for their evil intentions and actions.

25. Jesus stated over ten times that many unbelievers would hate Him and those who believe in Him. (Matthew 10:22, 24:8–11, Mark 13:13, John 15:18, 17:14)

26. The study of this doctrinal tenet that has infested all mankind must have had an origin. Sin was not created by God. What God created was *all good.* From when time was unmeasured and continuing to this day, some of God's creation, through free will, have chosen to reject God's love and holiness ... *None calleth for justice, nor any pleadeth for truth: they trust in vanity, and speak lies; they conceive mischief, and bring forth iniquity....* (Isaiah 59:4) It first appeared in the angelic host in heaven. Sin was personally conceived in a covering cherub, Lucifer.

27. This created being was the custodian of God's creation on earth, and instead of overseeing God's creation, Lucifer began to govern and direct the created beings. He instilled in them his own intentions and did not oversee God's will for them. It was the overwhelming power that Lucifer saw he began to have that drove him to the place of self-will and power contrary to God's purpose for His created beings. This influence over God's created beings welled up inside him as pride.

28. Furthermore, his magnificent beauty as a created cherub was no longer being reflected towards God but he claimed ownership of it, and thus self-indignation and pride hoisted him to a level he

assumed was rightfully his, namely, self-will and self-control of his eternal destiny.

29. Lucifer, in this self-elevated state, cultivated his selfishness and lust for more power. He let his self-worth, pride, and power turn into arrogance. He not only saw his achievements through God's created beings on earth, but he also convinced himself that he was equal to his Creator. Thus, the progression of sin conceived in the spirit grew into a desire to be like God and an uncontrollable lust to be God, even to sit on His throne. This corrupted the covering cherub, Lucifer, to believe in his self-worth as being equal with God.

30. A further extrapolation of this truth is that Lucifer contaminated the created beings with this lustful power urge. The created beings over which he had custody turned their attention to merchandising and power, and followed blindly after Lucifer, ignoring their Creator. God stopped Lucifer from continuing his mission and banished him from the presence of Almighty God. Lucifer's custodianship infested one third of the angelic host who believed in him and not God, their creator, whom God also cast out of heaven. It is therefore correct to say that sin had its origin in Lucifer's spirit, and he is the instigator of all sin. (Isaiah 14:12–15, Ezekiel 28:11–19, John 8:44, Jude 6)

31. It cannot be stressed too often the seriousness with which God considers sin and sinners. The rejection of Him, His love, and His goodness must result in God enacting on His Word that all who sin must *surely die.* (Genesis 2:17, Romans 6:23) The *death* spoken of in biblical terms is threefold: spiritual, physical, and eternal separation from God. Sin and its consequence of death began on earth in the first man, Adam, when he disobeyed God's command.

32. Isaiah speaks … *Your iniquities have separated between you and your God, and your sins have hid his face from you, that he will not hear....* (Isaiah 59:2) Spiritual death is the state in which a sinner finds himself while living in the flesh on earth. He is cut off

and incapable of a spiritual relationship with God until he repents. This "death" is the precursor to physical death.

33. The moment Adam partook of the fruit from the tree of knowledge of good and evil, he began to die physically, even though Satan lied, saying ... *You will not surely die.* (Genesis 3:4, Romans 5:12) Thus, the process of physical death began the moment sin entered him.

34. The evidence of both spiritual and physical death is ever apparent in the world. However, the most heartbreaking death is eternal death, namely eternal separation from God. The Bible calls this the *second death.* (Revelation 20:14–15)

35. God's punishment of sin is clearly proclaimed in the Word. It also explains the degrees of sin and the degrees of punishment *greater sins* will suffer. To this end, Spirit-filled believers understand the difference between sin, sins, and the meaning of *greater* sins.

36. All sin is punishable by God, and He will destine an unrepentant heart to eternal punishment. Irrespective of the degree of the punishment, the extent of the punishment for the least of sins will be so enormous because of one overriding factor: the constant reminder that they are eternally separated from God, and there will never be any opportunity afforded them to be released from eternal damnation.

37. At the outset, Spirit-filled believers know that they are born in sin which is the inherent sin within every human being. It is the human, fallen nature that comes from Adam. The Word says ... *All have sinned ...* (Romans 3:23), and this is so because the nature within every human is carnal and tarnished by the parents who conceived the newborn child. This heredity sin is what separates mankind from God and is the inherent nature that drives him to sinful thoughts and acts.

38. Inherent sin is exposed by the Holy Spirit who convicts man of his state and standing before God and offers him the pathway to rid the penalty from this inherent sin. (John 16:8–11) This is

the born-again experience Jesus speaks of when He talks with Nicodemus. (John 3:1–8) It is the Holy Spirit's convicting work that exposes the person's depraved and lost state without God that invites him to repent. The sinner repents of his inherent sin, asking God to forgive and cleanse him from all unrighteousness as he receives Jesus Christ into his heart. (Romans 10:9–10)

39. This is the first step the person takes towards his born-again experience. It is repentance from the heart because ... *godly sorrow worketh repentance to salvation, and not to be repented of*.... (2 Corinthians 7:10) Once there is confession, repentance, and acceptance of Christ's work on Calvary, the individual's inherent sin is blotted out by the shed blood of Jesus.

40. Thereafter, the road of salvation for the born-again believer begins with the sanctification process. The sins man commits after his born-again experience require confession to God and repentance towards God, so that he can be cleansed from all unrighteousness. (1 John 1:8–9)

Soulish Sins

41. Sin contaminates a person's entire being. It can be characterized into the sin of the soul, the flesh, and the spirit. To begin, because mankind is born in sin, their soul is conditioned towards fulfilling its craving to do what is contrary to God's holiness. It is fueled by the five senses of touch, taste, seeing, hearing, and smell. These outward influences fester in the soul and drive the desire within to partake of it.

42. Once an initial response towards the temptation is made, the sin-seed begins to germinate in the soul and it covets more, causing it to overtake rational thinking. The soul, which is the decision maker for the body, compels the body to act according to its sin-infested intentions.

43. The *fiery darts of the wicked* (Ephesians 6:16) are used to tempt a person into doing evil, penetrating a man's soul. These *fiery darts* enter the person's soul via the five senses and create a platform of ungodly desire that channels the person's thinking into evil deeds. Jesus said ... *I say to you that whoever looks at a woman to lust for her has already committed adultery with her in his heart....* (Matthew 5:28 NKJV) The soul becomes the breeding ground of evil intent that provokes the person into sinful acts.

44. The devil's treacherous act of *blinding* a mind is another method he uses to confound unbelievers ... *But even if our gospel is veiled, it is veiled to those who are perishing, whose minds the god of this age has blinded, who do not believe, lest the light of the gospel of the glory of Christ, who is the image of God, should shine on them....* (2 Corinthians 4:3–4 NKJV)

45. This blinding of the mind from the truth is not only aimed at unbelievers but is clothed in deceit towards believers when the devil launches an attack on them. Through false teachers, he deceives believers into believing a lie, corrupts the truth, and introduces false doctrine that confuses them. (2 Corinthians 11:1–4, Colossians 2:18, 1 Timothy 6:3–5, 2 Timothy 3:8–9) Tragic as it may seem, this confusion that causes some to be... *tossed to and fro and carried about with every wind of doctrine, by the trickery of men, in the cunning craftiness of deceitful plotting ...* (Ephesians 4:14 NKJV), results in the deceived making *shipwreck* of their faith (1 Timothy 1:19).

46. This deception is aimed at contaminating the mind ... *to those who are defiled and unbelieving nothing is pure; but even their mind and conscience are defiled. They profess to know God, but in works they deny Him, being abominable, disobedient and disqualified for every good work....* (Titus 1:15–16 NKJV)

47. The Bible states, *The soul that sinneth, it shall die.* (Ezekiel 18:20) *Jesus declares, depart from me, ye that work iniquity....* (Matthew 7:23) Iniquities are perceived in the soul and worked through the

flesh. It is from the evil soul that the flesh and the spirit are enticed to sin: *The labor of the righteous tendeth to life: the fruit of the wicked to sin* (Proverbs 10:16).

48. In the soul, the plotting and scheming of evil is devised; *He who plots to do evil will be called a schemer. The devising of foolishness is sin, and the scoffer is an abomination to men.* (Proverbs 24:8–9 NKJV) This platform of evil intention results in the blackening of a man's soul that encases his ability to think rationally ... *lest any of you be hardened through the deceitfulness of sin ....* (Hebrews 3:13)

49. The devastating consequences for a sinful soul are too terrible to contemplate. Irrespective of how minute the initial sinful thought might appear in the soul, once it takes root, its growth is phenomenal. It saturates the person's entire thinking and propels the flesh into acts of unrighteousness. It stains the heart (spirit) that results in cataclysmic separation from God ... *But each one is tempted when he is drawn away by his own desires and enticed. Then when desire has conceived, it gives birth to sin; and sin, when it is full-grown, brings forth death....* (James 1:14–15 NKJV)

50. It is no wonder that Apostle Peter sounds the call ... *Therefore gird up the loins of your mind* (soul), *be sober, and rest your hope fully upon the grace that is to be brought to you at the revelation of Jesus Christ....* (1 Peter 1:13 NKJV) Believers are called to do this, so that they do not conform themselves *...to the former lusts* ... (vs. 14), namely, the result of the soul's influence over the flesh and the spirit.

The Sins of the Flesh

51. The body is both a receiver and a transmitter of sinful lusts. The sensual feelings from touch, the aromas, the taste of iniquitous alcohol, the achievements of strength, and the satisfactions from

warmth all send a message to a sinful soul. On the contrary, the body is the servant of the soul, and does according to the soul's bidding.

52. The flesh, or body, is poisoned by the soul to do sinful acts. Apostle Paul records a number of these acts, calling them the *lusts of the flesh.*(Galatians 5:16–21) The result of these acts are that ... *they which do practice such things shall not inherit the kingdom of God....*

53. The sinful acts perpetrated in the body must come under the condemnation of the sin. These fleshy sins are witnessed by others and it is the most influential and enticing influence on mankind. Too often man has asked, "If he can do it, why can't I do it?"

54. The witnessing by others of someone's sinful acts motivates them to believe it is an acceptable practice. Believers are warned to never expose a weaker person to sinning because they observe the stronger person doing something.... (1 Corinthians 8:6–13)

55. The sins of the flesh invoke sensual satisfaction, create lustful habits, and always propose furtherance and greater involvement in the act. The disastrous consequences of alcohol, drugs, immorality, lust for power, etc., always entices the flesh to be more, have more, and do more.

56. The Bible teaches that believers ... *keep under my* (their) *body, and bring it into subjection....* (1 Corinthinas 9:27) The body is always subject to the soul's decisions. It is only when the spirit is born again that the soul receives its instructions from a heart which follows after righteousness (Psalm 15:2–5) and does works in their body (flesh) ... *There is therefore now no condemnation to those who are in Christ Jesus, who do not walk according to the flesh, but according to the Spirit....* (Romans 8:1 NKJV)

57. The Word is clear that overcomers of the flesh walk not according to sinful lusts because they overcome unrighteous desires as they ... *Walk in the Spirit, and ye shall not fulfil the lust of the flesh....* (Galatians 5:16)

Spiritual Sin

58. The most blatant spiritual transgression is the worship of false gods, idols, and counterfeit methods that some use to justify their salvation. God is forthright in His commandments and the first two are emphatic when He declares ... *You shall have no other gods before Me. You shall not make for yourselves a carved image— any likeness of anything that is in heaven above, or that is in the earth beneath, or that is in the water under the earth; you shall not bow down to them nor serve them....* (Exodus 20:3–5 NKJV)

59. Idolatry is an abomination in the eyes of God. This is categorized clearly in the Word that states if anything other than the Godhead, namely the Father, the Son, and the Holy Spirit is worshipped, then it is idolatry. There can be no excuse for those who blatantly worship other created beings, man-made figurines, and structures. Offering prayers, praising golden images, presenting sacrifices, making offerings to them, and accepting mythical interpretations from a man-made religion are spiritual sins.

60. Regrettably, in the church age, false gods and crooked and perverse teachings have saturated many believers' lives. They are told to hold graven images, call upon persons other than the Godhead, or cover themselves with "anointed" clothing to make themselves acceptable in God's sight.

61. One of the most grievous spiritual sins is spiritual pride. The attitude of "We are better than them" is rampant throughout some denominations. Instead of: *Examine yourselves, whether ye be in the faith* ... (2 Corinthians 13:5), they compare their beliefs to others. They condemn others because their beliefs are different, they pride themselves because they perform "righteous works," or they whisper amongst themselves dissention and lies to propagate their beliefs.

62. What they should be doing is entering the closet, being alone with God, and seeking His face for guidance and wisdom to be

a worthy testimony for Jesus Christ. *God resists the proud, but gives grace to the humble. Therefore humble yourselves under the mighty hand of God....* (1 Peter 5:5–6 NKJV) Therein is truth, and therein is the blessing of God.

63. Spirit-filled believers must always be conscious of the indwelling Holy Spirit's leading. There is no place for complacency and disregard for His guidance. Believers cannot elevate themselves above the work of the Holy Spirit by positioning themselves on a platform that ranks them equal with the Holy Spirit or better than any other believer.

64. All saved persons are *saved by grace through faith, and not of yourselves; it is a gift from God* (Ephesians 2:8 NKJV). There is no ground more level and equal than the ground upon which God's grace is imparted. No matter the person's wealth, poverty, lofty rank or position, education, and gender, everyone stands before God covered in the same inherent sin and needs the same cleansing. How apt that Apostle Paul says ... *Let nothing be done through selfish ambition or conceit, but in lowliness of mind let each esteem others better than himself....* (Philippians 2:3 NKJV)

65. Spiritual transgression is a vile transgression in God's eyes. *God is Spirit,* and Spirit-filled believers know that they are to walk *circumspectly, not as fools but as wise, redeeming the time, because the days are evil ... submitting to one another in the fear of God....* (Ephesians 5:15–16; 21 NKJV) God's holiness, righteousness, and sovereignty are precious to Him. Any neglect or sin against these attributes is a violation of who God is. Spiritual sin is a direct accost against the persons of the Godhead.

Degrees of Sin

66. There are degrees of sin, and the weight of the punishment is greater for greater sins. Jesus makes several references to the level

of sins. (Matthew 23:14, John 19:11) The punishment thereof is further defined when Apostle John was given the *Revelation of Jesus Christ, which God gave unto him;* (Revelation 1:1) ... *I saw the dead, small and great, standing before God, and books were opened. And another book was opened, which is the Book of Life. And the dead were judged according to their works, by the things which were written in the books.... And they were judged each one according to his works.* (Revelation 20:12–13 NKJV)

67. Sin is enacted in two ways: that which affects only the individual, and that which affects others through the sin the person commits. Herein is the difference Jesus spoke of when He tells Pilate ... *You could have no power at all against Me unless it had been given you from above. Therefore the one who delivered Me to you has the greater sin....* (John 19:11 NKJV)

68. When someone sins in their thought or action that does not affect anyone else, it is regarded as a personal sin. This is a lesser sin because it does not affect anyone else other than the person sinning. However, when someone sins and this sin affects others who follow in his path of sin, this is the *greater sin.*

69. Sin is defined further as an act or thought and a state. If one sins, it is the act of sin. If the person does not repent of their sin, they remain in the state of sin. Sin darkens the life of an individual. Satan is the prince of darkness, and he covers up the light of the gospel by shrouding it with his dark, evil deception.

70. This darkness results in separation from God and His holiness. This cataclysmic condition does not separate unrepentant man from God for a season, but it has eternal division from God's holy presence. Sin is laid at the feet of the sinner who is guilty before God because they have adopted the way of the devil and refused God's *gift of eternal life in Christ Jesus.* Ultimately, sin defiles the soul.

71. The end result of a sinner's soul is that it becomes utterly corrupt and full of rejection for all that God is ... *The fool*

has said in his heart, there is no God. They are corrupt, they have done abominable works, there is none who does good.... (Psalm 14:1 NKJV)

The Unforgivable Sin

72. Jesus taught the Pharisees that there was an unforgivable sin ... *Therefore I say to you, every sin and blasphemy will be forgiven men, but the blasphemy against the Holy Spirit will not be forgiven men. Anyone who speaks a word against the Son of Man, it will be forgiven him; but whoever speaks against the Holy Spirit, it will not be forgiven him, either in this age or in the age to come....* (Matthew 12:31–31 NKJV)

73. Over the centuries of the church, this statement has drawn confusion amongst believers. Many have misunderstood what Jesus was saying and thus, they were either wrongly informed or they personally condemned themselves by thinking they had committed this sin.

74. Any sin committed by mankind is against God. God is Father, Son, and Holy Spirit. When man sins, he sins against all three Persons of the Godhead. The unforgivable sin is directed at the Holy Spirit's ministry amongst the lost and believers, and not at the Person of the Holy Spirit.

75. In some cases, the unrepentant heart can be so callous and indifferent that it blasphemes the convicting power of the Holy Spirit, and he never accepts it throughout his life. Spirit-filled preachers have experienced the condemnation of the work of the Holy Spirit by some hearers, as He convicts others while the gospel is being preached. When a sinner never responds to the convicting power of the Holy Spirit and openly condemns His works and refuses to acknowledge the Spirit's representation of the Godhead, what results is the blasphemy of His works.

76. This is not merely rejection of the call to salvation; it is the total rejection of the work of the Holy Spirit in a person's life and the utter condemnation (cursing and cussing) that the Holy Spirit is not that part of the Godhead who is ministering to the lost person's heart. It is further with the tongue of an accuser that he blasphemes the Holy Spirit. He speaks against the holy sovereignty and divinity of the Holy Spirit, accusing Him of being false ... *whoever speaks against the Holy Spirit....*

77. This is what the Pharisees did when they witnessed Jesus casting out demons ... *Now when the Pharisees heard it they said, "This fellow does not cast out demons except by Beelzebub, the ruler of the demons...."* (Matthew 12:24 NKJV) They condemned Jesus and the work of the Spirit, stating it was not ... *by the Spirit of God* (vs. 24). Jesus made sure they understood that they were not to speak blasphemies against the work of the *Spirit of God.*

78. What the Pharisees said gave rise to the intent and state of their heart/soul, and thus poured out their contempt for Jesus' ministry. Jesus says to them ... *Brood of vipers! How can you, being evil, speak good things? For out of the abundance of the heart the mouth speaks....* (Matthew 12:34 NKJV)

79. The unforgivable sin is attributable to sinners and those who profess to be a Christian. An apostate is one who knows God and the Holy Spirit's gifts, and they have drawn back and walked no more with God and the Holy Spirit's teaching. Their plight is clearly defined in the Word ... *For it is impossible for those who were once enlightened, and have tasted the heavenly gift, and have become partakers of the Holy Spirit, and have tasted the good word of God and the powers of the age to come, if they fall away, to renew them again to repentance, since they crucify again for themselves the Son of God, and put Him to an open shame....* (Hebrews 6:4–6 NKJV)

80. While this tragic state is spoken of in God's Holy Writ, it is not entirely correct to include it in the context of the unforgivable sin.

Apostates have experienced and know the blessings of God and His forgiveness, and the work of the Holy Spirit in their lives. But they turn from this righteous walk and utterly condemn the Godhead and all His attributes and work in their life. The result of their enmity with God is irretrievable.

81. When considering the unforgivable sin, it is marked by the utter rejection and condemnation of the work of the Holy Spirit. An example of His work is ... *He will glorify Me, for He will take of what is Mine and declare it to you....* (John 16:14 NKJV) Furthermore, the Holy Spirit will ... *guide you into all truth ... tell you things to come....* (vs. 13) Spirit-filled believers understand that the work of the Holy Spirit goes deeper than this, and that believers have access into the church, the body of Christ through the baptism with the Holy Spirit ... *For by one Spirit are we all baptized into one body....* (1 Corinthians 12:13) Jonathan Black, in his book, *Apostolic Theology,* says "Therefore, to sin against the Holy Spirit is to willfully reject the Holy Spirit's ministry ... and then to attack that truth with blasphemy."

82. The unforgivable sin is not merely a person deciding not to accept the gift of salvation through Jesus Christ. Wayne Grudem, in his book, *Systematic Theology,* says, "Jesus is speaking about a sin that is not simply unbelief or rejection of Christ, but one that includes (1) a clear knowledge of who Christ is and the power of the Holy Spirit working through Him, (2) a willful rejection of the facts about Christ that His opponents knew to be true, and (3) slanderously attributing the work of the Holy Spirit in Christ to the power of Satan."

83. In essence, it is the total rejection and cursing (blaspheming) of the work of the Holy Spirit's presentation of salvation in Christ Jesus and His work amongst believers. The Dutch Reformed theologian, Louis Berkhof, in his book, *Systematic Theology,* approached this subject from a Calvinistic perspective, that out of hatred for the truth and works of the Holy Spirit, the confessor

attributes the Holy Spirit's works which testify to the grace of God in Christ to the devil.

God's Remedy for Man's Sin

84. Because God is aware of the depravity of man's conscience and the frailty of his abilities, from the very beginning God gave mankind laws which, if followed, would render him righteous. Dr. Henry Thiessen, in his book, *Lectures in Systematic Theology,* says, the law "was given to intensify man's knowledge of sin, to reveal the holiness of God, and to lead the sinner to Christ." (Romans 3:19)

85. Jesus as Son of Man fulfilled all the law, and in His death and resurrection tore down the curtain (partition) between God and mankind and opened the way of forgiveness and reconciliation. He annulled the law ... *For Christ is the end of the law for righteousness to everyone that believeth....* (Romans 10:4) From that moment, God's love and mercy produced grace by which man is saved. (Ephesians 2:8) Henceforth ... *sin shall not have dominion over you; for ye are not under law, but under grace....* (Romans 6:14)

86. During the Law of God and the Mosaic Law, man's works rendered him righteous before God. God covered up man's sin when he made an annual sacrificial offering to God. Thus, all that man did through obeying God's laws rendered him righteous in the sight of God.

87. Jonathan Black says, "The law shows what man hasn't done, can't do, and won't do. But the gospel shows what Jesus has done and has completed. The Law says 'Do!' but the gospel says 'Done!'"

88. In the dispensation of grace (the church age), man is saved by grace through faith and not of works. (Ephesians 2:8–9) This is the gift of God to a repentant heart who confesses Jesus Christ as

Lord. While works gave man a reprieve from his sin during the Old Covenant, now God's applied grace forgives him.

89. Calvary's Hill is the "Place" where the Father took care of man's iniquity. Jesus is the "Person" whom God used to reconcile man to Himself. And the Holy Spirit "Presents" this *unspeakable gift* to mankind.

The Doctrine of Hell

90. The Bible is filled with the message of God's love and His desire that He is ... *not willing that any should perish but that all should come to repentance....* (2 Peter 3:9) It is within this *agape* that His every impulse is that man whom He created be eternally in His presence. This presence He desires is with Him in a blessed unity and the bond of peace.

91. This unfathomable love is extended to every human being. However, God leaves the decision to everyone to decide whether they desire to be in His presence in a blessed eternal union or outside of His love, mercy, and grace. This decision is made by man and not by God.

92. The consequences of man saying yes to God's gracious offer of His Son Jesus Christ's redeeming work on Calvary is the promise of everlasting life in His presence in all holiness, purity, righteousness, and blessing. The consequences of man saying no to God's gracious offer of His Son's redeeming work on Calvary results in man existing eternally under the wrath of God in the Lake of Fire.

93. Scripture speaks of *Sheol* in the Old Testament Hebrew. This word incorporated the *grave, paradise, and hell*. The Greek translation in the New Testament of the same word is *Hades*, which also incorporates all three places. The place created by God for the wicked sinful dead is hell. Paradise was created by God for the righteous dead who died before Jesus was crucified. These

righteous dead were resurrected when Jesus was raised from the dead, leaving paradise empty.

94. There is another place created by God especially for the wicked angels, called *Tartarus*. They are the only inhabitants who are chained in this place of torment until the ... *judgment of the great day*.... (Jude 6)

95. This underworld consisting of hell is where the sinner's soul and spirit are cast, and it is the destination of those *cursed* by God (Matthew 25:41). It is a place of darkness, misery, and torment. As much as the love and compassion of God is evident when the righteous are taken into His heavenly presence, so is His wrath poured out on the sinner who rejected Christ.

96. Spirit-filled believers know and are assured that salvation and everlasting life are granted to them this side of the grave. Likewise, hell and its torment are chosen by the sinner this side of the grave. The moment the believer breathes his last breath, his soul and spirit are *absent from the body* and *present with the Lord*. (2 Corinthians 5:8) The sinner's demise is as instantaneous; his soul and spirit are immediately separated from his body and they are cast into hell.

97. Jonathan Black says, "In hell, the finally impenitent undergo 'the fiery indignation' of the terrible wrath of God. It is God who casts unrepentant sinners into hell (Mark 9:45, 47). The active punishment on God's part is just and righteous ... *It is a righteous thing with God to repay with tribulation those who trouble you ... in flaming fire taking vengeance on those who do not know God*.... (2 Thessalonians 1:6, 8)"

98. The righteous dead await the Judgment Seat of Christ at which time they receive a crown for their works from Jesus. The wicked dead must also undergo a judgment, only at a different time and under different circumstances. Their term in hell concludes at the Great White Throne Judgment where they hear their sentence from Jesus, and then cast into the Lake of Fire.

99. This subject has been relegated to the lowest level in many preachers' minds. They veer away from the truth that it contains and try to cover the reality of the lost soul's destination. Yet, even though the Bible speaks forcefully about the salvation of the believer, it speaks even more definitely about the lost sinner ... *Therefore consider the goodness and severity of God; on those who fell, severity; but toward you, goodness, if you continue in His goodness. Otherwise you also will be cut off....* (Romans 11:22 NKJV) And too many preachers will not declare *the soul that sins will surely die.*

100. Henry Ward Beecher said, "Future retribution is only alluded to: eternal punishment almost never taught in the pulpit today. Silence as to 'the weeping and gnashing of teeth' Jesus spoke of (Matthew 25:30) does more to populate hell than the blasphemies of Tom Paine and Robert Ingersoll combined."

101. The Bible states that hell is *beneath* (below) (Proverbs 15:24); its place is known as the *abyss*, meaning the destination where the lost sinner is separated from God and lives in torment and fear. The banishment of a sinner to this place of isolation is corroborated by the fact that everyone there is of the same condition and condemnation. Their ultimate punishment and eternal state is in the Lake of Fire.

102. Spirit-filled believers are acutely aware of the doctrinal facts that those who do not accept Jesus Christ as their Savior die in their sin, and they have no hope of everlasting life in the presence of God's glorious majesty. (Mark 9:43–48) Having said this, it is expedient that believers know that man's soul and spirit live forever. There is no death of the soul, but a separation from God's grace and love. The sinner's soul therefore lives forever outside of communion with God.

103. Finality of the everlasting torment of the sinner is without question. Their punishment is irrevocable and everlasting; there is no hope of any reprieve from their state beyond the grave.

104. This place called hell, the abyss or the destination of the sinner, is not everlasting. It has a termination date engraved on its door. It is when God has intervened for the last time on earth and ushers the Great White Throne Judgment onto the podium.

105. Here He will judge the wicked dead who are incarcerated in hell, as well as the fallen angels in Tartarus. Hell is emptied, and the occupants are paraded before the Judgment Seat to hear the extent of their everlasting punishment. The Lake of Fire replaces hell. With the judgment at the Great White Throne, hell and all its occupants are to be cast into the Lake of Fire (Revelation 20:14, 15; 21:8). Therefore, hell itself, the present abode of the lost, is not eternal but its torment is.

106. The Lake of Fire and the second death are in most cases identical to hell's doom. (Revelation 20:14; 21:8) A few differences are found: first, unlike hell, the judgment pronounced is final and without end; it is the place of everlasting punishment. Second, the judgment is metered out according to the wickedness done. Third, this is also the place of the devil and his angels (Matthew 25:41). Now the wicked dead are face to face with their accuser and deceiver, and they will be forever in Satan's presence.

107. Yet more engulf the sinner. They are acutely aware that they are in an everlasting state, and under God's curse, not His blessing. This torment stays with them every moment. They hear the pronouncement of their judgment ... *Depart from me, ye who work iniquity* ... (Matthew 7:23), and the penalty for their iniquity ... *Depart from me ye cursed into everlasting fire....* (Matthew 25:41)

108. Different from hell where they only have their soul and spirit, in the Lake of Fire they are now body, soul, and spirit. (Revelation 9:6; 14:11)

109. The Psalmist makes a statement worthy of further consideration ... *Where can I go from Your Spirit? Or where can I flee from Your presence? If I ascend into heaven, You are there. If I make my bed*

in hell, behold, You are there.... (Psalm 139:7–8) Jonathan Black says, "Revelation 14:10 describes hell as being ... *tormented with fire and brimstone in the presence of the holy angels and in the presence of the Lamb....* The wrath of God is poured out by God in His very presence in hell.

110. "The presence of God can refer to the blessed experience of the presence with His people. This is the 'comfortable presence' of God. Hell, then, is separation from the comfortable presence of God. Instead, the finally impenitent in hell experience the uncomfortable presence of God as He pours out His wrath. When Christ tells the wicked to *depart* (Matthew 7:23; 25:41), therefore, it is not a local departure from the omnipresent Christ, but rather they are cast out from communion with the Godhead through Jesus Christ the Son (the Lamb)."

111. The charge by Jesus Christ to the church ... *Go ye into all the world, and preach the gospel to every creature* ... (Mark 16:15) is the directive to believers to share the good news (*gospel*), so that many will turn from their wicked ways and follow in Jesus' steps and escape the wrath of God to come.

CHAPTER 27

THE DOCTRINE OF SALVATION

1. *How shall we escape, if we neglect so great salvation...* (Hebrews 2:3) The word in this text that needs to be focused on is *great.* The greatest Man ever to walk the earth is Jesus Christ. The greatest act that could ever have been done is the offering of the sinless Christ's life for the eternal salvation of wretched sinners.

2. No subject brings more joy to a sinner's soul. No expression of love is more pronounced and valuable than the enactment of God's salvation for mankind. The holy, divine *Word became flesh,* He left His throne in heaven where He was rich and highly esteemed to enter a lowly poor habitation as Son of Man (2 Corinthians 8:9) for one supreme purpose, *to seek and save the lost.* (Luke 19:10)

3. Jesus' mission was not that He came to earth to heal, deliver, and set captives free which He willingly did; His goal was the fulfillment of God's purpose that man be set free of the inherent sin. *This is a faithful saying, and worthy of all acceptation, that Christ Jesus came into the world to save sinners....* (1 Timothy 1:15) Hence, it is *great* salvation.

4. To begin this tenet, it is important to seal this fact: man has no possible way to redeem himself from his sin—only God could remedy the problem. The deplorable and despicable state of

man's rottenness severs the relationship and communication with his Creator. Only God, in His holiness and righteousness, could step into mankind's existence and fix the problem.

5. There was, is, and will ever be only one remedy for mankind's sin, the Master's sacrifice on Calvary's Hill where He shed His blood for the remission of sin. *Nor is there salvation in any other, for there is no other name under heaven given among men whereby we must be saved....* (Acts 4:12 NKJV)

6. Jesus, the Son of God, the almighty Creator, blessed Word, and righteous One left His kingdom and riches, became poor so that repentant man could become rich in salvation (2 Corinthians 8:9). Herbert Lockyer gives a great statement for the purpose of Christ's coming, "He did not leave the battlements above, where He was the Prince of Glory, to become a teacher, or a model for our obedience, or as a martyr willing to die for truths and principles He believed." (Luke 19:10)

7. Spirit-filled believers know, understand, and live the fact that God is love, and He who is love appropriates it towards wretched man when He shows him mercy. This mercy from a heart of love offers grace to the lost sinner. As the sinner recognizes the redemptive act of Calvary and that salvation is in no one else but the saving grace of God through Jesus Christ, he responds by repenting of his sin.

8. God, who is rich in love, mercy, and grace, hears a repentant heart's cry and pours out unconditional forgiveness that blots out his sin. This gracious act of forgiveness produces an unmerited favor of justification towards the believer: just as if he had never sinned. The saved person is not only justified in God's eyes because he believes in the finished work of Christ's sacrifice and His shed blood and confesses Jesus as Lord, but this holy endowment from the holy God confers upon the saved the unearned state of righteousness.

Atonement

9. It is fitting to study the path to this ultimate blessing of salvation found in the Holy Writ. God's appropriation of atonement towards His people, the Jews, is clearly evident in the Old Testament. It was a requirement of God's instructions to His people that they offer a sacrifice for the atonement of their sins. God's laws expose man's sin ... *What shall we say then? Is the law sin? Certainly not! On the contrary, I would not have known sin except through the law. For I would not have known covetousness unless the law had said, 'You shall not covet'....* (Romans 7:7 NKJV)

10. Jonathan Black in his book *Apostolic Theology* says, "The Law causes man to know his sin. Paul writes that God speaks by His Law so *that every mouth may be stopped, and all the world may become guilty before God....* (Romans 3:19) It is not that the Law creates guilt before God, but rather that we know our guilt before God through the Law, for by the Law we recognize sin to be sin." (Romans 3:20)

11. God's people were required to offer a sacrifice to God of an unblemished animal to receive from God the "covering" of their ignorant and intentional sins. This covering, referred to as "atonement," was made when the sacrifice was offered by the sinner in the hope that God would accept it and thus pardon him from his sin. When a sin offering was presented at the altar and the blood of the bull was sprinkled on the horns of the altar, God appropriated forgiveness to them. (Leviticus 4:13–20)

12. The application of the Hebrew word translated as atonement, *kaphar,* means, in essence, "to cover." It embraces the substitutionary act of a sacrifice of an animal, which is at a cost to the one making the sacrifice. This cost and offering of the animal was the action man performed in an attempt to seek God's covering of his sin. Thus, the sacrificed animal is the substitute

for the man's life which God accepted as sufficient for Him to cover the man's sin.

13. Atonement involved a substitutionary sacrifice and the shedding of blood. (Hebrews 9:22) The Word states ... *The life of the flesh is in the blood: and I have given it to you upon the altar to make an atonement for your souls: for it is the blood that maketh an atonement for the soul....* (Leviticus 17:11)

14. Clearly, the person who sinned was required to make a sacrifice and an offering (the animal is the offering, and the putting to death of that animal is the sacrifice the person made). This is regarded a "substitutionary" sacrifice and death of the animal for the person. Norman Geisler calls it a "perfect and sinless substitute." This means that atonement through the sacrifice of an animal that had no sin in it was "substitutionary atonement, symbolizing a transfer of guilt" to the sacrificial offering.

15. In summarizing the Old Testament's teaching on atonement, it is clear that God required His people to "do" something in order to appease His wrath. Their sin against God required them to offer a sacrifice and, upon acceptance by God, their transgression would be atoned for or covered up. Simply put, God would not hold their transgression/sin against them anymore.

16. This appropriation of the Old Testament's atonement is taken to a deeper level in the New Testament. The application of the substitutionary sacrifice does not merely atone man's sin, it is eradicated, blotted out, totally forgiven, and washed away in the blood from the sacrifice of Jesus Christ.

17. Believers cling to the Bible's statement that Christ died *for* them ... *And He took bread, gave thanks and broke it, and gave it to them, saying, "This is My body which is given for you; do this in remembrance of Me." Likewise He also took the cup after supper, saying, "This cup is the new covenant in My blood, which is shed for you...."* (Luke 22:19–20 NKJV) Jesus made the most loving

and compassionate statement when He said ... *I lay down my life for the sheep....* (John 10:15)

18. Jesus Christ fulfilled all the requirements of the Law, and His sacrificial death and resurrection extended beyond the law. It fully accomplished all the requirements God demanded so that He can forgive, justify, cleanse, and impute righteousness.

Salvation: Total Forgiveness

19. To return to the intent and origin of salvation, it must be clear from whom it comes, to whom it is appropriated, and for what purpose it is intended. Norman Geisler states, "The origin of salvation is the will of God, who decreed from all eternity to provide salvation for those who would believe: *Salvation is of the Lord.*" (Jonah 2:9) Apostle John says it best that believers are born-again and become ... *children of God... who were born, not of blood, nor of the will of the flesh, not of the will of man, but of God....* (John 1:12–13 NKJV)

20. It is God who determines the salvation of man's lost soul. This is not man's doing. God is the supreme and sovereign decision maker on this magnificent subject that turns man's everlasting destiny away from hell and into God's merciful and loving presence. While the purpose and implementation of the sacrifice is God's divine thought and application (Ephesians 1:5), it is man in his free will that chooses to accept or reject this divinely instituted purpose. (1 Peter 1:2)

21. Salvation is from the heart of God predetermined in the ageless past ... *the Lamb slain from the foundation of the world ...* (Revelation 13:8) and is offered to mankind. Jesus is the holy, worthy Lamb slain for the unworthy, unrighteous sinner. Calvary's Hill became the altar of this salvation act. Whereas man's offering of a sacrificial animal in the Old Testament was accepted by God

and the sin was "covered" (atoned), Christ's sacrifice includes more. When His sacrifice on Calvary is accepted by faith, His shed blood eradicates, blots out, and annuls every sin, never to be remembered again by God.

22. Knowing from whom salvation comes, it is then correct to inquire for whom salvation was purposed. God is the instigator of the purpose and man is the beneficiary. Every person born of the flesh is in need of this salvation offering. There are no nations, tribes, or religious beliefs that have a reason or an excuse to propagate their exclusion from this holy salvation offering. There is only *the way* and that is via the Cross of Jesus Christ, and His finished work that affords mankind no matter their race, age, gender, religious beliefs, and sin state to come into the presence of the Father through Jesus Christ and what He did at Calvary. That way, and only that *way*, will allow the grace of God to be shed abroad in the heart of a repentant sinner.

23. The only way man can receive the gift of salvation from God is through faith in the finished work of Calvary. No amount of good-doing, confession, or abstinence from evil can earn man salvation; it is appropriated to the heart through faith. Whereas the source of salvation is God's choice to save us, the nature of salvation is God's grace ... *and if by grace, then is it no more of works: otherwise grace is no more grace...* (Romans 11:6) Grace, then, is unmerited favor. What we work for we earn, and what we do not work for we do not earn. Since salvation comes to us without works on our part, it follows that we did not merit it: Salvation is *the gift of God* (Romans 6:23).

24. To solidify the definition of mercy and grace, it is summed up as: Grace is given from God to man who does not deserve it (salvation), while mercy from God towards man is not giving mankind what he deserves (condemnation).

25. God's gift of salvation is *freely given* and can only be worth something to man if he *freely receives* it. Centuries ago, Augustine

said, "God is said to be 'our Helper'; but nobody can be helped who does not make some effort of his own accord. For God does not work out salvation in us as if He were working in insensate stones, or in creatures in whom nature has placed neither reason nor will."

26. It is the conscious step of faith towards God's gift that man must take in order for the gift of salvation to be imparted to him. No man can ever say that they did not have faith to accept salvation ... *God hath dealt to every man the measure of faith....* (Romans 12:3) Man is saved through faith (Ephesians 2:8–9), and they are justified by faith (Romans 5:1). It is only when they believe in Christ that they can be saved (Acts 16:31). All this can only be the result of faith which each person has been given to believe. Geisler says that man does not ... "get saved in order to believe; rather, we believe in order to become saved."

27. God took care of sin, its penalty, and its effectual separation from Him when He sent His only begotten Son to die for the lost. Jesus was freely given as a sacrifice by His Father so that man could be once again reconciled to Him ... *For if when we were enemies we were reconciled to God through the death of His Son, much more, having been reconciled, we shall be saved by His life....* (Romans 5:10 NKJV)

28. God spared no pain, mental anguish, or spiritual separation of His Son to redeem mankind from his wretchedness. He permitted every possible sinful condition, sickness, and physical punishment to the extent that Jesus Christ became the cursed ... *Christ hath redeemed us from the curse of the law, being made a curse for us: for it is written, 'Cursed is everyone that hangeth on a tree....'* (Galatians 3:13) The holy prophet, Isaiah, sums it up the best ... *Surely He has borne our griefs and carried our sorrows; yet we esteemed Him stricken, smitten by God, and afflicted. But He was wounded for our transgressions, He was bruised for our*

iniquities; the chastisement for our peace was upon Him, and by His stripes we are healed. (Isaiah 53:4–5 NKJV)

29. God's whole being is *love*. He looks upon man with love and compassion, desiring to have fellowship with him again. Second, He shows man *mercy* which is God holding back the punishment due to the sinner. Flowing from this love, because man is pardoned from the punishment due him as a sinner, God then thirdly shows man *grace* and not only removes the punishment due to the sinner, but He also removes the guilt from the sinner's account. Grace is therefore the pardoning and removal of the sin which wretched sinners do not deserve to be granted.

30. Therefore, if these are the three aspects of God that reach into man's sinful life, namely love, mercy, and grace, what then prevails and makes it possible for man to be saved?

Repentance

31. It is a worthy acceptance that repentance is a God-given grant to all mankind. (Acts 11:18) God through Jesus made it possible for mankind to repent ... *Him God has exalted to His right hand to be Prince and Savior, to give repentance to Israel and the forgiveness of sins* ... (Acts 5:31 NKV) ... *repentance is unto life* ... (Acts 11:18), and ... *to salvation* (2 Corinthians 7:10).

32. The holy grant from God, repentance, is taught and delivered to the sinner in order that ... *God perhaps will grant them repentance so that they may know the truth, and that they may come to their senses and escape the snare of the devil....* (2 Timothy 2:25–26 NKJV) It is when the sinful spirit within man acknowledges God's grant that a man can receive it and apply the glorious effect to his life which is granted to him by God.

33. Repentance is the first step man takes when he responds to the Holy Spirit's convicting power that man is a sinner. Repentance

is not a man-made, human work, or man-induced idea that he repents. It is man applying the gift of repentance from God to him so that he can apply it towards God. John Calvin taught that "repentance is conferred on us by Christ."

34. Jonathan Black says, "Repentance means coming to Jesus for Him to crucify and bury our old sinful lives and raise us up with Him to a new life. Repentance is not a turning from works of sin to works of righteousness; it is a turning from sin to Jesus." In practice, it is when man turns to God, confessing Jesus as Lord of his life, and seeks God's forgiveness for his inherent sin. It is the turning from a sinful path towards the righteousness of God in Jesus Christ who *became for us righteousness....* (1 Corinthians 1:30) God's grant, and man's acting upon it, produces the fruit of righteousness. The analogy of a person receiving a gift and then using it to their benefit compared to the person who is given the gift and never accepts it, blatantly rejects God's gracious offer of righteousness being applied to a repentant heart. It takes two parties to fully realize the gift's potential.

35. One of the aspects of this subject is the consideration of the application of grace and who is involved in the process. This needs to be set out in such a way that Spirit-filled believers can be aware of both the sovereignty of God and the utter depravity of man's lost position in God's eyes ... *For all have sinned and fall short of the glory of God, being justified freely by His grace through the redemption that is in Christ Jesus* ... (Romans 3:23–24 NKJV) ... *except ye repent, ye shall all likewise perish....* (Luke 13:5)

36. The church has adopted two stances on the subject: God and man are the two parties who need to be involved in the appropriation of grace, or it is God alone who is the appropriator of grace and man has no part of it.

37. To support the position that grace works in tandem with man's free will, it is based on the premise that grace can only be effective when man applies his faith. The Bible declares that man is saved

through faith (Ephesians 2:8) and is *justified by faith.* (Romans 5:1) Grace is therefore only effective when man receives the gift of salvation from God who imparts it by His grace.

38. When looking at the second interpretation, God's sovereign grace is His doing, and He alone is the originator and the only One who applies grace to the lost and there is no involvement of man in the process. This is based on what Jesus said ... *No man can come to me, except the Father which hath sent me draw him: and I will raise him up at the last day....* (John 6:44)

39. This viewpoint is further supported by Scripture ... *But God, who is rich in mercy, because of His great love with which He loved us, even when we were dead in trespasses, made us alive together with Christ (by grace you have been saved)....* (Ephesians 2:4–5 NKJV) Apostle Peter confirms that it is God who reaches down into man's depraved state and saves him ... *Blessed be the God and Father of our Lord Jesus Christ, who according to His abundant mercy has begotten us again to a living hope through the resurrection of Jesus Christ from the dead....* (1 Peter 1:3 NKJV)

40. It is Jesus who said ... *Without me ye can do nothing....* (John 15:5) This does not imply that God dictates and forces salvation onto man, neither does it infer that man is created without having a free will. What is being said is that salvation by God's grace is from God alone ... *It is God which worketh in you both to will and to do of his good pleasure....* (Philippians 2:13)

41. To put it in its correct context, grace is a God thing. It is conceived in the heart of the sovereign God and is made available to everyone who believes and applies his faith in the finished work of Calvary. Be it known that God alone is the source of the application of grace. And it is the response in faith from man that this grace is applied to his life. D.P. Williams said, "God's effectual calling operates on human choice."

42. It is therefore appropriate to state that Spirit-filled believers know that grace is a sovereign work of God without man's assistance,

and that He alone is the Presenter of grace towards mankind. Man responds while in his sinful state to the call of the Holy Spirit and receives by faith God's grace. Thus, man receives God's grant of repentance by confessing Jesus Christ as Lord and is saved.

Justification

43. The moment man confesses his sin before God, he is forgiven. This forgiveness is from God, and man has no claim to its appropriation in his life. It is from the sovereign heart of God that forgiveness flows. Man can never apply forgiveness to himself for his inherent sin.

44. Upon his confession that Jesus Christ is Lord of his life, God eradicates the inherent sin and justifies him as sin-free. Herein is perfect love: God releases the sinner from the bondage of inherent sin and declares him to be guiltless. God therefore holds nothing to the account of a repentant heart; he is forgiven, and the guilt that sin imposed on man is blotted out. It is more than sin-free and guiltless: it is also the total pardon from the penalty of the inherent sin.

45. The most profound understanding is that God deals with man's repentant heart instantaneously. The very instant man repents and believes in his heart that God raised Jesus from the dead, he is forgiven. Without a further second ticking past the hour, man is justified in the presence of the Father "just-as-if-I'd" never sinned. (Romans 8:1)

46. The application of justification could only be effective if it came from a just God. God needed a sinless sacrifice to be offered as a just substitute. Only Jesus Christ, the Son of God, could do this. Without Christ paying the price for our sins, God could not be just and yet also be the Justifier of the unjust (Romans 3:21–25). Without the Just dying for the unjust, God's justice would not

be satisfied, and without justice being appeased, God's mercy could not be released to declare the otherwise unjust sinners to be justified in His eyes. (Geisler paraphrased)

47. Sin makes man a debtor to God, against whom man has transgressed. The price to remove the debt and set mankind absolutely free from any debt owed to God could only come from the just One, Jesus. Even though sin originated in Satan, Jesus paid the price for sin to God, and not to Satan. Satan was the cause of sin that mankind owed, but God set man free from that debt. Henceforth ... *For there is one God, and one mediator between God and men, the man Christ Jesus....* (1 Timothy 2:5)

48. Christ's mediation covers three major aspects: He is Prophet, High Priest, and King. As Prophet, He brings the message from God to man (Hebrews 1:2), as High Priest, He represents man to God (Hebrews 3:1, 9:15), and as King, He reigns over man (1 Timothy 1:17).

49. God predestined salvation from the foundation of the world, long before mankind was created. His foreknowledge enabled Him to purpose His salvation for them. It is Christ's work in perfecting salvation in His death, resurrection, and ascension that man accepts salvation by faith.

50. Man is justified the moment he accepts Jesus as Savior. This is the first enactment by God towards man. The repentant man is immediately redeemed, born again, and reconciled to God. This is only achieved by faith in Christ's work on man's behalf when the Just died for the unjust. It is only in this way that God's justice can be satisfied, and by His mercy, He justifies the unjust.

51. Man stands before God, the unjust before the Just. Reconciliation is needed, repentance is demanded, and redemption is applied. Mankind has no part in this process; it is God's divine purpose for mankind. He purposed salvation from the foundation of the world, and He reconciled man to Himself. Man could never do

this. God is not reconciled to man; man is, through Jesus Christ, reconciled to God—saved, justified, and made righteous.

52. As impossible as it may appear, man is totally justified before God and has all his sins eradicated, thus giving him, in the eyes of God, a justified status to now come once again into the presence of God.

The Possibility of Falling from Grace

53. The contentions that this subject creates within many believers is so great that sinful reactions, condemnation, and even hatred towards one another are evidenced throughout the church age. On the one hand, some believe that if they accept Jesus Christ as their Savior, they are saved eternally from the moment they confess Him as Lord. They are adamant that even if they sin and never repent of it, they are eternally saved.

54. On the other hand, there is the belief that a person who truly believes in Jesus Christ as their Savior, and they turn again to their wicked ways and never repent, there is the possibility of them falling from grace. Spirit-filled believers understand the principles that bind them to God's love, and if they decide to walk away from it, there is the possibility of falling from grace.

55. W.A.C. Rowe says, "It is possible for a believer to truly believe on and accept the Lord Jesus Christ as Savior, to experience and manifest the change of heart and life which are the evidences of sincere conversion and the New Birth; to be sanctified and to bear a testimony consistent with all the standards of Scripture; and yet to grow cold in the heart, backslide in experience, and ultimately fall entirely away from grace and return to a lost condition of soul."

56. God's Word is clear that any falling away from grace is the action man takes and not God ... *as His divine power has given to us all*

things that pertain to life and godliness, through the knowledge of Him who has called us by glory and virtue, by which have been given to us exceedingly great and precious promises, that through these you may be partakers of the divine nature, having escaped the corruption that is in the world through lust.... (2 Peter 1:3–4 NKJV)

57. God emphatically seals His promise and part of salvation to a repentant heart ... *No man is able to pluck them out of my Father's hand....* (John 10:29) Again ... *Now unto Him who is able to keep you from stumbling, and to present you faultless before the presence of His glory with exceeding joy* ... (Jude 24 NKJV), and ... *Faithful is he that calleth you, who also will do it....* (1 Thessalonians 5:24) Herein are the assurances that God will never renege on His part of His salvation offer.

58. However, it must not be overlooked that while God will never go back on His promise, man can walk away and fall from grace. While God will never remove the person from His hand and neither will He allow someone else to snatch them out of His hand, the person has free will to take themselves out of God's hand and ... *it would have been better for them not to have known the way of righteousness, than having known it, to turn from the holy commandment delivered to them. But it has happened to them according to the true proverb: "A dog returns to his own vomit," and, "a sow, having washed, to her wallowing in the mire."* (2 Peter 2:21–22 NKJV)

59. The rejection of Christ's grace that some believers did when they returned to and adopted Jewish practices of the Law was an outright refusal to accept the promises and privileges grace gave them. They were set free from the bondages of the Law but decided to return to it, and in so doing fell from grace ... *Stand fast therefore in the liberty by which Christ has made us free, and do not be entangled again with a yoke of bondage.... You have*

become estranged from Christ, you who attempt to be justified by law; you have fallen from grace.... (Galatians 5:1, 4 NKJV)

60. The clearest explanation of the possibility of falling from grace is expounded in Hebrews 6:1–6. It states that a person who turns from their experience of being born again, has received the baptism with the Holy Spirit and rejects the gift of God, the Scripture clearly states ... *For it is impossible for those who were once enlightened, and have tasted the heavenly gift, and have become partakers of the Holy Spirit, and have tasted the good word of God and the powers of the age to come, if they fall away, to renew them again to repentance, since they crucify again for themselves the Son of God, and they put Him to an open shame....* (Hebrews 6:4–6 NKJV)

61. The Word has numerous examples of those who were once in *the* faith and then departed from it and fell away. Apostle Judas was replaced by Matthias ... *to take part in this ministry and apostleship from which Judas by transgression fell, that he might go to his own place....* (Acts 1:25 NKJV) It states further ... *Now the Spirit expressly says that in latter times some will depart from the faith, giving heed to deceiving spirits and doctrines of demons....* (1 Timothy 1:1 NKJV) It is supported by the following Scripture ... *Let no one deceive you by any means; for that Day will not come unless the falling away comes first, and the man of sin is revealed, the son of perdition....* (2 Thessalonians 2:3 NKJV)

62. Rowe continues, "While the will of the believer is operationally active in his believing in Christ to be saved and thus his vital faith-union is maintained with the Lord, the prevailing ministries of grace are assured. It cannot be emphasized too strongly that man can only be received and continue to enjoy fellowship with God in Christ (1 John 1:7). God is ever and always the same to all who continue in faith in Christ and who are not moved away from that union."

63. There are born-again believers who did walk in the fullness of

Christ's grace and righteousness and have departed from the faith, returning to the wickedness of the world ... *Demas hath forsaken me, having loved this present world* ... (2 Timothy 4:10), Timothy is exhorted to contend for the faith, and not depart from it ... *Wage the good warfare, having faith and a good conscience, which some having rejected, concerning the faith have suffered shipwreck, of who are Hymenaeus and Alexander....* (1 Timothy 1:18–20 NKJV)

64. Then there are others who were walking in the fullness of God's grace and turned to the things of the world and were no longer fully committed to their salvation. It is Jesus who says it in the clearest manner ... *So then because thou art lukewarm, and neither cold nor hot, I will spue thee out of my mouth....* (Revelation 3:16)

65. W.A. C. Rowe says it in the following way, "Therefore God is ever and always the same to all who continue in faith in Christ and who are not moved away from that union. He is unchanging in His nature and attitude (Malachi 3:6), immutable in His promises through His only begotten Son our Lord (2 Corinthians 1:20) because of Christ's propitiatory work (Romans 3:25).

66. "(When a person moves) out of Christ, a different set of principles concerning righteousness and judgment and another relationship comes into being. It is possible for a believer to become an unbeliever. Nominal belief may be a mere mental husk completely lacking the will, trust, and desire of the whole personality. Therefore, a person so changed, falling back into a life of nonacceptance, places himself in a position where the grace of God is in vain (2 Corinthians 6:1). He gravitates into the same attitude of forgetfulness of the Lord, carnality, worldliness and sin that is the experience of the unregenerate man (1 John 2:15–19). Such souls are back to where they were before they first came to Christ." (2 Peter 2:15–22)

67. Perhaps the misunderstanding of a believer's commitment to the Lord Jesus Christ is that too many believe that salvation is

achieved when a person accepts Jesus Christ as their Savior and does not have to continue in the steps of the Master. Salvation is received the moment a person accepts Jesus as Lord, yet there is the continuance of the salvation walk through endurance and obedience to Christ's teachings ... *Whosoever transgresseth, and abideth not in the doctrine of Christ, hath not God....* (2 John 9)

68. The Word is clear that believers *contend, stand fast, endure to the end, hold fast the profession of their faith,* and *live and move and have their being* in Christ. Eternal life is a gift given to those who accept Jesus Christ and do not fall away, returning once again to the lost state of sin by taking themselves out of the hand of God.

69. God's precious gift of His Son, Jesus Christ as Savior, must never be taken lightly. It is the most glorious experience anyone can encounter. It is the displacement of the eternal destiny of an unrighteous person's destination, and the placement into the divine presence of Almighty God ... *And you, who once were alienated and enemies in your mind by wicked works, yet now He has reconciled in the body of His flesh through death, to present you holy, and blameless and above reproach in His sight - if indeed you continue in the faith, grounded and steadfast, and are not moved away from the hope of the gospel which you heard....* (Colossians 1:21–23 NKJV)

70. This gift should be treasured and cherished, kept and nourished every day until the day of Christ. It should never be treated and handled without ... *fear and trembling....* (Philippians 2:12) Because ... *how shall we escape, if we neglect so great salvation* ... (Hebrews 2:3), and ... *Do not give what is holy to the dogs; nor cast your pearls before swine, lest they trample them under their feet, and turn and tear you in pieces....* (Matthew 7:6 NKJV)

PART 8

The Doctrine of the Church

CHAPTER 28

THE DOCTRINE OF THE CHURCH

1. *I will build my church; and the gates of hell shall not prevail against it....* (Matthew 16:18) These are the victorious and dynamic words of Jesus Christ, the Son of God. It is a sovereign and divine proclamation directly from the depth of God's innermost being. Jesus empathetically declares that no one or nothing shall hinder His divine, spiritual church.

2. Not only did Jesus proclaim that He will be the builder, but He also revealed, through the Holy Spirit, to men exactly what the structure should be and who works in it to bring it to perfection.

3. This divine organism given to men from the Day of Pentecost is spiritual in its intent and humanly beneficial in its operation. It is the original Apostolic Church born on the Day of Pentecost, and which led the new converts into a new life in Christ Jesus. (2 Corinthians 5:17)

4. It must be clearly understood that the church is God's holy, divine purpose. It has nothing to do with man's inventions or intentions. This is God working through mankind on earth. If anyone dares to build on the foundation of Jesus Christ any other structure than that which is contained in the Word, they are transgressing God's holy ordinances for the church.

5. In the same way that the High Priest and priesthood in the Old Testament were warned, under the penalty of death, not to do anything contrary to God's divine ordinances for temple worship, so, too, must Spirit-filled believers understand this is Jesus' sovereign purpose and pattern for His church; be careful how it is structured, handled, and reverenced.

Church Government

6. Perhaps the most destructive attack on believers has been the interference of man's ideas in the structure of the government of the church. So many different denominations exist today, yet the church taught and declared in the Word is hardly found anywhere. There is a need to return to the Word and seek God's will for believers in the Church Age.

7. Jesus gave the *blueprint* of the church, and Apostle Paul is very clear in his letters about what that structure should be. Jesus Christ is the Head of the church (Colossians 1:18), and He will build His church (Matthew 16:18). The only way for the church to abide in the perfect will is to follow the pattern and plan Jesus has given to believers. Who gives man the right to build any other way? Where do church leaders get the idea that they can structure an entity like the church according to their whims and fancies, and then expect God to bless it?

8. The configuration of the church is God's business, and the believer's business is to listen to His commands and do what He desires. Frightening is the prospect that a day is coming when thousands of men who are called of God will stand before His Son and hear these words, "Why didn't you structure My church the way I told you in My Word?" What will their answer be?

9. This magnificent blueprint of the church needs dedicated, anointed men to handle it with reverence and respect. There is

no excuse for anyone called of God to declare that they were not given enough information and direction when they were called to build for Him.

10. Before studying the blueprint of the church found in the Word, it is important to understand the governmental structure and leadership God has for the church.

11. Let it be known and declared without controversy: the church is God's desire involving man, and God is the Supreme Overseer of its members ... *The government shall be upon His shoulder ...* (Isaiah 9:6), not man's or mankind's thoughts on how it should be governed.

12. Thus said, the application of the ordinances of the church that are entrenched in biblical doctrine are applied as governmental guides to help steer the church towards God's ultimate purpose. W.A.C. Rowe says, "The heavenly vision is the *eternal purpose of God.*" Apostle Paul explains ... *and to make all see what is the fellowship of the mystery, which from the beginning of the ages has been hidden in God who created all things through Jesus Christ ... according to the eternal purpose which He accomplished in Christ Jesus our Lord....* (Ephesians 3:9, 11 NKJV)

13. Rowe continues, "Thus divine government will always steer (believers) to that glorious and comprehensive end. It will steer away from the rocks and false doctrines and indifferent and lesser objectives, out into safety of the deep and eternal purposes of God. There can be no shallows, chancy channels or hugging the coastline...."

14. It is God's *eternal purpose,* not man's "personal purpose." It is God who lays the blueprint before man, and it is God who brings about His purposes and will amongst believers. There should be no interference from man in what God does in the church. This is His church and He will direct and guide it in His *eternal purpose.*

15. The members of the church must grasp this fact that Jesus Christ is the builder, and it is to be structured according to His instructions.

It is spiritual, without hypocrisy, and divinely anointed to perform His will. Jonathan Black says the church "is important because it is God's chosen instrument. Those who don't place emphasis on the *eternal purpose* may be more inclined to miss the importance of the church and view it simply as a means to an end."

16. The church is not part of man's daily life. It is not a reference to guide man to do good and no wrong. It is God's *eternal purpose*. It is the complete and perfect purpose God has for man and should never be regarded as an "add-on" to life. It is the fullness of life and the completeness of Christ in all that man thinks or does. It occupies the entire life of a Spirit-filled believer who ... *in him we live, and move, and have our being....* (Acts 17:28)

17. Regrettably, it is too often the case that many members of a local fellowship are inclined to be members of a fellowship with the express purpose of what they can get out of it and benefit from the membership. Some take delight in saying, "I am a deacon in my church." Others like to boast of the fact theirs in the "first church" in the city, and that it has enormous membership which they frequent. This is not God's intention for a local assembly.

18. Its purpose is to *preach the gospel to the poor, bind up the brokenhearted,* pray without ceasing, study the Bible to be approved of God, care for the widows, visit the prisoner in jail, and reach down into the miry clay, plucking a lost drunkard from his pigsty.

19. Governments enact rules and laws to which people must adhere. They lead the people into a direction according to the decisions they make on behalf of the people. Governments strike those who don't follow their rules, and punishment is inflicted upon those who transgress with crimes that violate the regulations and harm others. In God's divine government of the church, the spiritual standards and guidance are in the written Word and purposefully explained, preventing man from wandering off into false doctrine and wayward beliefs.

20. It is a shame that in today's church functioning, very little is aligned to the Bible's instruction for the church. John Piper, in his book *God's Passion for His Glory,* says (paraphrased), "This is especially true about doctrine. We are pragmatic. We demand quick solutions. We define success in measurable quantities. We have little patience with doctrinal precision. And pastors who are infected with the pragmatic virus tend to justify their indifference to doctrine mainly by the fact that such reception is not what the audience is looking for."

21. Too few ministers revert to the Word for guidance regarding the operation of the church. Their approach is tainted by what the world is saying pertaining to what they believe is right at a specific moment in time, and to which some ministers apply their church denomination's principles and beliefs—when instead, ministers should be referencing the original governmental instructions God desires which are found in His Word and applying them. Ministers should be constantly checking their operations regarding the church against the plumb line: God's holy Word.

The Foundation

22. Jesus proclaimed ... *I will build My church ...* and He uses men whom He has called to lay the foundation and raise a sovereign, holy church to His glory with Jesus Christ as its foundation ... *For other foundation can no man lay than that is laid, which is Jesus Christ....* (1 Corinthians 3:11) The delicate process of building on this foundation requires the finest materials and most specialized labor force in the history of mankind, namely, Holy Spirit-baptized, anointed men who reference the Word as their blueprint plan for their enormous task.

23. There is no greater honor for ministers, there is no more blessed

privilege for ministers, and there is no greater responsibility than for them to hold in their hands God's blueprint for the church.

The Differences in the Covenants

24. One of the biggest divisions man created was due to his ignorance of the difference between the covenant of Law and the purpose of the covenant of Grace. Getting this fundamental wrong, then untold troubles exist.

25. Any architect will attest that the foundation must be perfect, and its strength and purpose understood before he ever starts building. The church's foundation is perfect, yet many have not understood, grasped its purpose, or studied how they should build upon it according to God's Word.

26. In the glorious Word, God's orderly governing of people is ever present. These time periods are divided into ages and dispensations that were evidenced by certain instructions, laws, and grace. Each period is detailed in the Word with teachings and instructions for each age.

27. From Adam until Moses, man was governed by the Law of God. From the time Moses led the Israelites out of bondage, God gave His people the Law of Moses; and then after Calvary and the resurrection, God ushered in the church age, namely, the Dispensation of Grace.

28. This church age is the age of grace. In this dispensation, believers are led by the Holy Spirit, and love is the basis of all their actions. Jesus' entire discourse with the disciples in John's Gospel starting at Chapter 13 and ending at Chapter 17 implores mankind to entrench their spiritual walk in His love, in love for fellow believers, and in love for their enemies.

29. Indeed, the basis for the church age is love unconditionally, and it is the age of the perfect will of God.

30. The church age is the most dynamic age in which man has ever lived. It is a *better covenant* (Hebrews 8:6), and it is the spiritual reality of the body of Christ. However, the church's foundation principles got lost in the turmoil when humanity hungered to fulfill their own desires. Therefore, to return to the fundamentals of the church, the Word must be referenced to enlighten the path on how it is structured and what Jesus purposed for His church.

The Kingdoms and the Church

The Kingdom of Heaven - The Promise in the Old Covenant

31. Jesus came to this earth to do the will of the Father. He came to *save the sinners....* (1 Timothy 1:15) Furthermore, He came to the Jews as their Messiah and to present to them the Father's promise of the Kingdom of Heaven. This was not a spiritual kingdom but a literal one, a literal peace and harmony on earth. As part of this promise, they were to receive from God a Messiah who would bring relief from all their torment and fears: *There shall come forth a Rod from the stem of Jesse, and a Branch shall grow out of his roots. The Spirit of the LORD shall rest upon Him, The Spirit of wisdom and understanding, The Spirit of counsel and might, The Spirit of knowledge and of the fear of the LORD. His delight is in the fear of the LORD, And He shall not judge by the sight of His eyes, nor decide by the hearing of His ears; But with righteousness He shall judge the poor, and decide with equity for the meek of the earth; He shall strike the earth with the rod of His mouth, and with the breath of His lips He shall slay the wicked. Righteousness shall be the belt of His loins, and faithfulness the belt of His waist. "The wolf also shall dwell with the lamb, the leopard shall lie down with the young goat, the calf and the young*

lion and the fatling together; and a little child shall lead them. The cow and the bear shall graze; their young ones shall lie down together; and the lion shall eat straw like the ox. The nursing child shall play by the cobra's hole, and the weaned child shall put his hand in the viper's den. They shall not hurt nor destroy in all My holy mountain, For the earth shall be full of the knowledge of the LORD As the waters cover the sea. And in that day there shall be a Root of Jesse, Who shall stand as a banner to the people; for the Gentiles shall seek Him, and His resting place shall be glorious." (Isaiah 11:1–10 NKJV)

32. This rest from all their oppressors was promised more than one thousand years before Jesus was born. However, from the day Jesus was born, God's people never accepted Him ... *He came unto his own, and his own received him not....* (John 1:11) Their failure to accept Jesus as their Messiah translated into absolute rejection of Him and, consequently, the Kingdom of Heaven.

33. The Jews were so busy with their lives doing what they could to follow the Law. The nation's spiritual leaders got so wrapped up in their personal desires to reject Jesus that they never saw what was actually happening. When Jesus was led away to be crucified, all they saw "going on" was a criminal being put to death. They didn't see "what was happening": namely, salvation for mankind.

34. Jesus came to them fulfilling the entire Law. They marveled at His teachings, works, and His testimony, yet they never saw Him for Who He is. *Love your enemies* was what Jesus told them, a fundamental of the Kingdom of Heaven, where everyone lives in harmony and at peace with each other. This literal kingdom they could not see despite its needing no doctrinal interpretation or Rabbi to explain, and despite its being easy to understand.

35. Undaunted, Jesus confirmed His mission ... *The Spirit of the LORD is upon Me, because He has anointed Me to preach the gospel to the poor; He has sent Me to heal the brokenhearted, to proclaim liberty to the captives and recovery of sight to the*

blind, to set at liberty those who are oppressed; to proclaim the acceptable year of the LORD.... (Luke 4:18 NKJV)

36. From the moment that divine, sovereign, and profound statement in that historic moment was declared, Jesus then put His mission into action. He brought healing to the sick, He set the captives free, and He gave countless teachings of how they should walk in His steps. Despite all this, they threw Him out of cities, rejected His teachings, and begged Him to leave them alone (Luke 8:37). All that the Kingdom of Heaven offered, Jesus brought it to them in a practical way, but their blindness to the truth caused them to reject the Kingdom of Heaven; and in so doing, they rejected the promised Messiah.

The Kingdom of God - The Promise in the Age of Grace

37. Once the Jews had rejected God's Messenger and Messiah, God introduced to all mankind a new covenant. This new covenant was presented not only to the Jew, but also to whosoever would accept Jesus Christ as their Savior. This new covenant was not a literal, outwardly expressed kingdom like the Kingdom of Heaven, but a spiritual kingdom, namely, the Kingdom of God.

38. Jesus proclaimed this to the people when He said ... *Nor will they say, 'See here!' or 'See there!' For indeed, the kingdom of God is within you.* (Luke 17:21 NKJV) Apostle Paul confirms Christ's proclamation that the Kingdom of God is a spiritual Kingdom ... *for the kingdom of God is not meat and drink; but righteousness, and peace, and joy in the Holy Ghost....* (Romans 14:17)

39. Jesus said ... *You must be born again....* This is the born-again call for man to be spiritually reunited with God. It can only be accomplished through the repentant person coming to Calvary's Cross and confessing that Jesus Christ is Lord of their Life

(Romans 10:9–10). They confess their sin to Him (the inherent sin of Adam which all mankind has inherited from him) and accept Him as their Savior.

40. This step of faith is accepted by God, who instantly washes their inherent sin away in the shed precious blood of His Son, Jesus Christ (1 John 1:7, 9). It can only be given to man on the basis of faith: works can never be done by a man to buy his way into the Kingdom of God. Man's faith in the finished work of Christ at Calvary is the only way they can be born again.

41. This divine, spiritual step born-again believers take as they walk from darkness into His glorious light, and the awakening of the spirit within them to reconcile the relationship with God is the most important step man can ever take.

42. Every deed, thought, or achievement the person has ever made pales into insignificance when compared to this step they take. The Hill of Jesus Christ's sacrifice is the meeting place of the repentant heart and the most sublime expression of God's love, as it is poured into their heart. The new birth, the reuniting of Spirit to spirit, the casting off the old man and putting on the new man is by far the most essential and critical step anyone can ever take in their life.

43. As they enter the Kingdom of God, they are filled with God's love, forgiveness, justification, and righteousness. They reach deep into their spirit-man and submit to Christ who becomes their king. Their daily response is to the sanctifying process of the Holy Spirit in their life (2 Thesalonians 2:13) who draws them closer to Jesus and cleanses them daily from all unrighteousness as they repent of their sins. (1 John 1:7, 9)

44. The obedience to the Law to justify them through obeying it is no longer applicable. The subjects in the Kingdom of God are justified by grace and not of works. (Romans 3:24) The shackles of the Law have no hold on them; it is by grace that God's love is shed abroad in their hearts through faith. (Romans 5:5)

45. What is available to the "whosoever will" is a new covenant that reaches past the rule of the Messiah to the Jews and translates all people from the kingdom of spiritual darkness into spiritual light.

46. It is in the new birth that ... *the eyes of your understanding being enlightened* ... (Ephesians 1:18) are opened. From the new birth, the Spirit of Christ dwells in man's heart (Romans 8:9). Those who choose Jesus Christ as their Savior are subjects to the King of this Kingdom, who is none other than Jesus. He is the One to whom they submit, and He rules their lives according to His Word.

47. Born-again believers, the subjects in the Kingdom of God, serve the Most High God who has the right to command them to do whatever He desires. *The gift of eternal life* is given to all who accept Jesus as their Savior and who submit to His Word. God permits them from every nation under the sun, the privilege of accepting His Son's sacrifice as sufficient to blot out their sin.

48. Everyone born of the flesh has the inherent sin of Adam within that needs to be rooted out ... *For all have sinned, and come short of the glory of God....* (Romans 3:23) It is therefore not the obedience to the Law but rather the application of faith in the finished work of Jesus Christ that brings salvation and forgiveness to mankind ... *For the wages of sin is death; but the gift of God is eternal life through Jesus Christ....* (Romans 6:23) There is nothing a man can do in his own strength that will produce salvation. He must be *born again.*

The Difference between Law and Grace

49. The biggest difference between the two covenants, Law and Grace, is that the Law was the measurement that governed the peoples' actions, and transgression of the Law resulted in punishment. The Jews strove to achieve God's approval by obeying the Law.

50. The covenant of Grace, on the other hand, pardons anyone's sin

once they accept His sacrifice on Calvary's Hill for their sin. There are no laws mankind must adhere to for salvation to be applied; neither do humankind "qualify" because they are of a specific race. All God requires is that man accept Jesus' sacrifice and believe in the resurrection of His Son.

51. If a repentant heart does this, they are appropriating their faith in the finished work of Christ on Calvary's Hill, and that is the basis upon which He deals with mankind in the covenant of Grace. Man receives by faith the promise of eternal life once he accepts Jesus as Savior, and from that moment on they walk in a spiritual relationship with God as Adam did in the Garden.

52. Because the Jews rejected the Kingdom of Heaven, God offered to the "whosoever" the Kingdom of God, to both the Jew and the gentile alike. This necessitated that He delay the fulfillment to His promise of the Kingdom of Heaven. The Jews will have to wait until the Kingdom of God is fulfilled.

53. The Kingdom of Heaven has been postponed by God and will be ushered in at the Millennium Reign of Christ on the earth at His Second Coming (Acts 1:6–7). Because of the rejection of the first kingdom by the Jews, the entire world is given the privilege of entering into a relationship with God through Jesus, into the Kingdom of God.

54. The Kingdom of Heaven is now no longer available to anyone. It has in this church age been postponed. However, one day soon, at Christ's Second Coming, all will be partakers of the harmony and peace in that Kingdom for one thousand years. For now, the Kingdom of God is sufficient for the salvation of every race, and the Word is the guide on how born-again believers must walk in Him.

55. Within the Law, man was compelled to obediently keep all its rules and instructions which was literally impossible to do. Hence, the requirement for them to diligently bring sacrifices to the temple so that their sins could be appeased.

56. Conversely, in the age of Grace, there is no law governing the

forgiveness of sin. Believers are required to *examine yourselves, whether ye be in the faith* ... (2 Corinthians 13:5), and to bring repentance to God for their sins, who, in His matchless love and grace, will pardon a repentant heart ... *if we confess our sins, he is faithful and just to forgive us our sins, and to cleanse us from all unrighteousness....* (1 John 1:9)

57. The role of the born-again believer in the Kingdom of God is that of a subject who obediently does the will of the king. Subjects follow the king's commands and are at his beck and call. In the Kingdom of God, the subjects are born-again believers who are endowed with the spiritual ability, such as the fruit of the Holy Spirit to walk circumspectly in the steps of the King and Savior, Jesus Christ. (Ephesians 5:8,15)

58. Believers are the testimony (2 Timothy 1:8) to the lost world of their changed and new walk in the light of the Word (1 John 1:7), as the light of the world (Matthew 5:14), and by the Light of the Word. (John 8:12)

59. They walk by faith in the promises of God ... *that whosoever believes in Him should not perish but have everlasting life....* (John 3:16) Their unwavering commitment to the witness of the Holy Spirit upon their lives encourages them to strive to be more like Christ and draw the lost into the Kingdom of God.

60. The Kingdom of God is a spiritual kingdom within the spirit of the believer. They have no human or earthly changes, but in their heart, they no longer walk according to the flesh but according to the leading of the Holy Spirit ... *in righteousness, and peace, and joy....* (Romans 14:17)

61. This life as a *new creation* (2 Corinthians 5:17 NKJV) is accepted by faith, and believers look to the eternal promises of God that gives them hope to endure to the end. (Matthew 24:13, 1 John 3:2–3)

62. Yet, still more exists for believers who desire a deeper spiritual walk in Christ. When they accept Jesus Christ as their personal

Savior, the Kingdom of God is the spiritual place born-again believers enter. This salvation is freely given, and the conversion of a repented heart is welcomed with anthems heralded across the heavens by the angelic hosts. Once the decision to accept Jesus as Lord is made, the converted subjects inherit the gift of eternal life (John 3:36).

63. These born-again believers who seek more of God are led by the Holy Spirit to take the next step and enter the body of Christ, the church through the baptism with the Holy Spirit.

CHAPTER 29

THE DOCTRINE OF THE CHURCH —

CONTINUED

Christ's Promise Fulfilled

The Church ... which is His body....
(Colossians 1:18, 24)

1. *I will build My church....* How seldom Jesus ever spoke of what
   He would do for His own sake, almost always focusing on what
   the Father wanted Him to do. However, when He declares to
   the disciples, *I will build My church,* He asserts His personal
   involvement and His intent that His church will be built according
   to His instructions.

The Day the Church Was Born

2. His church began at a definite moment in history on the day of
   Pentecost in the Upper Room when one hundred and twenty
   believers, who were born again, gathered together and waited

for the promise Jesus said would be given to them ... *But you shall receive power when the Holy Spirit has come upon you; and you shall be witnesses to Me in Jerusalem, and in all Judea and Samaria, and to the end of the earth....* (Acts 1:8 NKJV)

3. The instant they received the baptism with the Holy Spirit became the defining moment they entered the church, the body of Christ. This spiritual translation was an act of faith by every born-again believer who, when they appropriated their faith in the promise of Jesus, were baptized with the Holy Spirit. Several things happened to them at the precise moment their baptism took place.

4. The baptism with the Holy Spirit is a "Christ-thing." Luke explains ... *John answered, saying to all, "I indeed baptize you with water; but One mightier than I is coming, whose sandal strap I am not worthy to loose. He will baptize you with the Holy Spirit and fire...."* (Luke 3:16 NKJV)

5. Jesus is the baptizer with the Holy Spirit, because believers are baptized into His church. Jesus is the One who offers the gift of the Holy Spirit's power. This blessed step is prepared for born-again believers and is taken when they prayerfully turn to the Lord and open their hearts to receive the Holy Spirit's indwelling. When Jesus baptized them with the Holy Spirit, first they were endued with power from God through the Holy Spirit. Then they were given a supernatural, new language called ... *other tongues, as the Spirit gave them utterance....* (Acts 2:4)

6. Finally, and more importantly, they were translated from the Kingdom of God into the body of Christ, which is the church. The Holy Writ confirms this important step ... *For as the body is one and has many members, but all the members of that one body, being many, are one body, so also is Christ. For by one Spirit we were all baptized into one body—whether Jews or Greeks, whether slaves or free–and have all been made to drink into one Spirit....* (1 Corinthians 12:12–13 NKJV)

7. From the Day of Pentecost, born-again believers who responded

to the Holy Spirit's leading prayerfully waited and received by faith the indwelling of the Holy Spirit into their bodies ... *Or do you not know that your body is the temple of the Holy Spirit who is in you, whom you have from God, and you are not your own?* (1 Corinthians 6:19 NKJV)

8. It is at the experience of the baptism with the Holy Spirit that transfers born-again believers from the Kingdom of God into the church, which is the body of Christ. Thus said, the church, although also spiritual in its organism, is therefore different from the Kingdom of God. The Holy Spirit is upon born-again believers in the Kingdom of God, whereas once they are baptized with the Holy Spirit, He dwells within them in their bodies.

9. Clarence Larkin in his book, *The Greatest Book on Dispensational Truth in the World*, says: "We see that it is the baptism of (with) the Spirit that incorporates us into the body of Christ. Therefore, there could be no church until the Day of Pentecost. (Acts 1:4, 5:1–4) Apostle Paul, in his letter to the Ephesians that deals mainly with the church, emphasizes this baptism ... *There is one body and one Spirit, just as you were called in one hope of your calling; one Lord, one faith, one baptism; one God, and Father of all, who is above all, and through all, and in you all....* (Ephesians 4:4–6 NKJV)"

10. This wonderful experience is the receiving of the *person* of the Holy Spirit into the believer's body. The Holy Spirit Himself takes up residence in the believer's body. He is no longer upon him, but now in him. The believer personally knows of the indwelling presence of the Holy Spirit because of the outward manifestation of the Holy Spirit speaking through the baptized believer's vocal chords in an unknown audible tongue.

11. Prior to the believer being baptized, he knows of the wonderful love of God and has a witness of God's love by believing in the love He expressed towards mankind at Calvary. Now, as a witness of the love of God through the indwelling Holy Spirit,

he becomes an empowered testimony to the *uttermost parts of the earth.* (Acts 1:8)

12. Contrary to many beliefs, the baptism with the Holy Spirit does not only involve the Holy Spirit of the Godhead. The entire Godhead is involved in the empowerment and indwelling. Jonathan Black says, "The Father gives the promise of the Son who pours out the Spirit. The outpoured Spirit glorifies Christ (John 16:14), who glorifies the Father in and through the church" ... *Now to Him who is able to do exceedingly abundantly above all that we ask or think, according to the power that works in us, to Him* (the Father) *be glory in the church by Christ Jesus to all generations, forever and ever. Amen.* (Ephesians 3:20–21 NKJV)

13. The most significant aspect witnessed by the people when they came in contact with those baptized with the Holy Spirit was their unconditional outpouring of love for one another and the lost. The extent of this love reached across cultural and racial barriers, Jew to gentile, free man and slave, and into the dark crevices of nations who had no knowledge of *Jesus Christ and Him crucified.*

14. The immensity with which the Holy Spirit engulfs believers in love is explained by Jonathan Black, (paraphrased) "The love which the Spirit pours out into our hearts is not merely a love from God; it is the experiential participation of the divine love itself, the loving fellowship of the Father, Son, and Holy Spirit. Therefore, to be baptized with the Holy Spirit is to be immersed in the Godhead."

15. Apostle Paul, the bastion of the first Apostolic church and foundation writer of the tenets of this doctrine, under the Holy Spirit's anointing, says ... *Now hope does not disappoint, because the love of God has been poured out in our hearts by the Holy Spirit who was given to us....* (Romans 5:5 NKJV) Undaunting love and unparalleled faith that clings to the eternal Word which declares ... *I will never leave thee, nor forsake thee ...* (Hebrews 13:5) is what propelled the Holy Spirit-baptized believers in the

early church to *launch out into the deep* and love the sinner for Jesus' sake.

The Commencement of the Church

16. Now endowed with *power from on high* ... (Luke 24:49) they stepped out from the Upper Room onto the balcony overlooking the crowd that had heard them speak with *other tongues*. The *devout men* (Acts 2:5) were intrigued by what had just happened to the disciples. This is all the empowered Holy Spirit-baptized men needed, unsaved inquisitiveness, for Apostle Peter to unload his message under the anointing and in the power of the indwelling Holy Spirit. And thus the church began its journey, spreading the gospel to the unsaved.

17. This was a whole new dimension for Jesus' followers. Prior to this experience, they were regarded as zealous followers and treated as outcasts because they followed Jesus. Then came Pentecost when, from the indwelling Holy Spirit, not from man or the Law, they got the power to perform miracles.

18. As members functioning in this divine entity, the church, they were filled with a new love and an eagerness that motivated them to spread their faith in Christ to the world. Thus, as believers baptized with the Holy Spirit, they went forth with boldness and proclaimed the message that thundered across the Judean Hills and into Samaria and the uttermost parts of the world. As the church, their foundation was in Jesus Christ, and with His authority they proclaimed the purpose of His church ... *Go ye into all the world, and preach the gospel to every creature* ... (Mark 16:15) and ... *teach all nations....* (Matthew 28:19)

19. This glorious church is Christ's Bride at the Marriage Supper of the Lamb; and while they are waiting for that great day, the Holy Spirit leads and guides its Spirit-filled believers into all truth.

With the quickening power of the Holy Spirit that dwells in them, they are empowered to be more than conquerors. As affirmed in Romans ... *But if the Spirit of Him who raised Jesus from the dead dwells in you, He who raised Christ from the dead will also give life to your mortal bodies through His Spirit who dwells in you ...* (Romans 8:11 NKJV) and ... *in all these things we are more than conquerors through him that loved us....* (Romans 8:37)

20. Looking further at this transformation in the lives of believers who are baptized with the Holy Spirit, while in the Kingdom of God, they are "subjects" of the King, Jesus. Henceforth, when they are in the church, which is His body, they no longer have a King but a Lord in their lives. Jesus is not the King of His church but Lord.

21. *And the Lord added to the church daily....* (Acts 2:47) As Lord of His church, Jesus does not have "subjects" in the church but "members." Apostle Paul describes them as *members in particular* and elaborates on each member's unique, as well as collaborative, function in the body of Christ ... *For as we have many members in one body, but all the members do not have the same function, so we, being many, are one body in Christ, and individually members of one another.*

22. He compares believers who are baptized with the Holy Spirit to a body with many members. None is more important than the other, and each member has something different to do than the next. It is important to read exactly what 1 Corinthians 12:13–27 (NKJV) says in this regard ...

    For by one Spirit we were all baptized into one body—whether Jews or Greeks, whether slaves or free—and have all been made to drink into one Spirit.

23. *For in fact the body is not one member but many. If the foot should say, "Because I am not a hand, I am not of the body," is it therefore not of the body? And if the ear should say, "Because I am not an eye, I am not of the body," is it therefore not of the*

body? If the whole body were an eye, where would be the hearing? If the whole were hearing, where would be the smelling?

But now God has set the members, each one of them, in the body just as He pleased. And if they were all one member, where would the body be?

But now indeed there are many members, yet one body. And the eye cannot say to the hand, "I have no need of you"; nor again the head to the feet, "I have no need of you." No, much rather, those members of the body which seem to be weaker are necessary.

And those members of the body which we think to be less honorable, on these we bestow greater honor; and our unpresentable parts have greater modesty, but our presentable parts have no need. But God composed the body, having given greater honor to that part which lacks it, that there should be no schism in the body, but that the members should have the same care for one another. And if one member suffers, all the members suffer with it; or if one member is honored, all the members rejoice with it.

Now you are the body of Christ, and members individually.

24. To understand the baptism with the Holy Spirit's process, it is important to observe the spiritual transformation within the lives of born-again believers. The moment a person accepts Jesus as Savior, they are born again and enter the Kingdom of God. Then, the leading of the Holy Spirit reveals the baptism Jesus is waiting to give a believer. Once accepted, they are baptized with the Holy Spirit that translates them from the Kingdom of God into the church which is the body of Christ.

25. When one grasps this intrinsic truth that they are now empowered members of the body of Christ, and that they have a specific function to perform to the glory of the Lord, their spiritual walk becomes more meaningful than ever before. The change in the people who were in the upper room attests to this transformation.

Their commitment to the *work of the ministry* (Ephesians 4:12) so intensified that they gave all they had to ensure that God's perfect will be done.

26. It must be emphasized that all who are born again, because they accepted Jesus Christ as their personal Savior, receive the gift of eternal life. Indeed, the Word confirms that they partake of the eternal promise of His eternal presence once they are born again. Yet God's perfect will offers more both now and in His presence when one is baptized with the Holy Spirit.

27. Added to that, their responsibility is greater because as they are empowered with so much more, more is therefore required of them. The New Testament is filled with examples of those who did not count the cost and gave their all for Christ's church. There are also examples of those who refused to *contend for the faith.*

28. God desires a people who will not consider the cost; neither will they think of themselves as too weak. They are confident in their God and say with Apostle Paul ... *Being confident of this very thing, that he which hath begun a good work in you will perform it until the day of Jesus Christ....* (Philippians 1:6) Furthermore, these Holy Spirit filled believers witness ... *I have been crucified with Christ; it is no longer I who live, but Christ lives in me; and the life which I now live in the flesh I live by faith in the Son of God, who loved me and gave Himself for me.* (Galatians 2:20 NKJV)

29. The spiritual momentum that the Holy Spirit provides for the believer in the body of Christ is primarily the leading He enacts to encourage believers to study the Word, and to be found on their knees in prayer before God. He constantly reminds them of the relationship that they must have with Jesus Christ their Lord, to enable them to be continually Christlike to a lost world.

30. The perpetual motion of the believer is based on the premise that they are endowed with power from on high, and that their walk is spiritual and not carnal ... *For they that are after the flesh do mind*

the things of the flesh; but they that are after the Spirit the things of the Spirit.... (Romans 8:5)

The Church – Its Operation

31. This magnificent, divine organism that is the church is not a structure that God designed merely for its followers to deem marvelous. He has a purpose for every member in it, and all who become part of the vibrant body of Christ are required to adhere to the commands from the Captain of their Salvation. This is not a membership that has "sleeping partners" or "silent partners." Every member has something God wants them to be involved in and has no limitations on them to what they can do when they walk in the Spirit.

The church has three basic mandates:

Go into all the world, and preach the gospel to every creature ... Ministers and members are to take the gospel to the unsaved, and never stop telling the lost about Jesus Christ, the Son of the living God (Mark 16:15).

Continue steadfastly in the apostle's doctrine and fellowship, breaking of bread, and prayers. Members in the body of Christ have a responsibility to care for one another, and they are to grow in grace and in the knowledge of our Lord and Savior Jesus Christ. This behavior is known as the maturing of the believer (Acts 2:42, 2 Peter 3:18).

Lift up the name of the Savior, Jesus Christ, that He may be glorified in all that the church does (Ephesians 3:21).

32. The success of a church is not measured by the amount of money it has in the bank or its having a huge parking lot and a building that seats thousands, or its having a preacher who has a doctor of divinity and lives in a plush suburb. What deems it a success in

the eyes of the Lord is the number of souls that are saved through the preaching of the Cross. It is successful when the majority of the members are found attending prayer meetings, fasting each week for the spreading of the gospel, and growing in the Lord.

33. Some churches have vibrant praise and worship as they glorify the name of the Lord, and such praise and worship are acceptable to God. However, a relationship with God is not established and nurtured through how great the musicians are or how many instruments they have. It is established and nurtured through sincere and spiritual members' hearts whose praise and worship are a sweet-smelling savor unto the Lord. It is established and nurtured through the depth of the spiritual velocity of believers who reach the heart of God, not the numbers, buildings, and image the world sees.

34. As they walk in the Spirit and glorify the Savior, their most important part in the church's ministry is their witness to a lost and dying world. There are countless numbers of the sinful catapulting into hell; while sleeping, stubborn members sit in their pews and do nothing but moan about the color of the new carpet in the sanctuary.

35. The members' instructions are clear, and they need to follow them to the letter in the Word. Jesus gave members their "marching orders" in Mark 16:15 ... *Go ye into all the world, and preach the gospel to every creature.* It is the tireless, constant message members have ... *For whosoever shall call upon the name of the Lord shall be saved....* (Romans 10:13)

CHAPTER 30

THE DOCTRINE OF THE CHURCH –

CONTINUED

The Church's Structure

1. The basis for setting in order the structure of the church comes from the New Testament. It is meticulously explained in the Holy Writ, as well as from the operation of the church from the Day of Pentecost, until human interference veered it from the course outlined in the Word.

2. The Age of Grace, the current age in which the church is operational, begins with the baptism with the Holy Spirit in the Upper Room, and the first message preached by those empowered by the Holy Spirit was done on the steps of this room to over three thousand people.

3. This divine organism has been bringing the lost to Calvary's Hill for almost two thousand years and will soon close at the rapture of the saints (1 Thessalonians 4:14–18). Even though many denominations have tainted the truth and operation of the first Apostolic church that began in AD 37, the salvation message is still saving lost souls.

4. Because of the many differences in various church denominations and the slanting of the truth, it is therefore prudent to study the exact structure detailed in the Bible that must be followed. It is particularly important for ministers to be effective members in the ministry, that they study what Jesus gave to them when he who has ... *been approved by God to be entrusted with the gospel....* (1 Thesalonians 2:4 NKJV part one) Their words should be ... *not as pleasing men, but God who tests our hearts* ... (vs. 4 part two).

The Church, which Is His Body ...

5. At the onset, the body of Christ is just what it says—the *body.* The head of the church is Jesus Christ Himself ... *And He is the head of the body, the church, who is the beginning, the firstborn from the dead, that in all things He may have the preeminence....* (Colossians 1:18 NKJV)

6. Headship means authority, control, and guidance. It is from Christ, as the head of the church, that all the operational procedures must flow. Just as the human head gives instructions and direction to the body, so the instructions and directions for the body of Christ come from Jesus. He gave these instructions for His church, and ministers must follow His teaching throughout every area of their ministry.

7. It must never be overlooked that Jesus Christ is the Son of God who is of the Godhead. The entire Godhead is involved in the operation of the church. Jesus is the head of the church, and the Holy Spirit is functional within and amongst the members, while the Father is the authoritative approver of all that is done in His Son's name, because ... *And Jesus came and spoke to them, saying, "All authority has been given to Me in heaven and on earth...."* (Matthew 28:18 NKJV)

8. To continue the analogy: joined to the head of the church, we have the shoulders and the Bible says ... *The government will be*

on His shoulder.... (Isaiah 9:6) From His shoulders and into His body, Christ delegates authority to men, for ... *When He ascended on high, He led captivity captive, and gave gifts unto men ... that He might fill all things....* (Ephesians 4:8, 10 NKJV)

9. Jesus gave authority to five kinds of ministries. They rest on the body's shoulders and are responsible to the head of the church *... And he gave some, apostles; and some, prophets; and some, evangelists; and some, pastors and teachers; for the perfecting of the saints, for the work of the ministry, for the edifying of the body of Christ: till we all come in the unity of the faith, and of the knowledge of the Son of God, unto a perfect man, unto the measure of the stature of the fullness of Christ: that we henceforth be no more children, tossed to and fro, and carried about with every wind of doctrine, by the sleight of men, and cunning craftiness, whereby they lie in wait to deceive....* (Ephesians 4:11–14)

Ministries in the Church – Jesus' Appointments

10. Ephesians 4:11 ... *And he gave some, apostles; and some, prophets; and some, evangelists; and some, pastors and teachers* ... is the divinely decreed proclamation of offices to men called by God, and given a ministry by Jesus, to hold a ministry office in the church of Jesus Christ.

11. These men—called, separated, and chosen by God for the task of perfecting His Scripture—are not just any men, not various and sundry ones, but only those who are hand picked by Jesus. Only those to whom Jesus has appeared and revealed ... *I have appeared unto thee for this purpose, to make thee a minister and a witness....* (Acts 26:16)

12. The all-embracing seal of these men's ministries, and the process of separating them for the purpose of making him a minister, is vital to the success of their calling. To be eligible for the tasks inherent in

Ephesians 4:11, to be worthy of the authority inherent in Ephesians 4:11, and to be empowered with the privilege of sharing the inherent truths in Ephesians 4:11, he must have the *calling* and gift of the ministry deeply embedded in his spirit by the Spirit of God.

Christ's Body – The Shoulder

13. The question needs to be asked: who has the right to ... *preach the unsearchable riches of Christ...?* (Ephesians 3:8) Then, who is enabled to understand how ... *the foolishness of preaching* (1 Corinthians 1:21) can turn men's' souls from eternal destruction to eternal life? Even further, it is only right to ask who has the audacity to mine ... *the depth of the riches both of the wisdom and knowledge of God...?* (Romans 11:33) And finally, who is granted the freedom to explore the *mystery of Godliness* (1 Timothy 3:16), *the treasures of wisdom and knowledge* (Colossians 2:3), and His unsearchable judgments *and ways past finding out?* (Romans 11:33)

14. Hear the Word of the Lord: *No man in heaven, nor in earth, neither under the earth* (Revelation 5:3). Yet, in His divine wisdom and matchless grace, God has been lifting the coals from off the altar and purifying men's hearts, permeating them with the oil of Gilead and filling them with a river of living water so that they can proclaim the *acceptable year of the Lord,* and *with God all things are possible,* and *Jesus Christ the same yesterday, and today, and for ever* (Hebrews 13:8 NKJV).

15. These *called* are men *separated* by the Holy Spirit, *sealed* by the Holy Spirit, and *sanctified* by the Holy Spirit, and thrust forward by the surging power emanating from the very heart of God. These are men separated from the womb of time in the predestined purpose of God's perfect will and elected by Jesus Christ with a God-given ability.

16. These are men burdened with the salvation of other men's souls. God wills that these men proclaim His truth, and thus it is appropriate to find in the Bible and discover what constitutes the character of these men—the servants of God chosen by Jesus Christ to institute the government of God.

17. The men called and chosen by God to establish the members of the church are structured governmentally to perfectly enact the purpose of the church. It is the Holy Spirit's task to *perfect the saints*, and He does this through the offices in the church that are given by Jesus Christ. The foremost ministry in the church is an apostle … *And He put all things under His feet, and gave Him to be head over all things to the church, which is His body, the fullness of Him who fills all in all....* (Ephesians 1:22–23 NKJV)

18. W.A.C. Rowe says, "They (apostles) are to have a preeminent place in church government as it is *first apostles* (1 Corinthians 12:28). Note that it is this preeminence in the part they take in doctrine, direction, and discipline in the New Testament. This office is a permanent and continuous function in the body of Christ … *till we all come in the unity of the faith, and of the knowledge of the Son of God, unto a perfect man, unto the measure of the stature of the fullness of Christ....* " (Ephesians 4:13)

19. Henceforth follows the ministry of prophet and teacher. (1 Corinthians 12:28) These three ministries are to the church universal, while the remaining two ministries, evangelists and pastors, are to a specific group and not the entire church.

20. From the shoulders, the local assemblies and fellowship of believers are served by elders who are the *overseers of the flock....* (Acts 20:28) Elders form the spiritual leadership of the local assembly with the pastor as the leader of them and the members in the assembly.

The Called

21. The ministers of Jesus Christ are not democratically elected, balloted, or selected. They are *called*. These men are servants of God, not servants of men. Too many who are in charge of the Lord's work are at the beck and call of the influential members of the church, and they serve the people as instructed by these influential members.

22. Conversely, men who are called justifiably listen to the voice of the Lord, not the rambling of the people. They take the message of God to the people and not the message of the people to the people. They listen to the instruction of God and inform the people no matter how difficult it is. Because they are held accountable to God, not the people, their priority is to *incline their ears* unto God's message and declare *thus says the Lord* to the people, irrespective of their response.

How Is He Called?

23. This is a question too few ask and too many evade. The servant of God is not encouraged by his own impulses or desires. He is not driven by an ideal or craving to be like another preacher. His motivation is more than that, and much, much deeper. Scripture is sound, and the teaching fundamental that God will always use man to voice His purposes and so, too, with the one who is to be a minister. Jesus Himself called the apostles to be fishers of men. Continuing from the birth of the church on the day of Pentecost, God *reveals* callings to His ministers who hold certain offices ... *which in other ages was not made known unto the sons of men, as it is now revealed unto his holy apostles and prophets by the Spirit....* (Ephesians 3:5)

24. It is the offices of the apostle and prophet who receive divine revelation from God concerning ministries and gifts. When prophets, teachers, and elders gathered in Antioch (Acts 13:1–2), Barnabas and Paul's ministry was revealed to the church. Although Jesus had met Paul on the road to Damascus and told him at his conversion what he must do, not until fourteen years later in Antioch was the revelation spoken as an utterance of the Holy Spirit … *Now separate to Me….* (Acts 13:2 NKJV)

25. This was the calling of God through the Holy Spirit's utterance in the voice of the prophet who was present. God in this way *reveals* to an apostle or prophet the ministry of a brother to whom *Jesus has given the gift.* The *Holy Spirit* works through the ministry office of an apostle or prophet to announce the *calling.*

26. Often, this calling is not known by the recipient. Conversely, if it is known, it is very childish, dangerous, and scripturally wrong for him to announce or speculate on what God has given through Jesus Christ. If God has indeed revealed a ministry to the man who is called, then he is to bury it in his heart until God is ready for it to be proclaimed in His time through His holy apostles and prophets (Ephesians 3:5).

27. Moreover, no man can buy his calling. No man can work to obtain a calling. No man can borrow a calling or earn it. It is a *gift* from Jesus Christ (Ephesians 4:8). Such gifts are given without charge and handed to someone whether he has earned it or deserves it or not. It is so precious to God, so miraculously created and given that those who grab or demand their ministry without it being revealed only cheapen and scar the divine, perfect will of God. A genuine calling is pure and from the heart of God. It is revealed to His servants who bring forth the utterance in His time.

28. The fivefold ministries rest, as it were, on the shoulders of the head of the church. These five ministries are responsible to the head of the church, Jesus Christ, for the governing of the members in the body of Christ. Certain ministries receive revelation regarding the

operation of the body, while others serve them as well as others reach the world for the gospel's sake.

Character of the Called

29. The man *called* has the instruction from the Word to *abide in his calling* (1 Corinthians 7:20) and *to make full proof of thy* (his) *ministry* (2 Timothy 4:5). This person is a *man* gifted by Jesus Christ (Ephesians 4:8), not a woman whose place is detailed by God in the Word to be *addicted to the ministry of the saints* (1 Corinthians 16:15), to serve the ministers (Romans 16:6) and attend to the comforts of the ministers of God (Romans 16:1–2).

30. The characteristics of the one called into the ministry are identical to the characteristics of an elder that Apostle Paul speaks of in 1 Timothy 3:1–7. He is blameless, the husband of one wife, temperate, sober-minded, of good behavior, hospitable, able to teach, not given to wine, not violent, not greedy for money, but gentle, not quarrelsome, not covetous, rules his own house well, not a novice, and has a good testimony.

Obedient to the Call

31. The main character trait of the *called* is *obedience*. He manifests obedience in three ways: First, to be obedient, he must "hear" the call of God and surrender to it. He must be spiritually separated and dedicated, *inclining his ear unto the Lord*, listening as the Master gently calls him. In addition, his sensitivity to the Holy Spirit's prodding must be of such that he recognizes the genuineness in the utterance of the revelation of his calling, and he comprehends the enormity of the task when the revelation is declared, *Now separate to Me....* (Acts 13:2 NKJV)

32. Second, to be obedient, he must "see" his calling (1 Corinthians 1:26). It is a calling that produces the fruit of the spirit and *signs and wonders following* the manifestation of Holy Spirit power that abides in the called minister. These fruits, signs, and wonders are the results he "sees" in his ministry.

33. Third, to be obedient, a called minister will "speak" his calling and profess, *I have not shunned to declare ... it....* (Acts 20:27) Not only is he privileged to proclaim the Word, but he also is responsible to fulfill the Word of God (Colossians 1:25). To speak in the Spirit, to speak from the Word, to speak Christ, the called man must be sealed, separated, sanctified, and found studying ... *to shew thyself approved unto God* (2 Timothy 2:15).

34. He knows the way to the heart of God and enters *the closet* and *shuts the door* (Matthew: 6:6). He knows and trusts like a well-disciplined soldier bent on the divine promise that God hears the righteous (1 Peter: 3:12) and that *the effectual fervent prayer of a righteous man availeth much* (James 5:16). The Word, prayer, and faith compel him to hear, speak, and see his calling.

35. To speak the Word *of* authority *with* authority,

   Apostles will "deliver" *that which he has received* (1 Corinthians 11:23);

   Prophets will "declare" *and the Holy Ghost said* (Acts 13:2);

   Evangelists will "demonstrate" the Holy Spirit's power with *signs and wonders* (Romans 15:19);

   Pastors will "detail" the Word as he shepherds, *and feed the flock of God* (1 Peter 5:2);

   Teachers will "describe" the scriptural diet needed (Acts 18:26).

36. A minister who abides in his calling will set his sights *toward the mark for the prize of the high calling* (Philippians 3:14), and in so doing, be counted worthy of this calling (2 Thessalonians 1:11). It is essential that he be a partaker of the heavenly calling (Hebrews 3:1) and ... *give diligence to make your calling and election sure....* (2 Peter 1:10) He must do this because he is

called with a holy calling (2 Timothy 1:9), and God bestows on him this supernatural gift which is preserved perfect. It should in no way be tarnished and abused by one not adhering to the detail and standards required by the Chief Apostle because *the gifts and the calling of God are without repentance.* (Romans 11:29)

37. Divinely immaculate, unique, and precious is this calling that in God's sovereignty, He places him in the body of Christ by the process of him being "set" into the body (1 Corinthians 12:28). This is part of the answer as to who has the right, understanding, audacity, and freedom to speak ... *Thus says the Lord....* He is the one *obedient* to the *call.*

Dedication to the Call

38. The minister who responds to the resounding *call* and commits himself to *the preaching of the cross* must, at the outset, grasp and experience the revelation *of the fellowship of the mystery* (Ephesians 3:9) and then, keeping his eyes *on the author and finisher of our* (his) *faith* (Hebrews 12:2), receives the vision of the divine purpose of the church of Jesus Christ.

39. This vision is none other than ... *to make all see what is the fellowship of the mystery, which from the beginning of the ages has been hidden in God who created all things through Jesus Christ; to the intent that now the manifold wisdom of God might be made known by the church to the principalities and powers in the heavenly places, according to the eternal purpose which He accomplished in Christ Jesus our Lord....* (Ephesians 3:9–11 NKJV)

40. It is further the implementation of God's instructions to build the church as structured in the Word. This embodies the constitution of the theocratic government built into a divine organism headed by apostles, prophets, evangelists, pastors, and teachers (Ephesians

4:11). This "Apostolic Vision" is so precious to God that it is shared only with those who are deeply dedicated to fulfilling the vision.

41. He is so dedicated that he will look at all his achievements in the world and *do count them but dung, that I may win Christ* (Philippians 3:8), and as the hymn writer says, "labor for the Master from the dawn till setting sun...."

42. He is unshakable in his faith, and his hunger to serve in the victorious army of God overshadows any worldly pleasure. He is not only a "starter" but is a "finisher" who endures making himself *complete in him, which is the head of all principality and power....* (Colossians 2:10)

43. He doesn't do his own will but God's will. He is dedicated to completing the mission entrusted to him by God, and he does not weaken because his strength is from the Lord. He does not waver and is not *tossed to and fro, and carried about with every wind of doctrine* (Ephesians 4:14); he is constantly seeking the face of God with such sincere dedication that he would receive *visions and revelations of the Lord* (2 Corinthians 12:1).

44. The called minister's dedication is so all-embracing that amid the stench and filth of the world, he determines *not to know anything among you, save Jesus Christ, and him crucified* (1 Corinthians 2:2).

45. He is a dedicated soldier continuously dressed in *the whole armor of God* (Ephesians 6:13), knowing that *no man that warreth entangleth himself with the affairs of this life* (2 Timothy 2:4). Also, he must be dedicated to making disciples of all nations; and nothing but nothing does he use as an excuse that begs the question ... *Ye did run well; who did hinder you that ye should not obey the truth....* (Galatians 5:7)

46. This one who is dedicated to the vision stands alongside Apostle Paul and professes triumphantly ... *Brethren, I do not count myself to have apprehended; but one thing I do, forgetting those things which are behind and reaching forward to those things which are ahead, I press toward the goal for the prize of the upward call of God*

in Christ Jesus. He further declares his dedication by explaining *I did... fight the good fight of faith, lay hold on eternal life, to which you were also called ...* (1 Timothy 6:12 NKJV), concluding, *I have finished the race, I have kept the faith* (2 Timothy 4:7 NKJV). Undoubtedly, the one who is called to the ministry grasps the vision and dedicates his earthly pilgrimage to be a *fisher of men.*

Commitment to the Call

47. It is not faith. It is *the faith* (Jude 3). The minister responds to the call, grasps the vision, and settles himself firmly in the starting blocks of *the* faith. The character trait here is total commitment to the call.

48. The minister does not contend for any faith, in any direction, nor does he diverge on a tangent while expounding a favorite passage of Scripture. He is exceptionally well balanced and will *keep that which is committed to thy trust* (1 Timothy 6:20). He knows that to be a *partaker of the benefit* (1 Timothy 6:2), he must ensure that he upholds *all the counsel of God* (Acts 20:27) and is not entangled with *profane and vain babblings* (2 Timothy 2:16). Rather, he does as Christ mandates him to *go into all the world.* He stands upright and is totally committed... *to preach the word! Be ready in season and out of season. Convince, rebuke, exhort, with all longsuffering and teaching....* (2 Timothy 4:2 NKJV)

49. He is one who is rooted and grounded in love, is immovable, and continues steadfastly in the apostle's doctrine, fellowship, breaking of bread and prayers. (Acts 2:42) All this constitutes *the* faith.

50. He knows the meaning of Jude's plea *that ye earnestly contend for the faith which was once for all delivered to the saints* (Jude 3), and his faith is not a wishy-washy, soggy belief that sways as a reed in the ill wind. Rather, he is planted by the river of life and is a towering, unshakable cedar of Lebanon, and his voice is an

accolade of supremely anointed words that reach the ears of the congregation as a two-edged sword.

51. The committed minister understands the meaning of doctrine, and that Jesus declared His teaching which became the Apostles' Doctrine for the church. This man does not *shun to declare* doctrine, is *not ashamed of the gospel of Jesus Christ* (Romans 1:16), and is persuaded that nothing *shall be able to separate us from the love of God, which is in Christ Jesus our Lord* (Romans 8:39).

52. He continuously *examine(s) yourselves* (himself) *whether he be in the faith* (2 Corinthians 13:5). He is not divided in his belief, but he is of a *sound mind* and is in absolute harmony with the silent hum of the mechanism of the church. He moves at God's speed while being fueled by the Holy Spirit. He is *filled with the Spirit, prays continually,* and understands that "knee-ology" (constantly kneeling before God) is more important than theology. He knows that the cry of the fervent intercessor reaches the hearkened ear of his Lord, and he trusts the Word as his road map, compass, and storehouse in his pilgrimage through his life.

53. To conclude, the minister who is committed to walking in *the faith* understands that this uncomprising faith is the undaunting belief and trust that God's Word is invincible when He declares in His Word *I will build my church; and the gates of hell shall not prevail against it.* (Matthew 16:18)

54. It is the conviction that the church is the government of God, structured by divine revelation and calling (Ephesians 3:5), a living organism pulsating the breath of the Holy Spirit through believers' bodies (1 Corinthians 6:19).

55. It is the unwavering belief *that Jesus Christ came into the world to save sinners,* and that God *desires all men to be saved ... and not willing that any should perish.* Believing in this, contending for this, professing this, is *the* faith. Nothing can make a person of *the* faith waver in his belief, contending or professing. So bold is his stand that compromise never enters his mind.

CHAPTER 31

THE DOCTRINE OF THE CHURCH –
CONTINUED

Ministries – The Purpose

1. It is only right that one considers these men who are called by God to fulfill His purposes. God is ever cognisant of man's capabilities, and He is also aware of their abilities once He endows them with His anointing to fulfill His purpose. It is therefore important to consider what makes up the character and integrity of such a man.

Truthfulness

2. The minister must purpose the entire will of God and not a portion of the promise. He cannot compromise or twist the truth of God to blend in with a half-truth; it is the whole truth, the wholesome truth; it is Jesus Christ Himself (John 14:6).

3. One who grasps the purpose is never blinded. He is bent on the pureness of naked truth. He knows that God desires that he ... *make all see what is the fellowship of the mystery, which from the*

beginning of the ages has been hidden in God who created all things through Jesus Christ.... (Ephesians 3:9 NKJV)

4. He realizes that he has the God-ordained privilege to explore and lead the way into the *mystery* which is *in* God. He is allowed to look with the "x-ray" eye into the hidden will of God, and then to know that the revelation of his vision is not for his own gain but for the purpose of God to *make all see.*

5. He shares this revelation because he has discovered the purpose which is *according to the eternal purpose which he purposed in Christ Jesus our Lord* (Ephesians 3:11). He knows that ... *For this purpose the Son of God was manifested, that he might destroy the works of the devil....* (1 John 3:8) Ultimately, he stands with the revelation from God of *the mystery of His will* (Ephesians 1:9) and proclaims the truth as God desires.

The Minister Speaks the Truth

6. The minister of God never guesses. He does not assume, he cannot lie, and he dare not presuppose the move of the Spirit. He does not speak to one person one way and to another in a different way. He is not biased or presumptious but truthful.

7. All truth is total honesty and total uprightness. No negatives, no shadows cross his actions or tongue, and he releases to God the control of his entire life. He knows ... *the tongue can no man tame* ... (James 3:8) and, therefore, he yields his voice to the Master who gives him both wisdom and utterance, resulting in truthfulness.

8. Lewis Chafer says, "A Spirit-filled, truth-imparting preacher will have little time or disposition to descend to mere controversy, but will give out the supernaturally efficacious message of God, against which no error can ever stand." His validity of his every utterance is never questioned.

9. He speaks only the Word, not an interpretation of the Word nor a translation of it. He does not bend the Word to suit the need of any individual by speaking it out of context. Rather, he lets it penetrate the heart of a hearer like a *quick and powerful ... twoedged sword....* (Hebrews 4:12) At all times, though, he speaks *the truth in love* (Ephesians 4:15).

10. The minister will at times reprove a member. Because of his concern and love for his sheep, he will administer a distasteful dosage which is bitter to swallow but kills the worms of corruption in the life of a member. Just as no doctor avoids prescribing medicine because of its taste, likewise, no minister should speak a half truth or water down the Word which is ... *life unto those that find them, and health to all their flesh....* (Proverbs 4:22)

11. He must learn that the application of the Word as liniment is as delicate an application as pronouncing an oracle or written law. Therefore, he does not speak the truth callously or "shoot off his mouth," but rather, that which has been entrusted to him he shares in absolute truth with the hearer. He knows that he never reacts to others when speaking God's Holy Writ; instead, he responds with the Word. Therein he is then an instrument of God to proclaim the purpose by *speaking the truth in love....* (Ephesians 4:15)

The Minister Lives the Truth

12. Beyond speaking the truth, the minister of God must also live the truth. He does not live two lives; one to the congregation and another in his home or private life. He is not reverent and pious when preaching the gospel and rough and ungodly behind the scenes. In all aspects of his life he understands that God knows the secret yearnings of the heart, that *His eyes are on the righteous,* and that nothing can be hidden from God. He knows that uprightness and godliness are of God, and sin and deceit are of the devil.

13. His life is therefore a well-lit room with no dark corners or crevices hiding some crooked deed or action. He lives therefore in truth, on truth, with truth, by truth, and for truth to fulfill the purpose of God.

14. God's minister knows the difference between the command given to every disciple to *Go ye into all the world, and preach the gospel to every creature* (Mark 16:15), and being bestowed with a gift from He who ascended also descended (Ephesians 4:9).

15. *Go into the world* is God's universal call to every believer to bring in the ready harvest, but the minister has added responsibilty because he is entrusted with the divine responsibility of governing with authority on behalf of God. With this divine charge, his ultimate purpose is to perfect the saints (Ephesians 4:12), and be a mouthpiece in the building of the church so that *the gates of hell shall not prevail against it.* (Matthew 16:18)

16. He lives the Word and never underestimates the power that resides in the name of Jesus. He knows the Name embodies *truth* and therefore condemns those with *itching ears* who refuse to submit to the whole truth. (2 Timothy 4:3) To *make all men see* (Ephesians 3:9) is a glorious challenge, and he lives determined to fulfill this purpose of God. To do this, he must be truthful.

The Minister's Challenge

17. While the entire Word of God is the road map, compass, and storehouse for every believer, Apostle Paul's letters to Timothy provide an outline of conduct for every minister.

18. This dynamic apostle, who endured many hardships, took under his wing the young, budding Apostle Timothy whom Apostle Paul guides through his learning years to become a seasoned disciple. So broad are his teaching to Timothy that they cover personal health (1 Timothy 5:23) all the way to *fight the good fight of faith*

(1 Timothy 6:12). Such diverse perspectives explain, then, that the challenge for the minister has many aspects which must be carefully understood.

Submission

19. Every minister of God must realize that he is called not by his own doing but by ... *Christ Jesus our Lord, who has enabled me, for that he counted me faithful, putting me into the ministry....* (1 Timothy 1:12) The minister is therefore in submission to Christ Jesus who is his Lord. Lords have the right to command those who serve them.

20. This submission turns into responsibility when the minister takes up his office and becomes accountable to those who send him out, and responsible to them for his actions, testimony, and work in the body of Christ. As he applies the teachings of the mentor who counsels him and guides him at all times, he is responsible to the presbytery of the local assembly of which he could be a "chief elder" or cochief elder.

21. Therefore his submission is not like that of a puppet on a string, but rather his actions and work that are in accordance with the Word are acceptable to those in authority over him. His submission is like that of Apostles Paul and Barnabus who returned to Jerusalem and reported to those who sent them forth. (Acts 15:4)

22. However, there is a distinction between the concept that the minister is subject to the leadership of the local assembly and the belief that they have the right to dismiss him if he does not preach what they desire to hear. They have no right to dismiss any minister who has been placed there by the Holy Spirit. Because the Holy Spirit called him to the position, only when God speaks through revelation can the minister be sent out. The leadership of

the local assembly needs to know that God is the appointer and the minister is His appointee, not the leadership's.

23. Still, the minister always looks to the leadership of the local assembly for guidance and correction, and together they forge a bond that cannot be broken by personal ideologies. Submission in a ministry goes both ways. The minister will have his assembly in submission to him as they respond to his counseling and teaching, and he knows to accept a *charge* from his mentor (1 Timothy 1:18–19) and to adhere to counsel lest he *suffer shipwreck* of his faith. To crash against a rocky coastline is virtually impossible if he has a minister, ministers or elders who are responsible for him, and he is in submission to them and to Jesus Christ. This is theocratic government.

24. Sincere, crisp, and caring advice is given to teachable ministers, such as *lay hands suddenly on no man ... do not neglect the gift that is in you ... take heed to yourself,* and *I urge you in the sight of God ... that you keep this commandment without spot, blameless until our Lord Jesus Christ's appearing. ...* These are not just spoken or written. They are divinely inspired by God and spoken by one who is sincerely responsible for a young man's ministry, which must mature.

25. Any minister who is on the receiving end of *I charge thee before God, and the Lord Jesus Christ, and the elect angels, that thou observe these things without preferring one before another, doing nothing by partiality* (1 Timothy 5:21) must be in submission to the giver of such a statement.

Temperance

26. A fruit of the Spirit, temperance, is a vital aspect in the minister's life. It does not matter what time of day or night it is or how much pressure exists, he must always be of the same mind and

attitude. He should never be allowed to let his temper rage and circumstances twist his responses into reactions. His Apostle and High Priest *is Jesus Christ the same yesterday, and today, and forever* (Hebrews.13:8).

27. Every assembly member has the divine right to call upon him. He must listen patiently (sometimes with longsuffering), and never must he say, "I don't have the time to listen or talk with you." A minister's learning to distinguish between urgent and important is the key to his being available to all, and his learning the art to listen is acquired while he is in his training years. Throughout all, though, the assembly knows that whenever or wherever they meet him, he is temperate; he is the same.

28. When a minister is preaching or teaching, he never has to act or perform. He never has mock gimmicks or puts on a performance. Because of his passion for the Word, he simply stands under the anointing of the Holy Spirit and *speaks* the Word (Acts 18:9).

29. Undoubtedly, the minister knows that *with God all things are possible* (Matthew 19:26), and he is therefore able to overcome all things. He is *persuaded ... knows whom he has believed* (2 Timothy 1:12), and is *more than a conqueror through Him that loved us* (Romans 8:37).

30. These are the challenges of the minister: to do God's will *according to his purpose* (Romans 8:28), *to run well ... to abide in his calling*, to do *what is well-pleasing in his sight* (Hebrews 13:21), to *stand fast therefore in the liberty wherewith Christ hath made us free and be not entangled again with the yoke of bondage* (Galatians 5:1), and *to make all men see* (Ephesians 3:9); what a challenge, what a privilege!

31. All these characteristics, concepts, and challenges apply to the fivefold ministries of apostles, prophets, evangelists, pastors, and teachers which Jesus gave to His church.

CHAPTER 32

THE DOCTRINE OF THE CHURCH —

CONTINUED

The Church's Ministries – The Offices

1. The authority of the ministry is conferred upon a child of God not because he is worth more than the next, not because he is favored (God has no favorites), not because he occupies a worldly office of authority, but because God, in His wisdom, by His grace, and according to His purpose, elects him (2 Timothy 1:9).

2. The chosen and called man is separated for the office. God, the Holy Spirit, searches the earth and selects the individual for the task. Then, the nail-scarred hand reaches into the world and he that is hewn from the rock and dug from the pit (Isaiah 51:1) is quickened by the Holy Spirit (Romans 8:11, Ephesians 2:1). This man who has entered through a supernatural, spiritual infusion into the holy body of Christ (1 Corinthians 12:13) by the baptism with the Holy Spirit stands in Christ, *not of works, lest any man should boast* (Ephesians 2:9), but under the mantle of love and cries, *Abba Father.*

3. All his achievements as a worldly lord, all his labors in the flesh

as a towering influence over humanity disappear, and he stands naked before God, *clothed with humility* (1 Peter 5:5).

4. With this character trait, a minister can steer the people's gaze from the "things of God" to the "God of things." People who sit at his feet, while he expounds the Word, glorify God about whom the minister preaches as he is led by the Spirit (Romans 8:14), causing them to seek the Giver of the gift rather than the gift.

5. Offices are given, and they have authorities attached to each of them. The authorities in the New Testament are evidenced whenever the ministries are functioning. It is vital that each minister remain within the authority of his ministry.

6. It is the office that gives the authority of a ministry. If he has been called to the office of one of the five ministries, then he must function in that office so that he can have the authority of that office.

7. For example, the president of a business is given authority by virtue of his office to make decisions and take certain steps which no other office (i.e. vice president) encompasses. They hold the office because they have been appointed to it by the head of that business, and in that office they have the authority to approve or deny certain requests and decisions. No one else has that authority in their area. It is no different in the church regarding the offices and their authority.

Offices of the Church
The Fivefold Ministries
APOSTLES in the Church

8. The first ministry God has "set" in the church is that of apostle (1 Corinthians 12:28). Those called to be apostles have a responsibility to Jesus Christ to build the church according to the blueprint that He gave in the Word. This is a ministry to the church as a whole, and is not confined to one local assembly.

9. The authority within the office of an apostle is derived from the

head of the church, Jesus Christ. It is Christ, *the Apostle,* who expresses His apostleship through men He has called to be apostles. Jonathan Black says, "Each apostle derives his authority only from Christ, the Apostle, and head of the church. The authority does not come from the man himself, nor does it come from the title (nor is it delegated by the church), but comes from (and belongs to) Christ."

10. Black continues, "The authority of the apostle comes from revelation… it is either the written Word of God in the Scriptures or prophetic revelation…."

11. An apostle can be compared to an architect. When a multistory building is designed for construction, the most important person in the project is the architect, the one who creates the "plans" of the building, the one instructing the bricklayers, carpenters, plumbers, etc. Every person involved with the construction project knows to take direction from the architect, for he has the final decision on all matters. After all, he has the plans in his control and is responsible as an architect to build according to that plan.

12. The Greek word *"ápostello"* explains "one sent forth." This ministry receives the blueprint of the church from the Lord. In addition, he must ensure that all necessary precautions and steps are taken so that the body of Christ is built on the sure foundation. Apostle Paul describes this concept as follows ... *For we are God's fellow workers; you are God's field, you are God's building. According to the grace of God which was given to me, as a wise master builder I have laid the foundation, and another builds on it. But let each one take heed how he builds on it. For no other foundation can anyone lay than that which is laid, which is Jesus Christ.* (1 Corinthians 3:9–12 NKJV)

13. W.A.C. Rowe says, "Apostleship always directs man's eyes to Him who is its fount. Apostleship ever exalts the Christ (Acts 2:32–33)." This divine gift from Jesus Christ to men is entirely sacred in its impartation. Rowe continues, "It is wholly of Him

and wholly to Him. Christ gives men to the church as apostles (Ephesians 4:8–11). Each apostle carries out a fraction of the whole which is, in entirety, in *the Apostle* ... (Hebrews 3:1) who is Christ Jesus." Apostles are therefore *part* of Christ's ministry, and are responsible for continuing His ministry to the church.

14. Apostles receive revelation from the Holy Spirit concerning the building of the church (Ephesians 3:5). They are also responsible for "setting in order" the spiritual leaders in a local assembly and for continuously overseeing their work (Acts 14:23). In doing so, apostles stay very active in the church universally and locally in establishing new assemblies. However, they do not stay at one local assembly; for as they build a work and it becomes established, they move on.

15. A telling example of apostolic functioning is found in Acts 8:1–17. This passage recounts the events of Philip, who was an evangelist, and was sent to Samaria to preach the gospel. Once the Samaritans received the gospel and were saved, Philip took them through water baptism, and signs and wonders followed his evangelical ministry. When news filtered back to the apostles in Jerusalem that the Samaritans had received Jesus as their Savior, apostles took the plan of the church structure to the new converts.

16. Once they were in Samaria, Philip acted just as he should. He did not stick out his chin declaring, "These are my sheep, leave them alone." Instead, he stepped aside, and the first offices in the church—the apostles, who have the authority to lay hands on believers to receive the baptism with the Holy Spirit—entered the city and laid their hands upon the people, and they received the Holy Spirit.

17. From that moment on, apostles became responsible for laying the foundation for the local assembly and setting the structure in order. To do this according to God's will, apostles have the ability to receive revelation from God concerning the workings

of the church. They focus on doing His will and ensure that all the counsel of God is declared (Acts 20:27).

18. In quoting W.A.C. Rowe, he says, "The substance of this ministry is Christ-imparted.... An apostle is the messenger of the Lord." In fulfilling this vital function, the enduring substances within this minstry are evident in various ways.

19. Apostles must handle the deep and innermost things of God with clean hands. Their motive is never from the flesh but bathed in the anointing of the Holy Spirit. Their dedication to being a worthy servant of God is drenched in His grace, and they firmly yet lovingly impart the truth no matter how difficult it might be.

20. Apostles are enabled to operate within the remaining four ministries during their building of a local assembly. There will, not as yet, possibly be other ministries set in the local assembly, thus causing an apostle to function as a pastor, teacher, prophet, or an evangelist. (2 Timothy 2:5) Rowe continues, "It is as the keystone of the arch of ministry interlocking all into a divine unity through which souls pass into the temple of God."

21. The revelation that apostles receive, whether it be for direction, instruction, or admonition, may be for the local assembly or for the body of Christ as a whole. It often comes through prophecy to the church, or it can be revealed separately to the apostle.

22. However, the prophetic utterance that comes from the office of an apostle is different from that used in the gift of prophecy. The gift of prophesy is used for edification, exhortation, and comfort for the people, while an apostle's prophecy tends to be about governmental matters and gives direction to the people (1 Corinthians 14:3, Acts 15:19–22). The awesome responsibilty rests on the shoulders of an apostle to correctly carry out the instructions and revelation from Jesus Christ.

23. These are men who have the whole body of Christ on their heart *... beside those things that are without, that which cometh upon me daily, the care of all the churches.* (2 Corinthians 11:28) Their

desire is that the gospel be preached to everyone through the work of the local assembly. They carry the burden of the lost to such an extent that they go to any length to share the gospel and show them *the Way*.

24. The burden on an apostle's heart is a universal one that desires to have the entire church acceptable in the sight of God, and they hold dear the mystery and deep truths they receive from God. They *run the race* well and *contend for the faith*, as they seek only the will of God and strive to be perfect.

25. Even though this office is of utmost importance in the church, it is not highly esteemed by both members of the church and the world. Apostles are called *the off scouring* of the earth, and as such they understand that no amount of praise or admiration can elevate *them ... being defamed, we intreat: we are made as the filth of the world, and are the off-scouring of all things unto this day....* (1 Corinthians 4:13)

26. This office in the church contains the dimensions of all the other ministries as well. At times an apostle will prophesy in the same depth as a prophet, and with the same "foretelling." On other occasions, he will preach to the lost with such an evangelical thrust and he will *do the work of an evangelist* (2 Timothy 4:5).

27. Often, once people have responded to the call of God, he will then teach them all the truths in the Word in order to root and ground them (Acts 11:26). Also, at other times, while he is building the work and establishing men into positions of leadership, he assumes the position of pastor until the Holy Spirit reveals an appointed pastor for the local assembly. This "role" as a pastor he occupies is that of an overseer. Nevertheless, an apostle knows he must keep his focus on the bigger picture all the time, knowing that he soon will be moved to start a new work somewhere else.

28. Some apostles grow into a more responsible position in their apostleship ministry and are deemed "chief men" or "chief

apostles" as referenced by Apostle Paul in 2 Corinthians 12:11 … *I am become a fool in glorying; ye have compelled me: for I ought to have been commended of you: for in nothing am I behind the very chiefest apostles, though I be nothing.*

29. This entitlement usually occurs when an apostle is responsible for several works he started and still keeps a watchful eye over them while a young pastor finds his feet. There is also the appointment of the apostolic leadership by an apostle who oversees the entire work of the Lord in a country, province, or on a continent. They have the greater responsibility for the entire fellowship, and his guidance and ministry are sought from many quarters.

30. It is in his assigned office that the apostle moves with the anointing, and the authority associated with his office blends in to all areas of his ministry as he serves the people. Just as the architect has authority to tell a contractor to break down a wrongly constructed wall, so must an apostle direct the elders and pastors to rebuild where they have not done the work of the Lord correctly. He must ensure that the perfect will of God is operational always acting as the situation warrants, *with a rod, or in love, and in the spirit of meekness*? (1 Corinthians 4:21).

31. While an apostle's ministry wields enormous authority, it likewise carries huge responsibility. The fact that he proclaims, "Thus says the Lord," is daunting because it compels the people to follow him. If he is not listening to the Spirit and speaks out of order, then the entire assembly he addresses will be led astray. Such is this responsibility that an apostle cannot afford to direct the people unless he is one hundred percent sure he has heard correctly from God. Conversely, if he hears from God and does nothing, then he is guilty of being disobedient.

32. Inherent in this office is a depth that allows an apostle insight into the perfect will of God to such an extent he is both privileged and empowered to share it with the members in the body of Christ. This depth manifests itself when divine revelation pierces the heart of

an apostle who gets insight from the Word through the Holy Spirit. This revelation is pure and sovereign, and because it is so awesome it could not come from man; it had to come from the Spirit.

33. Often apostles receive insight into situations of which they have no prior knowledge, and when they declare that they have *received of the Lord*, the members marvel that they know about it. An example of such an experience occurs in Acts 5:1–11 when Peter was given the revelation that Ananias and Sapphira hid things from the people.

34. Examples also occur with modern-day apostles who have received revelation concerning ministries for men called by God. The called man is separated by the Lord, and apostles are shown conclusively that he has a ministry. When the time arrives for the Holy Spirit to reveal the ministry, the man stands aghast at the revelation that confirms his calling.

35. Likewise, apostles are used by the Holy Spirit to impart spiritual gifts to members in the church. (Romans 1:11) They are led of the Spirit as they receive revelation regarding the gift of the Holy Spirit that is within a member. This function is imbedded in the ministry and is only available to apostles who, as the extension of the Holy Spirit's work, are given the revelation of the supernatural gift within a member.

36. This ministry is sacred and dear to the heart of God. He entrusts the building of the church into the apostle's hands, who must build according to the details found in the Holy Writ. He lays the responsibility of the members' growth, the impartation of all things spiritual, the continuance of the leadership attributes given to him by Jesus Christ, on the shoulders of an apostle. This fragment of responsibility imparted to him is done with love and protection from the Master Himself.

37. While the ministry of apostles in the church began with the Twelve Apostles whom Jesus called, and named them as such (Luke 6:13), the perpetuation of this ministry is continued through apostles, even in the church today.

Apostles of the Lamb

38. The original twelve disciples called by Jesus into the ministry of apostles were Jews who forsook their original faith, families, vocations, and ambitions (Matthew 19:27–28). These men were given the title *Apostles of the Lamb* for a specific reason, namely the future role in the eternal purposes of God pertaining to the Jews.

39. The first account is found in Matthew's Gospel where they are spoken of as the *judges* (rulers) of the twelve tribes of Israel during the Millennium Period. (Matthew 19:28)

Apostles of the Lamb in the Millennium Reign

40. During the Millennium Reign, God fulfills His promises of a Messiah and the establishment of the Kingdom of Heaven on earth. The apostles of the Lamb's function will be to oversee the twelve tribes of Israel. It is worth remembering that life continues for one thousand years on the earth, and the teachings of the Jewish faith that pertain to this period are in their custody.

41. However, what each individual apostle of the Lamb will be doing is not clearly defined. Suffice to say they will be governing the Jews with Jesus for one thousand years

The New Jerusalem

42. The only role recorded in the Word about the Twelve Apostles of the Lamb is found in Revelation 21:14: *And the wall of the city had twelve foundations, and in them the names of the twelve*

Apostles of the Lamb. These foundations are referenced with the twelve tribes of Israel, and according to Matthew 19:28, the Twelve Apostles of the Lamb will judge (rule) the twelve tribes.

New Testament Apostles

43. During the Millennium Reign, New Testament apostles, together with the saints who are caught up to meet Jesus in the air, return to the earth with Him and reign at His side. The church is no longer an entity, neither is the Kingdom of God, for Jesus will rule everyone which explains that both saints and Jews will glorify Jesus in the unity of the faith ... *Every knee should bow... and that every tongue should confess....* (Philippians 2:10–11 NKJV) This will, in effect, be the Kingdom of Heaven on earth.

44. During the New Jerusalem, there is no need for apostles, prophets, evangelists, pastors, and teachers, because believers are "perfect" in Christ (Ephesians 5:26–27), and there is no need for these ministries whose primary function in the church age was for the *perfecting of the saints* (Ephesians 4:12–13).

45. In essence, the entire structure of the church closes when the rapture of the saints takes place (1 Thessalonians 4:14–17). Jesus receives His Bride, namely the church at the Marriage Supper of the Lamb (Revelation 19:7–9). The church who, with the glorified saints, are continually in His presence, and there is no need for faith anymore, for He has fulfilled all things for them who are beloved ... *Beloved, now are we the sons of God, and it doth not yet appear what we shall be: but we know that, when he shall appear, we shall be like him; for we shall see him as he is....* (1 John 3:2)

46. Apostles, a vital, mighty office, yet one that is the least esteemed by anyone on earth.

47. It is tragic that the ministries of apostles and prophets have been

removed from almost every denomination. This disaster has left the church without the spiritual offices that are vital to the fulfilling of God's perfect will for the church.

Prophets

48. In the structure of the church, prophets hold the second office. To continue the construction analogy: just as an architect who has the plans for a multistory building and takes with him a quantity-surveyor to measure out and check the statistics of the requirements needed in the construction of the building, so does an apostle have at his side a prophet. In the same way that a quantity-surveyor tells an architect to "mix six cubic yards of crush with seven loads of sand," a prophet declares, *"Thus says the Lord ... separate me...."* (Acts 13:2)

49. Apostles and prophets are called "twin ministries" because they usually are found working side by side. Their overall thrust in the church is to build, prepare, reprove, rebuke, repair, and speak the oracles of God concerning His will.

50. The beauty of the two working together hand in glove is a marvel of God's handiwork. Scripture reveals this workmanship in Acts 15:32, 40 when Apostle Paul took with him the Prophet, Silas, and together they ministered to the people.

51. Another example of this is cited when, recently, an apostle received from the Lord a revelation about a calling that was on a certain brother's life. The apostle did not speak the revelation immediately. He received it and waited for confirmation to come through the office of a prophet who was ministering alongside him. Within days, the prophet informed the apostle and confided in him that the Holy Spirit had revealed a calling on the same brother's life. It was the identical revelation the apostle received.

52. A prophet is often found alone in prayer more than in the company of the saints. He continually seeks the face of the Lord for direction and supports the ministry of an apostle by confirming the apostle's leadership. He also receives revelation, as an apostle does.

53. The prophet hides *in the secret place of the Most High.* He abides under *the shadow of the Almighty.* He falls prostrate before the Lord and clings to the anointing of the Holy Spirit as he is commissioned to *go* and *tell.* Their pattern comes from the Old Testament when men were urged by the Spirit to speak ... *for the prophecy came not in old time by the will of man: but by holy men of God spake as they were moved by the Holy Ghost....* (2 Peter 1:21)

54. It is the righteous and holy state of the prophet's spirit that places him in a right standing to be used by the Spirit. W.A.C. Rowe says, "The Holy Spirit works upon holy channels. They must be pure, clean, and separated unto the Lord.... From the original words, a prophet is one who receives the whispers of God, the secret communications of the Most High. He is one who is enveloped by the Holy Spirit and in ecstasy spiritually appropriates the revelation of God."

55. He needs to be saturated in the anointing of God, because when he opens his mouth to prophecy to the people, he is as the voice of God and as the mouth of God. (Jeremiah 15:19)

56. He needs the progression of insight, then foresight that contains the prediction within the message. He speaks from the platform of holiness, and one without compromise.

57. Then, at the appropriate time, he will speak as the Spirit gives him utterance. He is patient as he waits for the Spirit's leading, and forthright in declaring *thus says the Lord.*

58. The prophet's ministry speaks prophetical utterances that are direction giving and forewarning to the people. His prophesying, therefore, is used in a capacity that is different from that of the gift of prophecy in that God reveals to a prophet details such as names,

places, events, and results that will come to pass at a future date. An example of this is in Acts 21:10–17 when the Prophet Agabus visited Apostle Paul and told him of his impending hardships that would come to pass when he entered Jerusalem.

59. It cannot be emphasized enough that God works in the church age through revelation to His people, and no democratic principle is available to any servant of God for any move of God. Instead, the entire church is spiritual and the head of the church, Jesus Christ, reveals through the Holy Spirit everything we need to know about the functioning of the work of the Lord.

60. Without the work of the prophet, members miss out on the fullness of the work of revelation. Prophets are used in a spiritual capacity more than any other way (i.e., materially or physically). They incline their ear to the spiritual desires of God for the people, and not so much to their material and physical needs. Prophets will "speak" when called on and "tell" what God desires.

61. It must be clearly understood that ministers who are servants of God are just that: *servants of God*. They are not the servants of *men*. In the case of the office of a prophet, he is as the voice of God to the people, not the voice of the people to God.

62. Because his is a ministry to the world as well as to the church, the prophet will always speak in accordance with Scripture. Every time he utters a prophetical utterance, the yardstick by which it is measured is the Word. He cannot foretell anything that is contrary to the Word, and he must not contradict the Word.

63. He speaks by revelation from God, the same God who is in the Word. Because his prophetical utterance cannot be half right and half wrong, his message is accepted in its entirety or not at all. Spirit-filled believers need not sift the *chaff from the wheat* in his utterances, because they must be from God with whom there is no confusion.

64. Truly, the prophet's ministry is one that requires utmost dedication and endurance as he spends endless hours in the presence of the

Lord receiving the message for the people of God. God's message is to the people, through His messenger, the prophet. They are so precious to God that He declares ... *Touch not mine anointed, and do my prophets no harm....* (Psalm 105:15)

Teachers

65. The third office in the church is a teacher. Considering the three ministries, namely, apostle, prophet, and teacher, it is clear from 1 Corinthians 12:28 ... *And God has appointed these in the church: first apostles, second prophets, third teachers,* that God has *set* in the church these three ministries. They are to the universal church and not to a local assembly. Their ministry is to the entire body of Christ, and as such it is to the entire church.

66. Evangelists are not to the church and should hardly ever be found doing any ministry to believers, unless they have fallen so far back into their sinful ways that they need to be plucked out of the fire. He belongs in the highways and hedges of the world where he finds sinners who need to repent.

67. Pastors, on the other hand, are not to the church universal; he is to the local assembly. He never roams around preaching all over the place. He is focused on feeding his own sheep and does not concern himself with another shepherd's flock.

68. Therefore, as with apostles and prophets, teachers are to the body of Christ universal and they are likened to the "specialist" who is called on by an architect when he is building his multistory building. For example, he might need a specialist to analyze the needs of his building for the air-conditioning. The architect does not have the know-how and intricate detail of the volume measurements and fan-power needed to keep the place at room temperature. He calls the one who has been schooled in that department to take charge of it.

69. That is how the teacher is in the church. A pastor might need help with teaching the people on the subject, "The Marriage Supper of the Lamb" and he knows there is a specialist in the body of Christ, the teacher, whom he calls to expound and break the Bread of Life (the Word) into portions that will be easily digested by the people.

70. Teachers are used exhaustively to expound the truths in such a way that the whole church is edified. Studying the Word on every occasion, never taking their attention from it, they research, search, scratch, seek, and *study to shew thyself approved unto God* (2 Timothy 2:15). They know that there is no end to the depths of the Word, and they continually seek God's face for the deeper truths that are like huge gold nuggets hidden in the caverns of the Word. Even the smallest clue is a boon as they study the Word to discover great truths that are beneficial to the children of God.

71. Teachers understand that their "research laboratory" is the never-ending depth of the Word. Just like a scientist researching a remedy for a dreaded disease buries himself for long hours in his laboratory, so a teacher spends hours in his study exploring the Word to find the nucleus of the truth.

72. Teachers have a love for the Word like no other ministry, and he lives and breathes it daily. He shows no end to his enthusiasm and desire to help someone understand a passage of Scripture. He is, in fact, *addicted* to the Word.

73. It is a marvelous experience for the pastor, as well as the people, to see these three ministries working together for the good of the church. The Word gives the same exaltation to this operation ... *Who then is Paul, and who is Apollos, but ministers through whom you believed, as the Lord gave to each one? I planted, Apollos watered, but God gave the increase. So then neither he who plants is anything, nor he who waters, but God who gives the increase. Now he who plants and he who waters are one, and each one will receive his own reward according to his own labor. For we are God's fellow workers; you are God's field, you are*

God's building. According to the grace of God which was given to me, as a wise master builder I have laid the foundation, and another builds on it.... (1 Corinthians 3:5–9 NKJV)

Summary

74. It is without doubt the biggest tragedy the church has faced: men have carved out ministries from the Holy Writ and lopped off vital functions that are critically essential to the *perfecting of the saints*. It is for this very reason Jesus gave five ministries ... *For the equipping of the saints for the work of ministry, for the edifying of the body of Christ, till we all come to the unity of the faith and of the knowledge of the Son of God, to a perfect man, to the measure of the stature of the fullness of Christ; that we should no longer be children, tossed to and fro and carried about with every wind of doctrine, by the trickery of men, in the cunning craftiness of deceitful plotting, but, speaking the truth in love, may grow up in all things into Him who is the head—Christ.* (Ephesians 4:12–15 NKJV)

75. Three vital ministries—the apostles, the prophets, and the teachers—are given to the church by Jesus and cast aside by men who deem them unessential. Man has thrown God's gracious power gifts onto the trash heap, declaring they don't need them. They have in ignorance, misconception, and sometimes arrogance cast aside His structure and desires, and fashioned the "church" in accordance with men's desires.

76. Consider this: Ministers will one day stand before the Master Builder, Jesus Christ, who will ask, "Why did you not build My church according to My Word?" What will their answer be?

CHAPTER 33

THE DOCTRINE OF THE CHURCH –

CONTINUED

Evangelists and Pastors

Evangelists

1. The ministry of an evangelist is a ministry to the world that is lost and dying, and not unto the church. If evangelists are found preaching to the local assembly, then they are in the wrong place. These are men who have an incomparable love for the lost sinner. They will spend hours in the presence of one lost soul, outlining to them the path of forgiveness in an effort to lead them to the Lord.

2. Salvation is their primary thrust, and they hunger and thirst to spread the gospel on every occasion. A vision of eternal life in Christ is at the forefront of evangelists' spirit, and the thought of souls being damned to hell drives them to share the good news with as many of the lost as possible.

3. They understand better than any other ministry the consequences of someone's not accepting Jesus as his Savior; their hearts are torn when they have preached the gospel and a sinner does not respond. As a result, the effort with which they exhort the sinner is matched only by the urgency of the hour in which they are preaching.

4. Evangelists do not see the crowd: they see the individual lost souls that do not respond. The burden weighs heavily on their soul when they are at prayer "in the closet" seeking God's guidance and wisdom to preach the gospel in such a way that it reaches past people's intellect and penetrates their hearts so that one of them may trust the promise quoted by Apostle Paul in Romans 10:9–10 (NKJV) ... *that if you confess with your mouth the Lord Jesus and believe in your heart that God has raised Him from the dead, you will be saved. For with the heart one believes unto righteousness, and with the mouth confession is made unto salvation.*

5. Evangelists possess an energy that converts into endurance as they tarry just prior to the moment they close the call to the lost to come to the Cross, issuing "just one last call, maybe there is someone here who has not made a decision. One last call..."

6. When one hears an evangelist appeal this way, the congregation should never mock his motivation or become impatient. He has seen the dilemma of the lost, and he is pleading with them in the best way he knows how so that they can escape the eternal flames of hell. Instead of getting impatient, the congregation should bow their heads and pray fervently, entreating the Holy Spirit to work with the stubborn hearted and convince them to turn from their wicked ways.

7. Evangelists are responsible to the local assembly's leadership and the members of that assembly who send them out to preach the Word. He is continually *filled with the Spirit* and listens to the call of the Holy Spirit to go here or there and proclaim the gospel. It does not matter where the call sends him; it matters that there are souls that need saving.

8. A model of the perfect work and support of an evangelist is Philip who was sent to Samaria. He did what he was sent to do—preach the gospel—and when he was finished, he left town. He never received a special camel or any "love gift": he *walked* out of Samaria ... *Now an angel of the Lord spoke to Philip, saying,*

"Arise and go toward the south along the road which goes down from Jerusalem to Gaza." This is desert. So he arose and went. And behold, a man of Ethiopia, a eunuch of great authority under Candace the queen of the Ethiopians, who had charge of all her treasury, and had come to Jerusalem to worship, was returning. And sitting in his chariot, he was reading Isaiah the prophet. Then the Spirit said to Philip, "Go near and overtake this chariot." So Philip ran to him, and heard him reading the prophet Isaiah....
(Acts 8:26–30 NKJV)

9. Philip was walking, and he *ran* to get to the eunuch. He was not sitting on a horse or chariot or any transportation from the people of Samaria; immediately when he had baptized the Ethiopian, the Spirit of the Lord *caught Philip away* (Acts 8:39).

10. The main focus of an evangelist is reaching the lost sinner. He focuses his entire ministry on the lost. He can be likened to the quarryman who is called by the architect to blast stone and gravel he needs for his new building. The quarryman is nowhere near the building to be constructed. He is out on the plains, digging deep into the ground for the correct stones the architect requires.

11. The same applies to this ministry. He is hewing lively stones from the highways and byways, the fields and the dirty gutters, the business office and the sports fields; he is everywhere other than preaching in a church building. He is where the lost are: in darkness and misery. He shines the light of the gospel into their lives and brings the good news that there is a Savior who loves them.

12. Too often people are drawn to a tent or a gathering to witness the signs and wonders that follow this ministry. Yet the focus is nowhere near that in the evangelist's heart; he can't wait to tell the lost about Jesus' saving grace. The miracles and signs are a by-product he doesn't even think of. Yes, the signs and wonders do follow this ministry. However, it is the miracle of the lost soul that responds to the gentle touch of the Holy Spirit on the convicted sinner's heart that fills the evangelist with joy unspeakable.

13. He knows man must ... *seek ye first the kingdom of God, and his righteousness; and all these things shall be added unto you....* (Matthew 6:33) He is conscious that man is born again ... *not of corruptible seed, but of incorruptible, by the word of God which liveth and abideth forever....* (1 Peter 1:23) He hungers and pines for the moment when a lost soul will raise their hand and accept Jesus as Lord. He is as excited about talking to one man about his lost state as he is talking to a crowd.

14. He is sensitive to the Spirit's leading and doesn't override the Holy Spirit's gentleness as He works with the lost one. He is void of arrogance, humble and blessed to share the life-changing gospel. His most precious possession is the Word, and he studies the pages of this Holy Writ for messages that will draw men to Christ.

Pastors

15. Referring to the church and the fivefold ministries, each ministry has an authority that accompanies the office and title. If God calls a man into the office of a pastor, He grants him certain authorities to function in that office. In fact, He delegates to the pastor the authority to shepherd and care for the sheep. That's the authority in the office of pastor.

16. Ministers must take their ministry very seriously and make sure that they fully understand the authorities within the ministry they occupy. They are to ... *give diligence to make your calling and election sure: for if ye do these things, ye shall never fall....* (2 Peter 1:10)

17. The office of pastor has the authority associated with it and is given the power to function accordingly. His primary function is to care for the people and feed them the Bread of Life. At times, he may show his people a way that seems wrong to them, but because he is God's servant and not man's, he will deliver to them whatever God wants them to have.

18. The message from God to the people is the responsibility of the pastor. He should never waver from his commitment to the ministry and shun to declare what the Lord has instructed him to tell the flock. It is in his faithfulness to preach only the Word that will turn his flock away from immaturity and an unsanctified walk.

19. Pastors, or more aptly translated, "shepherds," have a gentle spirit and a quiet and humble demeanor that should instill peace. He is passionate about the sheep and goes to great lengths to keep them spiritually sound and healthy.

20. He is aware of the importance of a spiritual diet for the flock, and he spends many hours studying the Word to find the message they need from the Bible. He studies to be a worthy pastor, and he seeks counsel from his elders on members of the flock when necessary.

21. Pastors have to do and say some very tough things at times to the people to rid them of their impurities, but all shepherds know how good a medicinal dipping is for the sheep.

22. The pastor's function is to feed the people the Word and not to be their crutch. He is the servant of God. His people must leave him alone at times to wait on the Lord and seek God's face in order to gather the finest meat of the Word for them.

23. The quality of the pastor's preached and taught Word he delivers each time he stands before the people determines the level of the people's spirituality. The more he leads them in the Word, and the deeper his messages delve, the deeper the people will thrive in the Spirit.

24. The more time he spends on his knees, seeking God's direction on a message for the sheep, the greater will be the impact on their lives. They will live spiritual lives to the level the pastor takes them. If he is shallow and unspiritual, his sheep will be the same. If he dodges the moving of the Spirit and ducks the call, his people will be lost in the desert of confusion.

25. The good pastor loves the sheep and shepherds them, tends to their spiritual needs daily. As a shepherd, his main function is

to mature the believer in Christ. To say as Apostle Paul did ... *I have not shunned to declare unto you all the counsel of God* (Acts 20:27) means just that. He has declared all the counsel of God; he has conveyed all the wisdom of the Word, and therein he has provided the catalyst for his people to mature as believers.

26. The greatest reward for a pastor who is spiritually minded is to see his members grow into spiritual giants for God. He longs to watch how the babes in Christ grow from the milk of the Word onto strong meat ... *For everyone who partakes only of milk is unskilled in the word of righteousness, for he is a babe. But solid food belongs to those who are of full age, that is, those who by reason of use have their senses exercised to discern both good and evil....* (Hebrews 5:13–14 NKJV)

27. The precious gathering of the sheep into the fold, and the nurturing of the young lambs as well as the old sheep, is a daunting task for anyone. How precious are the gifts that God bestows upon a man whom He calls into this office. He equips him to fulfill the office, authorizes him to do the *work of the ministry* (Ephesians 4:12), and endows him with a love for the sheep.

The Pastor's Duties

28. Primarily, this office is to one local assembly. The pastor's time is taken up by shepherding the flock entrusted to him by God. His time is consumed by the needs of his local assembly and he should never interfere with another pastor's flock.

29. Furthermore, too often pastors are laden with duties other than the spiritual needs of his flock. His primary purpose and responsibility is to *feed the flock of God* and not necessarily tend to the daily physical needs of the people. There are other offices of deacons and helps in the church to whom this responsibility is entrusted.

CHAPTER 34

THE DOCTRINE OF THE CHURCH –

CONTINUED

Offices in the Local Assemblies in the Church

Elders

1. According to the Word, the total responsibility of leadership rests not only with the fivefold ministries but also with other offices in the church. The first office is that of elder.

2. It is a tragedy that this spiritual office has been removed from almost every church denomination across the planet. For man-made reasons, and in some cases, for humanistic reasons, there are denominations that have walked away from this office. It can only be a selfish desire to exclude these offices, and in so doing, remove the spiritual leadership from their denomination. Those who remove this office prefer to run the denomination as a business and not apply God's holy purpose for the church.

3. The office of elder is a position of spiritual leadership in the local assembly and the church. Every local assembly should have

elders. It is divine in its call, operation, and reward. It is spiritual in its nature and led by the Holy Spirit in its functioning. The Bible refers to this office by three names: overseer, bishop, and elder. All three are one and the same.

4. At the outset, Spirit-filled believers know that it is God who calls man to repentance. Furthermore, they know that is it God who chooses men to hold office (Matthew 22:14).

5. Once called, and then chosen, the elder is to abide in the calling (1 Corinthians 7:20). This calling on a man's life is never removed; it is God-ordained and sealed. (Romans 11:29) Elders are God's choice from amongst the people; men selected by Him, not man (Acts 20:28). God chooses them to occupy this office; God gives them the responsibility embodied in the office (1 Timothy 3:1, Hebrews 11:6). Because they are called by God, it is important to see this calling in the same manner that God sees it.

Spiritual Calling

6. Eldership in the church is a spiritual calling from God. Therein, it is a holy calling (2 Timothy 1:9). Because it is a holy calling of God, it is, therefore, for His purpose that elders are called. The office of elder cannot be used for any personal gain or persuasion, for everything an elder does in this office is for God's glory, for His work, and in His Name.

7. An elder's purposes must be fulfilled for the extension of God's kingdom and church, and no glory or reward should ever be gleaned from this office towards the bearer. As overseers of the flock, elders have the responsibility of guiding and directing them spiritually (Acts 20:28).

8. If the man called to be an elder respects God, he will respect the office. If he respects the office, he will respect God's people. If he respects God's people, they will respect him as an elder.

God's Standards for Leadership

9. God calls men for this office, and He gives them the responsibility of having spiritual oversight over His people. God desires obedience to His Word from these men, and He expects nothing less, as was the case with His only Son. God expects active participation in the office from obedient men.

10. Elders are spiritually called by revelation, which is through the Holy Spirit. No place exists in the office of elder for man's carnality which induces a popular vote of the majority. Unconcerned with man's desire, God calls whom He desires to the office.

11. The original reference in the Word refers to the appointment of elders by apostles (Acts 14:23). Elders are men who are revealed through the ministry office in the local assembly to uphold the spiritual well-being of the people. They are separated by God and given the responsibility of assisting the pastor in his spiritual duties.

Seal of Eldership

12. The ultimate seal of eldership is in the evidence that he, as a servant of God, produces. It is the fruit of his labors that accentuates his seal in God. All his actions must equal his motives, and his decisions are Spirit-led, not voted upon (Acts 15:19–22).

13. His seal is in his contrite, humble application of the tasks he is assigned (Acts 20:19). The fruit of an elder is evidenced through his faithfulness to God first, then to the people. He oversees them with the love of Christ and guides them into the depth of the Word, encouraging them to continually fellowship with the saints.

14. An elder's leadership in the church is ultimately spiritual as they assist the pastor in nurturing and tending to the flock by following and applying the Word.

Qualifications of Eldership

15. God calls men who meet His standards and His qualifications into the office of elder. For a local assembly to have spiritual leadership, called elders must conform to the spiritual standards found in God's Word. To be chosen by God for this office, a man must be worthy in the following ways: he must have a thorough knowledge of the Word of God, and he must walk a holy life.

16. To begin, for the elder to counsel members in the assembly, he must have an advanced knowledge of the Word so that his entire reference for all questions he is asked remains the Word.

17. He does not need a worldly education to qualify him for the position, but he must have the Word so ingrained in him that it is the ultimate and only source to which he refers (2 Timothy 2:15). Therein his spiritual sources are Jesus Christ and the Holy Spirit who endow him with wisdom from above. (James 3:17) The office does not require a mind of reason but one of application; for in every situation the elder turns to the Bible for the answer and guidance.

18. Lack of the knowledge of the Word places a potential elder in the position of a novice, making him an unskilled counselor who gives his own ideas and experiences as solutions to questions, instead of the Word's answers. Also, never should an elder be in a position of doubt about his counsel. It must be biblically based so that he need never fear that what he says is wrong.

19. By having his spirit immersed in the Word, the elder will have less chance of giving incorrect advice and counsel. Further, such immersion creates a trust between him and the people, because they will soon understand that the counsel they receive from him is not his own ideas but rather, from the inspiration and guidance of the Word. Thus, the Word becomes *his refuge* and he stays in its *pavilion* (Psalm 27:5).

20. The Word declares that the people *are destroyed for lack of knowledge* (Hosea 4:6); that is, a lack of Godliness and of knowledge of God. It does not pertain to worldly knowledge or wisdom concerning earthly things, but it is centered on the spiritual knowledge of God and His Word.

21. Then, elders must live a holy life. God commands that believers be holy whether they are called to an office in the church or not (1 Peter 1:16). Even more so then must the leaders of God's people walk in holiness and purity. The elder must do more than tell the people what to do; he must walk in the holiness he professes so they will follow his example (Philippians 3:17).

22. A holy walk is not a gift from God. To be worthy of this holy walk, the elder must *lay aside every weight and sin,* and *cut off* any connection with those things that are contrary to God's desires for his life and *come out from among them* [the unbelievers] ... and *touch not the unclean thing* (2 Corinthians 6:17). By doing this, he walks the path of sanctification. As he cleanses himself of these things that are not acceptable to God, he focuses on the spiritual desires God has for his life, and then his vision becomes Christlike (1 Corinthians 1:30).

23. All of this translates as the purifying process (John 15:3), wherein the elder's thoughts and concerns become God-centered and Word-centered. By looking towards the spiritual things of God, he becomes involved with God's will and, as such, is found doing the things of God that enable him to walk the pure, holy walk in Christ (1 Corinthians 2:13).

24. Through this interaction, the elder develops a divine relationship with God as well as setting an example for the flock of God to follow. He constantly sets the example for the flock in living a holy life, and he is first to respond to the call to prayer and is a ready support to the pastor when he needs to counsel a wayward member.

25. Without doubt, as a leader in the assembly, the elder must be *filled with the Spirit* and walk in the anointing of the Spirit (Ephesians

5:18), thereby being sensitive to the Holy Spirit's bidding. He achieves this sustained filling of the Holy Spirit by staying in the presence of God and His statutes (Psalm 61:1–8).

26. Because he is continually filled with the Holy Spirit, an elder should never say that he is unavailable because he is not spiritually right in the Lord. The baptism with the Holy Spirit is therefore a prerequisite for a man to hold the office of elder, because he needs the continuous infilling of the Holy Spirit that will enable him to lead the people in the Spirit. The working of the Spirit in his life is vitally important to the edification of the body of Christ.

27. The gifts of the Holy Spirit are often in operation through the elder who helps, encourages, and guides the body of Christ. Many younger *babes* in Christ look to him for guidance about how to be used in the operation of the gifts of the Holy Spirit. He guides them by instruction and by example as the Holy Spirit flows through him. He sets the standard and is continually filled with the Holy Spirit to overflowing.

28. Furthermore, he is called by God to fulfill God's divine purpose, and he is obedient to the bidding of the Holy Spirit. God places the burden of many tasks on his shoulders, and He calls the elder to convey His ways, truth, and life to the people.

Elders – Their Duties

29. All men called of God and who hold a spiritual office (apostle, prophet, evangelist, pastor, and teacher) are also elders. Peter in his first letter explains that even though he holds the office of an apostle, he is still recognized as an elder because of the spiritual nature of the elder's office (1 Peter 5:1).

30. This is so because eldership is usually the "springboard" to a ministry. When a ministry is revealed, and the Holy Spirit reveals this man's calling to the apostles or prophets, they will set the man

called into the ministry aside, and when the Holy Spirit reveals the timing, they *set* (ordain) him as an elder in the local assembly.

31. The eldership in a local assembly usually includes all the men who are called into one of the fivefold ministries. These men support each other in every aspect of the spiritual well-being of the local assembly. As a group, they form the presbytery or eldership (spiritual leadership) and have specific duties to perform in supporting the pastor and the people of the assembly.

Duties That Support the Pastor

32. The pastor is the leader/shepherd of the people, and the elders form the nucleus of the pastor's spiritual influence within the local assembly. The elders support him as well as acquiesce to his guidance and leadership in all spiritual matters. Every spiritual decision that is made in the local assembly is made by the pastor, who is responsible to God as the shepherd for the members' well-being.

33. When he needs help with a spiritual decision, he should meet with the elders and weigh their suggestions, but the final decision is his and carries their unanimous support. Never should an elder say he went along with a decision because the rest agreed with the pastor, yet he himself did not agree. All the elders must totally accept and support every decision that the pastor makes (Acts 15:1–20). After all, is it not the same Holy Spirit who called the pastor into the ministry and who called elders to support him?

34. Elders are also duty-bound to serve the pastor spiritually, which means they assist him when he is unable to carry out any spiritual function, such as teaching or preaching, ministering at the Table of the Lord, performing baptisms, or presiding at funerals.

35. Whenever the pastor ministers to or prays for people who respond to the call of salvation, the elders support him in prayer while the

411

deacons help in the physical aspects of the ministry. Elders also have a duty to immediately bring to the pastor's attention any spiritual problem in the local assembly. If they are aware that a member is struggling and in need, they will first tell the pastor, who decides if an elder can take care of the matter. Never should an elder know about a situation and keep it from the pastor. Likewise, the pastor confides in his elders immediately when he knows of an issue. He has as much trust in them as they do in him.

36. Elders are to support every service and outreach that the pastor sanctions. In fact, every aspect of the local assembly's operation should have an elder present. If this is done, then this Scripture is applicable ... *Remember those who rule over you, who have spoken the word of God to you, whose faith follow, considering the outcome of their conduct.... Obey those who rule over you, and be submissive, for they watch out for your souls, as those who must give account. Let them do so with joy and not with grief, for that would be unprofitable for you....* (Hebrews 13:7, 17 NKJV)

37. Elders are the initiative takers. They respond immediately to any spiritual request the pastor makes in a service. The entire "spiritual barometer" of the assembly is measured by the level of the elders' spirituality. If the pastor is not spiritual, neither will the elders be. If the elders are not spiritual, then more than likely neither will the people be.

Duties That Support the People

38. Elders are on call twenty-four hours a day as they respond to the spiritual needs of the local assembly. Whenever members have spiritual needs, elders attend to them. They report the situation to the pastor and take the members into their care and see them through their struggles. Often, the members find themselves in dilemmas that cannot be solved by a single visit. Such situations

need to be in caring and nurturing hands until they are completely resolved. This is the elder's function.

39. Elders also are the ones responsible for visiting the sick as described in James 5:14 ... *Is any sick among you? let him call for the elders of the church; and let them pray over him, anointing him with oil in the name of the Lord.* Caring for those who are not well in the assembly is left in the hands of spiritual overseeing, which is the function of an elder. Sick people need the healing flow of the power in the Name of Jesus, and elders are the ones who administer this.

40. When someone is sick, they call for the elders (plural*)*, meaning that all, or at least two, are to take care of the sick person. Elders should never allow themselves to be exposed to any suspicion; they always work together.

41. In addition, elders stand in the gap for the pastor and teach the people the Word of God. They must be ... *apt to teach* (1 Timothy 3:2). They are the ones who teach the people in their homes. As new members join the assembly, elders visit them in their homes and explain the sacraments, ordinances, and operation of the gifts of the Spirit. They are the ones who feed the flock of God ... *over the which the Holy Ghost hath made you overseers, to feed the church of God, which he hath purchased with his own blood....* (Acts 20:28)

42. The responsibility of the people's spiritual well-being is the primary concern of elders. In this realm, they are charged by Apostle Paul to rule well. The doctrine they deliver is the Apostle's Doctrine and all the teachings by which the church is guided ... *Let the elders that rule well be counted worthy of double honor, especially they who labor in the word and doctrine....* (1 Timothy 5:17)

43. Elders must saturate their lives in the Word and the things of the Spirit so that they are above reproach. Never should the need arise

for 1 Timothy 5:19 (NKJV) to be applied ... *Do not receive an accusation against an elder except from two or three witnesses.*

Characteristics of Elders

44. It is acceptable practice that no minister holding an office of one of the fivefold ministries has been appointed without first being an elder. Jonathan Black says, "As the apostles are also elders among the elders (1 Peter 5:1) the qualifications for eldership apply to all five of the Headship ministries: apostles, prophets, evangelists, pastors and teachers."

45. These qualifications are detailed in two accounts in the Word: 1 Timothy 3:1–7, and Titus 1:5–9. Together, they deal with a total of sixteen characteristics.

Blameless

46. "Blameless" means he must be above reproach. Alexander Strauch in his book *Biblical Eldership* writes, "A man who is 'above reproach' has a good moral and spiritual reputation. He is a man with an irreproachable life in the sight of others." He is also without reproach to God. Strauch continues, "He is free from any offensive or disgraceful blight of character or conduct."

47. This keeps him from tarnishing the position of leadership ... *that ye may be blameless and harmless, the sons of God, without rebuke, in the midst of a crooked and perverse nation, among whom ye shine as lights in the world....* (Philippians 2:15)

The Husband of One Wife

48. Elders lead by Godly example and present to the church and to the world the God-ordained principles of marriage if they are

married. They are examples for the flock of God to follow and in so doing, there must be no question about their commitment to their marriage. The married elder is the husband of one wife and cannot hold office if otherwise. Anyone who has entered into the God-ordained institution of marriage, irrespective of whether he was born-again at that time or not, and then divorces his wife and marries another, may not hold office.

Temperate, Sober-Minded

49. The devil is out to destroy God's servants, and he will launch an all-out attack on those who hold office. Elders must be wide awake, careful, attentive, and fastidious. Alexander Strauch says, "Temperance is a much-needed quality if one is to stand firm against the devil's subtle attacks (1 Peter 5:8)."

50. A temperate/vigilant elder never drops his guard. He is *ready in season and out of season* to do God's work. He walks circumspectly and in self-discipline, never relenting to the onslaught that continually bombards his uprightness.

51. In the same way that he is temperate, an elder is sober-minded (prudent), of sound judgment, and never gets out of sorts and falls prey to false doctrine. Strauch continues, "Prudent means to be balanced, discreet, and controlled because of sound judgment, sensible thinking and reasonableness."

Good Behavior and Hospitable

52. The Elder must live an upright life that is self-disciplined and honorable before all men. An elder is not disorderly in conduct, speech, or dress, nor is he slothful in business, shoddy in keeping appointments, and reckless in handling his own affairs. His every step must be acceptable to God, and his lifestyle must

attract people to Godliness and induce them to turn from sin. (2 Thessalonians 3:6–7)

53. Scripture requires that an elder ... *be hospitable to one another without grumbling....* (1 Peter 4:9 NKJV) That is, as a leader of the church, he should receive the saints of God with warmth and goodwill. He should never begrudge the responsibility but rather celebrate the opportunity.

54. Being hospitable is not done as an act of obedience to the office; it should be done out of the love for his fellow man. This is a characteristic of an elder, not a demand.

Able to Teach

55. One of the most important characteristics of an elder is his ability to teach the flock of God on spiritual things. Again, Alexander Strauch gives an explicit analysis of this characteristic an elder must possess, "Elders must be able to teach which entails three basic elements: knowledge of Scripture, the readiness to teach, and the capability to communicate."

56. The elder's main duty is to lead the people closer to God and to do this, he is required to teach them. As a custodian of the doctrine, he must teach the people its contents. An elder teaches the people by showing God's instructions, and he teaches by example. Members will do what an elder does and say what he says. His example sometimes teaches more than what he expounds.

Not Given to Wine

57. An elder does not partake of alcohol in such a way that it causes him to lose his dignity. Further, he does not end up in an uncontrollable state that causes him to be a brawler because of the excess of alcohol. An elder has a divine responsibility to conduct himself in such a manner that it does not bring down a weaker

brother (1 Corinthians 8:7–13). The destruction that the devil brings about through alcohol is so great in the world today that any elder who partakes of it is identifying with a worldly practice that can so easily be the downfall of a weaker brother or sister.

Not Violent

58. The elder does not behave as a violent, short-tempered, quarrelsome person, and be prone to physical brawling. The fruits of such an elder will bring fear in God's flock who might expect an elder to assault them when correcting them. Instead, he should be gentle, gracious, and forbearing with the flock of God.

59. Their approach wins over the people's confidence because they have a sincere, gentle attitude and behavior. He does not bulldoze the people or use physical force to get them to follow God but in a gracious manner he leads them through the valley of the shadow of death and onto the mountaintop experiences. Because an elder is not violent, he is protective and does not allow the members to be battered and manhandled by anyone, knowing that they are easily affrighted.

60. It is appropriate to let the Word speak on this vital characteristic
 ... *The elders who are among you I exhort, I who am a fellow elder and a witness of the sufferings of Christ, and also a partaker of the glory that shall be revealed: Shepherd the flock of God which is among you, serving as overseers, not by compulsion but willingly, not for dishonest gain but eagerly; nor as being lords over those entrusted to you, but being examples to the flock....* (1 Peter 5:1–4 NKJV)

Not Greedy for Money

61. Nothing is more despicable than a man who lusts after money and lets it drive his every passion, mood, and craving. The love

of money is devilish in its origin and the result is evil (1 Timothy 6:10). The stewardship of God's money is given to deacons, yet the choice of the deacons to control the Lord's money is made by the elders.

62. If a man cannot control his greed for money, then he normally cannot make a responsible decision. Thus, the elder must continually guard himself against falling into the trap of lusting after money. They are self-disciplined, and not tempted into making debt. He is rather level headed and "cuts his coat according to his cloth" so that he is never financially overexposed.

Gentle, Not Quarrelsome, Not Covetousness

63. An elder must accept the reality that some members take longer than others to grasp the Word, and he is instinctively to ... *suffer fools gladly....* (2 Corinthians 11:19) To enhance his tolerance of the inadequate, an elder seeks to grow in grace towards God's people, and he exercises wisdom in every situation. He must be patient with them through every situation and fill them with encouragement at every opportunity.

64. The church's warfare is spiritual and requires the skillful use of the whole armor of God, not the conduct of brawlers and brutes. Such men who believe they must prove their manliness by being physical are mired in carnality which is at enmity with God (Romans 8:7) and shameful because they bring disrespect to the flesh. He does not enter into quarrelsome arguments with the flock, neither does he vent at apposing points of view. Furthermore, an elder knows that his body is the temple of the Holy Spirit and as such, must be kept wholesome and worthy to reverence God on every occasion.

65. The mere magnitude of the responsibility inherent in the office of elder should funnel all his attention and energy toward the duties and needs in the office. Those who covet have an addiction for that which they do not own or possess.

66. Never should he have the inclination to covet another's possessions, ways, or state. Because he is called according to God's purposes, he must be satisfied with what God has given him and never covet another's possessions. No matter what he has acquired in his life the Lord is satisfied with him, and he must never think that he should have more because he holds the office of elder. Covetousness desires what someone else has—and it is not the province of an elder.

He Rules His Own House Well

67. This is self-explanatory. They rule their own house well, and it has nothing to do with how others rule their house. How he manages his own household is a reflection of how he will shepherd the people of God. The manner of leadership within his home relative to his children and the relationship with his wife will testify to his ability to lead the people.

68. An elder's family life is clearly significant when considering his qualifications for eldership. He is required to be a loyal husband, patient, and given to hospitality, all hallmarks of managing his home well. This home environment is the base of God's law because He instituted the family, and it is to this divine example that pastors look and decide if a man is fit to be an elder, namely, if he rules his household well.

An Elder Must Not Be a Novice

69. Zealousness must not be confused with maturity. Many a new convert is on fire for God and may appear from his eagerness to be making great spiritual growth on a daily basis. At times, the devil may tempt this eager novice on tasks he is too immature to handle, setting him up for consequences he is unable to control.

70. To avoid such disaster, a new convert needs to walk in the

Master's steps and be seasoned in the work of the Lord before being worthy of eldership. Elders also need to be knowledgeable in the Word, so they will reject giving their own interpretation and ideas as advice instead of the Word's.

71. A novice is easily tripped up by pride, and Apostle Paul warns that this is why pastors need to be satisfied that those who are called as elders are not unskilled in the use of the Word.

He Must Have a Good Report from Without

72. A man's reputation before his Christian brethren must not be any different from that which he has in the world. The person who is caring, concerned, and righteous while he is in the presence of the saints but becomes cold, insensitive, and sinful when among the ways of the world is unworthy of the office.

73. The elder's character is on display no matter where he is, and the report from his fellow workers, superiors, and acquaintances must all reflect the same response, "He is upright, diligent, righteous, and not slothful." The elder's every action and words in the world are a direct reflection to the world what his local assembly stands for, and the opinion it forms of him is indirectly the opinion it forms of his assembly.

74. Therefore, the elder as a leader in the local assembly and the church must conduct himself in a manner that causes the world not to look upon him with disdain, but with respect and admiration because he embodies all the qualities of eldership.

75. In his letter to Titus, Apostle Paul lists many of the same qualities evident in the men who are called into eldership that are contained in the letter to Timothy. He enhances the spiritual requirements to include holiness, temperance, and the love of good men (Titus 1:6–9). While these are basic fundamental attributes of a Spirit-filled believer, they are more evident in the leadership of the church, and pose as an example for members to follow.

Other Offices in the Church

76. There are a few offices in the church pertaining to the material and physical aspects of its operation. These offices have specific responsibilities that encompass issues other than spiritual matters.

Deacons

77. Suffice to say the Word has strict guidelines for the assembly when electing deacons into the office that has no direct spiritual authority. Deacons' tasks are to care for the widows and see to the running of the church's lay concerns such as making sure the building and its operational aspects are in working order.

78. Apostle Paul gives a detailed explanation of the qualities a deacon must possess in 1 Timothy 3:8–13. These qualifications closely resemble the qualities of an elder. The most important quality being that they are men ... *of honest report, full of the Holy Ghost and wisdom....* (Acts 6:3)

79. A pastor does not have time to concern himself whether the microphones are working or whether the font is filled with water for the baptismal service. He must have his spirit in tune with what God has in store for the people, therefore he needs other men to take charge of those material matters that could be a hindrance to him.

80. The Word *declares ... Now in those days, when the number of the disciples was multiplying, there arose a complaint against the Hebrews by the Hellenists, because their widows were neglected in the daily distribution. Then the twelve summoned the multitude of the disciples and said, "It is not desirable that we should leave the word of God and serve tables. Therefore, brethren, seek out from among you seven men of good reputation, full of the Holy Spirit and wisdom, whom we may appoint over this business; but*

we will give ourselves continually to prayer and to the ministry of the word.... (Acts 6:1–4 NKJV)

81. By transferring the day-to-day operations of the church's functioning, it gave the apostles, other ministers, and elders the release to focus on the true purpose of their calling, namely prayer and the ministry of the Word.

82. It was the apostles who called the disciples (members) together and reported that their time was restricted and that they were led to spend time in prayer and the Word. They called on the *brethren* to choose men who had certain spiritual qualities to fill the role of deacon. Deacons were not balloted or voted into office. The *brethren* sought out these men who qualified for the office of deacon and had hands laid on them and were set in the body of Christ.

83. Deacons' authority does not include spiritual care or counseling. Some misinformed churches have transgressed the Word's instructions and favored deacons with spiritual obligations. Scripture assigns them as a help to the elders and ministers in a material way that relieves them of the burden of the material cares, allowing them to seek the face of God.

84. Deacons serve the people daily as well as the elders and the pastor, no matter what the hour. Deacons are not the ones who visit the sick in hospital, the elders are ... *Is anyone among you sick? Let him call for the elders of the church, and let them pray over him, anointing him with oil in the name of the Lord. And the prayer of faith will save the sick, and the Lord will raise him up. And if he has committed sins, he will be forgiven....* (James 5:14–15 NKJV)

85. Here is a biblical truth. The main reason David's army was so effective was because of the fundamental structure he had in place ... *All these men of war, that could keep rank, came with a perfect heart to Hebron....* (1 Chronicles 12:38) When a local assembly functions like this, each man abiding in his calling and doing the duties outlined in the Word, then it is abiding in the

perfect will of God and is a Spirit-filled assembly supported by Spirit-filled believers.

Helps and Governments

86. 1 Corinthians 12:28 speaks of two other forms of leadership in the local assembly. Those chosen for the position of "help" need no qualifications to hold this office. A "help" is someone who is asked to ease the burden on the leadership. A good example is the role of an usher in a church. They are asked to greet the people at the door and show them where to sit or where the restrooms are. Other "helps" are very good in the kitchen or with young children who need help with learning.

87. Many Sunday school teachers are "helps" as they train the young ones in the ways of the Lord. "Helps" are always assisting with the work of the church, enabling those in leadership to be free to concentrate on their ministry or office. There are no restrictions in the Word as to what, who, or how many "helps" an assembly should have.

88. "Governments" are members of the assembly who assist the fellowship on all the legal aspects the church must adhere to and conform to the laws of the land. They are the ones who interpret legal documents, understand accounting and tax laws, know about the financial workings of banks and other financiers, and advise the pastor on matters about which he may know very little.

89. Helps and governments are to the universal church. Their expertise can be used in any assembly. They are recognized by the leaders as having a God-given ability ... *God has set....* (1 Corinthinas 12:28) Their help with numerous tasks and their guidance on matters peculiar to their abilities is therefore used for the furtherance of the church.

90. Regarding tenure of the ministries and offices, no retirement age

exists for any of them. The reelection process and the voting methods in some churches today are not biblical in their application.

91. When God calls a man He calls him for life, and no matter where he is, he remains in his office.

Summary

92. The biblical structure for the church that is clearly given is what Spirit-filled believers adhere to. There is no *variableness, neither shadow of turning* (James 1:17) in their belief that everything they do must align with the Word of God. In reference to their total commitment to all things biblical: if they are to walk in righteousness, be holy, turn from their wicked ways, and follow after righteousness, then Spirit-filled believers are contending for *the faith* and following the perfect will of God.

93. As such, they know and believe that Christ is the head of the church which is His body, and that by one Spirit they are baptized into that body. They fully recognize and understand that the Apostles' Doctrine (Acts 2:42) is the plumb line and direct revelation imparted to holy apostles and prophets (Ephesians 3:5), and that five kinds of ministries are given by the head, Jesus Christ, to the church ... *for the equipping of the saints for the work of ministry, for the edifying of the body of Christ, till we all come to the unity of the faith and of the knowledge of the Son of God, to a perfect man, to the measure of the stature of the fullness of Christ; that we should no longer be children, tossed to and fro and carried about with every wind of doctrine, by the trickery of men, in the cunning craftiness of deceitful plotting, but, speaking the truth in love, may grow up in all things into Him who is the head—Christ—from whom the whole body, joined and knit together by what every joint supplies, according to the effective working by which every part does its share, causes growth of the body for the edifying of itself in love....* (Ephesians 4:12–16 NKJV)

CHAPTER 35

THE ORDINANCES

1. The church is not ritualistic. It is not fashioned on the "doing" but on the "being" of a believer. No ritual will ever secure salvation; it is only through the shed precious blood of Jesus Christ. Born-again believers are justified by faith and walk in the righteousness of Jesus Christ.

2. Thus said, every Spirit-filled believer clings to Jesus' teachings and obediently follows His command which is ... *Do this....* Jesus instructed His disciples to do two things for specific reasons: baptize believers and partake of the breaking of bread.

3. These are defined as ordinances and not sacraments, rituals, or symbols. A. H. Strong says it best, "It will be well to distinguish from one another the three words: symbol, rite, and ordinances. A symbol is the sign, or visible representation, of an invisible truth or idea. A rite is a symbol which is employed with regularity and sacrament intent. An ordinance is a symbolic rite which sets forth the central truths of the Christian faith, and which is of universal and personal obligation. Baptism and the Lord's Supper are rites which have become ordinances by the specific command of Christ."

Water Baptism

4. Scripture is definite and commanding that believers be baptized. Jesus gave the command, and He is the divine authority from which the command emanates. Baptism is not a man-made ritual, neither is it a heavenly revelation passed on to man via a prophetic utterance or vision; Jesus Christ Himself said ... *Go therefore and make disciples of all the nations, baptizing them in the name of the Father and of the Son and of the Holy Spirit, teaching them to observe all things that I have commanded you...* (Matthew 28:19–20 NKJV)

5. There is only one provision for this ordinance to be performed, and that is ... *you must be born again....* Those who have repented are born again and therefore testify to this by being baptized ... *Then Peter said unto them, Repent, and be baptized everyone of you....* (Acts 2:38)

6. W.A.C. Rowe says, "To give it less than its proper place and proportion is to treat the words of our Lord slightingly and to rob Christian experience of the satisfying conviction of having given a symbolic public confession of faith." While it is an activity the believer does, it must never be forgotten that it is a divinely commanded ordinance. Herein is the fundamental application of obedience.

7. While water baptism is a step of obedience, it is never an obligation that believers must do to be saved. Rowe continues, "Repentance and faith in the Lord Jesus Christ is the sole spiritual way of salvation (Romans 10:8–11)...." Therefore, salvation precedes water baptism. And more importantly, salvation is the only premise and grounds to justify the act of obedience of water baptism. Rowe says, "The Christian is not saved because he is baptized; he is baptized because he is saved."

8. The obedient child of God gives a public declaration that he has been truly born again. It is a statement that he is stepping

into the watery grave to be buried with Christ as the old man gives up his old ways of self, and now rises from the watery grave a new creation in Christ. He is testifying that by faith he believes he is washed clean of all the old man's ways and now is committed to the righteousness of Jesus Christ who is now in him. Rowe concludes, "As he rises out of the water, there shines upon his new elastic step the radiance and pulsating life of the resurrection morn."

9. It is not a sprinkle of water upon the forehead of a baby. Neither is it a ritualistic dunking three times in the water. The believer is fully cognizant of their born-again experience and is old and adult enough to know what they are doing and does not need a parent to perform the act on their behalf before they are even able to comprehend what is happening to them. Jesus instructed His disciples to baptize believers in the *name* not "names." Hence, the minister immerses the believer only once into the water.

10. The Greek word *baptizo* means to "immerse," "submerge," confirming the reason why Spirit-filled believers are completely immersed when baptized. The minister is under the instruction of Jesus to baptize the believer in the *name of the Father, and the Son, and the Holy Spirit.*

11. Apostle Peter says ... *Repent, and be baptized every one of you in the name of Jesus Christ....* (Acts 2:38) This does not introduce a new baptism. It is the application of the statement that believers are being baptized in the authority Jesus gave His disciples to baptize them. Henceforth, it is on the authority of Jesus Christ that they can baptize them in the name of the Father, and the Son, and the Holy Spirit.

12. It is tragic that so many receive Jesus Christ as their Savior, yet do not go through the waters of baptism. Many are led to believe that it is of no significance and as such they either procrastinate, postpone, or never do it. Yet, it is the Master Himself who commanded that believers be baptized.

13. This act of obedience should be one of the first steps the new convert takes. Rowe emphasizes that "the act of water baptism presents an opportunity for exact obedience on the part of the believer, about which there can be no doubt.... This pattern of obedience sets a standard right at the very threshold of Christian life. Finally, it increases our spirit of jubilation. There is real joy in obedience. The heart sings when completely yielded to the Lord's plan."

The Table of the Lord

14. There can be no more sacred a memorial than when Spirit-filled believers gather together at the Table of the Lord to celebrate what Jesus Christ did for mankind. Every aspect of their spiritual newness of life hinges on ... *the night in which He was betrayed....*

15. The sublime significance is the fact that Jesus Himself drew the disciples to Him after they had celebrated the Feast of the Passover and lovingly expressed the implementation of the New Covenant. Here was the threshold of the opening of the New Covenant and the closing of the Old.

16. Rowe says it like this: "It is in this service that we can undoubtedly enter into the deepest and sweetest experience of collective communion with Christ. To take part is an extremely high personal privilege. Because of the profound effect that the exercise of this ordinance must have upon church fellowship, there is absolute necessity for true conception and accurate practice. Our interpretation and application of the principles involved help to formulate the character of the church."

17. At the outset, let it be known Jesus instituted the Table of the Lord. It has nothing to do with man's desire nor his doctrinal influences. This is a God-thing, and man had better respect and handle it with the utmost holiness and contriteness of heart.

18. When looking in the Word and reading the actual, physical application of the bread and the wine, it is vital that Spirit-filled believers also consider the spiritual implications Jesus enacted during these moments in the Passover Feast.

19. It was Jesus who reached for the bread and He broke it ... *the Lord Jesus the same night in which he was betrayed took bread: and when he had given thanks, He brake it, and said....* (1 Corinthians 11:23–24) What He said as He reached for the bread was of huge spiritual significance. The ritual the Jews had religiously followed for centuries was about to be done away with.

20. Jesus moves the disciples' thoughts from the practical bread before them to His body, as a holy, sacrifice of His flesh. More so, Jesus is implicating His Father in His words when He tells them ... *this is My body* ... because whatever Jesus did, He always had the endorsement of the Father.

21. Jesus did not partake of the bread He had broken; He broke it and handed it to the disciples, telling them He was going to be the One broken. This sacrifice is not only going to be a physical suffering of His flesh on the Cross, but it will be a spiritual offering of His body to His Father as the sacrificial *Lamb of God slain from the foundation of the world.*

22. Had Jesus partaken of the bread, He would have inferred that His body was not part of the New Covenant. He does not confuse the disciples but allows them to partake of it so that they can identify with Christ's sacrifice of His body that was to be broken. Consequently, as He hands the bread to the disciples, He is telling them that it is His body that will be the sacrifice. *Do this in remembrance of Me....*

23. Under the Old Covenant of the Law, the breaking of the bread during the Passover Feast represented the sufferings God's chosen people endured. Yet now, Jesus is introducing a New Covenant which is spiritual in its intent and spiritual in its application. To achieve this spiritual breakthrough and reconciliation between

God and man, Jesus had to physically *suffer* (Hebrews 13:12). Thus, there is the fulfillment of the Old Covenant's sacrificial lamb being offered and the spiritual reconciliation with God in Christ's death, which the Old Covenant could never do.

24. Jesus also takes a cup containing wine from the table. The cup left on the table was the last of the three cups and was a symbolic cup representing the blessings God had bestowed upon His people. (1 Corinthians 10:16) As He hands the cup to the disciples, He tells them that it is ... *the New Testament in My blood....*

25. A divine, spiritual intervention by the Godhead is spoken of here. Jesus is the only begotten Son of God, conceived by the Holy Spirit, and executed by the Son of Man. The rejoicing by the Jews as they partook of the cup of blessing looked back to the time of their liberation and their current blessings from God. In this New Covenant, Jesus is telling the disciples that His shed blood will remove all sin and present the gift of everlasting life to whosoever believes in Him.

26. In the shedding of His blood, Jesus conquers death, opens the way to the Father, and saves the lost. This blessing from the Cup of Blessing is what the Spirit-filled believer receives and rejoices in their salvation through the shed precious blood of Jesus. It looks to the present and the future of everyone who believes.

27. The noteworthy statement Jesus makes is ... *This is my blood of the new testament, which is shed for many for the remission of sins....* (Matthew 26:28) The Word does not say that Jesus' blood was shed for all, but *many.* While the spiritual reconciliation is complete for all, not all will accept or receive Jesus as Lord and Savior. Henceforth, the shed blood of Jesus is for those amongst the many who receive Him as Lord ... *But as many as received him, to them gave he power to become the sons of God, even to them that believe on his name....* (John 1:12)

28. This divine ordinance is a proclamation and intent of the Spirit-filled believers' faith in the finished work of Calvary. Henry

Thiessen says, "The believer in partaking of the Lord's Supper sets forth in symbol all that the death of Christ signifies, in justification, sanctification, preservation, and glorification."

29. When focusing on the spiritual application of the bread and the wine, Spirit-filled believers unite their spirit with the deep spiritual intentions and application of the Table of the Lord. Then, when focusing on this aspect, the bread and the wine, symbolic of Christ's death, reveals the true intention of the *night in which He was betrayed.*

30. It is also a declaration by those partaking of the Table of the Lord to be "a death crowned with victory that Jesus died for our sins and lives for our justification." (Rowe) So vital was this testimony to the apostolic church in the first century that they gathered *daily* to *break bread* (Acts 2:46).

31. The emphasis Spirit-filled believers have is their attention to the experience that Jesus encountered while instituting the Table of the Lord. They consider with a fervent desire to know the thoughts and intent of Christ's heart as He reached for the unleavened bread that lay on a plate in the middle of the table.

32. It is vital that they look past their own application of the emblems and consider Jesus as He held the bread in His hands. The Word says ... *And he took bread, and gave thanks, and brake it....* (Luke 22:19) Holy hands held the stiff, unleavened bread as He closed His eyes and prayed a prayer of thanks over it. It was not a casual blessing whispered in appreciation for the bounty in His hands; it was a prayer that encircled the entire human race. Jesus gave thanks for the significance of who He was, and that He was the *bread of life.* (John 6:48)

33. The holy Son of God and Son of Man was filled with the enormity of the act He was about to do in the presence of His followers. At that moment when He took the bread off the table and held it between His fingers, He saw the reality of the *breaking of bread.* The Christ, Almighty God manifested in the flesh, held bread and

was about to signify the deepest spiritual schism that would create a canyon so deep and wide that there would be no way man could repair the breach.

34. As he snapped the bread in His hands, there was a spiritual thunderbolt that exploded in His heart. He saw, heard, and realized that the very action He had demonstrated to His disciples was in fact the most horrific spiritual breaking of the relationship He would experience from His Father. The sound of the breaking of the bread ricocheted in His ears, penetrated His heart, and resonated in His Spirit that this is what He came to do.

35. The Son of God felt the gravity of the moment and the consequences that must follow such a spiritual separation. To that end, He does not partake of the bread Himself, but *gave it to them* as He choked in the reality that began to seep into His Spirit.

36. It is of value to note that this institution of the New Covenant was enacted on the night the Jews celebrated the Passover Feast. This Feast was the celebration of the blood marked on the doorposts of the Jewish homes, and the angel of death passing over them as he saw the bloodstained doorposts. It was the symbol of the shed blood of a spotless lamb that gave the angel the reprieve to not kill the firstborn child in that home.

37. Now the *Lamb of God ... slain from the foundation of the world* (Revelation 13:8) steps into mankind's life and takes a piece of unleavened bread from off the Passover table and says ... *take eat, this is my body....* (Matthew 26:26) He then reaches for the cup and says ... *For this is my blood of the new testament, which is shed for many for the remission of sins....* (Matthew 26:28) In that moment, Jesus, the Lamb of God, effectively closes the Old Covenant and opens the New Covenant: a direct reflection of the Feast they had just completed.

38. With the heaviness of heart, the Son of Man reaches for the last cup on the table: the cup of blessing. In it is wine that was, to the Jew, an emblem that signified the blessing and victory God

wrought for His people. For Jesus, it had a more heart-wrenching significance.

39. The Word declares ... *And he took the cup, and gave thanks, and gave it to them....* (Matthew 26:27) Again, Christ's words of thanks are not for the refreshing of the body wine induces, neither was it for thanksgiving for the emancipation from slavery. He holds it closely to His bosom and prays to His Father, thanking Him for entrusting salvation's victory in His own shed blood. Yet, even as He understands that salvation is sealed in His own blood, it had to be His *shed precious blood* (Luke 22:20, 1 Peter 1:19). Only once His blood had been poured out could mankind be saved. The reality of the life-ebbing flow of His blood from His body causes Him, as Son of Man, to shudder under the weight of the ordeal.

40. Jesus, the holy Son of God, now in the Spirit, sees Himself as the *Lamb of God* crucified, and His blood flowing from every inflicted wound like a crimson river from Calvary's Hill. It rips in His heart as He leans forward and passes the cup around, saying, *This is my blood of the new testament, which is shed for many....* (Matthew 26:28)

41. How tragic it is to note that the pure, divine, and holy Son of God was *spat in His face and* (they) *beat Him; and others struck Him with the palms of their hands.* (Matthew 26:67 NKJV) And this was done by the most righteous Jewish members of the Sanhedrin, in the presence of the holiest office, the High Priest.

42. This precious gathering of believers around the Table of the Lord must be the center of attention at the gathering of the believers on the Lord's Day, the first day of the week. It is the express purpose for this gathering every Lord's Day ... *And upon the first day of the week, when the disciples came together to break bread...* (Acts 20:7) This memorial is celebrated every Lord's Day for one specific purpose: that believers never forget what Jesus did for them.

43. Consider this: since the inception of the church, countless thousands of events, salvation decisions, and miracles have taken place. They have not been recorded for posterity and are hidden in history's archives. But because of the diligent obedience of faithful believers who celebrate the Table of the Lord in remembrance of His death, resurrection *till He comes* (1 Corinthians 11:26), it has never been forgotten, neither cast aside and relegated to the annals of a historic event.

44. There is no excuse for any assembly not to break bread every *first day of the week.*

45. In as much as the Jews took great pains to care for and prepare a spotless lamb for the offering at the Feast of the Passover, so too should believers come prepared to the Lord's house to be of a right frame of mind when partaking of the Lord's Table. In their book, *Bible Doctrines, a Pentecostal Perspective,* William Menzies and Stanley Horton said, "Because the Lord's Supper is a solemn time for remembering the focal point of Christ's work on our behalf, it can become a time for great spiritual blessing, provided the participants come in the proper frame of mind and allow it to be an opportunity for worship and fellowship with the risen Christ and with each other."

The Emblems

46. It is a spiritual instruction that needs a called minister or elder to officiate at the Table. The Word of God is referenced at this time, indicating the instruction and importance of the memorial.

47. The bread and wine are "emblems" that represent the body and blood of Jesus. They are not the actual body and blood; they are partaken in accordance with the same significance that Jesus portrayed. He said, as He held the bread and wine, that they were to be a reminder of His body and blood that would be broken and

shed ... *Take, eat: this is my body, which is broken for you: this do in remembrance of me. After the same manner also he took the cup, when he had supped, saying, This cup is the new testament in my blood: this do ye, as oft as ye drink it, in remembrance of me....* (1 Corinthians 11:24–25)

48. It is of no significance whether the bread be unleavened bread, brown bread, white bread, cake, or wafer. It is a symbolic reminder of Christ's body that was broken for believers. What is of importance is the fact that those present partake of the bread. It is a physical application that has huge spiritual significance.

49. It must bring to remembrance the physical suffering Jesus endured. However, it must not deflect the attention away from the critical aspect, namely that Christ's death and resurrection burst open spiritual doors that returned mankind to a reconciled fellowship once again with the Father.

50. In this time of reflection and partaking of bread at the Table of the Lord, those present should be cognizant of the suffering Christ endured on their behalf. His body was mutilated, scourged (relentlessly whipped with a platted leather whip containing bits of bone, thorns, and iron), spat upon, pierced with thorns, and brutally scarred by nails through His hands and feet.

51. He was not led like a lamb to the altar that had its throat cut and died in an instant. His body went through hours of punishment and physical agony. (Isaiah 53:4–5) So gruesome was this infliction that the holy Savior carries these physical scars even now while resurrected and seated at the right hand of the Father in heaven.

52. It would be shortsighted to focus only on the *broken* body. Believers look to the resurrected and glorified Christ who, even though He still carries the scars of the suffering in His body after His resurrection, now possesses a glorified body that has no pain or suffering anymore. It behooves those partaking of the Table to always remember the finished work of Calvary.

53. Regarding the partaking of the wine, there have been more

divisions created in the church because of the inference that a chalice, not small cups, must be used; that real wine, not grape juice, must be poured, and that it must not be white wine but red wine. The list continues, and along its path many have argued and offered *vain babblings* to procure their standpoint. Yet it was with loving hands and a contrite heart that Jesus Christ took the cup in His hands and instituted the New Covenant.

54. There should never be a focus on the specific emblem or its qualities; there should be a direct focus on the reason for partaking of the emblem. Believers partake of the cup, whether a chalice or a small cup, for the specific reason to remember the *shed precious blood* Jesus spilled on that fatal day.

55. If believers are bickering about the method, then they have lost the purpose of the ordinance. God requires a contrite, humble, respectful, and grateful heart when partaking of the ordinance, not a stiff-necked arrogance that tarnishes the purpose.

56. Jesus' shed blood is the seal of salvation, the cleanser of sin, the life of the Savior poured out for humanity, and the ultimate expression of His love that renders a repentant heart justified in the sight of God. To that extent, it should always be the grateful heart of the saved who reaches forth with overwhelming joy that the cup they hold in their hands is an emblem that signifies their forgiveness.

57. These ordinances are the refractors that beam the light of the Christian into a dark world. Baptism publicly expresses a believer's faith in their Savior's finished work on Golgotha's Hill. The steadfast continuance of the Table of the Lord that believers share every Lord's Day not only commemorates but proclaims the Lord's death, His resurrection, and ascension, which is the foundation of their salvation and life.

58. There can be no minimizing the importance of these ordinances. They are God's instructions to the church and as such, they are to be enforced and not forgone. Thus, the Word says ... *And they*

continued steadfastly in the apostles' doctrine and fellowship, and in breaking of bread, and in prayers.... (Acts 2:42)

Stewardship

59. There is a spiritual call to every member of the body of Christ to walk circumspectly and with integrity as they *contend for the faith.* This responsibility rests with all, and is entrusted to the church to protect, be diligent, and respectful when handling the Word.

60. They are to take the gospel to the lost and be custodians of God's imparted gifts by caring and behaving appropriately. Likewise, believers are to support their storehouse with their presence and substance.

61. The Bible gives references to stewardship, and more so to good stewardship ... *As every man hath received the gift, even so minister the same one to another, as good stewards of the manifold grace of God....* (1 Peter 4:10) It is to be faithfully executed (1 Corinthians 4:2), and with all diligence ensuring that no one is adversely impaired in the fellowship.

62. Every member is called upon to ... *bring ye all the tithes into the storehouse....* (Malachi 3:10) Members bring their tithe to the *storehouse*, namely the place where they are received with the *right hands of fellowship* (Galatians 2:9). Attached to this tithe are *offerings*. Members share in their offerings with each other, and to the needs of the local assembly.

63. W.A.C. Rowe says, "It will be conceded that the Christian faith is essentially practical.... The believer wholly belongs to the Lord, with all his talents, powers, money and possessions to hold these as a steward (Luke 12:42–48), he is simply a trustee taking care of all upon trust (1 Thessalonians 2:4) for the rightful owner (*occupy till I come*—Luke 19:13)."

64. It must be carefully noted that believers do not "pay their tithe"; they "bring their tithe" to the storehouse. This is not a payment for membership, neither is it a payment for securing blessing and position in the church. It is done with a glad heart and without thought for gain ... *Honor the Lord with thy substance, and with the firstfruits* (tithe) *of all thine increase....* (Proverbs 3:9)

65. As to the offerings that members give ... *Every man according as he purposeth in his heart, so let him give; not grudgingly, or of necessity: for God loveth a cheerful giver....* (2 Corinthinas 9:7)

66. Let it be expressed in the simplest terms: a tithe is regarded biblically as ten percent of the overall earnings, product, or profit one has. Whatever the gross earnings of the wages are, or the crop in the field, or the profit gained, a tithe (ten percent) is first taken off and brought to the storehouse.

67. Again, offerings have no minimum or maximum attached it. It is according to the giver's heart that he gives an offering to the work of the Lord.

68. Rowe says that the Christian "is not free to seek his own particular leading as to how he shall make the application. *The tithes are the Lords....* (Leviticus 27:30) They are to be brought to His house, the church. It comes under the administration of those whom He has set in authority in His church to direct and use them for the purposes of the gospel and the body of Christ: *that there may be meat in mine house....*" (Malachi 3:10)

69. While many have stated tithing is an act of worship, and this might well be so conceived, it is in essence more so an act of obedience to God's holy Word. Let it be stated that it should be reverently and willingly given with a grateful heart and without the thought of gain. If this attitude of heart is regarded as worship, then there needs to be a question regarding the spiritual worship that is Spirit to spirit that should have no contamination of any monetary gain attached to it.

70. The church's focus is never placed on the tithes and offerings.

This principle is declared and taught to members when they are brought into fellowship, and the responsibility rests with them to be diligent and good stewards. Any variance from these fundamental responsibilities is to disregard God's holy Word and, consequently, rob the fellowship. Likewise, any minister who places more emphasis on the financial aspects of the fellowship than the spiritual has his vision dimmed by the glow of gold and the sparkle of silver.

71. Jonathan Black says, "Tithing is not a business transaction with God. It is not to be mistaken for financial investment. The saints do not secure God's blessing through their financial giving. (Acts 8:20–22) God's blessing is found only by His grace in Jesus Christ who died and rose again for us, and who gives Himself to us by His Holy Spirit through faith, so that in Him we are blessed." (Ephesians 1:3)

PART 9

The Doctrine of the Word of God: The Bible

36. DOCTRINE – Of the Word of God, the Bible
    a. This tenet is the basis and precept upon which every doctrinal tenet is based.
    b. It is studied from the aspects of *Revelation* and *Inspiration*.
    c. It declares categorically that it is God's word to man, and that man was merely an instrument who penned the revealed truths of God's intent and purpose.
    d. It is the defining doctrinal tenet in this book.

CHAPTER 36

THE DOCTRINE OF REVELATION AND INSPIRATION OF THE WORD OF GOD

1. When considering this holy and divine gift from God, namely His holy Word, it must never be forgotten who the Author is and for what purpose it is given. Therefore, to fully grasp the sovereignty of the Holy Writ, Spirit-filled believers must accept that the Bible is the revelation of God revealed through His divine inspiration and penned in the holy pages.

2. W.A.C. Rowe says, "The Scriptures of truth are pure revelation; they are God's approach to man, not man's approach to God: they bring certainty and brightness about Himself and His purposes. Only God can explain Himself: and only by His Holy Spirit can this be done ... *even so the things of God knoweth no man, but the Spirit of God....* (1 Corinthians 2:11)"

3. There are direct proclamations in the Bible as to its intent and how it is imparted ... *knowing this first, that no prophecy of the scripture is of any private interpretation. For the prophecy came not in old time by the will of man: but holy men of God*

spake as they were moved by the Holy Ghost ... (2 Peter 1:20–21) and ... *All scripture is given by inspiration of God, and is profitable for doctrine, for reproof, for correction, for instruction in righteousness....* (2 Timothy 3:16)

4. With this in mind, the attitude with which the holy Word is approached must be unequivocally pronounced, believed, and trusted that it is divinely inspired, totally void of errors, and is for instruction, reproof, and correction.

5. Spirit-filled believers are emphatic in their belief that there are no errors or omissions in the Word of God. Every word found in the pages of the Holy Writ are pure, holy, and infallible. It is God who chose the men to pen His Word. God separated them and anointed them to be used as instruments to convey God's holy and divine words that reaches every human being on earth.

6. This divine, holy Writ composed of sixty-six books can only be accepted and understood when the reader applies his faith in God, towards God, and towards His inspired Word. It is by faith alone, in the deep truths found in this fount of grace and love, that man is enriched, saved, and filled with eternal hope of things to come ... *Through faith we understand that the worlds were framed by the word of God, so that things which are seen were not made of things which do appear....* (Hebrews 11:3)

7. This eternal and majestic Word has been written and compiled for every created being on earth. Its readers include the Jews, the Gentiles, and the Christians. It also has the attention of the angels in heaven. Every living soul is incorporated in the Bible's message which is God's method of touching every heart that has ever lived.

8. Unregenerate man cannot receive nor understand the contents of the Bible until the Holy Spirit draws them to it ... *the natural man does not receive the things of the Spirit of God, for they are foolishness to him; nor can he know them, because they are spiritually discerned....* (1 Corinthians 2:14 NKJV)

9. Furthermore, the Word contains deep truths that are revealed by the Spirit of God to the righteous student. It is not revealed to those who walk as babes and carnally before Him (1 Corinthians 3:1–3).

10. History's hallways are covered with events engineered by man, victories achieved by conquering armies, valiant attempts to carve out a social enclave in which people can live in harmony, and tragedies soaked in blood and tears. Within these hallways, there is a record for all to see and read, namely that God's infinite love reaches past humankind's soul and places them in harmony and peace where the social fabric is of *one mind, one mouth, one Lord, one faith.* This record is none other than the Holy Bible.

11. In the Bible's purest form and most authentic languages, Hebrew and Greek, or the progression thereof (namely as expressions and words were enhanced or altered in meaning; for example, YHVH became Yahweh, and then became Jehovah), the message is unbridled by human interference. It is, therefore, of utmost importance that every Spirit-filled believer seek for the most perfect translation of the original Hebrew and Greek into their language. The deceiver, the devil, has infested too many men whose pecuniary interests have overshadowed the ultimate purpose of translating the Word by infusing an interpretation, instead of a translation, of the original languages.

12. In spite of these false works and the wayward teachings found in the interpretations of the holy Word, there are translations that are accurate and convey the true meaning of the Holy Writ. It is here that Spirit-filled believers find themselves engrossed in studying the Word and gleaning from its *God-breathed* message in their own language.

13. God has prevailed throughout mankind's existence and has always presided over His Word. He has preserved His message for all generations, and the Holy Spirit has, throughout these generations, guided men to translate the original languages into the language of the reader in its purest form.

14. At the outset, it is appropriate and correct to place the Word of God in its rightful place and standing in mankind's existence—in the past, present, and their future. W.A.C. Rowe says it best, "The Bible is supreme. This is the Book of God sent to men but is eagerly examined by angels (1 Peter 1:12) and demons (James 2:19 NKJV). It is not only a Book of this world (Psalm 119:103, 105), but of all worlds." (Revelation 4:1, 20:15) It occupies the loftiest pedestal, the highest position, and commands unparalleled respect from every human being. It is even higher than His name (Psalm 138:2).

15. There is no other book that can be compared to its message and value it has for mankind. It contains the inherent and intrinsic heavenly virtues, and moral, spiritual, and eternal values. (W.A.C. Rowe paraphrased) Nations throughout history have clung to its message and teaching. It has been the plumb line of moral virtue, social dignity, and everlasting hope throughout every race, culture, and creed.

16. The Bible is the declaration of who God is and how He deals with mankind's sin and sins. Explaining it more fully, Rowe says, "Its great subject is the Godhead, revealed in three persons, Father, Son, and Holy Spirit; the redemption of man from eternal misery and blackest hell, and his promotion to glory and the brightest heaven."

17. Not only does the Bible occupy the place of supremacy in the Spirit-filled believer's life; it is also the authoritative guide to every utterance and decision they make. Every doctrinal tenet, every measurement of good and evil, all applications of a spiritual relationship, and the standards of conduct are found in the Bible.

18. Lewis Chafer summarizes it in the following way, "In this Book, God is set forth as Creator and Lord of all. It is the revelation of Himself, the record of what He has done and will do, and, at the same time, the disclosure of the fact that every created thing is

subject to Him and discovers its highest advantage and destiny only as it is conformed to His will."

19. While it is important to consider the supremacy and authority of the Bible, it must never be forgotten that this divine Word was handed down to man by God. Thus said, it should be in the forefront of a Spirit-filled believer's mind that God's message ... *came not in old time by the will of man; but holy men of God spake as they were moved by the Holy Ghost....* (2 Peter 1:21)

20. It was God's predicted act and willful purpose that certain men be chosen for this holy task of recording the eternal Word. Herein came together the Holy Spirit's seal upon a man who was anointed by the Holy Spirit to receive revelation from the Godhead. Through the Holy Spirit's leading, the chosen vessel, in perfect unity with the Holy Spirit, received the inspired/*God-breathed* revelation of God's intent and purpose.

21. From the Bible's first book to its last, the focus is constantly on Jesus Christ and His works that ultimately saves believers. No other book can claim the authority that the Bible has on this subject. Many noted authors have published works that are like *sounding brass or a tinkling cymbal* (1 Corinthians 13:1) when compared to the Bible. Their message is compared to a shining moon against the brightness of the sun. Human authors are earthly bound, and so is their message. The Bible, on the other hand, is Authored by heaven's Supreme Commander, and directly from His throne.

22. Its message is interwoven with various frames and spans generations throughout history. Its message is instructional, promising, and filled with admonishment to those who are disobedient.

23. Ultimately, the Bible is the paramount record for every fellowship and individual believer. In every assembling of the saints, the Bible holds supreme place in the gathering. Every eye and ear are focused and tuned to its message in a meeting of saints. Nothing must ever displace the Word's supreme position in a gathering.

24. Likewise, for an individual who separates himself from the din of the world, he should turn to the lamp at his feet and the light on his pathway (Psalm 119:105) and hide in the shadow of the Almighty (Psalm 91:1). It is his shield and buckler in the time of trouble.

25. It is appropriate that this tenet focus its attention to the most exquisite explanation of the eternal existence of the Word ... *In the beginning was the Word, and the Word was with God, and the Word was God....* (John 1:1) Arthur Pink says, "The Scriptures reveal God's mind, express His will, make known His perfections, and lay bare His heart. This is precisely what the Lord Jesus has done for the Father."

26. There was always the existence of *the Word.* The holy manifestation of the oracle of God was revealed ... *God, who at various times and in various ways spoke in time past to the fathers by the prophets, has in these last days spoken to us by His Son, whom He has appointed heir of all things, through whom also He made the worlds....* (Hebrews 1:1–2 NKJV) The incarnate Christ thus manifested the living testimony of God in the flesh. Henceforth flowed the continuance of the Word through holy men of the New Testament.

27. Christ is the *Word made flesh.* Apostle John categorically states that John the Baptist was the *voice,* while Jesus is the *Word.* (John 1:1, 23) Man is but a voice anointed by God, while Jesus is the Word anointed by God.

28. While establishing a doctrinal tenet on the supremacy and authority of Scripture, it is important to establish the premise of revelation and inspiration. More succinctly, the focus must be on these two subjects as it pertains to the Word.

29. *Revelation.* While revelation is a vast subject that encompasses many aspects of a Spirit-filled believer's life, such as the things that have not yet taken place, the revealed wisdom to a believer on a certain subject, and the unveiling of a truth that is hidden

by someone else, this tenet is aligned to revelation from God regarding His Word.

30. Spirit-filled believers have no problem with the concept of revelation as it relates to God's holy Word. They are Spirit-led, and therefore are in tune with the spiritual message contained in the holy pages. The deep truths imbedded in the Bible are "opened" to the heart and mind of a Spirit-filled believer, as they immerse themselves in the message they are reading. (1 Corinthians 2:10–14)

31. The message printed in the words on the Bible's pages is not the sum of the message; it is the beginning of the passage along which a Spirit-filled believer begins a journey. They receive the Word they are reading and then seek the deeper truths within the written Word. These deeper truths are revealed to the heart that is seeking a deeper knowledge and relationship with Jesus Christ (2 Peter 3:18).

32. Revelation is what God reveals to man about subjects and situations he has no knowledge of, or insight. It is God drawing back the veil and showing the believer things they never knew or understood. This revelation which is spiritual is from God Himself and not from any particle of man's created structure. It is God revealing to man, and man is but the mere reciprocal.

33. Eugene F. A. Klug is quoted in the *Encyclopedia of the Bible*, "People have knowledge of God because of God's initiative and activity. God is always the initiator and author of revelation; men are the recipients. God discloses what otherwise would be unknown; He uncovers what would otherwise be hidden." (Deuteronomy 29:29, Galatians 1:12, Ephesians 3:3)

34. Revelation is Spirit-led insight granted to a believer that illuminates his understanding of the Holy Writ's message. The holy sanctuary of the Word is likened to the *secret place of the Most High*. (Psalm 91:1) As the believer enters into this divine place of solitude, he immerses himself in the presence of the Godhead and waits, meditates, worships Him. Here is the place

where Spirit-filled believers *dwell.* It is when he is under the anointing of the Holy Spirit that the believer receives God's revealed truths. God is constantly waiting for mankind to *enter in* and receive divine revelation from Him.

35. This is not an enhanced thought about the divine Creator and His handiwork. Even the world sees and receives the truth about creation and who is responsible for it. This is spiritual impartation from the Holy Spirit to the believer about something contained in the Word, and about which he knows nothing at all.

36. *Inspiration.* Now to the essence of the intrinsic values contained within the written Word. Spirit-filled believers are persuaded that the entire sixty-six books in the canon are God's revealed utterances given by God to men to record His thoughts, words, and promises that He wanted recorded and retained for all time. Eugene Klug continues, "Revelation and inspiration are necessary companions in God's disclosing of Himself and His will. They may differ in that, while revelation has to do with divine illumination (given by God in various ways) whereby prophets and apostles knew God and the things of God, inspiration is that divine agency employed by God in the recording of His Word. Thus, inspiration's focal point is first of all the written text; revelation's focal point is the information or disclosure God gives of Himself and His purposes."

37. Some reliable translations have taken the literal meaning of the Greek word *theopneustos*—God-breathed—and recorded it as *inspiration.* (2 Timothy 3:16 NKJV, NASB) In fact, what Apostle Paul is relating to Timothy is far more than an inspired utterance from God that He wants recorded for all ages.

38. Apostle Paul is laying down a foundational principle that seals the eternal existence of God's holy Word. The divine, holy words recorded in the Bible are of such importance to God that He personally induced His very *breath* into every syllable He dictated to holy men. Furthermore, the words so breathed by the sovereign, eternal God, have no beginning or end in their

existence; they are from the eternal God and therefore cannot be eradicated, removed, or altered. They are from the eternal God and are everlasting in their ability, application, and power. (Isaiah 40:8, 1 Peter 1:25)

39. When stating that God induced His very breath into every syllable, it is stating that the origin of the Bible is direct revelation from the eternal God to man. Benjamin B. Warfield, who is regarded by many as the authority on explaining "inspiration" and the original Greek word meaning "God-breathed" says in his book, *The Inspiration and Authority of the Bible,* "What it affirms is that the Scriptures owe their origin to an activity of God the Holy Ghost and are in the highest and truest sense His creation. It is on this foundation of divine origin that all the highest attributes of Scripture are built. They are from God, God-breathed, God-given, and God-determined."

40. To summarize the explanation, God-breathed (inspiration) in essence means that the Bible is not man's intelligence reduced to writing, but that the Bible in its every word is directly from God; totally His purpose, prose, and presentation without any human additives.

41. The God-breathed eternal Word is the bulwark that buttresses the divisions between truth from error, right from wrong, and good from evil ... *For the word of God is quick, and powerful, and sharper than any twoedged sword, piercing even to the dividing asunder of soul and spirit, and of the joints and marrow, and is a discerner of the thoughts and intents of the heart....* (Hebrews 4:12)

42. Spirit-filled believers know and seek the deep truths within these words. They understand that as man is tri-part (body, soul, and spirit) and at their rebirth, they are led by their spirit within that now communes with God who is Spirit. This division between spirit and soul is the most important focus they have because they know they must stay spirit to Spirit connected. Thus, there must

come a *division of soul and spirit.* This is done by the increase in their knowledge of the Holy Writ.

43. Every human thought, emotion, and natural impulse flows from the soul, while all spiritual impartation from the Holy Spirit is into the man's spirit. To be *led of the Spirit,* the believer's spirit needs to be filled to overflowing with things spiritual; thus, the need to divide the soul from the spirit. This calls for the believer to be spiritually in tune with the harmony of the Word as the Holy Spirit imparts the teaching and guidance from it.

44. There is no more fulfilling benefit for a believer than that they are endowed with the fullness of the Word pulsating through their spirit as they glean the truths from the Bible. This is the "routing out" of the emotional and egotistical attitude of the soul's desires as they empty their soul of all the fleshly lusts and desires and immerse themselves in the Word that has separated soul from spirit.

45. To take this verse even deeper in its application, the Holy Writ is *a discerner of the thoughts and intents of the heart.* The believer is led gently, but convincingly, to the fact that whatever egotistical ideals and imaginings he had of himself are vanity and useless in God's eyes. The Word exposes this to him.

46. Arthur W. Pink in his book, *An Exposition of Hebrews,* says, "He discovers what a vile, depraved, and hell-deserving creature he is. Though, in the mercy of God, he may have been preserved from much outward wickedness in his unregenerate days, and so passed among his fellows as an exemplary character, he now perceives that there dwelleth *no good thing* in him, that every thought and intent of his desperately-wicked heart had, all his life, been contrary to the requirements and claims of a holy God."

47. It is the Word that penetrates deep into the spirit and soul of a believer, bringing them to their knees in humble confession, causing him to seek the sanctifying process of the Holy Spirit.

It abases self-pride and self-recognition, and replaces it with a humble, contrite heart that seeks nothing else but *Jesus Christ and Him crucified.*

48. This magnificent holy Word, if allowed by the believer, will infiltrate the thoughts and intents of his heart and bring about the spiritual reformation of the soulish attitude to the place where it surrenders all personal, human, and selfish desires to the examination of the Word. Thus exposed, the believer humbly attests ... *Behold, thou desirest truth in the inward parts: and in the hidden part thou shalt make me to know wisdom....* (Psalm 51:6)

49. Spirit-filled believers must *enter the closet* and be alone with God, because that is the place where they glean the deep truths of the intent and will of God. The greatest example in the Bible is given when Isaiah has the vision of God's holy throne. He was a man who had audiences with royalty, noblemen, and the ordinary rank and file, a sought-after man in his generation.

50. Yet, when he enters the presence of God, he is granted permission to see the holiest place in heaven, and as he takes notice of its holiness, sovereignty, and righteousness, he immediately realized that everything he was, stood for, declared to others, and thought of himself was nothing but absolute *off-scouring* (1 Corinthians 4:13), to the point where he declares ... *Woe is me! for I am undone....* (Isaiah 6:5) He is literally saying, "Everything I have ever thought I was, have accomplished, could possibly do because of my position and qualifications, is torn to shreds, when I am in the presence of the Lord."

51. Every human sentence phrased in any human language is but a dry husk when measured against the nourishment and validity contained in the intrinsic ingredients of the Holy Writ. The Spirit-filled believer hungers and thirsts after its contents, and they bask in its glorious light that ... *is a lamp unto my feet, and a light unto my path....* (Psalm 119:105)

52. Scripture is compacted with goodness and instruction, ready to direct believers along the road of righteousness. It is laden with the ever-fresh wholesomeness contained in God's immeasurable love that causes them to ... *live, and move, and have our* (their) *being....* (Acts 17:28) Even as the threshing floor sorts the chaff from the wheat, so does the Word divide asunder and discern *the thoughts and intents of the heart.*

53. It is the undeterred and unshakable truth that will emerge on the Day of Judgment when Jesus, the Word, will tread *the winepress of the fierceness and wrath of Almighty God....* (Revelation 19:15) The winepress shows no mercy for the fruit; it has no hindrance that prevents it from pulverizing the fruit; and it is ruthless in its escapade ... *the word that I have spoken, the same shall judge him in the last day....* (John 12:48)

54. Authors have come and gone; man-made influences via the media have sown discord and confusion amongst generations; itching ears have gleaned false doctrines from smooth-mouthed talkers; some have strayed from the truth confessing that the truth is too hard to uphold; and some have tried to block out the sound of the Word. However, the time-worn sails of the holy, divine, sovereign Word of God have stood the test of time. Those who choose to stay in the ship of life have their faith rooted in the Bible's message and are ever strong, because the anchor holds. (Hebrews 6:19–20)

PART 10

The Doctrine of Last Things

39. DOCTRINE – Of Last Things: The New Heaven, New Earth, and the New Jerusalem
   a. The New Earth
   b. The New Heaven
   c. The New Jerusalem

CHAPTER 37

THE DOCTRINE OF LAST THINGS

1. When consideration and sincere spiritual examination is given to the doctrine of last things, no other tenet inspires a Spirit-filled believer more with hope. It is often the Bible's forthcoming promises that hold the believer on their course to stay faithful and committed to the cause *until the day of Jesus Christ.* (Philippians 1:6)

2. The most significant words from the Holy Pages regarding this subject, and that inspire believers to have their hope enriched, are found when Apostle John says ... *Beloved, now we are children of God; and it has not yet been revealed what we shall be, but we know that when He is revealed, we shall be like Him, for we shall see Him as He is. And everyone who has this hope in Him purifies himself, just as He is pure....* (1 John 3:2–3 NKJV)

3. God's predicted and promised events that will take place in the future encompass every aspect of human life on earth. They first give deep spiritual insight into Who it is that is over everything that will take place, and therefore has spiritual implications for the saved and the lost.

4. Second, it involves the natural state of earth and the cataclysmic changes God will enact during these times. Third, it focuses on the social fabric of the human race and its variances in their beliefs, cultures, and relationships with each other. Fourth, it is a time of the fulfillment of God's promises as to how He will deal with the enemy, the devil, and his cohorts. Fifth, it explains God's dealing with His wife, Israel, and finally, it brings into being the promises of a new heaven, new earth, and a new Jerusalem.

5. Throughout the Bible, the prophetical promises concerning the last things are related to everyone. They are not confined to only one book of the Bible or only one nation but are referenced time and again in different chapters and books. Yet they are all in step with God's promises of a final victory and of saints dwelling in His presence.

6. Let it be clearly understood that the only authentic revelation and detailed explanation of God's promises is the holy Word of God. No other account, additions, or modifications to the Word can ever add, change, or eradicate the fullness of the promises found in the Bible. Likewise, every contemporary prophetical utterance brought forth in an assembly regarding the future events of saints and sinners must always line up with the Word.

7. The study of last things is important to every Spirit-filled believer simply because it is God who says ... *Prepare to meet thy God....* (Amos 4:12) In addition to this command, Apostle Paul exhorts believers regarding the future to ... *comfort one another with these words....* (1 Thesalonians 4:18)

The Beginning of Last Things

8. The disciples who walked closely with Jesus during His time on earth were curious about the time of Jesus' return to earth. While they believed Jesus would be leaving them, they also believed He

would return. More so, they believed that God would intervene in this present age and bring it to an end ... *Now as He sat on the Mount of Olives, the disciples came to Him privately, saying, "Tell us, when will these things be? And what will be the sign of Your coming, and of the end of the age?"* (Matthew 24:3 NKJV)

9. Jesus taught them that certain things would precede His return ... *And Jesus answered and said to them: "Take heed that no one deceives you. For many will come in My name, saying, 'I am the Christ,' and will deceive many. And you will hear of wars and rumors of wars. See that you are not troubled; for all these things must come to pass, but the end is not yet. For nation will rise against nation, and kingdom against kingdom. And there will be famines, pestilences, and earthquakes in various places. All these are the beginning of sorrows. Then they will deliver you up to tribulation and kill you, and you will be hated by all nations for My name's sake. And then many will be offended, will betray one another, and will hate one another. Then many false prophets will rise up and deceive many. And because lawlessness will abound, the love of many will grow cold. But he who endures to the end shall be saved. And this gospel of the kingdom will be preached in all the world as a witness to all the nations, and then the end will come..."* (Matthew 24:4–14 NKJV).

10. Added to these cataclysmic events, many *false christs* and *false prophets* will appear, dragging many into a lost eternity. (Matthew 24:24–28) The detailed teachings of what happens after these introductory events are found throughout the New Testament. These events concern the moral state of the nations, the physical disruption of the earth, and the onslaught against Israel. Regarding man's moral state, Jesus said that it would be as it was during Noah's time. (Matthew 24:36–39)

11. These events taught by Jesus all precede the miracle God will enact with mankind. The dead in Christ are raised, and those who are alive are caught up and taken off the earth. The contemporary

word for this event is *the rapture*. (The catching away of the saints off the earth to meet Jesus in the air: 1 Thessalonians 4:17.)

12. The rapture is the first of seven events that will take place in the last days. These seven events happen in the following order:

    a) The Rapture of the dead in Christ and the living saints on earth

    b) The Judgment Seat of Christ

    c) The Marriage Supper of the Lamb

    d) The Great Tribulation

    e) The Millennium Reign

    f) The Great White Throne Judgment

    g) The New Heaven, the New Earth, and the New Jerusalem.

The Rapture of the Dead in Christ and the Living Saints on Earth

13. This miraculous event is the spiritual ending to the Dispensation of Grace which occurs when the dead in Christ and the church are raptured off the earth. (1 Thessalonians 4:13–18) This is a divine miracle that effects thousands on earth. Those who do not accept Jesus Christ as their Savior and do not walk in His finished work on Calvary will not be raptured off the earth.

14. This will be the time of great sorrow for those who were deceived, while for those who believed in *the way, the truth, and the life* will have a totally different experience. During this majestic experience in His presence, all the trials of their pilgrimage and even the blessed fellowship with believers will pale into insignificance as they stand before the holy Christ.

15. There will be no human, scientific, or social explanation for this miracle. It is a God-thing, and He is the Author of it. This is the first step Jesus takes on His return to earth. It is halted by an intermission

on the clouds. He steps forth from the right hand of the Father, tarries in the air, and meets His saints (1 Thessalonians 4:16–17).

16. The event is announced from heaven in three ways ... *For the Lord Himself will descend from heaven with a shout, with the voice of an arch-angel, and with the trumpet of God....* (1 Thessalonians 4:16 NKJV)

17. All the believers who died prior to this event taking place will be raised from the dead. Their graves will open, and their remains will be taken up in the clouds where their souls and spirits will be united with a glorified body. (1 Corinthians 15:21–23, 51–58)

18. Their glorified body is the same state that Jesus' body is at this present time. At the trumpet sound, God will perform the miracle and reunite the soul and spirit of every raptured saint with a glorified body. It is a promised gift from God to every believer ... *For our citizenship is in heaven, from which we also eagerly wait for the Savior, the Lord Jesus Christ, who will transform our lowly body that it may be conformed to His glorious body, according to the working by which He is able even to subdue all things to Himself....* (Philippians 3:20–21 NKJV)

19. This glorious experience promised to believers is not a protracted event that takes minutes or hours to perfect. God's instantaneous interference in normal day-to-day living is immediate, in the twinkling of an eye ... *Now this I say, brethren, that flesh and blood cannot inherit the kingdom of God; nor does corruption inherit incorruption. Behold, I tell you a mystery: We shall not all sleep, but we shall all be changed– in a moment, in the twinkling of an eye, at the last trumpet. For the trumpet will sound, and the dead will be raised incorruptible, and we shall be changed....* (1 Corinthians 15:50–52 NKJV)

20. There are aspects of a believer's walk that render them worthy to be partakers of the rapture. Finis Dake in his book, *Revelation Expounded,* says those who are counted worthy will have walked according to the Word of God ... *walk*(ing) *in the light as He is*

in the light, and will constantly be in Christ, be blessed and holy, be worthy, and purify himself even as He is pure; "We conclude that it is not receiving other experiences, whatever they may be, or however Scriptural they may be, that qualifies one to go up in the rapture, but it is the maintenance of a holy walk in Christ at the time of the rapture or at the time of death as the case may be."

21. The purpose of the rapture is to bring all the saints into Jesus' presence. This is termed *the Day of Christ.* (2 Thessalonians 2:2) It is the removal of the dead in Christ from their graves, and those who are alive and on the earth, from off the earth, to be present with the Lord. The place is in the clouds where they will meet Jesus *in the air* (1 Thessalonians 4:17).

22. It is during the rapture that physical death is annulled. As Jesus was raised from the dead, so too will the dead in Christ be raised from their graves and they will receive a glorified body. For those who are alive on the earth and are raptured, their bodies undergo a miraculous change and they receive a glorified body as well ... *For this corruptible must put on incorruption, and this mortal must put on immortality. So when this corruptible has put on incorruption, and this mortal has put on immortality, then shall be brought to pass the saying that is written: "Death is swallowed up in victory."* (1 Corinthians 15:53–54 NKJV)

23. Jesus said ... *"Let not your heart be troubled; you believe in God, believe also in Me. In My Father's house are many mansions; if it were not so, I would have told you. I go to prepare a place for you. And if I go and prepare a place for you, I will come again and receive you to Myself; that where I am, there you may be also...."* (John 14:1–3 NKJV) The idea that Jesus will prepare a place for His bride is often lost in the true understanding of the rapture. In fact, He is doing what any Jewish bridegroom would do as they prepare for their bride.

24. Jewish custom demands that the bridegroom prepares a place in his father's house for his bride. When the father is satisfied that

the place is suitable for his son's bride, he sends the best man to the bride's city and shouts from the gate with a loud voice for the bride to come forth and meet the groom.

25. Jesus is telling the disciples that He will do the same thing for His bride, and when His Father knows the time, He will instruct His Son to send for His bride. (Matthew 25:36)

26. It is therefore of utmost importance that the bride, while she waits for the bridegroom's call, be in constant readiness. Likewise, the church should be diligent and be prepared for that great day when they will be called with the shout, the voice, and the trumpet to meet Jesus in the air. It behooves believers to take *oil in their vessels with their lamps* (Matthew 25:4), namely, be in a state of preparedness for the time of Jesus' coming. (Matthew 25:13)

27. This is the anticipated moment Jesus longs for. This moment in the presence of the saints signifies He has completed His intercession for the saints, His work with all power and authority, and His saving grace has achieved its desired result. He stands before them with joy unspeakable, victory crowned in righteousness, and has ... *establish*(ed) *your hearts blameless in holiness before our God and Father at the coming of our Lord Jesus Christ with all His saints ....* (1 Thessalonians 3:13 NKJV)

28. Jesus stands before the righteous saints in all His glory that is now reflected in the glory of the saints and momentarily, He looks with thanksgiving: He is the Word; He is the Word made flesh; He is the sacrificial Lamb of God slain from the foundation of the world; He is the risen Savior; He is endowed with all power and authority from on high; and He is the Lord and head of the church; the king of the kingdom of God; and He is the all in all of God manifest in the flesh. He steps forth ... *like a bridegroom coming out of his chamber* ... (Psalm 19:5 NKJV), and He stands before the holy raptured saints and reaches and takes the hand of His bride as a bridegroom accepts His bride.

29. Heaven's angelic host, who rejoice over one sinner repenting, gather in heaven and gaze upon the glorious spectacle that unfolds before them. They have been anticipating this great day, and as they heralded the arrival at Jesus' birth and rejoiced as He ascended to the Father's right hand at His ascension, they now herald the arrival of the saints and their meeting with Jesus in the clouds.

30. This is heaven's business, and the entire Godhead and the angelic host in heaven witness God's promise being fulfilled.

The Judgment Seat of Christ

31. The manifestation of the glory of the Lord in the midst of the saints on the clouds and the presence of Jesus can never be expressed in human terms. The *Shekinah glory,* holy presence, and majestic appearance of the pure, righteous, and holy Jesus will leave every saint overawed.

32. The magnificence of His deity and sovereignty sheathed in love and consolation will exude forth from Him. The compassionate Christ will reach forth and embrace every saint in the most sublime and infusing love. The infusion of His grace into the saints' souls and spirits will seal His everlasting promise ... *I will never leave you nor forsake you....* (Hebrews 13:5 NKJV)

33. He leads the saints in gentleness and peace towards the Judgment Seat from which He will present to everyone a reward for their labors in Him. Motives will be examined and rewards for obedience and faithfulness will be given.

34. It cannot be emphasized enough that the raptured saints will not be judged for their sin and sins. Jesus Christ took care of it at the finished work on Calvary's Cross ... *Most assuredly, I say to you, he who hears My word and believes in Him who sent Me has*

everlasting life, and shall not come into judgment, but has passed from death into life.... (John 5:24 NKJV)

35. It is clear from the Word that Jesus was made *to be sin for us, that we might become the righteousness of God in Him....* (2 Corinthians 5:21 NKJV)

36. It is here that Jesus will display every saint's work and try it in the test of fire ... *Now if anyone builds on this foundation with gold, silver, precious stones, wood, hay, straw, each one's work will become clear; for the Day will declare it, because it will be revealed by fire; and the fire will test each one's work, of what sort it is. If anyone's work which he has built on it endures, he will receive a reward. If anyone's work is burned, he will suffer loss; but he himself will be saved, yet so as through fire....* (1 Corinthians 3:12–15 NKJV)

37. Every deed done since the believer accepted Jesus as Savior will go through the "fiery" trial. If what the saint has done is in accordance with God's standards and motives, their result will be a crown of gold, silver, and precious stones. If not done this way, their deeds will be judged as hay, wood, and stubble. (2 Corinthians 5:9–10)

38. This Seat is the "graduation ceremony" for all who are born again. There they will be rewarded for their labors for the Lord and in the Lord, when He the divine Judge will hand out their crown that is befitting the measure of their labors.

39. The crowning is, in essence, not a judgment but rather a rewarding of the deeds the believer has done. It is regarded as "judgment" because the individual will be "judged" as a faithful one who has met God's standards and is therefore judged as either a *good and faithful servant* or not. (Matthew 25:21 NKJV) It must be stressed, however, that while all who are raptured are saved, some will be rewarded with more than others. Jesus said, *For everyone to whom much is given, from him much will be required.* (Luke 12:48 NKJV)

40. Saints are given crowns as their reward for their works that are found to be acceptable by God, and for those who have obediently walked steadfastly in the Word. The Word promises five kinds of crowns.

41. The *crown of life* is presented to those for faithfulness unto death, and for those who love Him (Revelation 2:10, James 1:12). Those honored with this crown have dedicated their lives with zeal to serve God out of their unending love for Him. Their faithfulness is with such commitment and determination that even death (martyrdom) does not deter them ... *Greater love has no one than this, than to lay down one's life for his friends* ... (John 15:13 NKJV) ... *be faithful unto death, and I will give you the crown of life*.... (Revelation 2:10 NKJV)

42. The *crown of glory* is specifically for true shepherds who have labored with the right motive and diligence in serving God's people ... *Shepherd the flock of God which is among you, serving as overseers, not by compulsion but willingly, not for dishonest gain but eagerly; nor as being lords over those entrusted to you, but being examples to the flock; and when the Chief Shepherd appears, you will receive the crown of glory that does not fade away*.... (1 Peter 5:2–4 NKJV)

43. The *crown of rejoicing* is specifically handed to those who have spread the gospel of Jesus Christ, as they yield their lives as instruments of the Holy Spirit to reach the lost ... *For what is our hope, or joy, or crown of rejoicing? Is it not even you in the presence of our Lord Jesus Christ at His coming? For you are our glory and joy*.... (1 Thessalonians 2:19–20 NKJV)

44. The *crown of righteousness* is given to those who have shunned the world and its sin, and fervently lived in the hope of the promises of God and walked in the righteousness of Jesus Christ ... *Finally, there is laid up for me the crown of righteousness, which the Lord, the righteous Judge, will give to me on that Day, and not to me only but also to all who have loved His appearing*

.... (2 Timothy 4:8 NKJV) They have walked in righteousness to fulfill their purifying hope that drove them to live for Him and see Him in that Day ... *And everyone who has this hope in Him purifies himself, just as He is pure....* (1 John 3:3 NKJV)

45. The *crown of imperishableness* is awarded to those who have lived victoriously in Jesus Christ. (1 Corinthians 9:25) The onslaught of the devil and his attacks on the believers' life never overcomes them. They walk constantly in the promise that says *... Now thanks be to God who always leads us in triumph in Christ, and through us diffuses the fragrance of His knowledge in every place....* (2 Corinthians 2:14 NKJV) Their incorruptible steadfastness stands the test of life, and they are victorious in all their conflicts by remaining temperate.

46. The Judgment Seat of Christ is a joyous occasion in the presence of the Savior, Jesus Christ. Jesus will preside over the event, and Jesus will speak to the recipients. The long-awaited moment that is instilled in every believer's heart, the *hope of his* calling, will now take place. Apostle John says ... *We shall be like Him because we shall see Him as He is....* (1 John 3:1–4 NKJV)

47. Everyone present will be one of the "saints" who will reign with Jesus during the Millennium Reign. The moment is crowned with praise and worship to Jesus. (Revelation 19:7–9)

48. For Jesus, this is the moment when He stands before those who have fulfilled His desire to build His church. The saints have prevailed and are now in the physical presence of Jesus. Ultimately, this is the fulfillment of His statement: *I will build my church; and the gates of hell shall not prevail against it.* (Matthew 16:18)

The Marriage Supper of the Lamb

49. Following the Judgment Seat of Christ, the next event that takes place for the raptured saints is the Marriage Supper of the Lamb.

Every saint will partake in this event; some will be the bride while others will be the guests ... *Blessed are those who are called to the marriage supper of the Lamb....* (Revelation 19:9 NKJV)

50. The *bride* of Christ is the church. Ephesians 5:22–27 gives the comparison between the *church, which is His body*, and the union between a man and a woman. The work of the Lord and the Holy Spirit is focused on preparing the members to be spiritually ready for the Bridegroom ... *that He might present her to Himself a glorious church....* (Ephesians 5:27 NKJV)

51. The church is composed of all the believers who are baptized with the Holy Spirit and become members of the body of Christ, the church (1 Corinthians 12:13 NKJV). Those born-again believers who are not baptized with the Holy Spirit are subjects in the kingdom of God. They are saved and raptured, pass through the Judgment Seat of Christ, and invited as guests to the marriage supper of the Lamb. (Revelation 19:9)

52. Henry Thiessen says, "While the church is the bride, there will also be guests at the marriage feast. We must remember that although all saints of Old and New Testaments times will be raised at the rapture, not all these are a part of the church and so not of the bride."

53. It is here that Jesus, once He has completed His Judgment Seat, He, as the Bridegroom, receives His bride, the church, and He presents her to the Father. This glorious marriage takes place when Jesus takes His bride and the guests off the clouds and into heaven.

54. Scripture indicates the place of the marriage is in heaven. This is believed because Jesus presents the holy and blameless saints to the Father in heaven. (1 Thessalonians 3:13, Revelation 19:1–9)

55. This great event takes place in holiness and righteousness, entirely separate from all wickedness. It is the holy convocation especially prepared for Jesus and the saints in the presence of His Father and the Holy Spirit, which is witnessed by the holy angels.

56. There is no biblical evidence that anyone who is left behind on

earth after the rapture will see or take part in the marriage supper. This will be a holy time orchestrated by God, in the presence of God, for Jesus and the saints. (Revelation 19:1–9)

57. These two holy events are the culmination of the church age. They are the closing chapters of the New Testament and the beginning of the time of Righteousness on earth ushered in as Jesus returns to the earth with the saints. These two events with the saints in heaven takes place during the time that the Great Tribulation is happening on earth.

The Great Tribulation

58. Detailed events surrounding the Great Tribulation have not been expounded upon, but a mere synopsis of this time is given. It is summarized so that believers will have an outline of these events, giving them a glimpse of this seven-year period.

59. During the time of the heavenly celebrations of the Judgment Seat of Christ and the Marriage Supper of the Lamb, the remaining nations on earth experience the worst outpouring of evil, hatred, and dictatorship Satan can orchestrate. This is a period of seven years known as the Great Tribulation.

60. Both the Old and the New Testaments record the events that will engulf the nations that are left behind on earth after the rapture has taken place. No nation, whether Jew or Gentile, will escape the wrath that is to come during this period. Everyone living at the time of the rapture and who did not accept Jesus Christ as their Savior will be left behind. For those who lived a life without accepting Christ and died before the rapture took place, their bodies will remain in their graves, and their souls and spirits remain in hell until the Great White Throne Judgment.

61. This period in the Scriptures has a place of importance because it involves mankind. Although it is outside the events that affect

believers who will escape them, believers and the world need to be aware of the signs that precede the rapture and the Great Tribulation.

62. To begin this study, it is appropriate that the words of Jesus be the announcement of this time on earth ... *For then there will be great tribulation, such as has not been since the beginning of the world until this time, no, nor ever shall be....* (Matthew 24:21 NKJV) This prophetical utterance He gave confirmed the prophecy the Old Testament prophet, Daniel, brought forth (Daniel 9:26–27).

63. Jesus teaches His disciples that there will be signs preceding the rapture and the start of the Great Tribulation, which are ... *the beginning of sorrows....* (Matthew 24:3–8) The Old Testament prophets, Jeremiah, Ezekiel, and Daniel all refer to this period as a time of terrible tribulation for God's people, the Jews.

64. Jeremiah refers to it as the time of *Jacob's trouble* (Jeremiah 30:4–7 NKJV). Ezekiel says the Jews will experience this time as if they *will pass under the rod,* namely, suffer God's wrath (Ezekiel 20:37 NKJV), and Daniel says it will be a *time of trouble* for the Jews. (Daniel 12:1)

65. It is important to understand that everyone who was not raptured, whether they are Jew or Gentile, a follower of a religious faith that does not confess Jesus Christ as Lord, sinners who have not repented, and blatant heretics and atheists, will all be exposed to this impending time of trouble and great tribulation.

66. The Great Tribulation will last seven years. It is not the same as what is referred to in the Bible as *tribulation* which believers endure (Acts 14:22, 1 Thessalonians 3:4). These seven years are separate from the daily trials and tribulations believers experience. There is nothing that will ever compare to these cataclysmic events past, present, or future.

67. This period begins after the rapture of the saints. The world will seek answers to their social, political, and economic problems. The righteous will have been removed from the earth, leaving

nothing but evil and sin to remain. This causes the remaining people on earth to seek for answers to their problems. They will have no desire to look to God for their guidance (they are unrighteous) and as such, they turn to a man to lead them. This is the time when the Antichrist rises to power.

68. These seven years will be divided into two halves: the first half will be a time of recognition of the Jews, and they will restore their obligations of the Law such as the rebuilding of their temple in Jerusalem and the performing of animal sacrifices according to their Law.

69. At the beginning of the first three-and-a-half years, a man rises to the forefront and brings false peace that deceives the nations into believing he is the answer to their problems. To the world, it will appear that peace and harmony prevails throughout every nation. His motives and intentions are, however, contrary to his actions.

70. His true motives and intentions are exposed after the first three-and-a-half years, when he will begin his dictatorship and evil rule. (Daniel 9:27) His diabolical dominance is manifested as he sets about his Satan-infested hatred and idolatry (Revelation 17:8). The man who rises to power during the first three-and-a-half years of the Great Tribulation is possessed by the devil and declared to be the Antichrist. His every decision is driven by his evil possessor who dominates his authority and instructions.

71. It is during this time of the Great Tribulation that God deals with Satan who is in the heavens ... *And war broke out in heaven; Michael and his angels fought with the dragon; and the dragon and his angels fought, but they did not prevail, nor was a place found for them in heaven any longer. So the great dragon was cast out, that serpent of old, called the Devil and Satan, who deceives the whole world; he was cast to the earth, and his angels were cast out with him....* (Revelation 12:7–9 NKJV)

72. It is during the Great Tribulation that Satan, now on earth, manifests himself through the Antichrist who is a tri-part anti-God that is

a counterfeit of the holy Godhead. It is this false indoctrination when he declares himself to be the all-powerful God who rules the world that utterly deceives countless millions. His tri-part existence during this period is manifested as the dragon (anti-God) (Revelation 12:7–19), the beast (Antichrist) (Revelation 13:2), and the false prophet (anti-Holy Spirit) (Revelation 16:13).

73. It is worthy to note that there will be some who will not accept the Antichrist's rule, and because of their rejection of him they will be martyred, and their spirits will ascend to heaven and be under the heavenly altar of God. (Revelation 6:9–11)

74. During the latter period of the Great Tribulation, God pours out His divine wrath upon the earth, affecting both Jew and Gentile nations alike. There will be no sparing of His punishment that is brought onto the earth, and which all mankind must endure. (Revelation 16:1–21)

75. At the conclusion of the seven years, nations will have been filled with hatred and fear, and they live in a Satan-infested environment which produces evil and a lust for power and dominance. (Revelation 13:1–18) It is into this worldly state that Jesus Christ returns with the saints as King of kings and Lord of lords.

76. This triumphant return is completely different from Jesus' first arrival on earth in Bethlehem. At His first arrival, He came as a humble servant and went to the Cross for mankind. At His second coming, He returns to the earth to rule with the authority and power He has been given. (Revelation 19 1–16) His return will be as the *two men in white apparel* told the disciples when Jesus ascended to heaven ... *This same Jesus, who was taken up from you into heaven, will so come in like manner as you saw Him go into heaven ....* (Acts 1:11 NKJV)

77. His purpose for returning is to establish the Kingdom of Heaven on earth. This is the kingdom that God the Father promised the Jews He would give them but which they refused, and rejected Jesus as their Messiah. (Acts 1:6–7) Upon His return, Jesus takes

care of the unrighteous rulers and their rulership. It begins at the Battle of Armageddon. (Revelation 19:17–21)

78. It is during this time that Jesus casts the beast and the false prophet into the Lake of Fire, and an angel binds Satan and casts him into the bottomless pit where he remains for one thousand years. (Revelation 19:19–21, 20:1–3)

79. After this battle, Jesus returns to Jerusalem and the temple is rebuilt with a throne worthy of Jesus' dwelling. From His seat of authority in the temple, Jesus rules the world with the saints who returned with Him from heaven for one thousand years. Christ's righteousness and peace are enacted and ... *Therefore God also has highly exalted Him and given Him the name which above every name, that at the name of Jesus every knee should bow, of those in heaven, and of those on earth, and of those under the earth, and that every tongue should confess that Jesus Christ is Lord, to the glory of God the Father....* (Philippians 2:9–11 NKJV)

80. Jesus, King of kings and Lord of lords, recognized by the Jews as their Messiah, and to the gentile nations as the ruler of the world, now rules as king of the Father's promised Kingdom of Heaven on earth.

CHAPTER 38

THE MILLENNIUM REIGN

1. Throughout the ages and dispensations during which God deals with man, certain spiritual and physical events take place in each of these stages.
2. This dispensation is no different. During the church age, mankind experiences God's spiritual *grace* (Ephesians 2:8), whereas in the Millennium Reign God's *righteousness* will reign. Added to this, the natural and geographical state of creation will also change.
3. *Righteousness* is the final dispensation for mankind, and it is fitting that God Himself, through His Son Jesus Christ, enters the realm of man to rule and perfect all that man has debased, defiled, and destroyed through their sin-nature.
4. In every age and dispensation man has not been able to achieve the ultimate relationship with God, or perfect their conduct towards God. At this juncture, the Millennial Dispensation, when Jesus returns to the earth with the righteous saints, the curse on the natural/geographical state of creation, the natural intention of the beasts, fowls of the air, and creeping things, is renewed to its former state of peaceful existence, as it was in the Garden of Eden before Adam and Eve fell under the curse of sin.

5. In this dispensation, God Himself, the glorified Jesus Christ, returns to rule, and man's intentions, lust for power, and hatred for each other is subdued by the righteous governing power stemming from the earthly throne of God on which Jesus is seated ... *A King shall reign and prosper, and execute judgment and righteousness in the earth. In His days Judah will be saved, and Israel will dwell safely; now this is His name by which He will be called: THE LORD OUR RIGHTEOUSNESS....* (Jeremiah 23:5–6 NKJV)

6. The Millennium is not the *New Heaven* and the *New Earth*. The Millennium is the last dispensation on earth. The same sin-nature and attitude towards God is within remaining souls that survived the seven-year Great Tribulation and the Battle of Armageddon. It is into this worldly state where man's sin-nature rules his thinking that Jesus, together with His holy angels and the saints, returns to establish the Kingdom of Heaven.

7. The survivors who are on earth (in this world) will bow the knee and worship Jesus, thus subduing their sin-nature. In this dispensation, the rulership is no longer in the hands of man, but Jesus Himself will be the head of all things pertaining to man's existence on earth. This form of government will not be democratic, autocratic, or a monarchy. It will be theocratic: Jesus will reign over all the nations.

8. *When the Son of Man comes in His glory, and all the holy angels with Him, then He will sit on the throne of His glory. All the nations will be gathered before Him, and He will separate them one from another, as a shepherd divides his sheep from the goats....* (Matthew 25:31–32 NKJV)

9. The Old Testament gives extensive reference to the reign of the Messiah. Many prophets spoke of the promise of God to give His people, the Jews, a Messiah. These prophets spoke in detail about the Messiah's reign and the extent of His rulership.

10. Because of the rejection by the Jews of the Messiah, God postponed the Kingdom that would be ruled by the Messiah ... *He*

was in the world, and the world was made through Him, and the world did not know Him. He came to His own, and His own did not receive Him.... (John 1:10–11 NKJV) The Father now fulfills His promise as the Millennium Reign of His Son, Jesus Christ the Messiah, returns to the earth.

11. During the thousand years Jesus rules the entire world, and every nation will acknowledge His righteous rulership. The saints who return with Him are the ones who preside over all nations and enact Jesus' governance.

The Reason for the Millennium Reign

12. It is the *fulfillment* of God's promise to the Jews that He will give them a Messiah (the full meaning of this word incorporates every aspect of a King, a Priest, the Lord, and the Savior). (Isaiah 11:1–11, Daniel 9:24, Acts 3:20–21, 1 Peter 1:10–13) ... *Seventy weeks are determined for your people and for your holy city, to finish the transgression, to make an end of sins, to make reconciliation for iniquity, to bring in everlasting righteousness, to seal up vision and prophecy, and to anoint the Most Holy....* (Daniel 9:24 NKJV)

13. It is the establishment of righteousness for all nations and the sovereign reign of Jesus ... *He will be great, and will be called the Son of the Highest; and the Lord God will give Him the throne of His father David. And He will reign over the house of Jacob forever, and of His kingdom there will be no end....* (Luke 1:32–33 NKJV)

The Purpose of the Millennium Reign

14. To fulfill the everlasting covenants made with Abraham (Genesis 12), Isaac (Genesis 26), and David (2 Samuel 7).

15. To restore Israel and make them the head of all nations (Deuteronomy 28:1–2, 13) ... *And the Lord will make you the head and not the tail; you shall be above only, and not be beneath....* (28:13 NKJV) Until the Millennium, Israel has not been the *head* of all nations, and has been the *tail*. God has said they are like a treasure to Him ... *You shall be a special treasure to Me above all people; for all the earth is Mine....* (Exodus 19:5 NKJV) Again, *For the Lord has chosen Jacob for Himself, Israel for His special treasure....* (Psalm 135:4 NKJV)

16. It is further to vindicate the Lord Jesus Christ and His saints ... *And the high priest answered and said to Him, "I put You under oath by the living God: Tell us if You are the Christ, the Son of God!" Jesus said to him, "It is as you said. Nevertheless, I say to you, hereafter you will see the Son of Man sitting at the right hand of the Power, and coming on the clouds of heaven."* (Matthew 26:63–64 NKJV)

17. Finally ... *In the dispensation of the fullness of the times He might gather together in one all things in Christ, both which are in heaven and which are on earth—in Him ...* (Ephesians 1:10 NKJV) and restore all things. (Acts 3:20–21)

18. Here ends the present rejection of God's grace and the evil rebellion against God's love and mercy. This is done when God puts all these enemies under Christ's feet as He reigns on earth. (1 Corinthians 15:23–28, Hebrews 2:7–9)

19. The establishment of this rulership is set in order when Jesus Christ is honored by His Father to reign over all nations. Jesus does this by: judging the nations in righteousness and restoring the earth to its rightful condition; (Isaiah 11:1–11, Daniel 9:22–27, Matthew 25:31–46, Romans 8:18–23, 1 Corinthians 6:1–5,) as well as the establishment of His righteous government. (Isaiah 9:6–7, 11:1–9, Luke 1:32–33)

Israel's Role in the Millennium Reign

20. The Promised Land will be divided amongst the twelve tribes of Israel. Each tribe will settle in their portion of the land with Jerusalem as the chief city from which the Messiah, Jesus Christ, will rule. The land stretches from Dan in the north to Gad in the south. Then it spans the area from the Mediterranean Sea in the west to the Euphrates River in the east. (Ezekiel 47:13–23)

21. Israel will have earthly priests who will minister in the temple in Jerusalem ... *And He said to me, Son of man, this is the place of My throne and the place of the soles of My feet, where I will dwell in the midst of the children of Israel forever. No more shall the house of Israel defile My holy name, they nor their kings, by their harlotry or with the carcasses of their kings on their high places....* (Ezekiel 43:7 NKJV) During this time, the Jews who survived the end time wars and the Battle of Armageddon will return annually to Jerusalem to celebrate the Feast of Tabernacles as a memorial that celebrates their release and return from captivity.... (Zechariah 14:16–21)

22. Israel will declare to all the nations throughout the world the "good news" of the Messiah. They will spread the message and testify that Jesus is the Messiah and declare His glory. (Isaiah 66:18–21)

The Structure/Governmental Rule and Inhabitants during the Millennium Reign

23. God will send from heaven to earth His Son, Jesus Christ, with the mighty angels (Matthew 25:31) and all the resurrected and glorified saints. At the Battle of Armageddon all rebellion on earth will be conquered. (Zechariah 14:1–5, 9) Furthermore ... *and to*

give you who are troubled rest with us when the Lord Jesus is revealed from heaven with His mighty angels, in flaming fire taking vengeance on those who do not know God, and on those who do not obey the gospel of our Lord Jesus Christ. These shall be punished with everlasting destruction from the presence of the Lord and from the glory of His power, when He comes, in that Day, to be glorified in His saints and to be admired among all those who believe, because our testimony among you was believed.... (2 Thessalonians 1:7–10 NKJV)

24. The inhabitants will be on the earth for one thousand years. There will be three categories of people: resurrected saints who will reign with Jesus, the Gentile nations who will survive the Great Tribulation and the Battle of Armageddon, and the Jews who also survived.

Governmental Structure

25. No longer will man be governed by human rules and laws. No longer will they be subjected to cultural differences and intellectual interpretations. This is the Godhead's time and their governing of all the nations on earth. Almighty God will rule and reign by giving all authority and power to Jesus who will be on earth.

26. Jesus, King of kings and Lord of lords, will take up His seat in the Holy Temple in Jerusalem and rule the nations of the world from His throne. (Zechariah 6:12–13, Matthew 25:31–34, Revelation 11:15)

27. From His seat of authority, Jesus will rule with a *rod of iron ... Yet I have set My King on My holy hill of Zion. I will declare the decree: The LORD has said to Me, 'You are My Son, today I have begotten You. Ask of Me, and I will give You the nations for Your inheritance, and the ends of the earth for Your possession. You*

shall break them with a rod of iron; You shall dash them to pieces like a potter's vessel....' (Psalm 2:6–9 NKJV)

28. He will establish an order of government and place His rulers, the saints, over every nation. All the rulers/saints will be given directions from Jesus as to their rulership over the nations throughout the world.

29. The Jews will be ruled by the resurrected David. David, the king of Israel, will be appointed as Israel's ruler as prophesied in the Old Testament. (Jeremiah 30:9, Ezekiel 34:20–24, 37:24–28, Hosea 3:4–5) During this time, the Jews will testify that Jesus is the Messiah and continually proclaim Him as Lord of lords to the nations.

30. The twelve Apostles of the Lamb will each be given authority over the twelve tribes of Israel ... *So Jesus said to them, "Assuredly I say to you, that in the regeneration, when the Son of Man sits on the throne of His glory, you who have followed Me will also sit on twelve thrones, judging the twelve tribes of Israel...."* (Matthew 19:28 NKJV) Again, the Word declares ... *Now the wall of the city had twelve foundations, and on them were the names of the twelve apostles of the Lamb....* (Revelation 21:14 NKJV)

31. The resurrected saints who return with Jesus to the earth will be given rulership with Jesus over the nations throughout the world. (2 Timothy 2:12, Revelation 20:4–6) This privilege, reward, and honor will be given to those who have *endured* and did not *deny* Him.

Jesus' Authority and Reign over the Remaining Nations

32. Those who survive the Battle of Armageddon and remain on the earth during the Millennium will be subjected to Jesus' rulership and His governmental authority. Jesus' authority will command

peace on earth, resulting in no more wars being fought. (Isaiah 2:1–4, Micah 4:3)

33. These surviving nations will still possess their human nature that is anti-God, namely, their inherent sin-nature from Adam. They will therefore be compelled to submit to God's theocratic government and obediently follow Jesus' rulership. (Isaiah 45:23, Romans 14:11) They will not do this according to their free will: it is a command given to them.

34. Their free will has no evil deceiver, the devil, present to tempt them to walk away from Jesus. Those who do exercise their free will and reject Jesus' rulership will suffer the wrath of His punishment. (Isaiah 11:3–5, 16:4–5) Some will decide to physically worship Jesus, but in their hearts they will still cling to their old nature. Against these, Jesus will exercise justice and judgment upon them ... *till He has put all enemies under His feet.* (Isaiah 65:20, 1 Corinthians 15:25 NKJV)

The Spiritual and Material Complexity of the Millennium Reign

35. The Messiah brings universal religion, peace, and harmony to all nations. (Isaiah 9:6–7, Micah 4:3–4) The entire world will worship Jesus Christ as Lord of lords and King of kings ... *I have sworn by Myself; the word has gone out of My mouth in righteousness, and shall not return, that to Me every knee shall bow, every tongue shall take an oath* ... (Isaiah 45:23 NKJV) *that at the name of Jesus every knee should bow, of those in heaven, and of those on earth, and of those under the earth, and that every tongue should confess that Jesus Christ is Lord, to the glory of God the Father....* (Philippians 2:10–11 NKJV)

36. There will be universal knowledge of Jesus and His reign. (Isaiah 11:9, Zechariah 8:22–23) With this knowledge of Jesus

and His righteousness, there will be justice for all nations. (Isaiah 9:6–7, 11:3–5)

37. There will be significant natural and material changes during this period. Human life will be prolonged (Zechariah 8:2–6), and many will be born during the thousand years. (Isaiah 65:20) For those born during the Millennium, some will accept Jesus Christ and not be lured away once Satan has been released from the Bottomless Pit after one thousand years. (Revelation 20:1–3)

38. The trees will bring forth new fruit which shall be for meat and preservation of natural life for the nations. (Isaiah 55:12–13, Ezekiel 47:1–12, Joel 3:17–21, Amos 9:13–15) There will also be changes in the animal kingdom. (Isaiah 11:6–8) There will be no more fierce or poisonous creatures. It will be like the Garden of Eden was before the curse. The curser, Satan, will have been banished to the Bottomless Pit, and the threat of him infiltrating the lives of the nations during the Millennium is completely removed. There will be no more poverty, sickness, famine, plagues, or wars; only peace, prosperity, and tranquility. (Isaiah 11:9, 65:20–25)

39. At the culmination of the thousand years (Millennium Reign) the Bottomless Pit is opened, and Satan is given permission to deceive as many of the nations he can for a short while. His efforts are emboldened with hatred and deception that create a multitude of followers from the nations that become so enticed, they join him in the decision to declare war against the righteous Jesus Christ ... *Now when the thousand years have expired, Satan will be released from his prison and will go out to deceive the nations which are in the four corners of the earth, Gog and Magog, to gather them together to battle, whose number is as the sands of the sea....* (Revelation 20:7–8 NKJV)

40. According to the Word, this battle will not take place because God intervenes ... *And fire came down from God out of heaven and devoured them....* (Revelation 20:9 NKJV) This is the final stage of the Millennium. After God's intervention, the age of

righteousness closes. The next righteous act that must take place is the punishment of the wicked.

The Great White Throne Judgment

41. The Bible teaches that God intervenes at the proposed Battle of Gog and Magog and devours the enemies of Christ's righteous rulership. God ushers the next phase that deals with mankind and his earthly dwelling place. To begin, God's first order of business is to take care of the wicked. This is done at the Great White Throne Judgment.

The Purpose of the Great White Throne Judgment

42. God has always made it very clear to everyone that those who do not receive Jesus Christ as their Savior, *the wrath of God abides on them....* (John 3:36) God therefore uses this place as the final discourse with the wicked. (Revelation 20:11–15)

43. Its only purpose is to complete the Word of God's clear message about rejecting Him, and to announce the punishment the wicked were told they would receive.

44. This throne is "Great" because great will be the punishment, as well as the finality of the judgment/decision passed down upon everyone who stands before Him. It is "White" because the holy, pure, righteous Judge, Jesus Christ, presides over the judgment. God the Father, Jesus Christ the Son, and the Holy Spirit are the only pure, holy judges worthy of proclaiming the eternal doom of the wicked. This task is entrusted to the Son, Jesus Christ (Acts 17:31).

45. It is a "Throne" because the ultimate authority is vested in Almighty God and from His throne, which is His seat of authority, that Jesus decrees the wicked sinner's judgment and punishment

... because He has appointed a day on which He will judge the world in righteousness by the Man whom He has ordained. He has given assurance of this to all by raising Him from the dead.... (Acts 17:31 NKJV)

46. The torment in hell is halted for a moment in the wicked sinners' lives as they hear the seals of hell's doors being broken. They are blinded by the Shekinah glory beaming down from the throne as they stumble towards the place of judgment. Then the seals of the book are opened and the sound of the clasps ricochet in their ears as they are opened. They stand in awe in the presence of Jesus.

47. The Almighty Christ, in whom *all the fullness of the Godhead dwells bodily,* and in whom salvation is purposed and offered; the One chosen by His Father to be *wounded for our transgressions ... bruised for our iniquities, the chastisement of our peace was upon Him* and *despised and rejected by men ... oppressed and afflicted* is now the holy, pure, and righteous Judge. He leans forward and reads the wicked works of the dead to them and pronounces their punishment.

48. No heavenly seraphim, cherubim, archangel; no apostle, or no human being has the authority and capability of speaking the truth to each recipient. There is only One who holds the required office to do this: the *Christ, the Son of the living God* (Matthew 16:16 NKJV) *... because He has appointed a day on which He will judge the world in righteousness by the Man whom He has ordained. He has given assurance to all by raising Him from the dead....* (Acts 17:31 NKJV)

The Participants

49. All the wicked dead's graves are opened, and their soul and spirit reunite with a body and they stand before Jesus. All the angels who left their first estate are loosed from their place of

their captivity, Tartarus, and are called to appear before Jesus. (2 Peter 2:4, Jude 6–7)

50. This is the final discourse between God and the wicked. It is not a place of argument, neither a place to bargain with God. It is the *bema* "throne-platform" from which the sentence is proclaimed over wickedness. There is only one Source of Reference to which the wicked can look—the Word of Almighty God. There will be the wailing and gnashing of teeth as the wicked hear their punishment announced. (Matthew 25:30)

The Punishment

51. The contrast between the Judgment Seat of Christ and the Great White Throne Judgment can never be overstated. At this judgment, horror and damnation to an eternal Lake of Fire is pronounced. From there, torment and agony will persist for eternity for those who stand before Jesus and have their punishment metered out.

52. The extent of their punishment will be measured against their wickedness. However, no matter the extent, the peril of total expulsion from the presence of God for eternity is the worst torment anyone can ever experience.

53. There is no returning from the Lake of Fire. There is no further discussion that can be put forward to resolve any wickedness. Conversely, the rewards passed on to the righteous saints at the Judgment Seat of Christ are heralded with joy and praise to the Godhead. The rewards are also everlasting, and they are forever pleasing to the recipients. For those who stand at this judgment seat, the resultant effect is totally opposite to the Judgement Seat of Christ. They are cast away, and horror and regret accompany them to their destination.

54. The intensity of the Lake of Fire's torment is far greater than hell. Hell is the current place where the wicked dead's souls and spirits

wait for their judgment to be pronounced. There the torment is likened to being eaten by worms and existing in perpetual fire. (Mark 9:47–49) The Lake of Fire, on the other hand, brings *finality* and is *without end.*

55. The *death* (Revelation 20:14) spoken of is indescribable. It contains a finality that is expressed in the strongest spiritual terms, namely that the wicked sinners will never get a glimpse of the Shekinah glory again. They will never be given a release from their torment: it is everlasting. Added to that, their punishment and torment is forever ongoing; it will never let up in its intensity. The burning flames of the Lake of Fire bring suffering and pain to the wicked, while the torment in their soul intensifies with each passing moment as the two words beat like a pounding drum through their mind—*If only....*

56. When the last wicked sinner receives their punishment, the Book of Life (Revelation 20:12) is closed and once again sealed, never to be opened. Christ' work is concluded at the Great White Throne Judgment. Likewise, all His dealings with mankind starting from creation, through salvation, the building of His church, the Judgment Seat of Christ, the Marriage Supper, and His rule as King of kings and Lord of lords are complete. There will be no more sin, no more sickness, and no more hatred between men. What now awaits the saints and the nations is a *New Earth* and a *New Jerusalem.*

CHAPTER 39

THE NEW HEAVEN, NEW EARTH, AND THE NEW JERUSALEM

1. The eternal God, without beginning and end, great in power and majesty, holy and pure, divine and sovereign, brings to mankind the greatest expression of love and infinite deity: the recreation of heaven and earth and Jerusalem. This is a fulfillment of His promises to repentant born-again believers, now saints, totally unworthy of such a magnificent gift.

2. From the groanings of the earth and its travail through man's neglect and ravishing lust for all things imaginable, God reaches from His throne and restores earth so that it can be a habitation for His beloved Jews, saints, and saved nations ... *But the heavens and the earth which are now preserved by the same word, are reserved for fire until the day of judgment and perdition of ungodly men....* (2 Peter 3:7 NKJV)

3. The closing of the Age of Grace, and then the dispensation of righteousness in the Millennium Reign that culminates with the banishment of the wicked from the earth forever, Almighty God,

because *He is not slack concerning His promise*, (2 Peter 3:9 NKJV) sets the earth ablaze with fire from heaven, restoring this planet to once again be like Eden.

4. When the restoration is complete, God opens His heart to His people and leads them into the New Earth and the New Jerusalem, their new home forevermore. It is in this sublime paradise void of sin, shame, and hatred that man arrives and begins anew. The New Earth is the place where the nations who survived the Great Tribulation and the deceit of the devil when he was released after the Millennium Reign will live. The saints and the Jews live in the New Jerusalem.

5. It is here in the new earth and the New Jerusalem that mankind turns to the eternal Godhead and worships Him spirit to Spirit. There is no hindrance, static, or interference from any source that hinders the purest and most divine relationship that will flow from the hearts of Jews, saints, and the nations to God.

The New Earth

6. God opens this everlasting period with the proclamation that it is called the day of God. It is the closing of the day of the Lord. (2 Peter 3:11–13) This is the time when the righteous, immortal, and incorruptible saints dwell in the presence of Almighty God forever on the new earth ... *Behold, I make all things new....* (Revelation 21:5) Certain changes to the earth are made by God which are for His people.

7. There will be no more sin on earth. Righteousness will be prevalent everywhere. The inhabitants on earth will no longer have the sin-nature in them. Their everlasting body, soul, and spirit will now be focused on honoring God and to glorify Him.

8. An apt description of the real and spiritual change is given by Finis Dake in his book, *Revelation Expounded,* when he says,

"This New Heaven and New Earth are the result of renovation by fire. The complete destruction of all wickedness and the old order of things under the curse will make them new in freshness and character. This destruction will terminate the last time in all eternity that they will be marred by sin and rebellion of the creatures therein."

9. The inhabitants have an everlasting walk that will be one of joy as tears are wiped away, pain is no more, and sorrow disappears ... *And God will wipe away every tear from their eyes; there shall be no more death, nor sorrow, nor crying. There shall be no more pain, for the former things have passed away....* (Revelation 21:4 NKJV)

10. The nations will dwell throughout the renovated earth that will be void of seas. They will be about their daily tasks each with his own self-supporting homestead. (Isaiah 65:17–23) They will travel to the New Jerusalem and feed off the leaves on the trees growing along the banks of the river that flows through the new city. (Revelation 22:2)

11. Within the New Jerusalem, the saints will live and reign with God forever. (Revelation 22:5) What exactly saints will be doing is not made known. Suffice to say, the fact that they will be in the holy presence of God will surely involve much praise and worship. (Revelation 21:22–27)

12. While much is recorded in the Bible about God's saving grace and the everlasting state of saints, the duties and responsibilities they will have during this everlasting time have not been revealed. What is worthy to note is the fact that this new earth far exceeds anything man has ever imagined. There is no comparison on this current cursed earth to what the new earth will be like ... *Eye has not seen, nor ear heard, nor have entered into the heart of man the things which God has prepared for those who love Him....* (1 Corinthians 2:9 NKJV)

13. To even attempt to describe from a human's frail and puny mind what the fullness of God's presence will be like is impossible. The

Word says ... *Behold, the tabernacle of God is with men, and He will dwell with them, and they shall be His people. God himself will be with them and be their God....* (Revelation 21:3 NKJV)

14. The current curse that is on the present earth is removed. God's removal of the curse is one of most precious gifts to mankind He can give. (The most precious is the offering of His Son on Calvary for the forgiveness of sin.) There is no human comprehension for this fact.

15. Every second of every day while man lives on this earth, he lives with the fact that ... *cursed is the ground for your sake; in toil you shall eat of it all the days of your life. Both thorns and thistles it shall bring forth for you, and you shall eat of the herb of the field. In the sweat of your face you shall eat bread till you return to the ground, for out of it you were taken; for dust you are and to dust you shall return....* (Genesis 3:17–19 NKJV) How glorious is this promise that brings unfathomable relief ... *and there shall be no more curse, but the throne of God and the Lamb shall be in it, and His servants shall serve Him. They shall see His face, and His name shall be on their foreheads....* (Revelation 22:3–4 NKJV)

The New Heaven

16. The Word does not expound much on the New Heaven. Primarily, it is the abode of God and His angels, and therefore has little to do with man once *all is in all.* (1 Corinthians 15:28) God deals with heaven in a manner fitting to rid it of all the past sin that once existed there.

17. This renovation is a "cleansing" of the sin stain that originated in heaven. Now the abode of angels is free of any possible deceit and temptation, just as the New Earth is free of it.

18. These places in heaven are God's business, and man has no right to pry into things that do not concern him. The Word is filled with

examples of God's throne room and the angelic host that dwells in heaven with Him. One can only imagine how glorious it will be when it has been renewed and the angelic host glorifies God and constantly worships Him, knowing there is never going to be any possibility of deceit and sin to enter its corridors.

19. The New Heaven will therefore be "new" because the angelic host will be guaranteed by God that their future existence will be free of any possible deception and temptation. The glory of heaven and the everlasting presence in the fullness of God will be void of interference from sin.

The New Jerusalem

20. God prepares and delivers to the New Earth a New Jerusalem in which the Lamb's wife dwells. (Revelation 21:2, 9–10) This is a "new" city which is from God, and in contrast to the present Jerusalem filled with sin, hatred, and disbelief, the new city is a place of righteousness and peace where no sin is present.

21. It is a holy city because in it the holy God and His wife resides. The "city" is the place, but the inhabitants are what the "city" is about. Material existence of structure is the shell, whereas the inhabitants are the real essence of the city.

22. Furthermore, the unfathomable inability to comprehend it in this present cursed state that mankind dwells, namely that the righteous, saved saints will be present in the holy tabernacle of God, and God Himself will be in the midst of the people is profound ... *Behold the tabernacle of God is with men, and He will dwell with them, and they shall be His people. God Himself will be with them and be their God....* (Revelation 21:3 NKJV)

23. These inhabitants are the saints who were espoused to Christ at the Marriage Supper of the Lamb. Added to them, the Jews reside alongside the saints in the city. (Hebrews 9:11–16)

24. The Bible gives a clear explanation of the size and structure of the city. It has all things pure and perfect. Added to this, all the redeemed saints and Jews, now pure and perfect, dwell in it. To begin, this New Jerusalem was created in heaven, and it is brought to the New Earth. (Revelation 21:2, 10)

25. The explanation given to Apostle John in the book of Revelation explicitly details the most precious commodities God created, and with which He adorns the city. The size, layout, height, and width of the city is enormous. Human frailty cannot comprehend the magnificence of this God-structured habitation. (Revelation 21:9–27)

26. This city is different from the present and future earthly Jerusalem where a temple of God is constructed by human hands; there will be no earthly constructed temple in the New Jerusalem ... *But I saw no temple in it, for the Lord God Almighty and the Lamb are its temple....* (Revelation 21:22 NKJV)

27. Those who reside in the city are termed the *servants* of God (Revelation 22:3 NKJV) who will be at God's holy bidding. Their everlasting residence is in the midst of unimaginable glory and light ... *The city had no need of the sun or of the moon to shine in it, for the glory of God illuminated it. The Lamb is its light....* (Revelation 21:23 NKJV)

28. Revelation 22:1–6 explains the presence of the river that has the *tree of life* on either side of it. This tree bears twelve types of fruit and has leaves that bring healing to the nations. The "healing" is not for sickness (there is no sin present to cause sickness) but rather for the "preservation" of the nations.

29. While there is a vivid explanation of the physical structure of the New Jerusalem, it is as important to consider the spiritual implications of the city. The rulers in the city will be set in their positions by God. First, there will be twelve foundations for the wall that surround the wall and upon these foundations are the names of the twelve apostles of the Lamb. These are the eleven

apostles who were chosen by Jesus together with Matthias (Acts 125–26) who walked with Him while He was on earth.

30. Second, the saints reign with God in the New Jerusalem. (Revelation 22:5) Their everlasting presence with God will be the source of their reign. Suffice to say that worship and praise are the predominant activities with which they will be busy.

31. These three "new" places are outside man's current abilities to fully comprehend them. This is God's holy, divine presentation to His beloved. These places are of such magnificence that human understanding and appreciation is impossible to grasp. It will only be fully understood, appreciated, and applied when this *corruptible must put on incorruption, and this mortal must put on immortality....* (1 Corinthians 15:53 NKJV)

Beliefs and Principles of the Spirit-Filled Church

CHAPTER 40

TENETS OF THE CHRISTIAN FELLOWSHIP

An Apostolic Spirit-Filled Church

1. The eternal God, revealed as the Godhead in unity as three persons, namely the Father, the Son, and the Holy Spirit, who are one in substance and essence.

2. The Lord Jesus Christ is the only begotten Son of God and is unequivocally God; born of a virgin; sinless in life on earth; died by crucifixion; raised from the dead; and is seated at the right hand of the Father; soon to return to earth in the Millennial Reign.

3. The Person of the Holy Spirit is of absolute equality with the Father and the Son. He is sent by the Father and the Son to reveal the deep things of God, to empower believers, to lead and guide believers into all truth, and to convict the sinner of their depraved state unto repentance.

4. Man's human nature is totally depraved because of sin and can only be cleansed when repentance and regeneration is made through faith in Jesus Christ's finished work on the Cross. Redemption is only through the shed blood of Jesus Christ.

5. There is forgiveness, justification, righteousness, and sanctification in the finished work of Christ. The ever-present Holy Spirit is the Sanctifier who cleanses the person's soul and spirit with the Word of God.

6. A person who is born again is required to seek the baptism with the Holy Spirit with signs following; the reason being is that these two experiences are different and apart.

7. The evidence of the nine fruit of the Holy Spirit is testified by those filled with the Spirit which is contrary to the old nature.

8. There are nine gifts of the Holy Spirit desired by members in every local assembly where they operate decently and in order.

9. Absolute obedience to fulfill the commands of Jesus who instructs the church to uphold the ordinances of water baptism by single immersion of a believer and the Breaking of Bread on the Lord's Day.

10. The immutable, infallible and inerrant Word of God, the Bible, divinely inspired and authoritative reveals the will of God to man.

11. The church which is the body of Christ is a theocratic government with the Lord Jesus Christ as the head of the church to whom He gave ministries of apostles, prophets, evangelists, pastors, teachers, and offices of elders and deacons. Every person baptized with the Holy Spirit is a member of the body of Christ, the church. The church's commission is to glorify God, mature the believer, and go into all the world and make disciples of all nations.

12. Believers anticipate the lively and blessed hope of being reconciled to Jesus when they are raptured off the earth prior to the Great Tribulation taking place and will then return with Jesus to the earth after the Great Tribulation and rule with Him in the Millennial Reign.

Beliefs and Principles of the Spirit-Filled Church

1. *I will build My church....* (Matthew 16:18 NKJV) At the outset, be it clearly understood that the church is Jesus Christ's, and those baptized with the Holy Spirit are the channel and vessel through which Christ instructs and *builds.* This is His divine organism, and He is the one who directs and gives foundational beliefs and principles to which believers adhere. (1 Corinthians 3:11)

2. The Lord has chosen men who hold specific offices in the church to root and ground believers through His divine revelation to them *... How that by revelation He made known to me the mystery ... which in other ages was not made known to the sons of men, as it has now been revealed by the Spirit to His holy apostles and prophets....* (Ephesians 3:3, 5 NKJV)

3. These two offices of apostle and prophet have the responsibilities of implementing the beliefs and principles of Christ's church, and laying a perfect foundation for it to function ... *but fellow citizens with the saints and members of the household of God, having been built on the foundation of the apostles and prophets, Jesus Christ Himself being the chief cornerstone....* (Ephesians 2:19–20 NKJV) If the church does not have these two offices functioning, then it is void of the revelation it needs to operate effectively according to God's Word.

4. Ministries found in the Word: apostles, prophets, evangelists, pastors, and teachers (Ephesians 4:11) form the leadership of the church. They are supported by the spiritual office of elders who complete the leadership of the fellowship. The Bible declares that of the five ministries, three are to the universal church: apostles, prophets, and teachers. They minister amongst all the assemblies. The evangelists are to the world as he preaches the gospel to the lost. Pastors are usually confined to a local assembly where they shepherd the flock of God. This ministry of shepherding is supported by the spiritual office of elders.

5. Ministries are never voted into office; they are called by God through revelation by the Holy Spirit given to apostles and prophets. A shepherd, pastor of a local assembly, is called by God, revealed to the apostles and or prophets, and sent forth to the local assembly. This is a holy calling, and God does not need the members of the local assembly to cast their approval by voting on His appointment. Likewise, elders are called and made overseers by the Holy Spirit.

6. The only members of the local assembly who are chosen by the *brethren* are the deacons. These men are selected because they are *of good reputation, full of the Holy Spirit and wisdom,* (Acts 6:1–4 NKJV) whose function is to care for the material upkeep of the church and the caring of widows.

Church Membership

7. All believers, irrespective of their race, age, or gender, and who are born again, have the privilege of being part of this divine organism. The fellowship of believers is expressed in two ways: those who are born again are in the Kingdom of God (John 3:3, 5) and those who are baptized with the Holy Spirit are members of the body of Christ, the church. (1 Corinthians 12:12–13)

8. It is the responsibility of men called by God to hold office, to nurture and lead the members into a full and perfect standing in Jesus Christ ... *And He Himself gave some to be apostles, some prophets, some evangelists, and some pastors and teachers, for the equipping of the saints for the work of ministry, for the edifying of the body of Christ, till we all come to the unity of the faith and of the knowledge of the Son of God, to a perfect man, to the measure of the stature of the fullness of Christ....* (Ephesians 4:11–13 NKJV)

9. These divinely ordained offices must be equipped with God's holy anointing to ensure that the members stay on the path of

righteousness and not led away through deception ... *that we should no longer be children, tossed to and fro and carried about with every wind of doctrine by the trickery of men, in the cunning craftiness of deceitful plotting....* (Ephesians 4:14 NKJV)

10. Even though every born-again believer is personally responsible for their own spiritual growth and commitment to Jesus Christ, the church functions through the leadership of these five ministries who are given the spiritual responsibility of overseeing God's flock. They are supported by the spiritual office of elders in each local assembly.

11. Those who are born again and align themselves with a fellowship and have the intention to become a member who will submit to the leadership so appointed in the fellowship by God are given the right hand of fellowship by the ministerial offices in the assembly. (Galatians 2:9)

12. Membership therefore entails submission, participation, and involvement in every aspect of the fellowship of which they are a member. They participate in the spiritual application of the gifts of the Holy Spirit, prayer, study of the Word, and are a reliable support to all the activities of the local assembly. (Hebrews 10:22–25)

13. Because this membership is spiritual, every individual is in submission to the leadership and is guided by them into all truth. They must therefore abide in the spiritual direction given to them from the offices in the church. This entails more than willful following: it also includes spiritual counsel and discipline where necessary. (Hebrews 12:11)

Disciplining a Member

14. There is the possibility that members can be led astray and fall into sin, and the leadership of the assembly needs to counsel them and bring them back into order. It is appropriate that the

counseling of this member be done in the presence of two or three leaders. This is particularly proper when an elder has accusations brought against them. (1 Timothy 5:19)

15. The ministers need to constantly respond in love to a fallen member and should counsel them by exposing their transgression that is contrary to the Word. Malice and judgment should never be prevalent, but rather love and humility should be applied towards this member. If the member acknowledges their transgression and they repent of it, they are encouraged to continue in the faith.

16. However, there are times when members refuse the counsel of the ministers. If this prevails, then the disciplinary actions that must be applied are enacted by the fellowship's leadership. It is not a member of the local fellowship's responsibility to take disciplinary action against another member; it is the leaders' responsibility (ministers and elders). This disciplinary action can include the decision to ask the member to leave the fellowship.

17. While asking a member to leave the fellowship appears contrary to love and caring, there will be some who will not submit to the ministerial leadership of the fellowship. This blatant refusal by a member leaves the leaders no option but to remove them from the fellowship so that their transgression does not influence or entice others in the fellowship to follow their wayward path. (1 Corinthians 5:1–7, 11)

18. The counseling and disciplining of members must be done appropriately, taking into account upon whose shoulders the ultimate responsibility should rest to take such action. An example of this is when young adults, who are the responsibility of their parents, walk away from the household of God. It is the responsibility of the parents to discipline their children, and the parents seek the church's counsel on what action should be taken to bring the children back into a spiritual unity with the family and the members of the fellowship.

19. Likewise, when there is a problem between husbands and wives, the ministers will direct their counsel to both members. However, it is the responsibility of the husband and wife to remedy the improper conduct. Should one of them stray from the truth and be unfaithful, it is the minister's responsibility to direct them to the Word that exposes their error. The reconciliation of the couple is encouraged but remains in their hands.

20. When handling matrimonial problems, the leadership should always counsel both parties together and never talk to only one of the married partners. Likewise, it is always prudent that the leaders handle issues between a married couple in the presence of a witness.

21. Regrettably, it happens in many cases that the church becomes the crutch, parent, and spouse of the members, and members follow the minister as their dominant instructor. This is not the intention of the church. It is there as the beacon of light that draws the members into the fullness of God and ... *for the equipping of the saints for the work of ministry, for the edifying of the body of Christ, till we all come to the unity of the faith and of the knowledge of the Son of God, to a perfect man, to the measure of the stature of the fullness of Christ....* (Ephesians 4:12–13 NKJV)

Teaching Members of the Fellowship

22. Ministers and elders are the *overseers of the flock* (Acts 20:28). Their responsibilities include the teaching of the members ... *to shepherd the church of God which He purchased with His own blood....* (Acts 20:28)

23. It is appropriate that the younger members up to the age of understanding are taught in what is known by some as children's church or Sunday school in the church. The purpose of such a school is to teach the Word to the younger members and bring

them into a knowledge of the Word at a lamb's level. The church guides the children through Scripture, but the parents instruct them in the ways of the Lord.

24. However, the ultimate responsibility of training a child in the way of the Lord belongs with the parents. (Proverbs 22:6) Too often, the Sunday school becomes the only place young people ever hear about God and the parents abdicate their responsibility. The foundation of the child's spiritual life is formed and shaped by the example the parents bring to the family. Tragically, the children's church or Sunday school teacher becomes the alternate parent who is then the third party to the husband and wife as a parent of the child. This is not God's intention for a family.

25. Personal study of God's Word, constant prayer, and commitment to walking in the Spirit rests entirely on the heart of each member. There should be a constant hunger and thirst for the things of God as well as the God of things. The individual gleans from the teaching at a Bible study, Lord's Day services, prayer meetings, and outreaches to the lost. However, this should not be the only platform where they partake of the riches of the blessings of the Lord.

26. Every member should be constantly studying the Word, stay in prayer, and walk in righteousness. It is the most important responsibility of the leaders of the fellowship to teach and guide the members to a closer walk with the Lord. On the other hand, it is but a small measure of the time individual believers spend in their daily walk with the Lord and being taught by the leaders. Most of their spiritual growth is spent in personal prayer and study of the Word.

27. There is a practice of dedicating children to the Lord. This is done when the parents bring their newly born baby and present them to God with the members of the local fellowship as witnesses. At this time, they promise to God and the fellowship that they will train their child in the ways of the Lord and do what they can to

show them a righteous walk. While this is a precious and solemn promise they make to God and the members, there is no biblical evidence for this practice.

28. The birth of a child is a blessing from God and as such, it is fitting that the child be presented to the fellowship and the spiritual leader, the pastor, who prays a blessing upon the child, and God's guidance on the parents and the child as the members witness the occasion.

Laying on of Hands

29. The Bible has numerous examples of God's children laying hands on fellow believers. It is a specific instruction given by Jesus to His disciples to ... *lay hands on the sick*.... (Mark 16:18) Apostle Paul expresses to Timothy that hands were laid on him when a spiritual gift was given to him. (2 Timothy 1:6)

30. There are various practices that are aligned to the laying on of hands. First, it is when a blessing is invoked on a person by the leaders of an assembly. This is a solemn practice that is always done with fervent prayer while hands are laid on the recipient.

31. Second, ministers and elders are called to pray the prayer of faith (James 5:14–15) over the sick, and in so doing they will enact Jesus' instruction and lay hands on the sick. (Mark 16:18)

32. Third, ministers are called by the Holy Spirit and "set" in the body of Christ by the leaders of a fellowship who hold the office of apostle or prophet. This is done when they lay hands on the person as they pray over them. (Acts 13:1–3)

33. Fourth, it is performed when apostles and prophets lay hands on believers to receive the baptism with the Holy Spirit. It is a reverent duty that is done *in the Spirit* and is never taken lightly by these men. It is carefully done with the knowledge that their

hands are the extension of the Holy Spirit's presence and placed upon a person desiring the baptism. (Acts 8:14–25)

34. While the practice of laying on of hands is for all believers, Apostle Paul cautions Timothy to be conscious of doing this reverently and in the Spirit ... *Observe these things without prejudice, doing nothing with partiality. Do not lay hands on anyone hastily, nor share in other people's sins; keep yourself pure....* (1 Timothy 5:21–22 NKJV)

Material Support of the Fellowship

35. There should never be a member of the fellowship who lacks material and physical caring. The members take care of each other and are the ones whom the Lord uses to supply their every need. The leaders of the church will also call upon the members to share in the development and needs of the universal church.

36. Deacons are responsible for caring of the widows and serving of tables (taking care of the material needs of the fellowship), to relieve the ministers of this responsibility. The loving care of many other needs within the fellowship rests with each member.

37. While it is not wrong to share one's material things with institutions that are biblically based, it should always be the first thought of a member as to what the needs of their local fellowship are before they donate to these causes which are outside the local assembly. (Acts 4:32–37)

38. It is the responsibility of each member to ... *bring all the tithes into the storehouse....* (Malachi 3:10 NKJV) This is the stewardship the Word requires for all members to follow. Worthy to note is the fact that members *bring all the tithes*. This is not a payment, and members do not pay tithes. God's household never places a member in debt to Him and their local assembly. This is the

guiding responsibility every member must follow, and willingly do as they *bring all* to the Lord.

39. The place to which the member brings their tithe is to *the storehouse*. This is the place where they fellowship and align their membership. (2 Corinthians 8:1–4) Any other place they wish to support is not part of their tithe. It is the *offering* they make to those groups or institutions they feel led to support.

40. These tithes and offerings are a grateful expression of the believer's heart towards what God is doing in their life. It is not a sacrifice they make, neither is it a dominant condition of membership. This is done with a free heart and willful intention.

41. The custody of the tithes and offering rests with the leadership of the church. They make the decisions how it is distributed. The monetary disbursement of the tithes and offerings is always open for all members to see. In many cases, the leadership needs men who have experience in matters material and financial, and as such, even though they might not hold a spiritual office, they can be called upon to assist in matters of government and financial guidance. Hence, the Word speaks of men who are called into positions of helps and governments.

Christian Conduct

42. Spirit-filled believers' conduct is above reproach. It is a constant walking in the light and having fellowship with one another in this perfect light ... *If we walk in the light as He is in the light, we have fellowship with one another....* (1 John 1:7 NKJV) This is Spirit-led and divine fellowship from a heart drenched in God's holy love for one another.

43. Their walk is not worldly, rather Word-based ... *Do not love the world or the things in the world. If anyone loves the world, the love of the Father is not in him....* (1 John 2:15 NKJV) Because of

this righteous walk, they become a true witness of the Holy Spirit who leads and guides them into all truth.

44. Members of the fellowship are constantly guarding against corruption and a loose vocabulary ... *Let no corrupt word proceed out of your mouth, but what is good for necessary edification, that it may impart grace to the hearers.... Therefore be imitators of God as dear children. And walk in love, as Christ also has loved us and given Himself for us....* (Ephesians 4:29. 5:1–2 NKJV)

45. Their conduct is without reproach in every respect. They do not forbid marriage (1 Timothy 4:3), live a loose immoral life, or conduct themselves in the way of the world. (Galatians 5:16–21)

46. Believers are constantly aware that their path is different from the world's path. The light in which believers' walk is the true light, and darkness has no part in their being. This light exposes all their conduct, and it is the searchlight that is at their feet showing them the way. (Psalm 119:105) They separate themselves and live in righteous conduct that is never found in darkness ... *And have no fellowship with the unfruitful works of darkness, but rather expose them.... See then that you walk circumspectly....* (Ephesians 5:11, 15 NKJV)

47. It is therefore incumbent on Spirit-filled believers to walk uprightly before God and their fellow members. They do not have a façade while amongst believers and a reprobate lifestyle when away from them. Their righteousness is always evident, either when they are amongst believers or when they are alone.

48. Spirit-filled believers conduct themselves diligently according to the Word. They are careful to always be a righteous influence on their brothers and sisters. They guard against doing anything that could cause a weaker brother or sister to be drawn into situations that can lead them away from the truth. (1 Corinthinas 8:6–13)

49. Criticism is the threshold of division. Never should a Spirit-filled believer criticize or condemn the ministers and elders behind their back. *They should never let the sun go down on your wrath*

(Ephesians 4:26 NKJV), but when they have disagreement and an argument against the ministers and elders, they should rather immediately approach them to resolve the issue. If criticism festers, murmuring and complaining starts, and it breeds discontentment, which results in mistrust and gossip. (1 Corinthians 10:9–10)

The Lord's Day Services

50. From the earliest time of the church, and according to the Bible, believers gathered together on the ... *first day of the week to break bread*.... (Acts 20:7 NKJV) Their intention of gathering together was to partake of the Table of the Lord. It was the reason for the weekly gathering.

51. The church had grown to the point where the leaders could not visit everyone and celebrate the Table of the Lord. (Acts 2:47–47) Nothing was more valuable to them than remembering what Christ did for them on the Cross. They constantly met and kept in the forefront of their minds and hearts Christ's redemption for their souls. To ensure that all born-again believers could partake in the ordinance instituted by Jesus, they gathered on the first day of the week specifically to partake of the Table of the Lord.

52. This ordinance should never be forgotten. Neither should it become a ritual attached to the rest of the Lord's Day service; it should rather be the focal point of the gathering. While it is appreciated that the Word always takes precedent in every gathering of believers, the Table of the Lord should not be pushed aside and be excluded on the Lord's Day.

53. The gathering of Spirit-filled believers on the Lord's Day should be a joyous occasion. They should come prayerfully to the house of the Lord bringing the anointing with them so that the assembling of the saints can enter praise and worship in one

accord to the Lord. It is during this praise and worship that the gifts of the Spirit are operational.

54. There are certain aspects in a service that should always be present. These are the reverence for the Lord, the anointing on every believer, and the readiness within each one's spirit to desire united spiritual worship with fellow believers. This worship is never contingent upon the inducement of musical instruments, great choirs, and talented musicians; it is what flows from the heart that God sees and receives. It is acceptable to have great music and excellent choirs. However, this should never be the main reason why believers are blessed in a meeting.

55. The gathering of Spirit-filled believers is the time when the Holy Spirit leads them into one accord, and His anointing is what unites them to worship God in the Spirit ... *Be filled with the Spirit, speaking to one another in psalms and hymns and spiritual songs, singing and making melody in your heart to the Lord, giving thanks always for all things to God the Father in the name of our Lord Jesus Christ, submitting to one another in the fear of God....* (Ephesians 5:18–21 NKJV)

56. The harmony of the believers' spirit leads them to sing in the Spirit and brings them into oneness in Jesus Christ as they worship Him. This spiritual singing is never stirred up by great music and choirs; it is the harmony of the believers' spirit that is in tune with the Holy Spirit that causes everyone to sing in one accord. How tragic it is that so often the emphasis is on the musical abilities and grandeur of a great choir that overshadows the simplicity of an assembly that can enter the realm of the Holy Spirit's presence and sing from the heart by *making melody in your* (their) *heart to the Lord* as they sing in an unknown tongue. (Ephesians 5:18–19)

57. This is also the time when believers can bring their tithes and offerings to the *storehouse*. Nevertheless, this should never be an act that is pronounced; it is a believer's duty to bring their tithe to the storehouse and obediently place it in the reciprocal.

It is done reverently and with thanks and is never a showpiece in the Lord's Day gathering. Too often, time spent on pleading with those present to give more to God, and to place a burden that results in guilt, as the leaders beg for more, is nothing more than a diversion from the sweet and harmonious praise, worship, singing in the Spirit, the use of the gifts of the Spirit, the preaching of the Word, and the Table of the Lord.

58. To expand upon the mission of the church, it is important that the gospel be preached as often as possible. While there is the possibility that unbelievers could be in attendance in a gathering of believers, they would find the operation of the gifts foreign to them. As such, specific meetings are held when the gospel is preached, and the voice gifts of the Spirit are not used. The manifestation of the other gifts, such as the gifts of healing, the gift of faith, and the gift of discernment of spirits are operational ... *Let all things be done decently and in order*.... (1 Corinthians 14:40 NKJV)

59. Every gathering on the Lord's Day should always encompass the voluntary and willing participation of every member. They should be in prayer before they enter God's sanctuary and come reverently to gather with fellow-believers. Their intention of gathering together is not merely to receive an infilling of spiritual blessings; it is to bring to the gathering a heart that is already overflowing, and that can be a blessing and shared with the members.

Other Meetings

60. Members are encouraged to attend other meetings the local assembly holds. These usually include prayer and Bible study meetings. When members gather in prayer, there should be a mighty presence of the Lord who presides over the meeting. An

example of this is when members gathered together and called on the name of the Lord in fervent prayer. (Acts 4:23–31)

61. Prayer meetings, or the gathering of believers in one accord to pray, is crucial to the local assembly. It is the time when members dedicate time to be together in the presence of the Lord and seek direction and a deeper walk with Him.

62. Prayer meetings have, regrettably, become loathsome in many assemblies. They are regarded as unnecessary time which could be spent on something else more productive. Yet when a prayer meeting is called, and the members attend it with a divine infusion of the Holy Spirit's anointing, the gathering resounds with a unity of the faith, in one mind, one mouth, and one voice.

63. This is a time when members are expectant, waiting on the Holy Spirit to lead the gathering into a unity that is so strong no chords of dissension or disruption can separate them from each other. Their prayers are as firebrands, igniting the path of righteousness in each one ... *The effective, fervent prayer of a righteous man avails much....* (James 5:16 NKJV)

64. Without these prayer meetings, an assembly loses the binding force of unionism that builds up their most holy faith and is a refreshing of their spirit that enlightens their enthusiasm for more of God.

65. There can be no substitute for Spirit-filled believers' education of the Bible than a regular Bible Study gathering. The gathering is vital to their growth in the knowledge of the Word, in one accord, as the Word is shared and taught.

66. The pastor knows the spiritual needs of his flock, and it is in a Bible study meeting where the strong meat of the oracles of God (Hebrews 5:12–14) are delivered. The members know they need a constant refreshing, infusion of the Word. Their spiritual worthiness is not measured against their doing the things of God, but rather against their growing *in the grace and the knowledge of our Lord and Savior Jesus Christ....* (2 Peter 3:18 NKJV)

67. One of the most important reasons for this meeting is the teaching of God's Word to everyone at the same time. This brings the local assembly into one accord and places them altogether on one plain and knowledge of the Word. It is during these meetings that the sharpening of their *swords, the Word of God,* is done, and more so, done together. It enables them *to keep rank* and to stand together, all having the same level of knowledge of the Word.

Ministerial Responsibilities

68. Ministers have a responsibility to their members that involves marriage and burial. Both these aspects are biblically instructed and spiritual in their application. They are to be reverently conducted and always bring glory to the Lord.

69. The divine responsibilities entrusted to a minister are to be kept in all holiness and with righteous conduct. Never can frivolous or lukewarmness be adopted towards God's instructions to a minister ... *Be an example to the believers in word, in conduct, in love, in spirit, in faith, in purity.... Give attention to reading, to exhortation, to doctrine....* (1 Timothy 4:12–13 NKJV)

70. Their responsibility is first towards God, and second towards the members of the fellowship. Their personal conduct in their daily life, as well as their preaching and teaching of the Word, should always be acceptable in God's sight.

Marriages

71. Marriage is a God-ordained institution. It is God's fullest intention that man and woman become one in the eyes of the Lord ... *Therefore a man shall leave his father and mother and be joined to his wife, and they shall become one flesh....* (Genesis

2:24 NKJV) ... *Therefore what God has joined together, let not man separate....* (Mark 10:9 NKJV)

72. This is not a man-made institution but a God-ordained event that a man and a woman enter with the explicit intentions of including God in their union. It is incumbent upon them to have this marriage celebrated in the house of the Lord and in the presence of believers. (1 Corinthians 11:8–9)

73. The Spirit-filled church does not condone couples living together as husband and wife prior to them taking their marriage vows in the presence of the Lord. (1 Timothy 4:2–3, Hebrews 13:4)

74. Marriage is the foundation of God's purpose for mankind. It is in the household where parents live a Godly life and train the children in the way they should live. (Proverbs 22:6) It becomes the pillar of society. A sound biblically-based home is a stronghold for every member.

75. Any disgraceful and shameful conduct that degrades the union of a man and a woman in holy matrimony, such as adultery, disregard for each other, or two men or two women declaring they are married is a homosexual sinful act that transgresses God's purpose of marriage, and it is an abomination to Him. (Leviticus 18:22)

76. When the home is in spiritual order, society is in order. This is the purpose of God-ordained families. And marriage, in its fullest spiritual union, will keep the family in the presence of the Lord.

77. The tragedy of divorce is not permitted in God's eyes. Too often, a husband and a wife think too little of their vows they made before God and in the presence of members of the church. God will permit a woman to leave her husband if he abuses her, but neither party have permission to get divorced; they can merely separate. (1 Corinthians 7:10–11)

78. Marriage, while is first from God, is also in adherence to the legal statutes of the country's government. The universal legal recognition of the institution of marriage is, in part, what secular

law requires, while the real seal of a marriage is the spiritual vows made to God in recognition that it is God Himself who grants the union of a man and a woman.

79. God's purpose in permitting a man and a woman to *become one flesh* is a sacred and holy ordinance which should never be violated by carnal conduct. God never permits two people of the same gender to enter into the union of marriage; it is immoral and an abomination in the eyes of God, irrespective of what a country's laws might sanction. (Leviticus 18:22, Romans 1:27)

Burials

80. God has declared that man, in his flesh, will die. Furthermore, He has detailed the method in which the body will be taken care of once it is dead ... *In the sweat of your face you shall eat bread till you return to the ground, for out of it you were taken; for dust you are, and to dust you shall return....* (Genesis 3:19 NKJV)

81. The practice of burying a person's body is a divine instruction that it be laid in the ground from whence it was created. Dust is what God created, and from it He created man. Hence, He instructs that the body be returned to the state from which it was made.

82. The practice of cremation is not biblical. It is a man-made procedure that was adopted by pagan worshippers. Man was not and could not be made from ashes. Ash is a product of the burning of an artifact and is the residue of something that was made and burned. This product, ash, is therefore from something that was created and burned, and ash was not used to create mankind. If this were so, then it would mean that man was made from something that was already in existence and that had to be burned before man could be made. Neither was man made by man as an artifact is made. God is the giver of life, and He has said that the body must return to the ground to again become dust.

83. The words often quoted at burials, "from dust to dust and ashes to ashes" are not found in Scripture. It is therefore not included in a Spirit-filled minister's vocabulary when burying a member of the fellowship. Neither should the practice of cremation be the method of a funeral.

84. The purpose of the gathering of believers at a funeral is to honor the memory and testimony of the deceased, and also to minister to the grieving family. The support during this difficult time the bereaved experiences is comforted by those whom they know and fellowship with.

85. While it is a solemn time, it is also regarded as a time of spiritual celebration knowing that the Word is being fulfilled when a believer is called home by God ... *absent from the body and to be present with the Lord....* (2 Corinthians 5:8 NKJV)

The Way Forward

Therefore leaving the principles of the doctrine of Christ, let us go on to perfection; not laying again the foundation of repentance from dead works, and of faith toward God, of the doctrine of baptisms, and of laying on of hands, and of resurrection of the dead, and of eternal judgment.... (Hebrews 6:1)

It is within every Spirit-filled believers' grasp to *go on unto perfection.* They are to *commit their way unto the Lord, stand fast in the liberty wherewith Christ has made them free,* and *be filled with the Spirit* as they *contend for the faith.* There should be nothing that deters them from becoming fully clothed in all things spiritual and *come to the unity of the faith and to the knowledge of the Son of God, to a perfect man, to the measure of the stature of the fullness of Christ.*

Those reading this book are encouraged to become involved in a Spirit-filled church that contends for the perfect will of God. Become a humble, worthy, and useful instrument in the Master's hands as He guides along the path of righteousness for His name's sake.

There is no doubt so much more can be detailed in this volume. However, as the Holy Spirit leads and draws someone else to enhance the doctrines, give greater clarity, and expose the depth of the Word in a fathomless manner, let this book be the outline that gives the Spirit-filled believers a platform upon which they can build. It is also the intention that another book be written that will encompass other doctrinal tenets not included in this volume.

To God be the glory, honor, and grateful appreciation and thanks for permitting this book to be written.

BIBLIOGRAPHY

Arrington, French L. - *Christian Doctrine, a Pentecostal Perspective*. Pathway Publishers, Cleveland, Tennessee

Bergen, Robert D. Study Note contributor on Genesis. - *Holman Study Bible NKJV Edition*. Holman Bible Publishers, Nashville, Tennessee

Berkhof, Louis – *Systematic Theology*. Wm. B. Eerdmans Publishing Co. Grand Rapids, Michigan

Bishop, Jim – *The Day Christ Died*. Harper Collins Publishers, New York, New York

Black, Jonathan – *Apostolic Theology*. Published by The Apostolic Church Administrative office, Luton, Great Britain

Bromiley, Geoffrey W. General editor and associate editors – *The International Standard Bible Encyclopedia*. Wm. B. Eerdmans Publishing Co. Grand Rapids, Michigan

Buswell Jr. James, Oliver – *A Systematic Theology of the Christian Religion*. Zondervan Publishing House, Grand Rapids, Michigan

Chafer, Lewis Sperry – *Systematic Theology*. Kregel Publications, Grand Rapids, Michigan.

Chambers, Oswald – *The Complete Works of Oswald Chambers*. Discovery House Publishers, Grand Rapids, Michigan

Dake, Finis J. – *Revelation Expounded.* Dake Bible Sales, Inc. Lawrence, Georgia

Dick, John – *Lectures on Theology.* Applegate and Co., Cincinnati, Ohio

Elwell, Walter A. – Commentary in the *Encyclopedia of the Bible.* Baker Books; a division of Baker Book House Co., Grand Rapids, Michigan.

Erickson, Millard J. – *Christian Theology.* Baker Academic, Grand Rapids, Michigan

Gaebelein, Frank E. General editor – *The Expositor's Bible Commentary.* Zondervan Publishing House, Grand Rapids, Michigan

Geisler, Norman – *Systematic Theology.* Bethany House, Minneapolis, Minnesota

Grudem, Wayne – *Systematic Theology.* Zondervan Publishers, Grand Rapids, Michigan

Henry, Matthew – *Matthew Henry's Commentary.* Hendrickson Publishers Inc., Peabody, Massachusetts

Hopkins Evan – *The Law of Liberty in the Spiritual Life.* Andesite Press, Warsaw, Poland

Klug, Eugene F. A. – Commentary in the *Encyclopedia of the Bible.* Baker Books; a division of Baker Book House Co., Grand Rapids, Michigan.

Larkin, Clarence – *The Greatest Book on Dispensational Truth in the World.* Rev. Clarence Larkin Est. Glenside, Pennsylvania

Lockyer, Herbert – *All about the Holy Spirit.* Zondervan Publishing House, Grand Rapids, Michigan

Lockyer, Herbert – *All the Doctrines of the Bible.* Zondervan Publishing House, Grand Rapids, Michigan

Menzies, William W. and Horton, Stanley M. – *Bible Doctrines a Pentecostal Perspective.* Logion Press, Springfield, Missouri

Montgomery, G.E. – *Commentary on the Bible*. Wm. B. Eerdmans Publishing Company, Grand Rapids, Michigan

Murray, Andrew – *The Blood of the Cross*. Martino Publishing, Connecticut

Murray, Andrew – *The Power of the Blood of Christ*. Whitaker House, New Kensington, Pennsylvania

Nee, Watchman – *The Spiritual Man*. Christian Fellowship Publishers Inc. New York

Orr, James – *The Virgin Birth of Christ*. Hodder-Stoughton Publisher, London

Patterson, Richard D. - *The Expositor's Bible Commentary*. Zondervan Publishing House, Grand Rapids, Michigan

Pearlman, Myer – *Knowing the Doctrines of the Bible*. Gospel Publishing House, Springfield, Missouri

Pink, Arthur W. – *An Exposition of Hebrews*. Baker Book House, Grand Rapids, Michigan

Pink, Arthur W. – *An Exposition of the Gospel of John*. Zondervan Publishing House, Grand Rapids, Michigan

Piper, John – *God's Passion for His Glory*. Crossway Publishers, Wheaton, Illinois

Renn, Stephen D. – *Expository Dictionary of Bible Words*. Hendrickson Publishers Inc., Peabody, Massachusetts

Rowe, W.A.C. – *One Lord, One Faith*. Puritan Press LTD, Bradford, Yorkshire, England

Schaff, Philip – *History of the Christian Church*. Hendrickson Publishers, Inc. Peabody Massachusetts

Scofield, C.I. – *The Scofield Reference Bible*. Oxford University Press, New York

Scott, Martin J. – *The Virgin Birth*. P.J. Kennedy First Edition (1925), United States

Smith, James and Lee, Robert – *Handfuls on Purpose for Christian Workers and Bible Students*. Wm. B. Eerdmans Publishing Company, Grand Rapids, Michigan

Smith, Malcolm – *The Power of the Blood Covenant*. Harrison House Publishers, Tulsa, Oklahoma

Spence, H.D.M. and Exell, Joseph S. and various contributors to the volumes – *The Pulpit Commentary*. Hendrickson Publishers Inc., Peabody, Massachusetts

Strauch, Alexander – *Biblical Eldership*. Lewis and Wroth Publishers, Littleton, Colorado

Strong, A.H. – *Popular Lectures on the Books of the New Testament*. Griffith and Rowland Publishers, Philadelphia

Strong, A.H. – *Systematic Theology*. Wentworth Press, New York

Thiessen, Henry Clarence - *Lectures in Systematic Theology*. Wm. B. Eerdmans Publishing Company, Grand Rapids, Michigan

Torrey, Reuben A. – *The Fundamental Doctrines of the Christian Faith*. George, H. Doran Company, New York

Torrey, Reuben A. – *What the Bible Teaches – Updated edition*. Whitaker House, New Kensington, Pennsylvania

Williams, D.P. – Various Manuscripts and Articles from D.P. Williams' teachings available from the Apostolic Church of Great Britain, Luton, Great Britain

Wilson, Cyril D. – Article on *Jesus Christ Son of God, Son of Man* distributed by the Christian Fellowship, Durban, South Africa